The Chief Justiceship of
John Marshall, 1801–1835

CHIEF JUSTICESHIPS
OF THE UNITED STATES SUPREME COURT

Herbert A. Johnson, General Editor

The Chief Justiceship
of Melville W. Fuller, 1888–1910
James W. Ely, Jr.

The Supreme Court in the Early Republic:
The Chief Justiceships of John Jay and Oliver Ellsworth
William R. Casto

The Chief Justiceship
of John Marshall, 1801–1835
Herbert A. Johnson

Division and Discord:
The Supreme Court under Stone and Vinson, 1941–1953
Melvin I. Urofsky

The Chief Justiceship of John Marshall, 1801–1835

Herbert A. Johnson

University of South Carolina Press

Published 1997
First paperback edition 1998

©1997 Herbert A. Johnson

Published in Columbia, South Carolina, by the
University of South Carolina Press

Manufactured in the United States of America
02 01 00 99 98   5 4 3 2 1

ISBN 1–57003-294-7

Library of Congress Catalog Card Number 96-25201

To The Honorable William J. Brennan, Jr.,
Associate Justice of the United States Supreme Court, Retired,
with appreciation and thanks for his unfailing support and
encouragement to me in my study of United States Supreme Court
history

CONTENTS

Preface   ix

Acknowledgments   xi

Introduction   1

I   The Chief Justice and His Associates   9

II   Politics and Constitution in the Marshall Era   53

III   Marshall at the Matrix of Court Leadership   85

IV   The Circuit Courts and the Projection of Federal Power   112

V   Federal Supremacy and Judicial Power   138

VI   The American Common Market and Property Rights   162

VII   Fine-Tuning the Federal Common Market: Private Law in the Supreme Court   190

VIII   The United States in the Family of Nations   224

IX   The End of an Era   256

Appendix A: Points of Law Decided in the United States Supreme Court and the United States Circuit Courts, 1801–1835   265

Appendix B: Points of Law Decided by Supreme Court Justices in the United States Circuit Courts, 1801–1835   278

Bibliography   293

Table of Cases   305

Index   311

PREFACE

Each volume in this Chief Justiceships series is intended to provide a survey of the work of the Supreme Court of the United States during the presidency of one or more of its chief justices. The aim is to give a general reader information concerning the chief justice and his colleagues, explaining how together they shaped constitutional, international, and private law. Clearly there must be a biographical component to each volume, and each must deal with institutional changes in the way the Court conducted its business. Since the Court does not operate in isolation from other institutions in society, nor is it immune from political or cultural influences, some attention must be given to the general history of the period being considered.

Although all significant constitutional decisions must be included, balance requires that there be adequate attention to international and private law cases. The Constitution establishes the Supreme Court as the highest international law court in the United States, and its supremacy clause provides that federal treaties shall be the supreme law of the land. Traditionally the Court has deferred to the political initiatives of the president and the Congress in the area of foreign affairs, but a number of judicial situations arise where the outcome may well depend upon subordinating the private rights to the paramount needs of the nation.

Surprisingly, a large number of private law issues are litigated in the Supreme Court. This reflects the status of the Court as the highest federal court. In addition, its appellate jurisdiction makes it the court of last resort concerning federal questions raised in any state court proceeding. Federal questions include all decisions by the highest state court authorized to hear the matter. The Supreme Court may review all situations in which such a claim has been made under the Federal Constitution, under a treaty entered into by the United States, or under a federal statute. If the claim has been denied by the state court, an appeal to the United States Supreme Court is authorized.

The decision to divide the Court's history into periods defined by the chief justice's service should not be construed as giving undue emphasis to the personality or leadership of each chief justice. Over the Court's history its presiding officers have varied greatly in their effectiveness as leaders, in their talents for management of the Court's docket and in the administration of its business. Most importantly they have not been equally gifted at developing interpersonal relationships.

Given the tradition of secrecy concerning Court business and decision-making, it is difficult to discover the affinities and the conflicts between the justices. Even more tentative are any conclusions we might reach concerning the persuasiveness of one justice among his colleagues. On the other hand these factors are a vital part of the history of the Court, and any evidence that is available cannot be ignored.

This is the third volume to be published in a projected thirteen-volume series, and it exhibits many of the hallmarks of the previous two books. Attention to biography and consideration of the relationships between members of the Supreme Court has, once more, given human interest to what has previously been far too much a matter of intellectual and institutional history. Again we are reminded that famous decisions may be conditioned by the internal management of the Supreme Court and the personalities of its justices.

During the Marshall years we can trace jurisprudential change and shifting positions of power among the justices. The Court was very different in 1835 than what it had been in 1801, and that alteration was only partially due to the personality or authority of John Marshall. Given the political events of the day, Marshall's chief justiceship which began at a high water mark of nationalism, ended in a muddy ebb tide of nullification, growing moral debate over slavery, and rejuvenated enthusiasm for states' rights. There is pathos in the predicament of an aged chief justice reaching his last days only to see national life in such disarray and conflict. One suspects Marshall himself may have doubted the significance of his own chief justiceship, and felt betrayed by the nation, its institutions, and its people. It is in the retrospect of history that the Marshall Court's work becomes so central to our understanding of the Constitution of the United States.

ACKNOWLEDGMENTS

Several students have assisted in the ongoing research on this book and related projects. Tracy O'Kelly supervised the preparation of a computerized index to United States Circuit Court cases in the Marshall era and helped to update long unused data on the Supreme Court decisions of that era. J. Christopher Adams provided detailed briefs of Marshall Court cases after 1815, and several of his memoranda on the Court's work have proved invaluable. Toward the end of the project, some additional briefing and memorandum preparation was undertaken by Alexia Pittas, who has also done extensive bibliographic searching on the various decisions and topics discussed.

Professor Henry Joseph Bourguignon of the University of Toledo College of Law provided a careful critical reading of the materials in chapters 1 and 6. Dr. Charles F. Hobson, editor of *The Papers of John Marshall,* kindly shared his expertise on Marshall's life and career with particular attention to chapter 1. Professor Kent Newmyer of the University of Connecticut history department, the distinguished biographer of Justice Joseph Story, provided an excellent critique of the manuscript at the request of the University of South Carolina Press. Professor G. Edward White of the University of Virginia School of Law provided valuable comments that led to expansion of the bibliographic apparatus of the book and a number of modifications in earlier interpretations. Of course the author is responsible for any errors that may remain.

A generous grant from the Administrative Office of United States Courts permitted me to devote the summer of 1990 to preparing a machine-readable index to *Federal Cases, 1789 to 1880* (St. Paul: West, 1894–1898), and to work on the relationship between the Supreme Court and the circuit courts in the Marshall period. Gregg Gilbert, currently a biological statistician at the Medical University of South Carolina, performed yeoman duties in converting those materials and the Supreme Court database into the proper form for mainframe processing and then prepared several informative comparisons. Perry Simpson of Columbia, South Carolina, then utilized data to make comparisons of the type and number of cases decided by each justice in the Supreme Court and circuit courts, and the figures in chapter 4 are based upon his skillful manipulation of this data on the Lotus 1–2–3 system.

Dean John E. Montgomery of the University of South Carolina School of Law has made funds available to me for summer research over the past four years, freeing me from teaching duties and permitting me the luxury of working and reworking this manuscript.

The Chief Justiceship of
John Marshall, 1801–1835

INTRODUCTION

Because of the Marshall Court's significance to American legal and constitutional history, no single study can presume to satisfy the needs of all readers. Each will bring particular questions shaped by past knowledge of the Marshall Court, and of course, the nature of those queries will usually depend upon an individual's academic training and interests.

Although this volume makes its primary claim as a piece of history, its coverage would be incomplete without reference to the large and growing body of secondary material that has been published concerning the Court in the Marshall era. Much of this has been controversial, since the study of John Marshall's Court has been impacted by recent scholarly and lawyerly debates over original intention jurisprudence. Consequently much recent writing must be read with caution, and awareness of the fact that present-day current legal and political goals may dominate objective historical inquiry. Because these debates are among a group of extraordinarily talented people, many valuable historical insights have been expounded during constitutional argumentation. As far as possible these variant, and at times conflicting, views are discussed briefly in this introduction or identified briefly in footnotes.

THE MARSHALL COURT IN HISTORY AND RECENT SCHOLARSHIP

Few if any individuals have exerted a more profound influence upon the Supreme Court or the Federal Constitution than Chief Justice John Marshall of Virginia. As a consequence Marshall and his Court have become the focal point of study for a number of lawyers, judges, political scientists, and historians. The Chief Justice's captivating personality, emerging from documentary records and traditional anecdotes, has converted many into his partisan defenders, both during his lifetime and thereafter. Others (though very few of his contemporaries) have taken pains to criticize his abilities, his motivations, or his views of political life and constitutional law.

Even those who specialize in Supreme Court history may not be aware of the scarcity of original source material concerning the Chief Justice. Marshall's papers suffered dispersion and loss both during his lifetime and after his death. He was markedly indifferent to the state of his own files and records. Rarely did he retain file copies or drafts of his letters. The undoubtedly large and important files from his law practice are virtually non-existent. Letters he received, even from prominent statesmen of the day, were not systematically filed or retained. After his death what remained of Marshall's manuscripts were divided among family members, and some eventually found their way into libraries and historical society collections.

To the extent possible through modern photocopying techniques, this fragmentary documentation concerning Marshall has been assembled in the editorial offices of The Papers of John Marshall, maintained at the Institute of Early American History and Culture in Williamsburg, Virginia. The on-going publication of *The Papers of John Marshall*, with which the author was associated for a decade, promises to make this assemblage of materials more readily available for scholarly use. However, publication does not necessarily increase the sum total of knowledge concerning the man. Editorial work has unearthed some valuable new materials that expand our past knowledge of his career, but it still remains the case that a weak documentary foundation hampers efforts to understand John Marshall or to analyze fully his work upon the Supreme Court.

The institutional archives of the Marshall Court are sadly lacking in those records that would throw the greatest light upon the Court's activities from 1801 to 1835. Official records at the National Archives lack the type of comprehensive documentary coverage that historians need to write history "as it really was." Court rules did not require the filing of appellate briefs prior to argument, and relatively few survive. There are some terse notes made by the judges concerning arguments presented before them, but they are few and not necessarily related to the most important cases.

The justices must have prepared some draft opinions but these are virtually non-existent, and given the extensive oral communication between justices at their boardinghouse during the Marshall era, they might provide little assistance, and may have been prepared only on rare occasions. In addition, when final opinions were reduced to writing, they were handed to the reporter for editing, typesetting, and printing, never to be seen by the Court again, presumably having been consigned to the reporter's trash bin. An 1830 rule of the Supreme Court finally regularized the filing of manuscript opinions in the Court's records, but those subsequent opinions and all of the stray pre-1830 opinions that are in the National Archives, are simply clear copies and thus sanitized from handwritten insertions or deletions that would explain who wrote what and when during the Court's deliberations.

The original jurisdiction case records in the National Archives, even though few in number, might add much to our understanding of the Marshall Court's work. All of the Court's records were located in the Capitol when Washington was occupied by British troops in 1814. When the Capitol and White House were put to the torch in retaliation for American military depredations in Canada, the original jurisdiction files prior to that date suffered the greatest damage. Most are beyond any value in their current damaged state. The charred remains of the record of *Marbury v. Madison* provide a tantalizing example of what we might know except for the vagaries of "Mr. Madison's War."

For these reasons study of the Marshall Court must be in many respects inconclusive and tentative. Researchers must exercise both intuition and imagination in recreating the personality of the Chief Justice and the business of his Court. Intuition and imagination are, at best, subjective approaches to knowledge and can be easily warped by an author's predilections, personal experience, and false assumptions. Quite frequently, objective scholars working upon Marshall have been converted from impartial observers into impassioned Marshall advocates. The Chief Justice exerts as much charm posthumously over biographers as he did over his contemporaries in life. Senator Albert J. Beveridge was so affected. As a consequence his four-volume biography exhibits little criticism of Marshall, and scant sympathy for the Chief Justice's detractors and opponents.[1] Indeed, for the good senator, it would appear that Marshall exhibited all of the outstanding qualities of citizenship and duty that Progressives of Beveridge's day held in high esteem.[2]

The 1901 centennial of John Marshall's nomination and confirmation as chief justice, which occurred slightly more than a decade before Beveridge's biography appeared, coincided with what Professor Robert L. Clinton has identified as a qualitative and quantitative expansion in the use of judicial review by the Supreme Court.[3] Scholarly interest in judicial review rose to new levels, until the Court's activist use of the power precipitated the crisis between President Roosevelt and the Hughes Court. Perhaps some of the best work on judicial review, inspired by a wish to demonstrate the excessive and unprecedented use of Supreme Court power, was written

1. *The Life of John Marshall,* 4 vols. (Boston: Houghton Mifflin Company, 1916–1919).
2. Some more specific information is cited in Herbert A. Johnson, "Albert J. Beveridge," *Dictionary of Literary Biography: Twentieth-Century American Historians,* Vol. 17, 70, at 72–73.
3. Robert L. Clinton, *Marbury v. Madison and Judicial Review* (Lawrence: University Press of Kansas, 1989), 116–127.

in this period. The work of Edward S. Corwin is typical of this era, and well worthy of a reader's attention.[4] However it, too, bears the mark of present-ism in its interpretations, and must be read with caution.

Most recently Chief Justice Marshall and his Court have become focal points around which original intention arguments are fashioned and de-bated. The Bicentennial of the United States Constitution, begun in 1987 and continuing through 1991, was responsible for encouraging much of this renewed interest, and the political balance of those Reagan-Bush years fostered constitutional conservatism rooted in textual interpretation. Orig-inal intention, as its name implies, attempted to recover by historical re-search the true meaning of the Constitution from the papers of the members of the Philadelphia Convention and the various state ratifying conventions. Reflecting this nostalgic and largely ephemeral view of early constitutional history, many recent interpretations of *Marbury v. Madison* have contrasted the supposedly pure and unsullied judicial review of the Marshall period with the politically-oriented and anti-democratic exercise of judicial review in the twentieth century, particularly during Earl War-ren's chief justiceship.[5]

Reactions by scholars favoring modern "non-interpretive" construction of the Constitution, and those who wish to free constitutional history from an unhealthy political bias, have been inevitable. New rummaging through the Marshall Court's history has triggered new interpretations. Some au-thors have utilized a well-established technique of showing Marshall's de-fects as an architect of constitutional opinions, comparing his legal understanding and logic unfavorably with the attenuated and discursive judicial opinions of today.[6] Others have attempted to minimize the leader-ship and intellectual role that Marshall exercised as chief justice, pointing to the contributions of associate justices as being of greater significance and quality.[7] Most of this "lawyer's history" on both sides of the interpre-

---

4. *The Twilight of the Supreme Court* (New Haven: Yale University Press, 1934); *Court Over Constitution* (Princeton: Princeton University Press, 1938), Corwin's earlier works included *The Doctrine of Judicial Review and Other Essays* (Princeton: Princeton University Press, 1914), and *John Marshall and the Constitution* (New Haven: Yale University Press, 1919).

5. Examples are Christopher Wolfe, *The Rise of Modern Judicial Review: From Constitutional Interpretation to Judge-Made Law* (New York: Basic Books, Inc., 1986); Robert L. Clinton, *Marbury v. Madison and Judicial Review* (Lawrence: University Press of Kansas); and Sylvia Snowiss, *Judicial Review and the Law of the Constitution* (New Haven: Yale University Press, 1990).

6. One of the best examples of this approach is David P. Currie, *The Constitution in the Supreme Court: The First Hundred Years, 1789–1888* (Chicago: University of Chicago Press, 1985), 3–198. Currie's treatment of constitutional development in the Marshall period is nevertheless one of the best to appear in the past two decades.

7. On Joseph Story see James McClellan, *Joseph Story and the American Constitution: A Study*

tive spectrum has been quite good and has modified some of our earlier misconceptions concerning the Marshall Court. However, as Dean Alfange has pointed out in connection with recent monographs on *Marbury v. Madison*, these studies represent reworking of old materials, and in the long run, may not greatly increase our understanding of Marshall or the achievements of his Court.[8] In addition, anachronism can easily creep in when opinions written in the years 1801–35 are analyzed in the hindsight of subsequent legal or historical development.

Political scientists have engaged in a lively debate over the source of Marshall's constitutional ideas,[9] and a one volume popular biography by Leonard Baker[10] has kept John Marshall's personality before the public. Two volumes from the Holmes Devise *History of the Supreme Court of the United States* have been published, and provide a comprehensive coverage of the Marshall years.[11] The serious student of Marshall's career will wish to consult *The Papers of John Marshall,* Charles Hobson, et. al., eds., 8 vols. to date (Chapel Hill: University of North Carolina Press, 1974–) for documentary materials and useful editorial notes on the Supreme Court years.

Two of Marshall's associate justices have been the subject of exceptionally fine biographies. Joseph Story's life and work has been traced in works by Gerald T. Dunne, James McClellan, and R. Kent Newmyer. Judge William Johnson's biographer, Donald G. Morgan, gave us a study remarkable for its day in its comprehension of its subject and the operations of the Court during his thirty-four years of service.[12] No study of the Marshall Court would be complete without attention to the Newmyer and Morgan volumes.

---

in Political and Legal Thought with Selected Writings (Norman: University of Oklahoma Press, 1971); on Samuel Chase, see Stephen B. Presser, *The Original Misunderstanding: The English, the Americans and the Dialectic of Federalist Jurisprudence* (Durham: Carolina Academic Press, 1991).

8. Dean Alfange, Jr., *Marbury v. Madison and Original Understandings of Judicial Review: In Defense of Traditional Wisdom*, 1993 *Supreme Court Review* 329–446, at 329–330, 444–446.

9. Robert K. Faulkner, *The Jurisprudence of John Marshall* (Princeton: Princeton University Press, 1970); and Thomas C. Shevory, *John Marshall's Law: Interpretation, Ideology and Interest* (Westport: Greenwood Press, 1994).

10. *John Marshall: A Life in Law* (New York: Macmillan Publishing Company, 1974).

11. George L. Haskins and Herbert A. Johnson, *Foundations of Power, 1801–15* (New York: Macmillan Publishing Company, 1981); and G. Edward White, *The Marshall Court and Cultural Change, 1815–35* (New York: Macmillan Publishing Company, 1988).

12. Dunne, *Justice Joseph Story nd the Rise of the Supreme Court* (New York: Simon and Schuster, 1970); McClellan, *Joseph Story and then American Constitution: A Study in Political and Legal Thought with Selected Writings* (Norman: University of Oklahoma Press, 1971); R. Kent Newmyer, *Supreme Court Justice Joseph Story; Statesman of the Old Republic* (Chapel Hill: University of North Carolina Press, 1985); Donald G. Morgan, *Justice William Johnson, the First Dissenter: The Career and Constitutional Philosophy of a Jeffersonian Judge* (Columbia: University of South Carolina Press, 1954).

A volume of this size and scope cannot hope to deal with all of the new scholarship on John Marshall and the Court under his leadership. However, an attempt has been made to provide access to that work through footnote annotation and occasional references in the text. In keeping with the goal of this series, this volume is designed to describe the Court under Marshall, to provide insight into the relationship between the Chief Justice and his associates, and to explain the Court's work in the fields of constitutional, international, and private law. As a brief survey much of the material must be derivative from the published work of others, and readers are well advised to use the footnotes as guides for future study.

THE BUSINESS OF THE CIRCUIT COURTS

To the extent that space permits, this survey includes work in the circuit courts of the United States within its coverage. More of a Supreme Court justice's time was spent on the circuit than in residence at Washington, and the contribution of the judges to that work deserves far more attention than it has been given in the past. In keeping with this emphasis the terms "justice" and "judge" are used interchangeably when referring to members of the Supreme Court, for their work on the circuit stressed their shared labors with jurists who eventually would become "inferior court judges" to the Supreme Court and its members. In John Marshall's day the federal judiciary was not sharply divided into those who held commissions on the Supreme Court, and those who served in district and circuit courts. Then it was not true to say, as a federal judge quipped to me decades ago, "We're not justices, just judges. To get justice in the federal system you have to go to the Supreme Court." Under John Marshall, Supreme Court justices came to the people in the localities and there became judges to try both law and fact as appropriate.

THE BUSINESS OF THE SUPREME COURT

Books in this series are also designed to deal with the infrequently considered subject of how the Supreme Court conducts its business. For the Marshall era this requires some attention to statistics, coupled with attention to details in case reports that otherwise might be overlooked. With our knowledge of the personalities involved, and some guidance from the flow of cases before the Court, we can draw some tentative conclusions concerning the Marshall Court. Although Chief Justice Marshall's influence with his colleagues varied throughout his chief justiceship, it becomes clear that he was an effective leader and a reasonably good manager of the Supreme Court's business. On the other hand his associate justices were, in many cases, strong-willed individuals who made their views known and who did not hesitate to challenge the Chief Justice when the circumstances so dictated.[13]

Study of the Court's conduct of its business must begin with the Frankfurter and Landis monograph on the subject.[14] Modern methods permit us to move beyond that work, and beginning in 1968 the author began to assemble data on the opinions of the Court, and details concerning judicial attendance and disqualification. Using a rough categorization of the subject matter of cases, he was able to identify specific areas of the law in which each Supreme Court justice delivered opinions.[15] More recently the data has been expanded to include reported opinions of the circuit courts in the Marshall era, and some tentative conclusions are advanced in this volume concerning the degree to which circuit court work impacted upon Supreme Court opinion assignment.

This field of Marshall Court study deserves more widespread attention by scholars. Although the materials have long been available, the methods of data management and analysis promise to yield new insight into early Court administration.

ORGANIZATION AND FORMAT OF THIS VOLUME

Although a chronological format would simplify the presentation of some topics in this volume, the author has elected to deal first with the personalities and interrelationships of the Marshall Court justices, followed by a necessarily brief outline of the political circumstances that impacted upon the Court's operations and decisions. Within this chapter are the most extensive discussions of *Marbury* and *Martin*, with some attention to other constitutional cases such as *M'Culloch v. Maryland* and *Green v. Biddle*, which have broad political as well as legal implications. The materials on the business of the Supreme Court, followed by a consideration of the circuit court activities come next. They contain the most extended discussion of the most famous circuit court case, the treason trial of Aaron Burr. Finally, there is an admittedly abbreviated effort to cover the constitutional law opinions of the Court, followed by a consideration of the private law

13. It is inaccurate and misleading to describe Judges Johnson and Story as minor figures, as does Professor David P. Currie in *The Constitution in the Supreme Court: The First Hundred Years, 1789–1888* (Chicago: University of Chicago Press, 1985), 195.

14. Felix Frankfurter and James Landis, *The Business of the Supreme Court: A Study in the Federal Judicial System* (New York: Macmillan, 1928).

15. Conclusions up to 1815 are given in George L. Haskins and Herbert A. Johnson, *Foundations of Power, John Marshall, 1801–15*, vol. 2, *History of the Supreme Court of the United States*, 10 vols. to date (New York: Macmillan Publishing Co., 1981), 380–389.

decisions of the Court. The final substantive chapter covers the significant contributions made by Marshall and his colleagues to international law. Readers wishing to study only one case are referred to the Table of Cases, and hopefully the topical index will serve as an adequate guide to points of law or historical subjects touched upon in the text.

I

THE CHIEF JUSTICE
AND HIS ASSOCIATES

"I believe I must nominate you" were the words that announced to Secretary of State John Marshall that he was to become chief justice of the United States Supreme Court.[1] There was an element of expediency in the comment, for both Marshall and President John Adams realized that time was of the essence. Should the outgoing president not act promptly, he very likely would lose the opportunity to appoint a new member of the Supreme Court and would be limited to selecting the next chief justice from among the currently sitting associate justices. The controversial Judiciary Act of 1801 provided that the Supreme Court would consist of one chief justice and four associate justices. When Marshall and Adams spoke, the chief justiceship was vacant by virtue of Oliver Ellsworth's resignation, but five associate justices remained on the Court. Former Chief Justice John Jay's letter declining reappointment had just been received, and President Adams was faced with a dilemma.[2]

Given the situation, John Marshall's availability in Washington may be credited with his selection to serve as chief justice of the Supreme Court for the next thirty-four years. He was in the right place at the right time. In fact, he was in a perfect place. Serving as Adams's secretary of state in the waning months of Federalist control, Marshall had been an effective and loyal subordinate. During the president's frequent absences from the capital, it had fallen to Marshall to handle appointments and other matters

1. Leonard Baker, *John Marshall: A Life in Law* (New York: Macmillan, 1974), 353, quoting John Stokes Adams, ed., *An Autobiographical Sketch by John Marshall* (Ann Arbor: University of Michigan Press, 1937), 29–31.

2. The bill was passed on February 13, 1801. Among other provisions, its most controversial section created distinct circuit courts staffed by three circuit judges for each federal district. Hitherto the Supreme Court justices rode the circuits as part of their judicial duties. 2 Stat. 89–100, at 89–91. The situation is discussed fully in Kathryn Turner [Preyer], "The Appointment of Chief Justice Marshall," 17 *William and Mary Quarterly*, 3rd Series, 143–163 (1961).

that normally would have occupied the president's attention. Secretary Marshall's good judgment and loyalty had been a solace to President Adams, whose moderation in political matters alienated the more conservative Hamiltonian wing of his party and ultimately contributed to the Federalist Party's loss of the 1800 presidential election.

Among Virginia Federalists, Marshall was unique. He was elected to Congress in November 1798 by a district dominated by Jeffersonian Republican majorities. Campaigning at the express request of George Washington, Marshall benefited from the public acclaim for his conduct as one of the commissioners to France during the XYZ Mission (1797–98). The publication of their correspondence with the French Directory earned the commission public acclaim in America for its rejection of French intimations that bribes would be an appropriate preliminary to negotiating a new treaty. In his stand on domestic issues, Marshall had been modest but firm in his opposition to the controversial Alien and Sedition Acts passed by the Federalists as a means of diluting Republican popular votes and silencing antiadministration newspaper editors.[3] In the House of Representatives, Marshall was effective in defending key administration positions. He helped fend off Jeffersonian Republican attempts to abolish the small standing army for budgetary reasons. When President Adams acquiesced in the extradition of Thomas Nash (also known as Jonathan Robbins) to stand trial in Britain for murder committed on a British vessel on the high seas, Marshall's defense of the decision on the floor of the House was so persuasive that it was published in pamphlet form.[4]

John Adams decided to reorganize the cabinet he had inherited from President Washington and began the process in the spring of 1800. For secretaries who owed their appointments to Washington and their political allegiance to Alexander Hamilton, Adams sought out more moderate members of the Federalist Party. At first he chose Marshall to be secretary of war, but the freshman congressman refused the tender of office, preferring to attempt the reconstruction of his Richmond law practice. When it became obvious to Marshall that this would be impossible in light of his absence from Washington on public business, he was prepared to accept the next offer from the president—to serve as secretary of state. At the time the State Department performed a variety of domestic functions not assigned to other agencies. These included issuing commissions and land patents and patenting inventions. As secretary of state Marshall also served

---

3. For a discussion of the campaign see Herbert A. Johnson, Charles T. Cullen, William C. Stinchcombe, Charles F. Hobson, et al., editors, *The Papers of John Marshall*, 8 vols. to date (Chapel Hill: University of North Carolina Press, 1974–date), vol. 3, 494–502 (1979).
4. *Ibid.*, vol. 4, 53–58, 61–74, 76–79, 82–109.

as the keeper of the Great Seal of the United States. By virtue of his office, Secretary Marshall also acted as the conduit for requests for appointment to federal office. During the frequent absences of President Adams from the new capital at Washington, much of the direct control of patronage fell into the hands of John Marshall. His political acumen and good judgment earned him the strong support of Adams during the difficult period preceding the election of 1800.

In diplomatic affairs Marshall negotiated the United States position on neutrality in the seemingly endless series of wars between revolutionary France and the allied powers led by Britain, whose fleets dominated the high seas. Pursuant to earlier initiatives of the president, Marshall guided the last stages of negotiating a new treaty with France, the Convention of 1800, that would stabilize international relations with that nation for the first time since Marshall and his fellow XYZ commissioners had returned to the United States in June 1798. These achievements in diplomacy, coupled with his service in the House of Representatives, marked Marshall as someone of accomplishment but in themselves did little to recommend him to become chief justice.

Since a judicial appointment was contemplated for Secretary of State Marshall, President Adams might take some assurance from his subordinate's earlier career as a practicing lawyer. With relatively little formal training in law, Marshall launched a modest law practice in 1784; he rapidly became one of the leading appellate counsel before the Virginia high courts. When new federal courts were established under the Federal Constitution in 1790, Marshall's practice expanded to include a large number of cases in which he defended Virginians against the claims of their British creditors. Ultimately Marshall argued his clients' states' rights position before the United States Supreme Court in the landmark case of *Ware v. Hylton*. Despite the ingenuity of his arguments against the peace treaty of 1783 and the Jay treaty of 1794, Marshall lost in what would be his only appearance as an attorney before the Supreme Court.[5]

No discussion of Marshall's legal abilities would be complete without a mention of the complex and interminable litigation concerning the vast territory known as the Fairfax Lands. Held by the family of Thomas, sixth Lord Fairfax of Cameron, on the eve of the American Revolution, these vast tracts of land in northern Virginia and the eastern portion of what

---

5. For a discussion of Marshall's law practice see *ibid.*, vol. 5, li–lx; *Ware v. Hylton* is reported at 3 Dallas 199 (1796); Marshall's newly discovered argument is documented at *Marshall Papers*, vol. 5, 295–329. In addition to private practice, Marshall served for two and a half years as recorder of the Richmond City Hustings Court, which exercised limited criminal and civil jurisdiction within the city limits. See *ibid.*, vol. 1, 169–174.

would become West Virginia were to occupy John Marshall's attention and legal acumen from 1786 until the day he died. Not only was the new chief justice a native of this region, but his father, Thomas Marshall, was surveyor of the territory during the late colonial and confederation period. In the 1786 Virginia Court of Appeals case *Hite v. Fairfax*, John Marshall defended the Fairfax titles against claimants under a colonial patent. In 1793 Marshall, his brother James Markham Marshall, and his brother-in-law Rawleigh Colston contracted with Fairfax's devisee to purchase the Manor of Leeds and South Branch Manor. These choice parcels had been set aside by Lord Fairfax for his personal use well before the Revolution broke out and thus in law were distinguished from the so-called waste lands that remained undistributed and in the proprietor's possession when Virginia became independent.[6] The issues were complex, but they may be summarized briefly. At common law, aliens might hold title to real property, but at the owner's death the land reverted to the Crown. This rule applied to Virginia land, but there was some question whether Lord Fairfax or successors to his title were or were not aliens at critical times during the Revolution. It was also unclear what procedures were needed, if any, to vest title in the newly independent state of Virginia. And finally, both the 1783 treaty of peace and the 1794 Jay treaty guaranteed to Britain that lands then belonging to British subjects would no longer be subject to state confiscation or seizure. This last question was to involve a substantial portion of the U.S. Supreme Court's time during Marshall's chief justiceship, and while Marshall was active in counseling his fellow investors and former clients, he himself did not take part directly or indirectly in the decision of any cases involving the Fairfax titles. However, personal financial interest in the Fairfax lands matter, coupled with professional involvement in his pre-Court career, meant that Marshall spent a lifetime studying international law and the English and colonial law of real property.

One factor in Marshall's appointment that remains obscure is the degree to which President Adams accurately assessed his secretary's leadership qualities. We do know in retrospect that Adams considered the appointment to be one of the most important acts of his presidency.[7] Certainly the two men were quite different in personality and background, but their association during Marshall's nine months as secretary of state provided the president with ample evidence of Marshall's capabilities and character. Historians must depend upon a fragmented collection of documents and a collection of anecdotes from which to draw their conclusions. Unquestionably Marshall's personality was an essential ingredient in his

6. *Marshall Papers*, vol. 1, 150–164; vol. 2, 143–156.
7. Baker, *Marshall*, 354.

management of the Supreme Court and his overall influence upon its decisions.

A MARSHALL VIGNETTE

Familiarity with Chief Justice Marshall's published judicial opinions permits us to make some assumptions concerning his intellectual inclinations and abilities. Professor Robert Faulkner concluded that Marshall shared with the Founding Fathers, a generation senior to him in most cases, a Lockean view of politics and constitutional government. With them he saw individual self-interest as the driving force of political life. In John Locke's social contract theory a primitive form of self-interest once existed, but human beings had found it wise to surrender the free but dangerous state of nature for a more orderly social existence. Thus the social compact was formed, and it, in turn, supported a political agreement that provided protection for both the lives and the property rights of its individual members. Marshall and his contemporaries felt that economic self-interest would result in American prosperity and would guarantee the United States enhanced credibility and power among the nations of the world. Governmental and societal respect for property rights and contractual obligations was essential to social and economic stability and growth.[8] In addition, the realization of a common market among the American states, contemplated by the Philadelphia Convention, would increase economic development and be strengthened by the diversification of the American economy into commercial and industrial enterprises. State initiatives that inhibited free trade within the Union were both unwise in terms of political policy and unconstitutional under the Federal Constitution.

The written constitution that played such an important role in Marshall's jurisprudence was the product of a wise and commendable second social contract to erect a new form of national state. At the same time, there were certain innate rights and general principles that undergirded the formal constitutional provisions. These sound legal principles were fundamental to the existence of a well-ordered society, and they were to be supported by the exercise of a natural judicial power that arose by virtue of the social contract. In his later years Chief Justice Marshall witnessed the rise of popular majorities that jeopardized property rights and ended the traditional identification of political power with wealth and social position.[9] Marshall persevered as chief justice in spite of severe illness and pain rather

---

8. Robert Kenneth Faulkner, *The Jurisprudence of John Marshall* (Princeton: Princeton University Press, 1968), 3–44.

9. *Ibid.*, 59–79, 165–173, 193–226.

than allow President Andrew Jackson to appoint a successor who did not share Marshall's views of government and the Court's mission.

More recent scholarship has begun to question Faulkner's interpretation of Marshall's political philosophy. Drawing primarily upon the Chief Justice's biography of George Washington, Professor Thomas Shevory found strong elements of classical republicanism in Marshall's thought. These include an emphasis on the influence of great men upon history as well as the importance of civic virtue on the part of the common man. In addition, Marshall saw hard money—gold and silver currency—as the bedrock of financial and political rectitude, and in the issuance of paper currency the republic sewed the seeds of its future decline. Finally, the Constitution provided a stabilizing force against the excesses of the people, demonstrated in the French Revolution, which Marshall deplored.[10]

Subsequently Professor Shevory has pointed to the republican heritage of English law, indicating parallels between Marshall's thought and that of Sir Edward Coke on the one hand and Sir William Blackstone on the other. He finds a paradox in Marshall's thought between the republicanism of legal tradition and the liberal-rationalist positions adopted by Thomas Hobbes and John Locke. While he still finds republican elements in Marshall's thought, they are present primarily in matters of constitutional interpretation and political participation. In economic matters the Chief Justice was a liberal of the Hobbes-Locke school, but even there his liberalism was shaped and limited by his republican fear of ultimate political decline and decay.[11]

Professor Shevory's later construct of Marshall's political theory is not only more balanced but also suggestive of the likelihood that in all of these matters the Chief Justice simply reflected ideas current in his own time. We know that he owned and read Blackstone's *Commentaries,* and there is a strong likelihood that Lord Coke was well known to him. However, he lacked the traditional collegiate education in the classics, and there is no record of his owning or even reading the works of Hobbes, Locke, or Machiavelli.

The classical liberalism central to John Locke's political theory, unlike modern liberal thought, stressed individualism and limited interference by

10. Thomas C. Shevory, "John Marshall as a Republican: Order and Conflict in American Political History," in *John Marshall's Achievement: Law, Politics, and Constitutional Interpretation,* Thomas C. Shevory, ed. (Westport: Greenwood Press, 1989), 75–93.

11. Thomas C. Shevory, *John Marshall's Law: Interpretation, Ideology, and Interest* (Westport: Greenwood Press, 1994), particularly 3, 9, 75–98. Richard A. Brisbin, Jr., shares Shevory's understanding of Marshall as a republican, but he also sees the Chief Justice as a transitional figure in American political thought. "John Marshall on History, Virtue, and Legality," in *John Marshall's Achievement,* 95–115.

government in the life and freedom of an individual. In this sense Chief Justice Marshall was a liberal. On the other hand, in contrast to those who supported Thomas Jefferson, Marshall was clearly against permitting free rein either in economic activity or in the political process. He saw law, and particularly the Federal Constitution, as a necessary restraint upon the freedom of individuals and groups. However, the Chief Justice was willing to exercise a more general laissez-faire attitude toward economic activity than in the political sphere. In part this was due to a Lockean emphasis upon the benefits of self-interest and competition in business, but it also found support in the traditional view that the possession of property, either real or personal, made an individual a more responsible and thus a more virtuous member of society. As Jennifer Nedelsky has suggested in regard to the Founding Fathers, the variations among personal political philosophies of early American leaders was quite broad, and in Marshall's case it is wise to avoid attaching either the Lockean liberal or the classical republican label to his views of government and society.[12]

As we shall see in subsequent chapters, Marshall's Court shaped a federal government that reflected extant principles of separated powers and balanced government. That is, following Montesquieu, there should be a clear demarcation between legislative power, which made law, and the judicial power, which applied the law to individual cases. Going beyond the French aristocrat's concept, the Court fostered an American priority of legislative policy over executive power. The Marshall Court also drew the lines of limitation between areas of state sovereignty and those activities that fell within the proper boundaries of federal authority.

In extrajudicial writings, however, the Chief Justice emphasized the role of civic virtue in a healthy republican society. His monumental biography of George Washington set forth his paragon of civic virtue. In this five-volume work,[13] Marshall extolled the first president's sound judgment and

---

12. Jennifer Nedelsky, *Private Property and the Limits of American Constitutionalism: The Madisonian Framework and its Legacy* (Chicago: University of Chicago Press, 1990), particularly chapters 1–4; Professor William W. Fisher III provides a helpful guide to early American political theory in "Ideology, Religion, and the Protection of Private Property, 1760–1860," 39 *Emory Law Journal* 65, at 71–82.

13. John Marshall, *The Life of George Washington.* . . , 5 vols. (Philadelphia: C. P. Wayne, 1804–7). Shortly after the publication of the first edition, Marshall began revisions for a second edition, which appeared posthumously: *The Life of George Washington.* . . , 2d edition, revised and corrected, 2 vols. (Philadelphia: James Crissy, 1836–39). From the first edition he extracted an extensive body of material on colonial history, which was published as *A History of the Colonies Planted by the English on the Continent of North America.* . . . (Philadelphia: A. Small, 1824). Marshall and Bushrod Washington planned to edit the first president's papers but eventually gave up that project to the younger and more diligent hands of Jared Sparks.

perspicacity in political matters and found reason to praise his simplicity and quiet dignity of manner. On the other hand, as biographer, Marshall saw no reason to comment on Washington's lack of intellectual attainments; his indifference to art, literature, and music; or his lack of interest in philosophical subjects.[14]

To a degree, a Washington type of stolid practicality characterized the Chief Justice's own personal and political life. His written work lacks the classical adornment and flourishes typical of his day, and his demeanor and modesty resulted in a reputation for simplicity and rural charm. Letters between Polly Marshall and her sister Elizabeth Ambler Carrington show that, well before he was appointed to the Court, Marshall exhibited an indifference to matters of dress. Even after he occupied the highest judicial office in the land, he exhibited no inclination to dress for success. The story is told about a gentleman newly arrived in Richmond who purchased a chicken at the Shockhoe Street Market and sought out someone to carry it home for him. Seeing a humbly dressed "countryman" standing nearby, he struck an agreement for the man to run this errand, only to discover after Marshall delivered the bird that his poultry transporter was none other than the Chief Justice of the United States.[15]

Paradoxically, Marshall was careful to conform to his personal standards of dress when presiding in the federal courts. On his way to North Carolina in January 1803, he discovered that his breeches had been left at home, leaving him with only new-fashioned trousers to be worn to court. He directed a brief reprimand to Peter, the slave who was his manservant, and then decided to make the best of it and to obtain a new pair after he arrived. But, as he explained, "the greatest of evils I found, was followed by still greater. Not a taylor in town cou'd be prevailed on to work for me. They were all so busy. . . . I have the extreme mortification to pass the whole term without that important article of dress I have mention'd."[16] On the bench his concern for his office dictated that he should wear the traditional knee britches rather than the newer style of trousers in which he traveled.

This aura of agrarian humility apparently carried over into Marshall's patterns of speech. In 1803 William Wirt, a fellow member of the Richmond bar, described Marshall as being "tall, meager, emaciated—muscles relaxed & joints so loosely connected to prevent any graceful action. . . .

14. Faulkner, *Jurisprudence*, 128–129. Marshall was not indifferent to traditional education, and he evidenced respect for New England's educational leadership. *Ibid.*, 141–145.

15. Frances Norton Mason, *My Dearest Polly: Letters of Chief Justice John Marshall to his Wife.* . . . (Richmond: Garret & Massie, 1961), 203.

16. January 2, 1803, to Mary W. Marshall, *Marshall Papers*, vol. 6, 146.

Without advantages of Person, voice, attitude, gesture or any of the ornaments of an orator—one of the most eloquent men of the world."[17] Despite the unflattering nature of the portrayal, Marshall remained a close and devoted friend to Wirt throughout their lives.[18] Marshall's magnanimity in this regard is also evidenced by an anecdote concerning his appellate practice. He had been retained by a farmer to argue an appeal in one of the higher courts, but while the man was seated in the courtroom listening to arguments in prior cases, he decided to switch to another, seemingly more elegant, counsel. Having spent his last cent retaining the second lawyer and dismissing Marshall, the former client was appalled when Marshall defeated the second attorney in still another pending case. When the farmer asked Marshall to accept his case for a second time, Marshall did so, agreeing to argue without a fee since the man had impoverished himself in the course of his negotiations. The future chief justice then went on to win the man's case and to teach him a lesson about retaining legal counsel by physical appearance.[19]

Marshall's magnanimity in dealing with the vicissitudes of life is best shown in the evolution of his unusual relationship to his distant cousin President Thomas Jefferson.[20] Never closely affiliated, the two were separated by their political differences, but it is noteworthy that Jefferson was one of the few Virginians not on cordial social terms with the Chief Justice. On inauguration day of 1801 Marshall confided to Charles Cotesworth Pinckney, "The democrats are divided into speculative theorists & absolute terrorists. With the latter I am not disposed to class Mr. Jefferson."[21] After Jefferson's retirement to Monticello, the former president's continued influence in Republican politics led Marshall to comment to Justice Story that he was "among the most ambitious, & I suspect, among the most unforgiving of men."[22] Yet Marshall could be forgiving, and his name was among those listed to take up a subscription to relieve the former president from insolvency or debtor's prison shortly before death ended Jefferson's financial troubles.[23]

Simplicity in Marshall's manner was a product of his upbringing and his

---

17. William Wirt, *The Letters of the British Spy*, 9th ed. (Baltimore: 1831), 110–112; Albert J. Beveridge, *The Life of John Marshall*, 4 vols. (Boston: Houghton Mifflin, 1916–19), vol. 2, 168–169.

18. Mason, *My Dearest Polly*, 264.

19. Beveridge, *Marshall*, vol. 2, 166–167.

20. The two were related through the numerous and prolific Randolph line, one branch of which produced the chief justice's mother, Mary Randolph Keith, and the other Thomas Jefferson's mother, Jane Randolph. Mason, *My Dearest Polly*, 204–205.

21. March 4, 1801, to Charles C. Pinckney, *Marshall Papers*, vol. 6, 89–90.

22. July 13, 1821, Story Papers, Massachusetts Historical Society.

23. Mason, *My Dearest Polly*, 295.

preferred environment. Even when he was in political opposition to his fellow Virginians, he sought their company and enjoyed their companionship. Unlike his cousin Thomas Jefferson, Marshall did not move comfortably into the high society of Philadelphia and Paris. His preferences are readily apparent in his letters to Polly. While awaiting his ship for France in 1797 he wrote of Philadelphia and its social whirl, "This dissipated life does not long suit my temper. I like it very well for a day or two but I begin to require a frugal repast with good cool water. I wou'd give a great deal to dine with you today on a piece of cold meat with our boys beside us & to see little Mary running backwards & forwards over the floor."[24] If Philadelphia was bad, Paris was predictably much worse, and six months later he was informing Polly that "Paris represents one incessant round of amusement & dissipation. . . . The most lively fancy aided by the strongest description cannot equal the reality of the opera. All that you can conceive & a great deal more that you conceive in the line of amusement is to be found in this gay metropolis but I suspect it would not be easy to find a friend. I would not live in Paris to be among the wealthiest of its citizens."[25] Raised in a four-room frame house near Marshall, Virginia, Marshall preferred simple surroundings. His home in Richmond bears the mark of his character in its simple floor plan and its lack of pretentiousness. Yet he cannot be truly considered a product of the frontier, for his tastes reflected an appreciation of good wine and the enjoyment of the pleasant company of both sexes.

Wine and women, in fact, played a significant role in Marshall's life. He was attracted to his future wife when she was only fourteen, and her name adorns the pages of his law notebook. Even allowing for the flattery of portrait painters, Polly was an extraordinarily attractive woman.[26] The couple married in her eighteenth year, and Marshall lavished a lifetime of devotion upon her. When she was taken chronically ill of an unidentified malady, Marshall undertook the management of their household affairs, content to have her company for evenings, when they read by the fire. Marriage did not dull Marshall's enjoyment of the society of women, but with the possible exception of a weekend tryst with his Parisian landlady, he seems to have been faithful to his Polly.[27] As a young man he enjoyed attendance at balls and dancing assemblies, and while he was chief justice he reported to Polly his innocent flirtations with the young belles of the nation's capital.[28]

24. July 11, 1797, to Mary W. Marshall; Mason, *My Dearest Polly*, 98; *Marshall Papers*, vol. 3, 99–100.

25. November 27, 1797, to Mary W. Marshall, *ibid.*, vol. 3, 299–301.

26. See the frontispiece in *ibid.*, vol. 2.

27. See editorial note, *ibid.*, vol. 3, 155.

28. Fees for attending dances are scattered through Marshall's account book. *Ibid.*, vol. 1,

Marshall's wine purchases from 1783 to 1795 are documented in his account books, which show a steady consumption of the fruit of the vine with occasional purchases of rum and brandy.[29] A charming anecdote survives from his days as chief justice. Apparently it became the custom for the Court to consume a bottle of wine when its conferences fell on rainy days. At one time after Justice Story joined the Court in 1812, the conference was ready to begin when Marshall asked the junior justice to check the weather. When Story reported clear skies, Marshall hesitated for only a moment before he observed, "Such is the broad extent of our jurisdiction that by the doctrine of chances it must be raining somewhere."[30] Without a single dissenting voice the Court adopted this reasoning, and the conference proceeded on a more sociable note.

Marshall's sense of humor emerges clearly from his extant writings as well as from anecdotes concerning him. As a young member of the Virginia House of Delegates, he reported to his classmate James Monroe concerning a debate on the imposition of taxes: "Mr. [Patrick] Henry arrived yesterday & appears as usual to be charged high with the postponement of the collection of taxes."[31] Commenting upon the numerous marriages in February 1784, he told Monroe, "This excessive cold weather has operated like magic on our youth. They feel the necessity of artificial heat, & quite wearied with lying alone, are all treading the broad road to Matrimony."[32] At times Marshall's ebullient behavior provided amusement for others. As a Continental Line lieutenant in the Revolution, he ran footraces at Valley Forge, wearing white-heeled socks knitted by his concerned mother; for some years thereafter he was known as Silver Heels. Even while bearing the dignity of old age and high judicial office, he could be found on hands and knees measuring the winning distance in a quoit-pitching contest.[33]

For all of Marshall's extroverted behavior, he was also a man of deep compassion and understanding. Legend has it that he was frequently asked to resolve controversies between fellow officers in the Virginia Continental

317, 320, 346, 372. For his meeting with three young ladies at Secretary of State Van Buren's dinner party see Mason, *My Dearest Polly*, 391. Marshall also enjoyed male society, as evidenced by his subscription to membership in Formicola's Club and his leadership in the Richmond Masonic lodge and the Virginia grand lodge of Freemasons. See *Marshall Papers*, vol. 1, 329; vol. 2, 128–129, 131, 386.

29. *Marshall Papers*, vol. 1, 297, 302, 304, 306, 365; vol. 2, 376, 378, 382, 445, 496.

30. Beveridge, *Marshall*, vol. 4, 88. Story's role becomes more humorous when it is known that he abstained from alcohol until age thirty-two—possibly at the time he joined the Supreme Court. Thereafter his weak digestive system confined him to a little wine diluted with water at dinner. *The Life and Letters of Joseph Story*, William W. Story, editor, 2 vols. (Charles Little and James Brown, 1851), vol. 2, 104–105.

31. May 15, 1784, to James Monroe, *Marshall Papers*, vol. 1, 123.

32. *Ibid.*, vol. 1, 116.

33. Beveridge, *Marshall*, vol. 1, 117–120, 132; vol. 4, 76–78.

Line, and a letter to Major Thomas Posey written after the storming of Stony Point on July 16, 1779, illustrates Marshall's ability to smooth ruffled feelings.[34] In 1827 attorney Littleton Waller Tazewell was deeply offended when Justice Story referred to his arguments as "subtle." After reading the draft opinion, Tazewell objected to Marshall, who interceded with Story and convinced his colleague to delete the objectionable word. Apparently Tazewell had been called subtle during political debates and was particularly sensitive to an implication that Story did not intend.[35]

Marshall's ability to handle difficult situations can be further documented in his frequently being called upon to comfort the bereaved members of his extended family, which included his brothers, sisters, and their children.[36] We have already mentioned his devotion to his chronically ill wife, which at times led him to the the extreme of transporting her out of Richmond when noisy holidays approached and of securing the removal or silencing of a neighbor's dog that disturbed her sleep.[37] His letter to Justice Joseph Story on the death of a Story child reveals Marshall's pain on the 1792 deaths of two of his own children.[38] The first child's death had caused Polly great distress, and when she feared the second had died, she fled the house and took shelter with a neighbor. The second child lived two more days under his father's care, but Marshall did not notify his wife lest she build up false hope, since she already thought the child was dead. When the boy finally died, Marshall wrote Polly a note informing her that he and the other children needed her at home and begging her to return. Together they mourned their loss, but she never knew of her husband's protective actions on her behalf.[39] Marshall's letter reveals his own emotional distress at recalling the death of a child, and it also exhibits extraordinary empathy with the suffering of his younger colleague as well as a willingness to reveal to Story the devastating impact that the children's death had caused in Marshall's life.

---

34. September 1, 1779, to Thomas Posey, *Marshall Papers*, vol. 1, 32–34.
35. Tazewell to Marshall, January 18, 1827; Marshall to Tazewell, January 19, 1827; Tazewell to Marshall, January 20, 1827; Marshall to Tazewell, January 20, 1827. Collection of Littleton T. Wickham, Richmond, Va. This tempest in a teapot concerned *The Palmyra*, 12 Wheaton 1–18 (1827).
36. An example is his ride to Petersburg to be with "sister Taylor" (Mrs. George K. Taylor) on the death of her son Thomas Taylor. July 1, 1820, Marshall to Agatha Marshall, Collection of the late Margaret Cardwell, Cambridge, Mass. (photocopy in The Papers of John Marshall editorial office, Institute of Early American History and Culture, Williamsburg, Va.).
37. To [?] Rawlings, July 25, 1829, Mason, *My Dearest Polly*, 308–309.
38. Marshall's account book for August 1792 reflects the purchase of coffins for his son and daughter. *Marshall Papers*, vol. 2, 444.
39. Beveridge, *Marshall*, vol. 4, 73–74.

In dealing with his associate justices, Marshall showed great modesty concerning his intellectual attainments. As we shall see later, he sought advice from Joseph Story and Bushrod Washington concerning admiralty cases. Other letters show that while Marshall may have circulated his opinion to the other justices with a strong sense of its rectitude, he was nevertheless willing to yield to their arguments and even a contrary decision if they were sufficiently persuasive. This characteristic may well have led to historian William W. Crosskey's suggestion that Marshall surrendered his strongly held views to expediency when that was necessary to obtain unanimity in Supreme Court opinions.[40] Quite the contrary seems to have been the case. Natural modesty and a willingness to remain open-minded even after having ventured an opinion were responsible for Marshall's attitude of cooperation with his colleagues.

Much of the foregoing summary of what we know concerning Marshall's personality suggests that he was what twentieth-century psychologists would call a people person—an individual with great ability to relate to others in a constructive and understanding way. Easygoing, generous, ready to laugh at himself as well as others, he inspired confidence and trust and elicited a warm and supportive response from others. Even under provocation he found it hard to carry a grudge, and he took pains not to give offense or embarrass others. Upon John Marshall rested the responsibility of guiding the United States Supreme Court through thirty-four difficult years until his death on July 6, 1835.

Marshall's Associate Justices

It is impossible to contradict John Donne's observation that no man is an island, and this is nowhere more apparent than in the work of the United States Supreme Court. The chief justice and his associate justices work together closely both on and off the bench in hearing and deciding the controversies brought before them. That interrelationship is an important factor in the development of precedent before the Court, in the conduct of business within the Court, and in the public image the Court presents to the world. No study of the United States Supreme Court can ignore the personalities of all justices on the Court, nor can it fail to explore how they influenced each other.

Yet to bend Donne's aphorism beyond what he intended to say, we may also claim that the United States Supreme Court collectively *is* a sort of island. The judges are isolated by protocol and professional rules from free

---

40. William W. Crosskey, *Politics and the Constitution in the History of the United States,* 2 vols. (Chicago: University of Chicago Press, 1953), vol. 2, 1080–1081.

and untrammeled social intercourse with the other branches of government, members of their profession, and the litigants whose cases are heard before them. Even in Marshall's day, when Supreme Court justices rode circuit to the state capitals in their assigned region, they had a sense of being set apart. Distinctions of office and restrictions upon behavior all worked to draw the judges into their own unique and cohesive group.

Realistically, we must also concede that, contrary to Donne's view of the human condition, all individuals *are* islands—special and unique blends of intellect, emotions, and personality comprehended, if at all, only by the persons themselves and seen only remotely by their contemporaries.

All of the foregoing is to suggest that to comprehend the dynamics of the Marshall Court, it is necessary to look beyond the personality of John Marshall. The other justices must be described and placed in the context of the Supreme Court environment as well as in relationship to each other and their chief justice. Finally, the isolation of the Court from many of the influences of everyday life, and the impact that collegial life had upon the judges, must be considered before a clear picture of the Marshall Court can emerge.

Marshall's Federalist Legacy

When Marshall took his seat as chief justice, he inherited something of a mixed blessing in his Federalist associate justices. The senior associate justice, both in age and service, was William Cushing of Massachusetts. He had been appointed to the original bench of the Court in 1789 and was sixty-nine years old in 1801. Next in order of precedence was William Paterson of New Jersey, who received his appointment in 1793 and was ten years older than Marshall. Judge Samuel Chase of Maryland was appointed by President Washington in 1796 and passed his sixtieth birthday in 1801. Bushrod Washington of Virginia was President John Adams's first appointee to the Court in 1798. Washington, the favorite nephew of the former president, and John Marshall were both candidates for election to the United States House of Representatives when the death of Judge James Wilson created a vacancy. Marshall had first refusal of the appointment, which he declined in favor of Washington, who then withdrew from the congressional election. Marshall went on to win in his campaign for the Richmond area seat in the House.[41]

---

41. Dates of birth and appointment have been taken from *Justices of the United States Supreme Court, 1789–1969*, 4 vols., Leon Friedman and Fred L. Israel, editors (New York: Chelsea House, 1969), vol. 1, *passim.* In my discussion of these judges I have drawn heavily upon the summary biographies in George L. Haskins and Herbert A. Johnson, *Foundations of Power, 1801–15*, vol. 2 of *History of the Supreme Court of the United States*, 10 vols. to date

Judge Alfred Moore of North Carolina was the last of President Adams's nominations for the Court. A half-year older than the incoming chief justice, Moore wrote but one opinion in his five years on the Supreme Court bench and was the least impressive of Adams's appointees.[42]

Of the five, Judge Washington was the best known to Marshall. A fellow Virginian, the thirty-eight-year-old justice was already at work with Marshall on a proposal to edit the papers of his famous uncle, and it was with the full cooperation of Judge Washington that Marshall published his multivolume *Life of Washington* beginning in 1804. Judge Washington's career had converged with that of the new chief justice on several occasions. Both served in the 1787–88 session of the Virginia House of Delegates, and both sat in the Virginia convention that ratified the Federal Constitution in June 1788. Bushrod Washington graduated from the College of William and Mary in 1778, but he returned for George Wythe's three-month series of law lectures in 1780, which Marshall also attended. Washington then went on to a clerkship with Philadelphia attorney James Wilson, who was an associate justice of the Supreme Court from 1789 until his death in 1798.[43]

President Adams ignored sectional balance when he appointed Washington, then practicing in Alexandria, Virginia, to Wilson's vacant seat on the Court. However, Washington's ties to Philadelphia were strong, and he subsequently excelled as the circuit justice for the busy Pennsylvania federal circuit court.

Judge Washington was mild and conciliatory in outward appearance, and his diligence in studying law had blinded him in one eye. In 1808 freshman Congressman Joseph Story described him as "of a very short stature, and quite boyish in his appearance. Nothing about him indicates greatness, he converses with simplicity and frankness, But he is highly esteemed as a profound lawyer, and I believe not without reason. His written opinions are composed with ability, and on the bench he exhibits great promptitude and firmness of decision. It requires intimacy to value him as he deserves."[44] Sallow of complexion, Washington was an inveterate user of snuff and an untidy dresser. However, he was methodical in his habits and filed even the smallest piece of correspondence; surprisingly, very little

(New York: Macmillan Publishing Company, 1981), 84–102. On Marshall's role in securing the Supreme Court appointment for Washington see *Marshall Papers*, vol. 3, 507–508 (September 21 and 28, 1798).

42. Leon Friedman, "Alfred Moore," in *Justices*, vol. 1, 268, at 273.

43. The two had also argued cases before the Virginia Court of Appeals, and Bushrod Washington edited a two-volume set of reports of that court. Lawrence B. Custer, "Bushrod Washington and John Marshall: A Preliminary Inquiry," 4 *American Journal of Legal History* 34, at 36, 39 (1960).

44. February 25, 1808, to Samuel P. P. Fay, *Story Letters*, vol. 2, 167.

of his correspondence with Chief Justice Marshall has survived. As a trial judge, Washington locked his attention upon the proceedings and took few notes. He virtually ignored the courtroom audience and on occasion exhibited exemplary courage in passing sentence upon criminal defendants with a large public following.[45]

Like Marshall, Judge Washington was a voice for unanimity. In 1818 Judge Story complained that Washington had prevailed upon him not to dissent in *Olivera v. United Insurance Company,* even though "I was never more entirely satisfied that any decision was wrong, than that this is."[46] Eulogizing Washington after his death in 1829, Story wrote of his longtime colleague that "his mind was solid, rather than brilliant, sagacious and searching, rather than quick and eager; slow but not torpid; steady, but not unyielding; comprehensive, but at the same time cautious; patient in inquiry, forcible in perception, clear in reasoning. He was, by original temperament, mild, conciliating and candid; and yet he was remarkable for an uncompromising firmness." Judge Story went on to comment that Washington did not wish to shape the law to his own views but rather to follow its precepts with sincere good faith and simplicity.[47]

Very likely it was Judge Washington's concern for the integrity of the states and the regularity of contractual rights that led him to oppose Chief Justice Marshall in *Ogden v. Saunders* (1827). In effect he held that as long as a state insolvency law was prospective in its operation, it would not violate the contract clause of the Federal Constitution. For the most part, Washington's conservatism and nationalism aligned him with Marshall and Story, but his respect for *stare decisis* made him somewhat inflexible and narrow in his approach to new interpretations of the law.[48]

Next to Chief Justice Marshall, Bushrod Washington was Story's closest friend on the Supreme Court bench.[49] Together these three presented a strong chorus of Federalist ideology, and as we have seen, Washington was effective in at least one instance (and probably in many others) in restraining the young and impetuous Story from issuing a dissenting opinion. Marshall relied upon both Story and Washington for advice on admiralty and maritime law, and their understanding and support in other matters undoubtedly made it easier for him to control dissent in the Supreme Court.

Modest in demeanor, diligent and professional in the conduct of trials,

---

45. Albert P. Blaustein and Roy M. Mersky, in *Justices,* vol. 1, 243, at 250–251; Gerald T. Dunne, *Justice Joseph Story and the Rise of the Supreme Court* (New York: Simon and Schuster, 1970), 262.
46. April 8, 1818, *Story Letters,* vol. 1, 303.
47. *Ibid.* vol. 2, 30–31; quotation at 30.
48. Blaustein and Mersky, "Bushrod Washington," in *Justices,* vol. 1, 252–254, 256.
49. Newmyer, *Story,* 158.

and professionally circumspect in advancing new concepts of law, Bushrod Washington was by far the best legacy left to John Marshall by the two Federalist presidents. Among the four other judges on the Supreme Court in 1801, two were sufficiently uncontroversial to pose no threat to the Court's public position. At the same time, they would contribute little to its eminence. Of the two, Judge William Cushing at nearly sixty-nine years of age was well past his prime. Associate Justice Alfred Moore, appointed late in 1799 to succeed Judge James Iredell of North Carolina, had virtually no impact upon the Court's work before he resigned because of ill health in February 1804, giving President Thomas Jefferson his first opportunity to appoint a Supreme Court justice.

Judge Cushing had been nominated to succeed John Jay as chief justice in 1795 but declined the promotion. He continued to serve as an associate justice on the Marshall Court until his death on September 13, 1810, having completed twenty-one years of judicial service. The demands of riding circuit rested heavily upon him and depleted his health to the point that he often contemplated resignation, but financial need forced him to remain on the Court. Cushing received his first judicial appointment from Massachusetts's royal lieutenant governor, Thomas Hutchinson, in 1772. When the colony declared independence, he was recommissioned as a justice of the Superior Court. He rose to become chief justice of the Supreme Judicial Court and continued in that office until his appointment to the United States Supreme Court by President Washington. As a state judge, Cushing exhibited indomitable courage in facing rioters during the Berkshire Rebellion (1779) and Shay's Rebellion (1786). He was noted for having decided, in Quock Walker's Case (1780), that the Massachusetts Constitution, by declaring men free and equal, had abolished slavery in the Bay State. However, while the Massachusetts Ratifying Convention debated great issues of constitutional government, delegate Cushing doodled to pass the time and did not contribute to floor debate. As a colonial lawyer he enjoyed only modest prosperity, moving to Maine in an effort to gain more business. His greatest success was in commercial enterprises, but even these nonprofessional activities barely permitted him to make ends meet. His royal appointment was a welcome reprieve from what promised to be a lackluster career at the bar.[50]

Given Cushing's modest achievements prior to his appointment to the Court, the reason for his preferment must be found in President Washington's standards for selection. Of the five original appointees in 1789, four, including Cushing, had prior experience in judicial office; only James Wilson, a prominent Philadelphia attorney, lacked experience as a judge. All

---

50. Herbert A. Johnson, "William Cushing," in *Justices*, vol. 1, 57–70.

five were born between 1732 (John Blair and William Cushing) and 1745 (John Jay). Jay and Wilson were from the Middle States, Blair and Rutledge were from the South, and Cushing represented New England. Jay, complaining of the hardship of riding circuit, resigned to become governor of New York. John Rutledge resigned after one tour of the southern circuit to become chief justice of the South Carolina Court of Common Pleas. John Blair, exhausted from circuit riding, submitted his resignation in 1796 and died four years later. James Wilson, hounded by creditors acquired through his land speculations, died in office in 1798. James Iredell of South Carolina, though a relatively young man, was exhausted by his circuit-riding duties and died a year after his friend and Court colleague Judge Wilson. Cushing lived on and remained on the Court as the senior associate justice.

The two other associate justices on the Court that welcomed John Marshall were William Paterson and Samuel Chase. Paterson, appointed in 1793, served as attorney general of revolutionary New Jersey (1776–83) and, by the end of the Revolution, was the best-known lawyer in the state. Paterson was secretary to the First, Second and Third Provincial Congresses in New Jersey and represented the state in boundary controversies. As a delegate to the Philadelphia Convention he prepared and introduced the "small states" or "New Jersey Plan" as a conservative method for strengthening the Articles of Confederation. His most recent biographer, John E. O'Connor, considers Paterson to have been the major strategist and principal floor manager of the "small state" group in the convention. According to O'Connor, Paterson's deft handling of the representation issue led ultimately to the "Great Compromise" that gave each state an equal vote in the Senate but retained proportional representation in the proposed lower House. After ratification of the Federal Constitution, Paterson was elected a senator from New Jersey and played a critical role in drafting the Judiciary Act of 1789. While serving a term as governor of New Jersey, he was appointed to the United States Supreme Court by President Washington in 1793 and was considered by some to be a leading contender for promotion to chief justice in 1801.[51] President Adams's animosity toward the Hamiltonian wing of the Federalist party, to which Paterson belonged, was partially responsible for his being passed over for nomination. However, equally pressing were the president's wish to avoid insult to the senior associate justice, William Cushing, and the fact that Marshall was ten years younger and hence more likely to serve a longer term on the Court.[52] Paterson also

51. John E. O'Connor, *William Paterson: Lawyer and Statesman, 1745–1806* (New Brunswick: Rutgers University Press, 1979), 32, 47, 57, 75, 118–199, 151–154, 168, 171–173, 199–200, 221–222.

52. *Ibid.,* 261. On the nomination see also Michael Kraus, "William Paterson," in *Justices,* vol. 1. 172–173.

had a reputation for overbearing and punitive behavior as a circuit court judge disposing of Sedition Act cases.[53] This notoriety he shared with Associate Justice Samuel Chase of Maryland. Both were vulnerable to executive and legislative reprisals from the incoming president, Thomas Jefferson, and the Republican-dominated Congress.

William Pierce, a Georgia delegate to the Philadelphia Convention, described Paterson as "a Man of great modesty, with looks that bespeak talents of no great extent,—but he is a Classic, a Lawyer, and an Orator."[54] Some of these characteristics may have emerged from the future judge's undistinguished family background. The first son of an immigrant Irish tin worker turned general storekeeper, Paterson was ill at ease among his socially prominent contemporaries. Professor O'Connor documents Paterson's efforts, usually rebuffed, to maintain correspondence with his Princeton College classmates after graduation. There was a lack of self-assurance about the man. Even as a member of the United States Senate, he shunned attendance at parties, dinners, and other social events that did not require his official presence. Habitually cautious, he avoided the temptations of land speculation and manufacturing. Implicated as a surety in the financial embarrassments of two brothers, he was profoundly disturbed by the threat to his own credit and reputation for probity. When the American Revolution seemed inevitable, Paterson reluctantly joined the patriot ranks, fearing all along that the resultant disorder would destroy deferential politics and threaten the sacred rights of property ownership. That same mind-set moved him into the nationalist camp and brought him to the Philadelphia Convention. In common with virtually all present there, he believed that "unless the popular will, as expressed through the elected legislature, was limited with respect to property rights, the essential principle of republican government would be destroyed.[55] Paterson's early education impressed upon him the concept of a fundamental natural law, and from this grew his conviction that free government depended upon an institutional separation of fundamental (that is, constitutional) law from the day-to-day operations of government on one hand and the hasty decisions of legislative majorities on the other.[56] When those dearly held beliefs were threatened through the rise of partisan politics in the United States and by the excesses of the Reign of Terror in France, Paterson reacted defensively. While he was presiding over the trials of Republican editors

53. Kraus, "William Paterson," in *Justices*, vol. 1, 163–173; and O'Connor, *Paterson*, 235–248. The trials included those of Matthew Lyons and Anthony Haskell in Vermont and those of the Pennsylvania Whiskey Rebels, held earlier in 1795. *Ibid.*
54. Quoted at O'Connor, *Paterson*, 134.
55. *Ibid.*, 126.
56. *Ibid.*, 129–130.

who challenged the Federalist-based political order of the day, his hostility to partisan politics and radical political thought became manifest. He served on the Marshall Court until his death on September 4, 1806, but ill health prevented him from sitting with his colleagues at the 1804 term, and instinctive caution in the face of Republican legislative majorities caused him to play a minor role in the Court's deliberations when he was present.[57]

Native caution and sharing the Supreme Court bench with Judge Samuel Chase of Maryland shielded Judge Paterson from the full impact of Republican wrath. Judge Chase was anathema to Republicans throughout the United States. He was obese in figure, boorish in manners, and bitingly sarcastic to attorneys who appeared before him in treason and Sedition Act cases. The son of an Anglican rector in colonial Maryland, he studied law by clerkship and was admitted to the bar in 1761. In company with William Paca, he organized the Arundel County Sons of Liberty and actively participated in demonstrations opposing the Stamp Act. Prominence in the patriot cause earned him election to the First and Second Continental Congresses, where he was a member of the commission sent to Canada in an unsuccessful attempt to persuade French Canadians to join the American revolt. In 1778 he was accused of conspiring with his business partners to monopolize the wheat crop, using information available to him as a member of Congress. While the charge was later investigated and Chase was acquitted, the matter stained his reputation for the rest of his life.[58]

After the Revolution, Chase became active in land speculation, and Maryland entrusted him with an agency to regain possession of Bank of England stock owned by the state and seized by the British authorities during the war. Both ventures turned out unsatisfactorily, and Chase teetered on the brink of bankruptcy until he finally succumbed in 1788 and sought insolvency relief from his creditors. Appointments as chief judge of the Baltimore County Court of Oyer and Terminer and Gaol Delivery (1788) and chief judge of the General Court of Maryland (1791) provided him with a modest salary while he continued to importune President George Washington for an appointment to the U.S. Supreme Court. Eventually the president agreed, and the Senate confirmed Chase as an associate justice of the Court on January 27, 1796. Washington's hesitation was very likely based in part upon Chase's opposition to ratification of the Federal Constitution, which developed from his conviction that the proposed document

---

57. *Ibid.*, 7, 21, 23, 86, 121, 126, 129–130, 165–167, 174–175; quotation at *ibid.*, 126; Kraus, "William Paterson," *Justices*, vol. 1, 173.

58. Jane Schaffer Elsmere, *Justice Samuel Chase* (Muncie: Janevar, 1980), 1, 5, 10, 20–21. Chase was born in 1741, and his mother died shortly after his birth. *Ibid.*, 1.

lacked adequate guarantees for the liberties of the people.[59] On the other
hand, it is likely that executive caution was also attributable to Washington's reflection upon Chase's checkered and somewhat unsavory background. As early as 1778, when Chase served in Congress, he suffered from
gout. It is reported also that "his temper became unusually short, and he
could tolerate neither fools nor inefficiency."[60] As a judge of polls in a 1792
Maryland election, he had been so overbearing toward opposition voters
that some tradesmen threatened to carry him to the river for an involun-
tary swim. Considering Chase's weight, Dr. Elsmere comments, "Fortunately for Chase's dignity and their backs they were persuaded not to carry
out their intentions."[61] Witty and learned in his conversation, Chase could
also be boorish and insulting to hostesses.[62] Gout and sciatica kept him out
of regular circuit court duty once he had his Supreme Court appointment
and made him irritable when he presided at trials. He missed riding circuit
in 1798 and 1799, but his presiding over circuit courts in 1800 provided
him with adequate opportunity to balance the account with an extraordinary quantity of boorishness, overbearing comments, and browbeating of
Republican attorneys.

Chase's habitual behavior on the bench is graphically illustrated by an
undated letter of Uriah Tracy. Since Chief Justice Ellsworth is mentioned,
the incident must have occurred shortly after Chase took his place on the
Court.

> At times Chase's brusque manner on the bench was a trial to his brother
> judges. Neither coolness toward him nor tactful hints to mend his ways
> deterred him from showing irritation toward counsel who spoke too
> long or otherwise seemed to abuse their position. Chase was displeased
> particularly when counsel argued at length on the merits of a point
> which he considered settled. . . . On one occasion Chase presided with
> Chief Justice Oliver Ellsworth at a case heard in Philadelphia. [Jared]
> Ingersoll reportedly persisted in arguing about a point of law which
> Chase told him was settled. Three times Ingersoll brought the matter to
> the Court's attention and three times Chase chided him, each time
> more sharply. Ellsworth grew angry with Chase for interrupting Inger-
> soll's argument and thus prolonging it. At the end of his patience the
> Chief Justice took out his snuff box and, giving himself time to gain
> control of his temper, tapped the box on its side before he took a pinch

59. *Ibid.*, 25–26, 31, 34–36, 38, 44, 56.
60. *Ibid.*, 19.
61. *Ibid.*, 45.
62. *Ibid.*, 68, 87.

of snuff from it. Looking at Ingersoll, the Chief Justice said meaning-fully, "The Court has expressed no opinion, Sir, upon these points, and when it does, you will hear it from the proper organ [the Chief Justice] of the Court." Ellsworth then directed such a "withering look of re-buke" upon Chase that the latter "with all his nerve and daring, fairly quailed.[63]

During 1800 Judge Chase presided over the treason trial of John Fries and his associates in Northampton County, Pennsylvania, where the judge behaved in his usual brusque and partisan manner. District Judge Richard Peters, who joined Chase in the subsequent Sedition Act trial of editor Thomas Cooper, felt that the fine imposed by Chase was unduly severe. The capstone of Chase's judicial activities for the year came in Virginia when he rode roughshod over three leaders of Virginia's Republican bar to secure a conviction of a virtuoso of political libel, James T. Callender. Highlighted in the national press, the case focused attention upon Judge Chase and heightened Republican resolve that the judiciary had to be brought to heel once the election of 1800 was won by Thomas Jefferson. As for Chase himself, the *Philadelphia Aurora* resorted to verse to convey its contempt: "Cursed of thy father, scum of all that's base / Thy sight is odi-ous, and thy name is Chase."[64]

Contrasting behavioral patterns and judicial manners divided incoming Chief Justice Marshall from Judge Samuel Chase. Quite likely a patronage decision during the summer of 1800 also contributed to tension between the two men. Chase had importuned President John Adams to appoint his son Thomas Chase to the position of United States marshal for Maryland. Although the president was inclined to accommodate Chase, John Marshall as secretary of state was delegated the final responsibility of deciding on the recipient of the office. After consulting with Secretary of the Navy Ben-jamin Stoddart, who was a citizen of Maryland, Marshall came to the con-clusion that the appointment should go elsewhere.[65] As a perennial and persistent place man, the Judge would not take kindly to such a rebuff.

Such was Chief Justice Marshall's legacy from the ranks of Federalist appointees to the Supreme Court bench. Among the associate justices, only Bushrod Washington held promise as a vigorous jurist who shared Mar-shall's political and economic views. Cushing's advanced age precluded him from playing an active role. Paterson seems to have accepted gracefully his being passed over for appointment to the chief justiceship, but his age

---

63. Quoted from an extract in *ibid.*, 65–66.
64. *Ibid.*, 95–122, quotation at 123.
65. *Ibid.*, 131.

and susceptibility to illness hampered his activities. He also evidenced a diffidence attributable to his modest family background, which destined him to a limited part in early Marshall Court decisions. Paterson was tainted with having presided vigorously at criminal trials under the Sedition Act and may have felt himself under the same threat of impeachment that focused more directly upon his pompous and overbearing colleague Samuel Chase.

Judge Chase certainly retained much of the intellectual vigor and physical energy of his youth, but the full significance of Thomas Jefferson's political victory seems to have chastened if not silenced him. His contribution to Supreme Court jurisprudence from 1801 to his death in 1811 was far more limited than might have been anticipated in 1801. In brief, the Federalist legacy, with the exception of Judge Washington, was not a very positive factor in strengthening the Court as an institution or in aiding the new chief justice in navigating the heavy seas of political opposition and reprisal.

Jefferson's Appointees: William Johnson, Brockholst Livingston, and Thomas Todd

During his eight years as president, Thomas Jefferson had the opportunity to appoint three associate justices to the Supreme Court. Two vacancies occurred early in Marshall's term as chief justice. Alfred Moore of North Carolina resigned in 1804, making way for the appointment of William Johnson of South Carolina; and William Paterson of New Jersey died in 1806, leaving a place on the Court to be filled by H. Brockholst Livingston of New York. Jefferson's third appointment, Thomas Todd of Kentucky, was made possible by Congress's authorization of a western circuit and adding an additional Supreme Court justice to preside in those circuit courts.[66]

Although it was inevitable that there would be attrition among the Federalist justices, the arrival of Jefferson's first appointee, William Johnson, was a turning point in the history of Marshall's chief justiceship. From 1805 forward Jeffersonian political values could find expression in constitutional law, and the promise of more Republican appointees anticipated a time when the Federalist judges might become dissenters.

In retrospect it is apparent that Marshall's Court was only moderately affected by these shifts in political power. This was due in part to the slow

---

66. An Act Establishing Circuit Courts. . . , February 24, 1807, 2 Stat. 420–421. The new circuit covered the states of Kentucky, Tennessee, and Ohio; previously these states had been served by district courts authorized to exercise circuit court jurisdiction.

turnover of Court members, providing Jefferson and his successors with a limited number of opportunities to nominate. When the 1805 Republican campaign to impeach and convict Judge Chase failed, the judiciary gained additional strength and security against wholesale dismissal of judges whenever the political balance of power shifted. Another factor providing stability in the federal judiciary was the gradual disappearance of the Federalist party as a viable opposition to the Jeffersonians. This permitted a more broadly based Republican party in which elements of Federalist political and economic thought once more became respectable. Symbolic of this rapprochement was the Republican Party's selection of John Quincy Adams, son of the last Federalist president, to be its presidential nominee in 1824. Within the group of Supreme Court justices, a similar type of reconciliation took place, resulting in a substantial alignment in constitutional thought between Marshall's remaining Federalist judges and their newly appointed Jeffersonian colleagues.

The first of Jefferson's appointees, William Johnson, provides an excellent illustration of this process. As the son of a blacksmith, the new justice lacked the social standing common to all of his Court colleagues except Judge Paterson. However, he came from good revolutionary stock. His father organized the Charleston mechanics for Christopher Gadsden, and with the 1780 fall of Charleston to the British, young William accompanied the family into exile in British-held Florida. Educated at Princeton and by clerkship in the law office of Charles Cotesworth Pinckney, Johnson was admitted to the bar in 1793. Beginning in 1794, he was elected and reelected to the South Carolina House of Representatives until 1799, when he was elected a judge of the Court of Common Pleas by the House. Since membership in the Common Pleas Court carried with it a seat on the highest state appellate court, the Constitutional Court, Johnson was in an ideal position to gain Jefferson's nomination in 1804.[67]

Judge Johnson believed in legislative predominance in the affairs of government. The 1790 South Carolina Constitution perpetuated and strengthened the traditional control of the legislature over the election of the governor and the selection of judges. As a member of the House of Representatives who rose to the position of speaker before his elevation to the bench, Johnson was a product of this system and firmly believed that the people's legislative representatives should be the major policy-making com-

---

67. Donald G. Morgan, *Justice William Johnson, the First Dissenter: the Career and Constitutional Philosophy of a Jeffersonian Judge* (Columbia: University of South Carolina Press, 1954), 1–40. Morgan has written an excellent short sketch of Johnson's life that appears in *Justices*, vol. 1, 355–372. For a brief introduction to Johnson's constitutional thought, see Herbert A. Johnson, "The Constitutional Thought of William Johnson," 89 *South Carolina Historical Magazine*, 132–145 (1988).

ponent of republican government. When he joined the Supreme Court, his preference for legislative primacy impelled him to condemn President Jefferson's claim to exercise executive discretion in administering the Embargo Law. It also led him to seek the legitimacy of federal judicial power in express statutory provisions. Judge Johnson's solicitude for legislative power also generated disagreement with Chief Justice Marshall over the scope of the contract clause of the Federal Constitution. Since the contract clause operated as a restraint upon state legislative activity, Johnson was inclined to construe it narrowly. Consequently, as Marshall's opinions gradually expanded the contract clause limits on state legislative action (in *Fletcher v. Peck* and *Dartmouth College v. Woodward*), Johnson was forced into dissent or concurrences.[68]

Johnson brought South Carolinian views of legislative dominance to his work on the Supreme Court, but he concurred neither with the states' rights theories that were becoming popular in the agrarian South nor with efforts to expand state police power limits on the interstate commerce clause. His commitment to nationalism brought him to deny the validity of South Carolina's Negro Seaman's Act in the 1823 case *Elkison v. Deliesseline*. These strongly held convictions eventually brought him to such a tense relationship with his Charleston neighbors during the nullification crisis that Johnson left home to spend the summer in New York City. There he died in August 1834, having submitted to surgery from which he did not recover.[69]

William Johnson's appointment to the Court introduced a forceful personality into the hitherto restrained atmosphere that welcomed Marshall's leadership. John Quincy Adams characterized Johnson as "a man of considerable talents and law knowledge, but a restless, turbulent hot-headed, political caballing Judge."[70] There is compounding evidence concerning Judge Johnson's quick temper. In 1823 the Charleston newspapers made public a heated correspondence between him and President Thomas Cooper of South Carolina College.[71] Another contemporary described him as "bold, independent, eccentric and sometimes harsh."[72] Professor Morgan comments, "William Johnson had little of the disarming charm of manner or the simple clarity of expression characteristic of the great Chief Justice. He was scarcely the man to inspire disciples. This Johnson could boast no Boswell!"[73]

---

68. Johnson, "Constitutional Thought," 134–137; Morgan, *Johnson*, 75–92, 115–121, 192–218, 280–298.
69. Morgan, *Johnson*, 192–206, 268–281.
70. From an 1820 memoir entry quoted in Dunne, *Story*, 169, and at Morgan, *Johnson*, 107.
71. Morgan, *Johnson*, 141–143.
72. Charles J. Ingersoll, quoted in *ibid.*, 75.
73. *Ibid.*, 284.

Some of Judge Johnson's eccentricities became manifest in his relationships with colleagues on the Court, especially Joseph Story. When the two first met, in 1808, Story noted that Johnson had "a strong mathematical head, and considerable soundness of erudition." In time Story would assert that Johnson's opinions were lacking in precision and certainty. Johnson, in turn, seems to have been aware of Judge Story's friendship with Court reporter Henry Wheaton, and this knowledge may have given rise to resentment against both of them. On occasion Judge Johnson referred to Story's opinions as being loaded with dicta; his reference to "themes" and digest systems could be seen as barbs directed at Story's practice of writing anonymous notes or appendices to the Supreme Court's printed reports.[74]

In March 1820 Judge Johnson verbally attacked Chief Justice Marshall from the bench when the continuance of the *Amiable Isabella* case was announced. Johnson persisted in reading his personal opinion in the case and then ridiculed the arguments of William Pinkney, who was counsel for one of the parties. Writing of the incident to Joseph Story, Henry Wheaton commented, "The judges lament this extravagant sally, which was the more unfortunate as great numbers of persons were assembled for the purpose of hearing the decision of the Court. Judge Washington assures me that everything was done that *could be done, to prevent it, but in vain.*"[75] A few months later Wheaton apologized to Judge Story for printing Johnson's "crudities" in the Supreme Court case reports, concluding, "He has great strength of mind, but the defects of his early education predominate and he has unfortunately most conceit where he is most deficient—But what can't be cured must be endured."[76] The charged atmosphere between Story and Johnson may have gained much energy from their conflict over two matters: the nature and extent of admiralty jurisdiction and the existence of a federal common law, particularly in the area of substantive criminal law. In addition, as we shall see in discussing Judge Story, his quick mind and encyclopedic knowledge of the law were at times accompanied by an ability to irritate others. Given the evidence, it would seem unfair to blame the situation entirely on Judge Johnson. Rather it is likely that the strong personalities of Johnson and Story clashed after 1812, presenting a substantial challenge to the conciliating powers of Chief Justice Marshall.

President Jefferson's second appointment to the Supreme Court was Henry Brockholst Livingston, a member of the Manor Livingston family of New York and brother-in-law of former Chief Justice John Jay.[77] An early

---

74. Story to Samuel P. P. Fay, February 25, 1808, in *Story Letters*, vol. 1, 168; Morgan, *Johnson*, 283–284; Dunne, *Story*, 168–169. 201.
75. Discussed and quoted in Dunne, *Story*, 280–281.
76. July 2, 1820, quoted in *Ibid.*, 202–203.
77. Gerald T. Dunne, "Brockholst Livingston," in *Justices*, vol. 1, 387, at 387–388.

recruit into the American Revolution, Livingston served as a staff officer in the Continental Army and rose to the rank of lieutenant colonel before he accompanied Jay on his abortive mission to induce Spain to support the American cause. During the course of that diplomatic mission, the twenty-two-year-old officer became extremely sullen and temperamental, casting frequent aspersions upon the Continental Congress. This behavior drew the sharp disapproval of his sister and ultimately provoked a rupture between Jay and Livingston that resulted in the young man's return to the United States. During Jay's 1792 campaign for the New York governorship of New York, Livingston worked diligently to prevent the election of his brother-in-law. Subsequently he joined those who openly attacked the treaty Jay had negotiated with Great Britain. Around this time he dropped his first name and became simply Brockholst Livingston, adopting for public use the name earlier used in family circles.[78]

Livingston served in the New York Assembly from 1800 to 1802, when he was appointed an associate justice of the New York Supreme Court. Already on that bench were two Livingston in-laws, Chief Justice Morgan Lewis and Associate Justice Smith Thompson. Judge Livingston was energetic and visible; in his four years on the court he wrote 149 opinions, many of them expressing his independent concurring or dissenting views. Conspicuously mentioned for appointment to fill the vacant seat of Alfred Moore in 1804, Livingston was passed over when sectional considerations led to the appointment of William Johnson from South Carolina. Upon the death of Judge Paterson, Livingston received Jefferson's nomination and took his seat for the commencement of the February 1807 term.[79]

Shortly after his appointment, Livingston was described by then congressman Joseph Story as follows: "Livingston has a fine Roman face; an aquiline nose, high forehead, bald head, and projecting chin, indicate deep research, strength, and quickness of mind. I have no hesitation in pronouncing him a very able and independent Judge. He evidently thinks with great solidity and seizes on the strong points of argument. He is luminous, decisive, earnest and impressive on the bench. In private society he is accessible and easy, and enjoys with great good humor the vivacities, if I may coin a word, of the wit and moralist."[80] Story's initial impression was strengthened after he joined Livingston on the Court in 1812. Their surviving correspondence shows an easy familiarity and comradeship between

78. *Ibid.*, 387–389; for more detail on Livingston's relationship to the Jays in Spain see *John Jay, The Winning of the Peace: Unpublished Papers, 1780–1784,* Richard B. Morris, ed. (New York: Harper & Row, 1980), 168, 188–194.

79. Dunne, "Brockholst Livingston," *Justices,* vol. 1, 389–391.

80. *Story Letters,* vol. 1, 167.

the New York aristocrat turned Republican and the Massachusetts banker and lawyer. Accompanied by Story and Judge Thomas Todd, Livingston traveled to Mount Vernon to visit Bushrod Washington during his illness in February 1821.[81]

According to biographer Gerald Dunne, Livingston exhibited a pattern of rugged independence upon appointment to the New York Supreme Court and subsequently on taking a seat on the United States Supreme Court. However, as his service on each tribunal continued, he increasingly participated in joint opinions. Dunne suggests that Livingston's congenial nature made concurrence easier; he also notes that "Livingston can serve as an illustrative example of how the Federalist Chief Justice dominated and made dominant a tribunal largely appointed by his political opponents." On the other hand, Dunne is quick to point out Livingston's gradual return to the conservative, Federalist-oriented views of his youth.[82]

Although Judge Livingston was expert in admiralty and prize law, there is no evidence that he was consulted by John Marshall for advice in those fields. Since the Chief Justice frequently asked either Story or Washington for advice in deciding maritime cases, we may assume that there was greater distance between him and Livingston or, that if such consultations did occur, the fragmentary correspondence of both men does not contain any record of it. On the other hand, the web of personal relationships between justices clearly included Livingston. The Chief Justice's closest associates were Judges Washington and Story; Story in turn provided a link to Judge Livingston, and Washington and Todd may well have been included within a wider circle of friendship by 1821 when Washington was visited by the other three.

Judge Livingston was an active member of the Supreme Court bench and an effective trial judge at the circuit court of New York. The broad array of Livingston family interests, ranging from Louisiana real-property matters to encouragement of steamboat navigation, occasionally raised complaints of financial interest in cases tried before him. However, he seems to have been careful to avoid any direct conflicts, and he earned the esteem of the bar and his colleagues on the bench, who mourned his death in 1823.[83]

Unlike Brockholst Livingston, Jefferson's last Supreme Court appointee, Thomas Todd, left a meager impress upon the history of the Court.[84] Born

---

81. Dunne, "The Story-Livingston Correspondence (1812–1822)," 10 *American Journal of Legal History* 226–236 (1966); Story to Sarah W. Story, February 27, 1821, *Story Letters*, vol. 1, 398.

82. Dunne, "Brockholst Livingston," *Justices*, vol. 1, 391–392, quotation at 391.

83. *Ibid.*, 392–397.

84. Except as otherwise indicated, the details are from Fred L. Israel, "Thomas Todd," in

in Virginia in 1765, Judge Todd received a modest education in the classics and then became a clerk to Harry Innes, an attorney who moved to Kentucky, taking young Todd with him. Admitted to the Virginia bar in 1788, Todd was a highly successful litigator in the field of contested Kentucky land titles, the area in which he made his most significant contribution to Supreme Court opinions. He served as a judge and subsequently as chief judge of the Kentucky Court of Appeals from 1801 until he was appointed to the United States Supreme Court in 1807. Difficulties of travel and ill health caused him to miss the 1809, 1813, 1815, and 1819 terms in Washington. His wife's death in 1811 made him one of two single Supreme Court justices, and in March 1812 Joseph Story wrote his wife that Todd was "violently affected with the tender passion." Story continued, "The wisdom of years does not add anything of discretion to the impatience, jealousies, or doubts of a lover."[85] The lady of Judge Todd's desire was Lucy Payne, a sister of Dolly Madison, and the couple were the first to be married in the White House. Unfortunately, no biographer has dealt at length with the life of Judge Todd, whose social and marital activities seem to have eclipsed his practical contributions to the history of the Supreme Court.

Joseph Story and Gabriel Duvall: The Strong and the Silent

Among the justices who served on Marshall's Court, two stand out as preeminent in his affection—Joseph Story and Bushrod Washington. To them the Chief Justice signed his letters "affectionately," and with them he enjoyed a particularly close fellowship. Marshall's ties to Judge Washington were rooted in Virginia and his treasured but rather formal friendship with President George Washington.

Judge Washington and the Chief Justice were contemporaries in age, and they shared both Virginia nativity and practice in the Virginia court system. When Joseph Story was born in Marblehead, Massachusetts, in 1779, Captain John Marshall of the Seventh Virginia Continental Regiment was resting on his arms after the capture of Stony Point. During Marshall's later years, a British traveler seeing Marshall leaning on Story's arm as they walked thought the two of them looked more like father and son than judicial colleagues. When Joseph Story took his place on the Supreme Court, he was thirty-two years old; both Marshall and Washington were

---

Justices, vol. 1, 407–412; Todd was appointed to fill a new seat on the Supreme Court authorized by Congress on February 24, 1807, 2 Stat. 420, at 421. Frank Easterbrook considers Todd, whose entire Supreme Court output was limited to opinions in real-property cases, to be the most insignificant Supreme Court justice in history. "The Most Insignificant Justice: Further Evidence," 50 *University of Chicago Law Review* 481, at 483, 496 (1983).
85. *Story Letters*, 219.

already well past fifty. Yet despite these and other differences, the three remained close personal friends and confidants until Judge Washington's death in 1829 and Marshall's demise slightly less than five years later. Washington's decisions on the bench so closely paralleled those of Marshall that their Jeffersonian-Republican colleague William Johnson observed that the two were considered to vote as a unit.[86] No such unanimity existed in Judge Story's voting patterns and opinions, but the relationship between Marshall and his young associate grew only stronger through their years of judicial service together.

Joseph Story was appointed to the Supreme Court in November 1811, following a long period of indecision concerning who would succeed Associate Justice William Cushing, who had died in 1810. President James Madison, acceding to the wishes of his predecessor, Thomas Jefferson, nominated Levi Lincoln of Massachusetts, who declined because of poor eyesight. He then sent the name of Alexander Wolcott to the Senate, but Wolcott was denied confirmation. Next on Madison's list was John Quincy Adams, who had already moved into Jeffersonian-Republican party ranks. In the early stages of contemplating a campaign for the presidency, Adams asked that his name be withdrawn. Madison then forwarded the name of his fourth nominee, Joseph Story, to the Senate, which confirmed the appointment. Along with Story, the Senate confirmed Gabriel Duvall of Maryland, the latter to fill the associate justiceship left vacant by the death of Samuel Chase in June 1811.[87] The position Story would occupy had been vacant for nearly two years, and the dockets of the United States circuit courts in New England were filled with pending cases because no Supreme Court justice was available to tend to this business.

President Jefferson's opposition to Story's appointment was based on the nominee's opposition to the embargo, enacted during his single term as a congressman from Massachusetts. As Story explained that situation to Edward Everett in 1829, "The whole influence of the Administration was directly brought to bear upon Mr. Ezekiel Bacon and myself to seduce us from what we considered a great duty to our country and especially to New England. We were scolded, privately consulted, and argued with, by the Administration and its friends. . . . I was satisfied . . . it would be ruin to the whole country. Yet Mr. Jefferson, with his usual visionary obstinacy, was determined to maintain it; and the New England Republicans were to be made the instruments."[88]

86. *Marshall Papers,* vol. 1, 34; R. Kent Newmyer, *Supreme Court Justice Joseph Story: Statesman of the Old Republic* (Chapel Hill: University of North Carolina Press, 1985), 5; *Story Letters,* vol. 1, 2; Dunne, *Story,* 347; Johnson's comment on Marshall and Washington is in a December 10, 1822, letter to Thomas Jefferson, extracted in Morgan, *Johnson,* 182.

87. Dunne, *Story,* 78–80; Newmyer, *Story,* 70–71.

88. *Story Letters,* vol. 1, 187.

Apparently the new judge's independence of Republican Party discipline was established well before the nomination was forwarded for confirmation.

One of Story's biographers asserts that Story was "nervous" upon taking his Supreme Court seat in the early months of 1812 and was then on the "low side of the cycle of alternating cheerfulness and depression which persistently beset him." Such feelings of inadequacy, if they existed, were doubtless of short duration for, with the exception of Marshall, Washington, and Johnson, the sitting justices were at best "only solidly competent." Story's youth was more than counterbalanced by a strong classical education at Harvard, apprenticeship to two leading Massachusetts attorneys, and an extensive admiralty practice before the federal District Court for Massachusetts.[89]

Almost immediately Judge Story was a presence to be reckoned with in Court conferences and during oral argument. His loquacious personality and boundless energy transformed the sedate and rather elderly tribunal into a vibrant forum for debate. When he was in a room, few others found opportunity to speak, but those present reportedly did not resent Story's mannerisms because he talked not to dominate others but simply because he could not help it.[90] His enthusiasm and energy found expression in a growing number of Court opinions studded with references to English common law, continental civil law, and numerous historical sources. Chief Justice Marshall promptly harnessed Story's impressive legal knowledge to the heavy task of opinion writing that confronted the Court. Reportedly on one occasion early in Story's career on the Court, Marshall announced the decision and then commented that "Brother Story, here . . . can give us the cases from the Twelve Tables down to the latest reports."[91] Increasingly Supreme Court opinions evolved into comprehensive discussions of a field of law rather than ad hoc determinations of the matters at issue. Professor Newmyer observes that Story approached the law "comprehensively and architecturally—that is to say he consciously sought to put each rule, each case, in the fullest context of authority: to define by elimination, support by analogue, expand by extrapolation."[92] Not content with writing within the limitation of issues raised before the Court, Story contributed extensive notes and appendices for inclusion in Wheaton's Supreme Court reports. These were published anonymously, but Story's account book identifies ten

---

89. Dunne, *Story*, 25, 65, 91; Newmyer, *Story*, 77.

90. Dunne, *Story*, 33. Newmyer comments that Story's health began to decline, but he still avoided physical exercise: "Unfortunately, recreation for him was talking, not walking." Newmyer, *Story*, 157; see also Dunne, *Story*, 33, and *Story Letters*, vol. 2, 106.

91. Newmyer, *Story*, 81, 176, 197; Dunne, *Story*, 91.

92. Dunne, *Story*, 237–238; quotation at Newmyer, *Story*, 112–113.

appendices and notes written by him for the first five volumes of Wheaton's *Reports*.[93] An "artesian well" of legal knowledge, Story freely gave advice to countless lawyers he knew personally and several he knew only by correspondence.[94]

Undoubtedly, intellectual brilliance and scholarly achievement were Story's most outstanding personal attributes, but his experiences in life made him sensitive and responsive to others. "Congeniality, simple punctuality, dependability, careful management and even good manners paid off for Story in his law practice."[95] A reputation for sensitivity and statesmanlike discretion resulted in Story's selection to mediate a disputed Massachusetts election in 1806 and the impeachment charges against Moses Copeland in 1807. As a young man, Story was somewhat debonair in dress and was taken aback by Thomas Jefferson's negligent dress when the president received him in the White House.[96] Apparently similar lapses on the part of Chief Justice Marshall were either unnoticed or more quickly forgiven. As Dane Professor of Law at Harvard later in life, Story was extremely popular with his students, who found him demanding but at the same time a man with a sunny, smiling face whose heart was as full of kindness as his mind was full of law. He became a friend to each one of them, treating them with respect and thoughtfulness, but at the same time he never lost their respect. A Unitarian, he argued persuasively for toleration of Catholicism in correspondence with British statesmen and believed in freedom of opinion and inquiry in religious matters.[97] Despite his associations with the leading mercantile and industrial figures in New England, Story exhibited great interest in all classes and occupations. His colleague Judge Smith Thompson claimed that Story knew their trades and businesses as well as they did.[98]

Like John Marshall, Judge Story was a devoted family man, and his letters to his wife, Sarah Waldo Wetmore Story, contain careful descriptions of the social life of the justices as well as discussions of matters pending before them and the other branches of government. Schooled with girls at

---

93. They are as follows: On practice in prize cases, 1 Wheaton; on *Duvall v. Craig,* on *Liter v. Green,* and an appendix on prize practice and principles in 2 Wheaton; notes on *Robinson v. Campbell* and *Lanusse v. Barker* and an appendix on patent law in 3 Wheaton; an appendix on the law of charitable uses in 4 Wheaton; a note on piracy and a note on admiralty jurisdiction in cases of crime in 5 Wheaton. *Story Letters,* vol. 1, 283.

94. *Ibid.,* 176.

95. Newmyer, *Story,* 67.

96. *Story Letters,* vol. 1, 150; Dunne, *Story,* 125.

97. Newmyer, *Story,* 29, 253; *The Miscellaneous Writings of Joseph Story,* William W. Story, editor (Boston: Charles C. Little and James Brown, 1852), 5; Story to J. Evelyn Denison, M.P., January 20, 1826, *Story Letters,* vol. 1, 486–492.

98. Newmyer, *Story,* 121.

Marblehead Academy, Story recognized equal intellectual ability in men and women. He felt premature termination of female education was responsible for any difference between the sexes in mental acuity. Like the Chief Justice, Story and his wife lost several children to disease, and Sarah Story, like Polly Marshall, suffered from chronic illness.[99] Both Story and Marshall were devoted to home and hearth, and sharing their burdens and sorrows strengthened the growing affection between them.

In political and constitutional thought, Joseph Story was first and foremost a nationalist, exceeding even Chief Justice Marshall in his enthusiasm for the new federal republic. "Story's nationalism involved a mystical, almost religious, strain in an exulting nationalism," comments biographer Gerald Dunne.[100] In the case of wartime prize cases, Story's sense of nationalism, combined with a reliance upon the Spartan rules of international maritime law espoused by Cornelius van Bynkershoek, drew him into dissent against many of Marshall's more moderate decisions. Story dissented seven times in prize cases and wrote a growing number of Court opinions in this area: two in 1812, six in 1813, twelve in 1814, seven in 1815, and nine in 1816.[101] Nationalism was also a factor in Story's lifelong campaign for a recognition of a federal common law of crime, evidenced by his circuit court opinion in *United States v. Coolidge* (1812).[102]

Viewing with alarm the growing democratization of American political life, Story sought refuge in the law as a means to preserve the republican heritage of the American Revolution. Because of his commercial and in-

---

99. Dunne, *Story*, 94; *Story Misc. Writings*, 10–11; Newmyer, *Story*, 157; *Story Letters*, vol. 1, 314. Perhaps somewhat uncharitably, biographer Gerald Dunne comments that "one suspects that Mrs. Story rather enjoyed her poor health, wearing the martyr's crown in her frequently husbandless parlor." *Story*, 253. The same could be said of Polly Marshall, who may have suffered from a gynecological malady but seems also to have had some symptoms of mental illness.

100. Dunne, *Story*, 194. While Story's nationalism and decrees on the circuit court bench alienated New England secessionists during the War of 1812, Marshall kept intact his ties to the dissidents. Newmyer, *Story*, 94.

101. Dunne, *Story*, 113–114; Newmyer, *Story*, 83, 86, 93, 95.

102. Dunne, *Story*, 90–91, 107–109; Newmyer, *Story*, 101. The controversy over federal common-law crimes prior to 1801 is surveyed in Robert C. Palmer, "The Federal Common Law of Crime," 4 *Law and History Review* 267–323 (1986); and the Story-Johnson conflict is discussed in Kathryn Preyer, "Jurisdiction to Punish: Federal Authority, Federalism and the Common Law of Crimes in the Early Republic," 4 *Law and History Review* 223–265 (1986). Recently Michael Conant has argued forcefully that, based upon the commerce power and the supremacy of the federal government in international law matters, the federal courts should have developed a federal common law concerning commercial paper and other mercantile law topics. "The Commerce Clause, the Supremacy Clause and the Law Merchant: Swift v. Tyson and the Unity of Commercial Law," 14 *Journal of Maritime and Commercial Law* 153–178 (1984).

dustrialist connections, he favored economic enterprise but withdrew his support when new initiatives threatened property rights. The scientific development of the law was, to Story, the means by which the excesses of majoritarian government might be controlled. This would be through expansion of judicial power on one hand and, on the other, through public acceptance of the need for judicially determined predictability in economic relationships.[103]

Study of natural law heightened Story's sense of abstract justice. In 1821 he addressed the following rhetorical question to the Suffolk County (Massachusetts) bar: "What, indeed, can tend more to exalt and purify the mind, than speculations upon the origin and extent of moral obligations; upon the great truths and dictates of natural law; upon the immutable principles, that regulate right and wrong in social and private life; and upon the just applications of these to the intercourse, duties, and contentions of independent nations?" In his inaugural lecture as Dane Professor, he asserted that Christianity provided the very foundation upon which the common law was erected, for Christianity "now repudiates every act done in violation of its duties of perfect obligation. It pronounces illegal every contract offensive to its morals." In 1822 Story's circuit court opinion in *United States v. La Jeune Eugenie* condemned the slave trade as "repugnant to the general principles of justice and humanity." Small wonder that Story joined Judge Smith Thompson in dissent when Chief Justice John Marshall held that the Cherokee Nation was not an independent nation for purposes of asserting federal jurisdiction.[104]

The difference between Marshall and Story over the *Cherokee Nation* case is illustrative of more than their varied views of natural law. It shows very clearly their divergent approaches to adjudication. As Professor Newmyer suggests, Marshall was moderate and cautious, while Story was a proponent of purity. At times Story could provoke antipathy, and his scholarship and garrulous tendencies were overpowering to many. As in the case of Littleton Waller Tazewell, it frequently fell to the Chief Justice to soothe the ruffled egos of fellow justices and members of the Supreme Court bar.[105] While the Supreme Court gained intellectual power with the arrival of Joseph Story, it needed more than ever the moderation and political deftness of Chief Justice Marshall to temper Story's enthusiasm and doctrinaire ad-

103. Newmyer, *Story*, xvi, 38, 66–67, 99, 116–117, 144, 148, 178; Dunne, *Story*, 235. See also Story's essay "Characteristics of the Age," in *Story Misc. Writings*, 344–345, 350, 355–356 (1826).

104. *Story Letters*, vol. 1, 409; *ibid.*, vol. 2, 8–9; Newmyer, *Story*, 166; see the discussion of *Cherokee Nation v. Georgia* and *Worcester v. Georgia* at 81–84, 94, 248–255.

105. Newmyer, *Story*, 82, 197; Dunne, *Story*, 94; see discussion at 19–20.

vocacy of controversial views concerning law and constitutional government.

Judge Story's appointment was combined with that of Gabriel Duvall of Maryland, one of the less verbal justices in the history of the Court. By virtue of his earlier birth date (1752), Duvall was considered senior to Story. In every other way Story was the dominant twin. Duvall deserves the epithet "the Silent," for it was he who, following Marshall's extensive majority opinion (and Story's not inconsiderable concurring opinion) in *Dartmouth College v. Woodward,* noted that "Mr. Justice Duvall dissented." Why, we shall never know, for he did not elaborate. Duvall had some law training before the American Revolution and was admitted to the Maryland bar in 1778, having already served as clerk of the Maryland Convention and the Council of Safety. He served in the Supply Corps of the Continental Army and as a private in the Maryland militia during the battle of Brandywine. He was elected to the Maryland legislature, serving from 1787 to 1794, and as a member of the United States House of Representatives (1794–96). His judicial experience came during his tenure as chief justice of the General Court of Maryland (1796–1802), a position he resigned to become the first comptroller of the Treasury (1802–11). He was appointed to the United States Supreme Court to succeed Samuel Chase, who died on June 19, 1811. Duvall was almost sixty years old when he took his place on the bench, and he served for more than twenty-three years, resigning at the age of eighty-three on January 10, 1835.[106]

Duvall's years on the Court were marred by progressive deafness, and as he aged there were speculations that he might retire. When assured that President Jackson intended to appoint Roger B. Taney to his place, Duvall was convinced to step down, living out his days at his ancestral home until he died at the age of ninety-two. Political complications faulted the promise to appoint Taney, and Duvall's seat went instead to Phillip Barbour. Taney succeeded Marshall as chief justice in 1836.[107]

On the Court, Duvall supported Marshall's nationalism and rarely dissented from the Chief Justice's position. In *Mima Queen v. Hepburn* Judge Duvall refused to accept Marshall's view that the hearsay evidence rule was not relaxed in actions to obtain release from slavery.[108] He argued that the Maryland rule permitted hearsay testimony in regard to ancient transactions and matters of family genealogy when the witnesses were unlikely to

---

106. Irving Dilliard, "Gabriel Duvall," in *Justices,* vol. 1, 419–429. Professor David P. Currie claims that in his Court work Duvall "achieved an unenviable standard of insignificance against which all other justices must be measured." "The Most Insignificant Justice: A Preliminary Inquiry," 50 *University of Chicago Law Review* 466, at 466 (1983).

107. Dilliard, "Gabriel Duvall," *Justices,* vol. 1, 427–428.

108. 7 Cranch 290, at 298–299 (1813).

be alive at the time of trial. Since Maryland law was generally applicable to Washington County of the District of Columbia, where the case arose, Duvall's dissent cast serious doubt upon the wisdom of the Court's adherence to the hearsay evidence rule.

The appointments of Duvall and Story were the last for more than a decade. Perhaps fate decreed that a Court with Story as a member had more than enough "new blood" to last a decade. The appointments made by Presidents Jefferson and Madison altered the political alignment of the Supreme Court but did little to counterbalance its property oriented nationalism or its systematic assertion of authority to review states in their exercise of economic regulation. Indeed, the addition of Story strengthened the Court's support for stability in commercial relationships, just as the opinions of William Johnson did much to enhance the national bias of Court opinions. Little wonder that in 1822 former president Jefferson took Judge Johnson to task for his failure to write more separate opinions.[109]

The Last Republican Appointees: Smith Thompson and Robert Trimble

When Brockholst Livingston died in 1823, his colleagues spent three months fretting over a possible successor. Rumors repeated by Daniel Webster to Judge Story suggested that President Monroe would call upon Nathaniel Macon. On the other hand, there was a general feeling that the president favored his secretary of the navy, Smith Thompson, who resided in Livingston's circuit. The judges were appalled that Macon, a longtime Republican zealot and a vocal enemy of the Court, might be appointed. After an uncomfortable summer of doubt, all were relieved at the announcement of Thompson's name.[110] Undoubtedly Thompson was among the most reluctant Court nominees in the Marshall era, his indecision lasting four months despite constant encouragement from Monroe to accept his appointment.

Thompson was born in Dutchess County, New York, in 1768 and graduated from Princeton in 1788. He could boast strong antifederal connections through his uncle, Melancthon Smith, and his marriage to Sarah Livingston in 1794 united him to the powerful Manor Livingston clan. Thompson

---

109. See Morgan, *Johnson*, 168–189.

110. See Charles Warren, *The Supreme Court in United States History*, revised edition, 2 vols. (Boston: Little, Brown, 1922–26), vol. 1, 587–594, which incorrectly identifies Thompson as Monroe's secretary of war. See also Warren, *The Story-Marshall Correspondence (1819–1831)*, Anglo-American Legal History Series, series 1, no. 7 (New York: New York University School of Law, 1942), 19; Marshall to Story, July 2, 1823, Story Papers, Massachusetts Historical Society; Marshall to Washington, August 6, 1823, Morristown National Historical Park Library, Morristown, N.J.

had studied law with James Kent and with Sarah's father, Gilbert Livingston, and became his future father-in-law's partner in 1793. He left practice in 1801 to take a seat on the New York Supreme Court, where he served for sixteen years, delivering nearly 250 opinions. As a member of the state supreme court he also served on the Council of Revision, which reviewed legislative acts for conformity to the New York Constitution. He was appointed Monroe's secretary of the navy in 1818 through the influence of Martin Van Buren, and his national career was for a time tied to that of the future president. Ultimately Thompson's own interest in the highest executive office caused a breach with Van Buren, but not before Thompson had accepted his Supreme Court appointment.[111]

As might be anticipated from his active role on the New York Supreme Court, Thompson would have a substantial impact upon the U.S. Supreme Court and its constitutional law decisions. While economic conservatism made him solicitous for property rights, the new associate justice's views of the nature of the Union, the interpretation of the contract clause, and the negative impact of the interstate commerce clause were quite different from those of Chief Justice Marshall. Essentially, Thompson felt that state legislatures should be permitted to take any action that did not conflict with the exercise of a federal power. This became evident in his opinion on tax immunities in *Brown v. Maryland,* and it also colored his view of the "exclusive power" of the federal government. By his definition, an exclusive power was one that had been granted to the federal government, that had never been exercised by the state, and that was beyond the authority of the state. Because of this limited definition of exclusive powers, it was easier for Thompson to uphold all state insolvency laws in *Ogden v. Saunders.* In the same case he held that contracts were governed by the law of the state in which they were executed and that state legislatures should be permitted discretion in setting the manner in which property might be taken in satisfaction of debts. In the copyright case *Wheaton v. Peters* Thompson held that a common-law copyright existed at state law and took precedence over copyright provisions in the Federal Constitution, at least in the absence of express legislation to the contrary. Professor Roper observes that "to Thompson the common law was considerably more than a mere guide to judicial statutory interpretation. . . ; it was rather 'the application of the dictates of natural justice and of cultivated reason, to particular cases.' "[112]

---

111. Donald M. Roper, *Mr. Justice Thompson and the Constitution* (New York: Garland, 1987), 2, 8, 17, 23–24, 50, 55; on Thompson's nomination and relations with Van Buren see Dunne, "Smith Thompson," in *Justices,* vol. 1, 475, at 479–482.

112. Roper, *Thompson,* 63, 72, 78, 100–101, 124, 141–142, 146, 159, 177–178, 186, 189–193, 198, quotation at 192.

In the politically sensitive area of Indian rights, Smith Thompson proved to be more activist than his colleagues. Contrary to his usual concurrent view of the commerce clause, he held that commerce with Indian tribes was within the exclusive jurisdiction of the federal government. He also eschewed the "political question" position taken by Judge Johnson and noted that when private rights of property or person were involved, the Supreme Court could exercise jurisdiction over treaty matters. Approaching slavery with an unwillingness to rock the politically unstable boat of the Missouri Compromise, Thompson held in *The Antelope* (1825) that slavery was not, as such, contrary to international law and that those engaged in the international slave trade could be punished only under the municipal laws of their nation. While he was a member of Monroe's cabinet, Thompson had been vigorously opposed to the international slave trade, but on the Court his concern for state authority, his views of the commerce clause, and his political sense of caution prevented him from acting upon his earlier convictions.[113]

Judge Thompson in many ways represents a transitional figure between the Marshall Court of the "golden years" of 1815–24 and the Taney Court that would follow Marshall's death. Like the Court under Taney, Thompson was willing to accord greater latitude to state police powers when they clashed with congressional authority over interstate commerce. He was also willing to permit state alterations in the hitherto sacred rights of contract. These constitutional views found their counterpart in Thompson's views of the judicial function. For example, he felt that statutes should be read with full weight being extended to the intent of the legislature that passed the measure. Similarly, his dissent in regard to the validity of Florida land titles (*United States v. Arredondo,* 1832) was based upon the intention of the negotiators rather than upon the text of the Adams-Onis Treaty of 1819.[114] Deference to executive and legislative power, a landmark of the Taney era, was part of the judicial style of Monroe's only Supreme Court appointee. The winds of fundamental change were beginning to blow through the sedate chamber of the highest court in the land and were undermining the one-time judicial unanimity of the Court's conferences.

To the extent possible in his two terms on the Supreme Court, Robert Trimble contributed to the changed emphasis upon states' rights and state regulation of contractual obligations. His major opinion, as part of a majority in *Ogden v. Saunders,* held that a state insolvency law was a valid exercise

---

113. *Ibid.,* 27, 29, 208–209, 238–244, 255.
114. *Ibid.,* 56, 57, 195–196.

of state power and not contrary to the obligation of contract protected by the Federal Constitution.[115]

Born into a Kentucky frontier family of modest means, Trimble saved enough money to provide himself with a classical education and law apprenticeships with George Nicholas (first professor of law at Transylvania University) and James Brown. He began his practice around 1800 and served briefly on the Kentucky Court of Appeals. He was federal district judge for Kentucky from 1817 to 1826, weathering an extremely heated dispute over federal admiralty jurisdiction in Kentucky and the invalidation of Kentucky's land laws by the U.S. Supreme Court. Trimble's support for federal authority in the face of bitter and threatening opposition earned him President Adams's nomination to the seat left vacant by the death of Judge Todd. Unfortunately, Trimble died in August 1828 of a "malignant bilious fever," having shown his substantial abilities in his separate opinion in *Ogden v. Saunders* (1827) and his opinion for the Court in *The Antelope* (1827). Had he survived beyond 1828, he would undoubtedly have made significant contributions to the Court and its published opinions.[116]

The Incoming Jacksonian Tide: John McLean, Henry Baldwin, and James Moore Wayne

Although President John Quincy Adams made an effort to appoint Judge Trimble's successor, the Democratic majority in the Senate blocked nominations until Andrew Jackson occupied the White House. In the maneuvering for cabinet positions, Postmaster General John McLean was disappointed, and Jackson awarded him a seat on the Supreme Court as compensation for McLean's assistance in the 1824 and 1828 elections. Born in New Jersey in 1785, McLean migrated in his youth first to Kentucky and then to Ohio. His legal training began with two years as an apprentice to a clerk of court, coupled with law studies supervised by attorney Arthur St. Clair, Jr. (1804–6). He then opened a printing office but was admitted to practice law in 1810 and combined the activities for several years before surrendering the printing business to a brother. Elected to the U.S. House of Representatives for two terms (1812–16), McLean returned home to Ohio when the legislature selected him for membership in that state's supreme court. Six years later he was appointed to federal office as commis-

115. 12 Wheaton 213, at 312–331 (1827). Trimble spent considerable time attacking Marshall's natural-law view that contracts exist by virtue of the act of the parties rather than by force of law. *Ibid.*, 318–324.

116. Fred L. Israel, "Robert Trimble," in *Justices*, vol. 1, 513–519.

sioner of the Public Land Office (1822–23), followed by a long and extremely successful tenure as postmaster general of the United States (1823–29).[117]

A deft politician, McLean survived in federal appointive positions under Presidents Monroe and John Quincy Adams while seeking the election of Andrew Jackson. Even after joining the Supreme Court, McLean nursed presidential aspirations. These were set back by his equivocal behavior during the early years of Jackson's administration, and by 1830 McLean was already seeking preferment from those who would ultimately become Whig Party leaders.[118]

McLean also proved apostate to the Jacksonian faith in some of his early decisions from the Supreme Court bench. As a westerner he held close to the Jacksonian preference for paper money. Thus in *Craig v. Missouri* he joined Judges Thompson and Johnson in a dissent against the Court's holding that Missouri's loan certificates were currency and thus violated the Federal Constitution's prohibition against states' issuing coins or currency. However, his moral attitude in support of Indian treaty rights, supplemented no doubt by his strong Methodist religious convictions, caused him to join the Marshall majority in *Worcester v. Georgia* (1832). Gradually he became a close friend of Judge Story, and their jurisprudential affinity increased as McLean drew further away from Jacksonian ideological and political positions.[119]

McLean's political ambitions continued until his death in 1861, but he was valued by fellow professionals for his diligence and broad acquaintance with the law and even more for his wide experience in public affairs. According to one account, "He was not a great judge, but he was a safe judge. His decisions were right even when the opinions by which he supported them were open to criticism."[120] Usually mild and urbane in his deportment and patient and decorous in conducting court business, McLean could be tenacious on a matter of principle. In his judicial work, contemporary observers saw him as one who would decide a case not only upon precedent but also with a view toward essential justice and common sense.[121] Large in physical stature and in the size of his head, McLean was remarkable for his "Websterian eyes, Roman nose, full lips, and firm

---

117. Francis P. Weisenberger, *The Life of John McLean: A Politician on the United States Supreme Court* (Columbus: Ohio State University Press, 1937), 2–8, 9, 18, 33, 47, 66–67; Frank Otto Gatell, "John McLean," in *Justices*, vol. 1, 535–545, at 535–539.
118. Weisenberger, *McLean*, 53, 68, 73–74.
119. *Ibid.*, 156–157; Gatell, "John McLean," 540. McLean also found Judge William Johnson a worthy and agreeable colleague. Weisenberger, *McLean*, 154.
120. The opinion of Manning Force, quoted at Weisenberger, *McLean*, 186–187.
121. *Ibid.*, 227–228.

jaw."[122] While his limited formal education hindered him in providing erudition to the Supreme Court, his political sensitivity was invaluable to his
colleagues. Very likely his strong sense of morality was felt by his associates
in the Marshall Court, as it would be later when he dissented from proslav-
ery decisions of the Taney Court.

The second justice appointed by President Jackson was Henry Baldwin
of Pennsylvania. A 1797 graduate of Yale, Baldwin took his law clerkship
under Alexander J. Dallas of Philadelphia and joined the Allegheny County
bar in 1801, soon forming a partnership with two other lawyers, Tarleton
Bates and Walter Forward. Together they dominated the Pittsburgh legal
community, and Baldwin became well known for his scholarly briefs. He
also became the owner of a woolen mill and several iron-rolling mills located in western Pennsylvania and Ohio. He served in the U.S. House of
Representatives from 1816 to 1822, resigning because of ill health. Thereafter he actively supported the presidential aspirations of Andrew Jackson,
and for his efforts he was nominated to succeed Bushrod Washington on
the Supreme Court in 1830. The new justice promptly steered his own
rather eccentric course through the law, its inconsistencies caused in part
by his insistence upon his peculiar approach to constitutional adjudication
and in part by periodic attacks of insanity. President Jackson was appalled
at Baldwin's support for rechartering the Bank of the United States and
irked by his support for Marshall's position in the Cherokee cases. Apparently the relationship between Baldwin and Marshall developed in spite of
the Pennsylvanian's many separate, and at times highly critical, opinions.
When Marshall died in Philadelphia in 1835, it was Henry Baldwin who
attended his bedside.[123]

Judge James Moore Wayne of Georgia was President Jackson's last appointment to the Supreme Court during Marshall's chief justiceship. Succeeding to the seat vacated by the death of Judge William Johnson, Wayne
took his oath of office at Marshall's last term of Court. Suffering from the
illness that would cause his death the following summer, Marshall administered the oath to his young colleague. They must have presented a physical
contrast: Wayne was described as having "almost the air of a dandy" in his
dress and as a man who carefully cultivated his whiskers. Despite variances
in dress, Marshall seems to have taken to the Georgian, who remembered
him with affection. A native of Savannah, Wayne graduated from Princeton
in 1808 and then studied law with Judge Charles Chauncy of New Haven,
Connecticut (1809–10). In 1813 he married Mary Johnson Campbell, the

---

122. *Ibid.*, 226.
123. The material on Baldwin is extracted from Gatell, "Henry Baldwin," in *Justices*, vol.
1, 571–580.

daughter of Alexander Campbell of Richmond. Mrs. Wayne's father was an attorney who practiced at the Richmond bar and frequently opposed John Marshall in the trial of British debt cases.[124]

Wayne served in the Georgia legislature in 1815–16 and was alderman and mayor of Savannah from 1816 to 1819. Elected judge of the Court of Common Pleas and Court of Oyer and Terminer for the city of Savannah, he continued in that position until 1822, when he was elected judge for the Eastern Circuit Superior Court. Wayne emerged upon the Washington scene as a member of the House of Representatives elected with Andrew Jackson in 1828. In Congress he supported the programs of President Jackson. When Jackson nominated him to succeed Judge Johnson in 1834, Wayne was promptly confirmed by a Senate controlled by the Whig Party, and his selection was widely acclaimed. He had been a strong unionist during the nullification controversy, and his loyalty to the central government persisted through the secession crisis of 1861. Wayne remained on the Court throughout the Civil War and died in office in 1867. He was a strong nationalist and generally accepted Marshall's views concerning the contract and commerce clauses of the Constitution.[125]

CONCLUSION

The Supreme Court over which John Marshall presided did not lack for forceful personalities, although some of the justices left a meager mark upon American law or the federal system. We have noted the personal charm and easy manner of the Chief Justice, but it has also become clear that he and his colleagues had serious differences of opinion concerning the role of the judiciary, the nature and application of the commerce clause, and the interpretation of the contract clause. Dealing with international law, he and Judge Story sparred over the draconian innovations in prize law introduced by the works of van Bynkershoek. Briefly, Marshall seems to have preferred the older positions advocated by Grotius and Vattel, which were more solicitous for the rights of neutrals and nonbelligerents. Story and Judge Johnson maintained a running quarrel over federal common law, particularly as it related to common-law crime. In his only constitutional law dissent, in *Ogden v. Saunders*, Marshall built upon a natural-law concept that contract arose entirely from the voluntary agreement of the parties. His associates, especially Judge Thompson, saw contract as a

---

124. Alexander A. Lawrence, *James Moore Wayne, Southern Unionist* (Chapel Hill: University of North Carolina Press, 1943), 3, 11–13, 19.
125. *Ibid.*, 26–28, 32, 42, 214–216. See also Gatell, "James M. Wayne," in *Justices*, vol. 1, 601–611.

product of positive law, without any life of its own. To add other examples would only corroborate the undeniable evidence that Chief Justice Marshall did not "dominate" his colleagues; the domination theory has been so thoroughly refuted that Professor David Currie referred to it as the story of "John Marshall and the Six Dwarfs."[126]

Despite the influx of Jeffersonian and Jacksonian appointees, the Marshall Court changed very gradually in the 1820s. By the end of Marshall's tenure, the new presidential appointees had succeeded in undermining some of his original constitutional holdings. However, the initial Jeffersonian goal was to alter constitutional law totally, to make the Court subject to the Congress, to hold it answerable to popular majorities, and to neutralize the "federalist influence" on the bench. Why did Jefferson, his political partisans, and his successors in the presidency, fail in this effort?

One reason emerges from our brief review of the appointees to the Court. All were members of the bar; most came from respectable middle-class or upper-class (almost aristocratic) backgrounds; all had some legislative and judicial experience. They were men who had arrived at a stage in their lives at which they enjoyed professional success and had accumulated both property and family obligations. Marshall's associates had far more similarities than differences, and this drew them together into a cohesive social and professional group.

Another commonality was their standing at the bar, based upon proven ability in the courtroom and the esteem of their clients and neighbors. They knew the art of compromise, they understood the role of *stare decisis* in Anglo-American law, and they appreciated the need for reasoned decisions and the maintenance of a fundamental law. Each judge was either a participant in the generation that drew the state and federal constitutions or belonged to the next generation, which began filling in the interior walls of those governmental superstructures. They were men who saw the future greatness of America in the purity and practicality of her legal system. Finally, they were realists who recognized the need for economic growth and diversification. While they might differ concerning the means to be utilized, each sought the stability and security in financial relationships that could exist only when the law accepted responsibility for protecting private property.

It is also important to note that, by virtue of their office, Marshall and his associates were united in their defense of the judicial branch of the federal government. From 1801 until Marshall's death there was extreme external pressure upon the Court to conform to currently popular views. This was backed by threats of impeachment, refusal to increase judicial

---

126. Currie, "Most Insignificant Justice," 469.

salaries, attempts to alter the appellate jurisdiction of the Court, and count-less other initiatives. These influences constituted real and present dangers to the institutional future of the Supreme Court, but they also made the justices, however they had been appointed, fellow combatants in its de-fense.

II

Politics and Constitution in the Marshall Era

At no other time in its history was the United States Supreme Court as vulnerable to political reprisals as it was during the chief justiceship of John Marshall. Undoubtedly the Court was then, and always has been, located at the nexus between law and politics; it has been the forum in which important issues of national life were debated and resolved. What made the years from 1801 to 1835 such a critical time was the evolution of the Court into a powerful instrument for imposing constitutional norms upon a rapidly expanding and constantly changing nation. At the outset there was no agreement that the Court should perform this function. Neither was there a consensus concerning the proper relationship between state and federal authority. Understandably, the decisions of the Supreme Court were of critical concern to Americans in various walks of life, and their reception generated reactions in public opinion that frequently supported limitation of judicial power.

For these reasons, no consideration of Marshall's work as chief justice would be complete without some attention to those political events that had the most profound impact upon the Supreme Court as an institution. The Court was a relatively powerless branch of government when Marshall became chief justice, and part of its situation could be attributed to unwise public relations choices made by his predecessors. Earlier chief justices were inattentive to the political and constitutional views of the people and their elected representatives. As a consequence, when popular opposition to the Supreme Court's decisions manifested itself, Marshall's predecessors were taken aback. The ratification of the Eleventh Amendment (1798), which canceled the Supreme Court's authority to hear cases in which a non-resident sued a state of the union, provided stark evidence of the nation's rejection of Chief Justice Jay's view of a unified national state. At the same time, the issue of federal-state balances of power remained open to future determination, and it was within this framework that most of the Marshall Court's decisions were made.

Marshall's leadership of the Supreme Court was firmly established upon his assessment of the political framework within which it had to operate. He expended considerable effort to achieve what was possible within the Court's limitations. Indeed, given the degree of public outcry against the Court's decisions, we may assume that he led the Court to the very outer limit permitted to him. Exceeding those limits imposed by the political process would have caused a sharp restriction on the Court's appellate jurisdiction and perhaps even impeachment of one or more of its justices. As it was, the Supreme Court rarely issued an opinion that was not severely criticized or denounced in the newspapers and in legislative halls. However, the litmus test of success was not damping the cycles of public opinion; rather it was the maintenance of sufficient congressional goodwill to preclude any inroad upon the Court's jurisdiction other than those already incorporated in the ambiguities of the Eleventh Amendment.

Chief Justice Marshall's first concern was to deal with the awkward situation that arose from judicial reforms and appointments effected in the last weeks of the Adams administration. Personally and by virtue of his prior office as secretary of state, he was directly involved in many of those Federalist efforts to retain control of the judicial branch of government. He was also faced with the admittedly partisan behavior of several of his associate justices, who had become overly zealous in their support for prosecutions under the provisions of the Alien and Sedition Acts. Finally, he knew that the Jeffersonian Republican majority in Congress was available for use against the Court or against him or his colleagues individually. Circumspection was clearly the way to move ahead, but with Marshall's leadership even circumspection proved to be constructive of a stronger Supreme Court.

COURT REFORM, MIDNIGHT JUDGES, AND THE JUDICIARY ACTS OF 1801 AND 1802

The 1789 Judiciary Act established a three-tiered system of federal courts: the United States Supreme Court, the district courts, and the circuit courts. It provided for a chief justice and five associate justices on the Supreme Court and for a district judge to be appointed for each state (that is, for each federal district that was contiguous with the boundaries of each state). The district courts in turn were to be grouped into three geographical circuits, and a circuit court would be held twice yearly in each circuit. These circuit courts were to be staffed by two Supreme Court justices and the district judges of each district in the circuit.[1] In March 1793, responding to pleas from the justices, Congress provided that only one Supreme Court justice need be present at the circuit courts.[2] Even with this reduced need for circuit riding, the expansion of American territory west of the Appalachian Mountains made the duty burdensome. Congress had had the circuit court issue under consideration since 1798, but it was not until the waning days of Federalist control that the Judiciary Act of 1801 became law, establishing independent circuit courts and relieving the Supreme Court justices of circuit duty. Although the Judiciary Act of 1801 can be defended as a valid reform measure,[3] it had been passed by a lame duck Federalist majority and provided for sixteen new federal judgeships, to which President Adams promptly named prominent Federalists. Jefferson and others correctly asserted that, having lost the 1800 election, the Federalists "retreated into the Judiciary as a stronghold, the tenure of which renders it difficult to dislodge them."[4]

Needless to say, one of the first items on the agenda of the incoming administration was the repeal of the Judiciary Act of 1801. In providing for more thorough review of federal and state court actions by the newly independent United States circuit courts, the 1801 act ran directly counter to the wishes of the incoming congressional majority. Repeal was accomplished on April 29, 1802, by a statute that expressly repealed the earlier act and directed the resumption of circuit court duty by members of the Supreme Court.[5] The enactment of this Judiciary Act of 1802, coupled with its cancellation of the June 1802 term of the Supreme Court, forced the Supreme Court justices to consult by mail concerning the situation. Taking the lead, Chief Justice Marshall raised with his colleagues the questions of whether they might proceed to hold circuit courts without statutory autho-

1. Sections 1–4, Act to Establish the Judicial Courts of the United States, September 24, 1789, 1 Stat. 73, at 73–75.

2. Section 1, An Act in Addition to "An Act to Establish the Judicial Courts of the United States," March 2, 1793, 1 Stat. 333, at 333–334.

3. An Act to provide for the more convenient organization of the Courts of the United States, February 13, 1801, 2 Stat. 89–100; see George L. Haskins and Herbert A. Johnson, *Foundations of Power: John Marshall, 1801–15*, vol. 2, *History of the Supreme Court of the United States*, 10 vols. to date (New York: Macmillan Publishing Company, 1981), 107–126, and Kathryn Preyer, "Federal Policy and the Judiciary Act of 1802," 22 *William and Mary Quarterly*, 3d series, 3 (1965).

4. Sections 6, 7, An Act to provide. . . , February 13, 1801, 2 Stat. 89, at 90–91. See also Charles Warren, *The Supreme Court in United States History*, revised edition, 2 vols. (Boston: Little, Brown & Co., 1922–26), vol. 1, 185–189. The Jefferson quotation is at *ibid.*, 193.

5. Sections 1–3, An Act to amend the Judicial system of the United States, April 29, 1802, 2 Stat. 156, at 156–157; Haskins and Johnson, *Foundations*, 126–151, 163–168; Kathryn Preyer, "The Midnight Judges. . . ," 109 *University of Pennsylvania Law Review* 494, at 494–495 (1961).

rization to do so (the 1802 act had not reauthorized the justices to hold circuit but merely canceled the 1801 act, which relieved them of that duty) and whether a special commission as circuit court judge was required. He suggested that since the Supreme Court justices had, before the 1801 act, participated in holding circuit courts, the position that they could not do so was much weaker than it otherwise would have been. In any event, he was willing to abide by the views of the majority of his colleagues. All but one of the associate justices agreed with Marshall that it would be unwise and perhaps unlawful not to be guided by the Repeal Act of 1802, and thus it was their duty to hold circuit courts as directed by that act and the revived portions of the Judiciary Act of 1789. Only Judge Samuel Chase presented a lengthy and forceful argument that the Judiciary Act of 1802 was unconstitutional and that it would be unlawful for the Supreme Court justices to preside again over the circuit courts. Any other course would in effect do injury to the rights of the already commissioned circuit court judges. Chase urged that the judges convene in Washington during the summer of 1802 to set upon a joint plan of action. True to his word, Chief Justice Marshall acted according to the views of the majority, and thereafter, in accordance with the 1802 act, he and the others held the scheduled circuit courts.[6]

On December 2, 1802, the validity of the Judiciary Act of 1802 was challenged in the United States circuit court for Virginia, held by Chief Justice Marshall. In 1803 this litigation would come before the Supreme Court as *Stuart v. Laird*. In an earlier circuit court held by the circuit court judge appointed under the provisions of the 1801 Judiciary Act, the plaintiffs had obtained judgment by default on a forthcoming bond.[7] Before Marshall, the defendant (judgment debtor) opposed the application to collect on the bond, asserting that Marshall's circuit court was unconstitutional. He also claimed that the court over which Marshall presided could not lawfully act as a successor to the circuit court in which the bond had been posted. Marshall overruled the defendant's demurrer, and the case was appealed to the Supreme Court. Because of Marshall's participation in the case below and Judge Cushing's absence from the bench, Judge Paterson delivered the opinion of the Supreme Court. The opinion established that the

---

6. Haskins and Johnson, *Foundations*, 168–180. A petition by circuit court judges appointed under the 1801 act, claiming violation of good behavior tenure, was presented to Congress in January 1803, but no action was taken to redress the alleged grievance. *Ibid.*, 177–180. The correspondence is printed at *The Papers of John Marshall*, Herbert A. Johnson, Charles T. Cullen, William C. Stinchcombe, Charles F. Hobson, et al., editors, 8 vols. to date (Chapel Hill: University of North Carolina Press, 1974–date), vol. 6, 105–106, 108–118.

7. A forthcoming bond guarantees the surrender of property to satisfy a judgment outstanding against a party to the litigation.

circuit court held in accordance with the 1802 Judiciary Act was constitutionally authorized and functioned as the lawful successor to the short-lived circuit court.[8]

Ostensibly *Stuart v. Laird* demonstrated Supreme Court acquiescence in the Republican-dominated Congress's riding roughshod over the good behavior tenure of the federal circuit judges. This represented a serious threat to judicial independence as well as a potential taking of property without due process. However, to have decided otherwise would have triggered a direct confrontation with Congress and the president, a course approved only by Judge Chase. On the other hand, six days before the *Stuart v. Laird* opinion was delivered, Chief Justice Marshall announced his famous opinion in *Marbury v. Madison,* firmly recognizing judicial review as a part of American constitutional law.[9] *Marbury* as such was not confrontational because it was self-executing; refusing to grant relief ended the proceeding, leaving no action to be taken by any executive officer of the government. On the other hand, *Marbury* raised the bid in the political poker game between the Court and the Jeffersonians. It diverted Republican energies into the task of impeaching Federalist-appointed officials, not to exclude the possibility of removing one or more Supreme Court justices.

MARBURY AND THE CONTOURS OF CONSTITUTIONAL GOVERNMENT

The mandamus case, like *Stuart v. Laird,* involved judicial appointments made by President Adams under authority of the statute organizing the District of Columbia.[10] William Marbury, a prominent landowner in the Maryland (Washington County) half of the District, had been appointed to a five-year term as justice of the peace. His commission, duly signed by the president and sealed with the Great Seal of the United States by authority of Acting Secretary of State John Marshall, was one of several overlooked in the rush of business in the last days of Federalist rule. Upon assuming office, President Jefferson ordered his secretary of state, James Madison, to withhold all of the undelivered commissions. Joined by three other disap-

8. See *Stuart v. Laird,* 1 Cranch 299 (1803), and Haskins and Johnson, *Foundations,* 180–181, 630–631, 650.

9. 1 Cranch 137 (1803). H. Jefferson Powell asserts that the primacy of judicial construction of the Federal Constitution was not a matter of argument, even for most Jeffersonian Republicans. "The Political Grammar of Early Constitutional Law," 71 *North Carolina Law Review* 949, at 984–985 (1993).

10. Sections 3, 11, An Act concerning the District of Columbia, February 27, 1801, 2 Stat. 103, at 105–106.

pointed J.P.'s, Marbury brought a petition to the Supreme Court asking that it issue a writ of mandamus directing Madison to make delivery. A hearing on the petition was delayed until the February 1803 term because the Judiciary Act of 1802 had canceled the intervening terms of the Supreme Court.

Marbury placed the Supreme Court in direct conflict with the Jefferson Administration, and there is some reason to suspect that some Federalists sought such a confrontation as a means of embarrassing the Republicans. As a matter of abstract justice, William Marbury had an appealing case. It could be pictured as a crass use of political power to deny judicial office to a worthy appointee. It could also be seen as Republican disregard for property rights, judicial independence, and the ideal of impartiality in government. On the other hand, as one of the largest landowners in the District of Columbia, Marbury was not destined to live a life of poverty if he never became a justice of the peace. All of these points suggest that Chief Justice Marshall had a broad spectrum of possibilities available to him in deciding Marbury's case, and uncertainty predicting the Court's action led to increased Republican trepidation.

In what would become characteristic of Marshall's style, the Court adroitly avoided a conflict with the executive branch over enforcement. Delivering the Court's opinion, Marshall pointed out that with all of the preliminary steps completed, Marbury was entitled to his commission, and the laws of the United States should provide a means for him to assert that right. He further held that the delivery of a commission was not a matter of discretion on the part of the president or his subordinate. Such executive actions were not subject to judicial control; they were what future courts would term "political matters" left by the Constitution within the exclusive power of the executive or legislative branches of government. However, the delivery of a commission was a ministerial act, not involving any discretion, and would be subject to Court mandate providing the Court had jurisdiction of the matter.[11]

This lengthy discussion, viewed by some Jeffersonians (and many future

---

11. David E. Engdahl traces the origin of judicial review in federal and state courts before 1803 and concludes that Marshall's position, affording each branch the right to construe the Constitution, is "Jeffersonian" in contrast to Federalist views of judicial supremacy that have again become current under *Cooper v. Aaron* (1957). "John Marshall's 'Jeffersonian' Concept of Judicial Review," 42 *Duke Law Journal* 279, at 279–289, 333–339 (1993). Professor Powell notes Marshall's deft juxtaposition of presidential discretion with the rule of law in "Political Grammar," at 1004–1006 (1993). Professor Robert L. Clinton, in *Marbury v. Madison and Judicial Review* (Lawrence: University of Kansas Press, 1989), argues that prior to the Civil War the U.S. Supreme Court utilized judicial review only when federal statutes touched upon questions of federal court jurisdiction.

scholars) as a brazen judicial attempt to lecture Thomas Jefferson concerning his duties and moral obligations, led directly into a consideration of the mandamus provisions in Section 13 of the Judiciary Act of 1789[12] and of Article III of the Federal Constitution. Marshall compared the constitutional article with the statutory authorization for mandamus. Not finding the mandamus power within the original jurisdiction of the Supreme Court as stated in the Constitution, he held that the statute could not supply the defect and refused to issue the writ. Since the Constitution was the supreme law, which judges were sworn to uphold, they could not act in accordance with a statute that was in conflict with the fundamental written law of the Constitution.

As a consequence of Marshall's opinion in *Marbury*, the disappointed justices of the peace never got their commissions, and the Republicans were able to appoint others to their vacant positions in the District of Columbia government. So much was clear. However, the full scope of Marshall's doctrine was far from certain. Narrowly construed, *Marbury* was simply a self-imposed limitation on the Supreme Court's jurisdiction and an assertion that Congress could not increase the constitutionally determined boundaries of that power.[13]

The broader implications of *Marbury* become obvious in a line of monographic treatments initiated by the late Professor Alexander Bickel in 1962. Pointing to the fact that Marshall failed to explain why the Supreme Court should be the ultimate determiner of constitutionality, Bickel showed that Marshall's position was by no means dictated by constitutional doctrine. Furthermore, the *Marbury* opinion did not establish textual or functional underpinnings for the Supreme Court's exercise of that role in the federal system. On the other hand, judicial review appeared to be one of the assumptions the framers made in erecting the federal structure. While Bickel was willing to concede Judge John Bannister Gibson's point that judicial review could not withstand determined majoritarian pressure in the legislatures and polling places of the nation, he nevertheless argued that it provides a legitimating function for government—it provides principled as well as democratically responsible authority.[14] More recently, Professor Jesse H. Choper has argued that while majoritarian rule is a principal aspect of American democracy, it is not without countering influences, including that of the use of judicial review to protect individual rights.[15]

---

12. 1 Stat. 73, at 81.

13. This view is amply argued by Clinton in *Marbury v. Madison*, 97–101.

14. Alexander M. Bickel, *The Least Dangerous Branch: The Supreme Court at the Bar of Politics* (Indianapolis: Bobbs-Merrill, 1962), 3, 5, 7, 15, 23, 29.

15. Jesse H. Choper, *Judicial Review and the National Political Process: A Functional Reconsideration of the Role of the Supreme Court* (Chicago: University of Chicago Press, 1980).

The traditional view of *Marbury* and judicial review has been that the case was simply the natural development from prior case law in the states, as well as a natural evolution from the practice of Privy Council review of colonial court decisions before the American Revolution. Recently, however, Sylvia Snowiss has advanced a persuasive argument that *Marbury* represents not only an abrupt change in earlier approaches to judicial review but that it also provides a key to Marshall's unique contribution to constitutional history. She argues that earlier principles of judicial review looked to constitutions as embodiments of social contract and accorded no particular respect to their existence as written documents. While a concededly unconstitutional legislative enactment would be denied validity and not be enforced in the courts, there was considerable reluctance to take such action in doubtful cases. Chief Justice Marshall, on the other hand, substituted the positive law restraint of a written constitution and textual interpretation in place of a traditional preference for resort to "first principles" drawn from natural law. Judicial review thus became "an external, continuously operating legal restraint on legislative and majority will." By reading the Constitution and construing it as one would interpret a statute, Marshall began the process of "legalizing" the Constitution. Snowiss argues that Marshall's technique of textual exposition in constitutional cases was particularly effective in construing the contract clause issues before his Court in *Fletcher v. Peck* and *Dartmouth College*. It also utilized commerce clause and supremacy situations that arose in *Gibbons v. Ogden* and *M'Culloch v. Maryland*. The Chief Justice's use of this method, coupled with his dominance in writing majority opinions for the Court, had great influence upon the course of judicial review in the United States even though his associate justices rarely if ever followed this innovative approach to constitutional adjudication.[16]

Professor Snowiss correctly points out that modern writers on judicial review have been misled by intervening nineteenth-century glosses on Marshall's opinion. Others have highlighted changes in judicial review that have occurred since Marshall's day, with particular attention to the years

16. For a good detailed presentation of the traditional view see Haskins and Johnson, *Foundations*, 182–204; earlier Edward S. Corwin asserted that the principle of judicial review was generally accepted by the Founding Fathers. "Marbury v. Madison and the Doctrine of Judicial Review," 12 *Michigan Law Review* 538–572, at 538, 562–563, 571–572 (1914). Akhil Akmar correctly points out that Marshall's opinion broke little new ground and was uncontroversial in 1803. "Marbury, Section 13, and the Original Jurisdiction of the Supreme Court," 56 *University of Chicago Law Review* 443, at 446. For the new interpretation by Sylvia Snowiss see her *Judicial Review and the Law of the Constitution* (New Haven: Yale University Press, 1990), 3–5, 29–31, 34, 105, 119 (includes quotation), 120–123, 169–171, 172–175.

1890 through 1910.[17] Consideration of twentieth-century concepts of judicial review are beyond the scope of this work, but what is of great pertinence is that Snowiss's insight into *Marbury* provides a key to Marshall's subsequent development of judicial review. It also serves as a reasonably consistent distinction between his approach to decision making and that of his colleagues.[18]

Much recent writing on *Marbury v. Madison* has been triggered by a conservative reaction to the activism of the Warren Court. Among those treatments, the best-known is Christopher Wolfe's *The Rise of Modern Judicial Review*, which highlights *Marbury* as the inception of a moderate form of judicial review that best accords with the intention of the Founding Fathers and the proper construction of the Federal Constitution. Wolfe provides a careful description of the Chief Justice's approach to constitutional interpretation, which stressed at the outset the intention of the Founding Fathers as expressed in the language of the Constitution. Beyond such textual study, Marshall had resort to other techniques. He considered the context in which a word or phrase was used in the Constitution, and the placement of the provision within the four corners of the document was also important, as was the context being considered by the passage. Finally, the Chief Justice was aware that the Constitution had to be expressed in general and fundamental terms, leaving to the Congress and the courts the task of filling in details.[19]

While Professor Wolfe makes no bones about his view that judicial review triumphed through Marshall's decision in *Marbury,* he also stresses the fact that it was moderate judicial review that was characteristic in this period. Normally the Court would defer to legislative decisions except when unconstitutionality was clear. Drawing upon *Marbury*'s distinction between ministerial and discretionary executive action, the Court refrained from deciding political questions. Finally, the Marshall Court only rarely mentioned natural-law principles in its utilization of judicial review. Consequently Wolfe finds the Marshall period, and indeed most judicial review in antebellum America, to be of the moderate type and a worthy foil against which to posit the decline of Supreme Court judicial review into twentieth-century noninterpretive natural-law judging.[20]

---

17. Clinton, *Marbury v. Madison,* 207–233; Christopher Wolfe, *The Rise of Modern Judicial Review from Constitutional Interpretation to Judge-Made Law* (New York: Basic Books, 1986), 323–356. There is a second edition of Wolfe, published in New York by Rowan and Littlefield in 1994, that is substantially similar in its discussion of the Marshall Court.

18. On the historical development of judicial review after Marshall's years on the Court see William E. Nelson, "Changing Concepts of Judicial Review: The Evolution of Constitutional Theory in the States, 1790–1860," 120 *University of Pennsylvania Law Review* 1166–1185 (1972); and Clinton, *Marbury v. Madison,* 161–233.

19. Wolfe, *Rise of Modern Judicial Review,* 39–56.

20. *Ibid.,* 91–113.

Both Snowiss and Wolfe focus upon Marshall's interpretive methods, one to establish the originality of Marshallian judicial review, the other to apotheosize it as the essence of constitutionalism. Professor James O'Fallon, on the other hand, finds *Marbury* to be a decision driven by the necessities of the day and shaped by Federalist political concerns and theories. Another scholar, Akhil Akmar, has suggested that Marshall misread Section 13 of the Judiciary Act and that Congress had no intention of conferring original mandamus jurisdiction upon the Supreme Court. These and countless other close studies of *Marbury* confirm Professor Alfange's observation that the case will remain controversial and continue to have great attraction for scholars.[21]

The centrality of *Marbury* to the work of the Marshall Court is obvious from the amount of scholarly effort lavished upon its rationale and its details. Very likely the full story and a complete understanding of the opinion will never be achieved, but as the effort continues, it becomes quite clear that the mandamus case contains much that will inform us concerning Marshall and his Court. At the same time, a single issue analysis or explanation of *Marbury* appears to be hazardous. To say that Marshall proceeds by textual interpretation explains much, but even in *Marbury* there are overtones of "higher law" thought, and these become manifest in Marshall's *Ogden v. Saunders* dissent in 1827. Like the blind men seeking a description of the elephant, those who approach *Marbury* and its significance for understanding Marshall and his Court must exercise care and caution. To one the elephant is like the snake of Federalist political partisanship; to another it is the tree of judicial objectivity; and to a third, an innovative approach to judicial review that feels like a rock—it all depends on what one grabs first.

THE CHASE IMPEACHMENT

Twentieth-century constitutional scholars seem to have more interest in *Marbury* than President Jefferson manifested when the opinion was read. On the other hand, the possibility that judicial review would negate Jefferson's legislative initiatives could not be ignored by the president. Although President Jefferson originally had reservations about using impeachment

---

21. James O'Fallon, "Marbury," 44 *Stanford Law Review* 219–260 (1992); Akmar, "Marbury, Section 13," 454–458, 461–462, 468–474; Dean Alfange, Jr., "Marbury v. Madison and Original Understandings of Judicial Review: In Defense of Traditional Wisdom," 1993 *Supreme Court Review* 329, at 329. The claim has also been made that prior to *Marbury* the Court had issued a mandamus in exercise of original jurisdiction. Susan Low Bloch and Maeva Marcus, "John Marshall's Selective Use of History in Marbury v. Madison," 1986 *Wisconsin Law Review* 301–337.

to remove Federalist judges, after *Marbury* was decided he urged Republicans in the House of Representatives to commence impeachment against one or more of the Federalist-appointed federal judges. District Judge John Pickering of New Hampshire was an easy, albeit pathetic, target. Elderly, insane, and habitually drunk even when he had moments of sanity, Pickering was famous for his inability to remain awake on the bench during the course of trials. His inability to perform his office became less disruptive during the brief period in which the Judiciary Act of 1801 placed a circuit court judge in place for New Hampshire. Circuit Judge Jeremiah Smith presided in Pickering's absence, and the court's business moved forward with expedition. However, the repeal of the Judiciary Act of 1801 forced Judge Pickering back on the bench, and the obvious need to do something about the situation triggered legislative action against him.

On February 4, 1803, Jefferson sent a message to the House, urging that it investigate the possibility of removing Pickering through impeachment. Two weeks later the Supreme Court opinion in *Marbury* was issued, perhaps alerting Republican legislators to the possibility of impeaching one or more of the Supreme Court justices. On May 2, 1803, Judge Chase intemperately charged the Baltimore grand jury concerning what he considered the dangerous democratic activities of the Jefferson administration. He denounced proposals to adopt universal manhood suffrage in Maryland and also attacked the discharge of the sixteen circuit court judges by the enactment of the Judiciary Act of 1802.[22] Chase told the jurors and others in the courtroom that "the late alteration of the federal Judiciary, by the abolition of the office of the sixteen Circuit Judges, and the *recent* change in our State Constitution by establishing *universal suffrage;* will, in my Judgment, *take away all security for property,* and *personal Liberty,*—The independence of the National Judiciary is already shaken to its foundation; and the virtue of the people alone can restore it."[23] It was this charge that focused all previous resentments against Chase and brought the House to consider impeaching him on charges that covered not only the "seditious" grand jury charge but also his conduct in the trials of the Northampton County, Pennsylvania, rioters and the Sedition Act trials of James Callender and others.[24]

Judge Pickering was tried on impeachment charges and convicted by the Senate on March 12, 1804, providing a precedent for misbehavior and

22. The House brought charges for trial in the Senate, which, despite evidence of Pickering's insanity, found him guilty as charged. Based upon this precedent, impeachment was a valid method for removing a judge unable to conduct his duties, and insanity cease to be a defense. Haskins and Johnson, *Foundations,* 211–223. 234–238.

23. Quoted in *Ibid.,* 218, from Chase's manuscript notebook in the Maryland Historical Society.

24. *Ibid.,* 219–223.

inability to perform the duties of office as sufficient grounds for removal by impeachment. The following day Uriah Tracy wrote to Robert Goodloe Harper that impeachment charges against Judge Chase had been presented to the Senate.[25] Thereafter a series of amendments, coupled with pamphlet and newspaper exchanges between Chase and various members of the House, delayed proceedings. As Tracy explained to Harper, the Jeffersonian strategy was to delay the impeachment trial until after the November 1804 presidential elections. The prediction proved correct, for on December 12, 1804, close upon the heels of that election, the final charges were presented to the Senate.

Chase was arraigned before the Senate on January 2, 1805, and given until February 4 to file his answer. The trial began on February 8, and the extended testimony suggests that the judge was ably represented by some of the best counsel in the nation, while the House's presentation was badly mismanaged by Congressman John Randolph. Despite the weaknesses of the House's case, the Republicans in the Senate had more than the required two-thirds vote to convict Chase of one or all of the charges. However, the refusal of some Republican senators to vote for conviction resulted in his acquittal on all counts.[26]

Chase's acquittal removed the immediate threat that impeachment, perhaps following colonial usage, would be used for the removal of unpopular judges and other officials. The defensive position of Chase's counsel—that impeachment required that there be proof of an actual crime committed by the defendant—evolved into the law of the case. In the short run, the failure to impeach Chase provided a degree of safety to the Supreme Court. Ultimately it provided greater independence for judges and gave greater stability to judicial tenure. By exposing the poor manners and overbearing behavior of Judge Chase, it provided an incentive for improvement in judicial decorum and for the separation of partisan politics from the courtroom.[27] What once posed the most serious threat to Marshall and his colleagues now became a powerful illustration of the need for judicial independence as well as for proper behavior on the part of those who held judicial office.

---

25. March 13, 1804, Uriah Tracy to Robert G. Harper, Morristown National Historical Park, Morristown, N.J. The author is grateful to Professor William R. Casto for calling this letter to his attention.

26. Haskins and Johnson, *Foundations*, 238–244; see also Albert J. Beveridge, *The Life of John Marshall*, 4 vols. (New York: Houghton Mifflin Company, 1916–19), vol. 3, 169–222; Herbert A. Johnson, "Impeachment and Politics," in 63 *South Atlantic Quarterly*, 552–563 (1964).

27. Haskins and Johnson, *Foundations*, 244–245; for impeachment proceedings in general see Peter C. Hoffer and N. E. H. Hull, *Impeachment in America, 1635–1805* (New Haven: Yale University Press, 1984).

Although the impeachment did not remove Chase from the Supreme Court bench, it appears to have sharply restricted his participation in Supreme Court decision making. It will be recalled that it was Judge Chase who advocated defiance of Congress over the reinstitution of circuit riding for the Supreme Court. He also played a formative role during Chief Justice Ellsworth's tenure on the Court and might have continued to do so except for the threat of impeachment after 1804. Even his acquittal did not rejuvenate his combativeness. While the Jeffersonians had not gained a conviction, they succeeded in their purpose—to virtually silence Chase and neutralize his influence among his colleagues on the bench and the people at large.

THE BURR TRIALS AND THE SUPREME COURT

As president of the Senate, Aaron Burr presided with dignity and objectivity over the impeachment trial of Judge Chase. It was not an easy time for the vice president, who had fatally wounded Alexander Hamilton in a duel on July 11, 1804. During and after the Chase trial an arrest warrant was outstanding against him, preventing his return to his native state. His four years as Jefferson's vice president were marked by political neglect and rejection. The final insult was Jefferson's selecting Burr's New York rival, George Clinton, to occupy second place on the Republican ticket in the 1804 presidential election. After Jefferson's inauguration Burr left Washington and travelled through the Ohio and Mississippi River valleys, gaining support for a project which continues to remain a mystery even after the labors of countless historians. Although the details of Burr's subsequent trial before Chief Justice Marshall in the circuit court for Virginia will be considered in detail later in this volume, the political significance of the case demands some comment in the present discussion.

Without exception the Burr trial was the most direct conflict that occurred between the Marshall Court and the executive branch of government. President Jefferson took an active role in assembling evidence concerning Burr's activities. He closely supervised the investigation of the various cases and provided both advice and direction to those involved in the prosecutions. There is reason to suspect that the central trial, that of Burr for treason, was located at Richmond so that Marshall as the circuit judge would be directly involved.

When the trial began Marshall's conduct was closely watched, and to a degree it provided Jefferson's supporters with plausible grounds for complaint. Although the chief justice had exercised care to avoid giving basis for charges of favoritism, his easy convivialtiy undermined his resolve, and he found himself sharing the dinner table with Aaron Burr and his attor-

neys. John Wickham, Marshall's close friend and next-door neighbor, periodically held "lawyers' dinners." When Marshall arrived for such a meal
while the grand jury proceedings were in progress, he found Aaron Burr,
free on bail, among the assembled company. Reluctant to embarrass Wickham, Marshall remained until the conclusion of the meal, giving the Jeffersonian press ample opportunity to editorialize about the presiding judge's
favoritism to the accused.[28]

Burr's trial ended on August 31, following Marshall's lengthy opinion
clarifying and expounding the American law of treason. Since the opinion
narrowly restricted the definition of treason, the jury had no choice but to
hold the former vice president not guilty.[29] Although excitement over the
threat of war with Britain diverted public attention from the president's
wish to impeach John Marshall, the judge was not to escape ridicule. Along
with representations of Burr and his attorneys, Chief Justice Marshall was
hung in effigy by the Baltimore mob on November 3, 1807. For two months
after the end of the Richmond trial he was denounced on the floor of the
United States Senate. Closer to home, the Republican-controlled *Richmond
Enquirer* published two "Letters to John Marshall" that sharply criticized
his protection of Aaron Burr and deemed him a "traitor" along with the
former vice president.[30]

At the very least, President Jefferson succeeded in his effort to subject
the Supreme Court, and Marshall in particular, to popular hatred and journalistic attack. On the other hand, enthusiasm for impeachment waned,
and to many observers, Jefferson's prosecution of Burr seemed inept at
best and vindictive at worst.

THE EMBARGO AND PRESIDENTIAL DISCRETION

Few if any efforts to exert national control in peacetime equal the Jeffersonian embargo, initiated by the enactment of a congressional statute in
December 1807 and terminated by the passage of the Non-Intercourse Act
of March 1, 1809. The embargo was an effort to halt all transoceanic carriage of goods to either belligerent in the Napoleonic War then raging.
Because of the proximity of English, French, and Spanish colonial possessions to American seaports, the embargo would have been difficult to enforce under any circumstances. American sea captains were raised in a long
tradition of smuggling, first as colonial subjects of Britain desperate for a

---

28. Beveridge, *Marshall*, vol. 3, 395.
29. *Ibid.*, vol. 3, 470, 505–509, 513; 4 Cranch 469–508 (1807); *Marshall Papers*, vol. 7,
74–119; see the discussion at chapter 4, 126–128.
30. *Marshall Papers*, vol. 3, 533–542.

source of specie and a favorable balance of trade, then as revolutionaries engaged in running gunpowder and weapons for a hard-pressed Continental Army, and later as merchants who, because of diminished trading opportunities after 1783, embraced smuggling profits as essential to their survival.

As the first effort to exert comprehensive national control through bureaucratic action, the embargo presented a formidable challenge to Congress and President Jefferson. The underlying legislation contained a number of oversights or omissions that permitted widespread evasion. A substantial effort was made to tighten enforcement procedures and fine-tune the definition of illegal trade.[31] However, the major political threat was the contention by many Federalists, and by virtually all New Englanders regardless of their party affiliation or economic involvement, that the embargo was unconstitutional. For this reason Jefferson and his fellow partisans braced for still another clash with the judiciary. The conflict that came was less clearly defined than earlier differences between the executive, Congress, and the Court, but it nevertheless posed still another external threat to the Supreme Court.

Ironically, the first decision adverse to the embargo came from Jefferson's first appointee to the Court, Judge William Johnson. Sitting in the May 1808 circuit court for South Carolina, Johnson was asked to issue a mandamus to a collector of customs who refused to issue a sailing permit to one Gilchrist. The collector cited instructions from the secretary of the treasury that forbade this action, even though the collector himself felt the merchant had no intention of breaking the embargo. Judge Johnson issued the mandamus, pointing out that the statute vested discretion in the collector and did not subject that official to supervision or direction by the secretary. At President Jefferson's urging, Johnson was attacked in the press by Attorney General Caesar Rodney. The judge duly defended himself in the Savannah and New York press, causing a rupture in his relations with Jefferson that lasted for several years. A Georgia grand jury issued a presentment against Judge Johnson for "improper interference with the Executive," and Johnson again made a strong public reply.[32]

A Federalist judge in Massachusetts was given the first chance to declare the embargo unconstitutional, and he declined to do so. In October 1808 District Judge John Davis, in *United States v. The William*, upheld the embargo as a valid congressional exercise of the commerce and war powers.[33] The decision gave comfort to the Republican administration at a time when comfort was needed. A month earlier, Jefferson's second appointee to the Court, Brockholst Livingston, while sitting in the Vermont circuit

31. Haskins and Johnson, *Foundations*, 298–302, 415–432.

32. *Ibid.*, 298–302; Warren, *Supreme Court*, vol. 1, 324–338.

33. 28 Federal Cases 614 (16,700) (Cir. Ct. Mass., 1808).

court, had thrown out a treason prosecution based upon a smuggling arrest.[34] The nonpartisan character of these decisions suggests that the Supreme Court justices were dealing with the embargo in terms of a quasi-criminal statute to be enforced as a matter of law and not as a Jeffersonian political initiative. They were beginning to distinguish between law and politics. Under the Federalist presidents, the federal courts had considered it their duty to support the political positions of the executive and legislative branches. Understandably President Jefferson wished to secure similar support for his diplomatic and legislative initiatives, despite the altered relationship between the judicial branch and the political arms of government.[35]

Following so closely upon the Burr trial, the embargo cases and the attendant publicity kept the Supreme Court justices in a defensive position. Partisan ties did not protect individual judges who decided cases contrary to Republican policies. Indeed, the attack upon such apostasy seemed even more vicious than against Federalist-appointed judges. President Jefferson's two terms in office began with uncertainty concerning the future activities of the Supreme Court. Beginning with *Marbury*, the Court strengthened its position, even as it strove to avoid conflict with the new president or Congress. The ill-advised and inept impeachment effort against Chase actually emphasized the value Americans of both parties placed upon the ideal of an independent judiciary. It also practically eliminated future recourse to impeachment, as Jefferson realized during the course of the Burr trial. On the other hand, the president insisted upon micromanaging the treason prosecution of his political rival Aaron Burr, creating a sharp division in his party's ranks and casting suspicion on his personal motives.

The eight years of Jefferson's presidency rule generated a cohesion among Supreme Court justices that developed, to a considerable degree, as the result of the extreme forms of political and psychological pressure brought to bear upon them. Ironically, it was Jefferson's struggle to discredit the Court that strengthened John Marshall's leadership position and weakened the president's influence with his own Supreme Court appointees.

MARTIN V. HUNTER'S LESSEE:
STATE POWER AND NATIONAL INTEGRITY

Undoubtedly the most significant events affecting the Court during the War of 1812 were internal rather than external political conflicts. There was a notable rise in the number of concurring and dissenting opinions,

---

34. See Warren, *Supreme Court*, vol. 1, 342–351; Haskins and Johnson, *Foundations*, 305–311.

35. Haskins and Johnson, *Foundations*, 297–298, 309–311.

particularly in prize cases. Important archival materials, including file papers in original jurisdiction cases, were burned when British forces captured Washington and put the Capitol to the torch. The Court moved to makeshift quarters, and business resumed as usual.[36]

Among the unfinished business from the 1813 term was the outstanding Supreme Court mandate in *Fairfax v. Hunter,* directing the Virginia Court of Appeals to reverse its decree upholding Virginia's seizure of Fairfax proprietary lands during the Revolution. Because of Chief Justice Marshall's professional and financial connections with the case, he had not participated in hearing or deciding the *Fairfax* appeal before the Supreme Court. Judge Story wrote the Court opinion, based on the 1794 Jay Treaty with England, which precluded any seizures of British-owned lands after 1783. In December 1815, after a series of delays, the Virginia Court of Appeals formally declared that it would not execute the mandate from the United States Supreme Court. Led by Justice Spencer Roane, the Virginia judges asserted that the Supreme Court had no constitutional basis to exercise appellate jurisdiction over the highest courts of the states.[37]

This development in the complex series of law cases concerning the Fairfax lands was not totally unexpected. Indeed, much of the opposition to Virginia's ratification of the Federal Constitution in 1788 revolved around two issues: the collection of prerevolutionary debts owed by Virginians to British merchants and the possibility that federal courts would invalidate Virginia's seizure of British-owned real property during the Revolution. Ironically, it was John Marshall who unsuccessfully argued the case for Virginia debtors in *Ware v. Hylton* (1796). At the same time, he was scheduled to argue an earlier version of the *Fairfax* case before the Supreme Court, but it was postponed indefinitely. While the state's resentment was left to smolder over the debt issue, collections, such as they were, proceeded slowly. The Supreme Court's 1813 *Fairfax* decision raised once more the specter of a national government trampling Virginia sovereignty under foot to appease the despised enemy of revolutionary days. Coupled with this political environment was the personal tension between Chief Justice Marshall, a popular and influential Virginian, and the state's Republican leadership, still swayed by the opinions of Thomas Jefferson and under the control of Judge Roane, a disappointed aspirant for the chief justiceship of the United States in 1801.[38]

36. For the rise in concurring and dissenting opinions concerning prize matters, see chapter 3. It was not until 1819 that the Court moved back into a newly redecorated chamber to begin its "golden age." G. Edward White, *The Marshall Court and Cultural Change, 1815–35,* vols. 3 and 4, *History of the Supreme Court of the United States,* 10 vols. to date (New York: Macmillan Publishing Company, 1988), 158–159.

37. Haskins and Johnson, *Foundations,* 514–518; 1 Wheaton 304 (1816).

38. *Ware v. Hylton,* 3 Dallas 199 (1796); Marshall's argument is at *ibid.,* 210–215; Beveridge, *Marshall,* vol. 3, 20, 113, 178; vol. 4, 157–164.

Historians as well as contemporary commentators differ concerning the role Marshall played in *Martin v. Hunter's Lessee*. Promptly after the Virginia court's decision, John Marshall prepared a writ of error, which was signed by Judge Bushrod Washington. Although Professor White cites Marshall's preparation of the writ as evidence of his undue (and improper) influence in the decision to appeal the case to the Supreme Court, it was the usual practice for the Supreme Court justice assigned to a circuit to approve the writ of error to the Supreme Court. His sending the document to Washington for approval was an effort not to conceal his identity but rather to insure impartiality in the pro forma step of allowing the appeal. There was nothing surreptitious about the procedure.[39]

Far more damaging to Marshall's reputation were contemporary assertions that he wrote or dictated the opinion issued as that of Joseph Story. On this the evidence is inconclusive. Dunne suggests that Story's son and biographer had some doubts concerning the authorship of the opinion, and the judge himself wrote several years later that Marshall concurred in every word of it. On the other hand, the opinion's assertion that the Constitution compelled Congress to give a full range of judicial power to the federal courts points to the nationalistic Story as its author. Professor David Currie, a close student of the judicial craftsmanship involved in the Marshall Court opinions, comments that *Martin* demonstrates a striking difference from the Chief Justice's earlier opinions, which Currie terms "curt and conclusory." Perhaps the most persuasive evidence of Marshall's inclination to avoid involvement in this category of litigation is Beveridge's observation that when, in an 1805 North Carolina circuit court case, Marshall had an opportunity to pass upon a state sequestration of British-owned realty, he declined to do so, citing his interest in the Fairfax lands.[40]

Absent discovery of new evidence concerning authorship, or perhaps some convincing word-content analysis of the *Martin* opinion, we can only speculate concerning Marshall's role, if he had any, in its preparation. The Story opinion undoubtedly bears similarities to Marshall's analytical style, particularly in the first portion, dealing with the definition of what constitutes the judicial power of the United States and why powers not specifically granted to the Supreme Court must be distributed either in that Court or in some lower federal court. However, it is this very portion of the opinion that Dunne identified with Story's ultranationalist position. Sena-

---

39. White, *Marshall Court,* 167–168, 169–173.
40. Gerald T. Dunne, *Justice Joseph Story and the Rise of the Supreme Court* (New York: Simon and Schuster, 1970), 135–136; Beveridge, *Marshall,* vol. 4, 154; David P. Currie, *The Constitution and the Supreme Court: The First Hundred Years, 1789–1888* (Chicago: University of Chicago Press, 1985), 95–96.

tor Beveridge also pointed out that in 1822 Marshall wrote his brother that Story should have based his opinion not upon the 1794 Jay Treaty but rather upon the Peace Treaty of 1783.[41]

Historians may temporize about the Chief Justice's involvement in *Martin*, but his Republican contemporaries were not inclined to give him or his judicial colleagues the benefit of the doubt. Sectionalism was on the increase after the War of 1812 drew to a close. The embargo before the war and the war itself were extremely unpopular in New England. Eventually a secessionist convention was organized to meet at Hartford, Connecticut, to deal with New England's profound dissatisfaction with the war. A last-minute effort by Federalists to reestablish their political power, the Hartford Convention lost its reason for being when news of the Treaty of Ghent arrived, ending the War of 1812.

Coupled with the possibility that Aaron Burr might have succeeded in establishing a secessionist republic in the West, the War of 1812 and the Hartford Convention established an aura of states' rights and sectionalism that permeated the postwar years. The temper of the times favored states' rights posturing, and Virginia's opposition to the 1783 and 1794 treaties with Britain focused upon the Fairfax land litigation.

The 1813 mandate in *Fairfax v. Hunter* upheld the treaty rights of the Fairfax family, but it was never executed by the Virginia courts. Consequently, title to the Fairfax lands remained in question and continued so until well after Marshall's death in 1835. Defiance by Virginia's highest court was but one phase of a persistent political and ideological effort to isolate Virginia law from external control.[42] Virginia lawyers were forbidden to cite *Martin v. Hunter's Lessee* as precedent in state courts. The Old Dominion's newspaper editors chose to print Judge Johnson's concurring opinion, which suggested that the Supreme Court's mandate was entitled to comity (and no more) in Virginia courts.[43] They totally ignored Story's opinion for the Court, and the matter was still at issue in 1821 when *Cohens v. Virginia* again raised the question of Supreme Court appellate jurisdiction over state courts.

---

41. 1 Wheaton 304, at 331, 336–339, 342; Dunne, *Story*, 135–136; Beveridge, *Marshall*, vol. 1, 164.

42. The Virginia stance is well described in F. Thorton Miller, *Juries and Judges versus the Law: Virginia's Provincial Legal Perspective, 1783–1828* (Charlottesville: University Press of Virginia, 1994).

43. White, *Marshall Court*, 504; H. Jefferson Powell suggests that the Virginia judges objected to federal court interference with "autonomy of process" in state court proceedings. Thus while they did not challenge the supremacy of congressional power, they did assert state independence from federal court jurisdiction. "The Oldest Question of Federal Constitutional Law," 79 *Virginia Law Review* 633, at 675–681 (1993).

The *Martin* opinion raised Virginia's wrath against the Court, and a smattering of critical articles appeared in the *Richmond Enquirer,* the foremost Republican newspaper in the state, which was edited by Judge Spencer Roane's cousin Thomas Ritchie. At the federal level Congress took no action on a bill increasing the justices' salaries, causing Judge Story to remark in 1818 that they were starving in splendid poverty.[44]

This impasse over the Supreme Court's appellate review of federal questions raised in state courts highlighted a trend that was characteristic of the Court's caseload under John Marshall. Before Marshall became chief justice, the major confrontations between the Court and the states had been in original jurisdiction matters in which one or more of the states were parties. After 1801 the number of appeals from state courts increased gradually, but the bulk of appellate business before the high court came from the federal circuit and district courts, with the District of Columbia circuit heavily represented. Before 1801, 8 percent of the Supreme Court's docket consisted of appeals from the highest courts of the states; for the period of 1801–15 only 4.5 percent of the cases before the Court were appealed from state courts.[45] During the entire history of the Supreme Court, from 1789 through 1813, the Court had taken appeals from state courts in sixteen cases without any serious objection.[46] This acquiescence reflected the views of the first Congress while enacting the Judiciary Act of 1789. The Supreme Court's authority to hear appeals from the highest courts of the states was considered necessary to insure uniformity in the interpretation of the Federal Constitution and to maintain federal supremacy in national and international affairs.[47] Nevertheless, Virginia's persistent defiance of the *Fairfax* mandate brought into question the Court's ability to provide a uniform interpretation of federal law throughout the United States.

---

44. Beveridge, *Marshall,* vol. 1, 146, 166–167.

45. See Haskins and Johnson, *Foundations,* 377–380, indicating that 60.5 percent of the appellate caseload in the period 1801–15 was from the federal circuit courts, and another 35 percent originated in the District of Columbia circuit.

46. For details concerning legislative efforts to alter Supreme Court appellate jurisdiction under Section 25 of the Judiciary Act, see Charles Warren, "Legislative and Judicial Attacks on the Supreme Court of the United States—A History of the Twenty-fifth Section of the Judiciary Act," 47 *American Law Review* 1–34, 161–189 (1913), and Warren, *Supreme Court,* vol. 1, 443. Akhil R. Akmar argues that the Judiciary Act of 1789 created a two-tiered concept of federal judicial power. The first and most significant area of Supreme Court jurisdiction was involved with foreign affairs. "The Two-Tiered Structure of the Judiciary Act of 1789," 138 *University of Pennsylvania Law Review* 1499, at 1501–1508, 1513–1515 (1990). For a contrary argument see Martin H. Redish, "Text, Structure and Common Sense in the Interpretation of Article III," 138 *University of Pennsylvania Law Review* 1633, at 1635–1641 (1990).

47. Haskins and Johnson, *Foundations,* 378.

M'CULLOCH V. MARYLAND **AND THE FRIEND OF THE UNION**

Given the uncertainties of the Fairfax lands litigation in Virginia, it was inevitable that issues of federal supremacy would be litigated more frequently in the Supreme Court, with attendant resentment and localism in the states. The great term of 1819, marked by Supreme Court opinions in *M'Culloch v. Maryland,*[48] *Dartmouth College v. Woodward,*[49] and *Sturges v. Crowninshield,*[50] emphasized this judicial authority over the States in a dramatic way that was bound to attract controversy and political retribution. Two of these cases were heard on writs of error to the highest courts of the states involved. *M'Culloch* and *Dartmouth* reversed state decisions that represented significant local interests—the power of taxation in the first and the authority of the state over its domestic corporations in the second. In *Sturges* a sharply divided Court agreed with Marshall that a state insolvency law that operates retroactively to discharge an obligation violates the contract clause of the Federal Constitution. Although it was only a partial solution to the complex commercial situation created by the absence of a federal bankruptcy statute, *Sturges,* like the two other cases, did severely restrict the ability of New York State to provide relief to debtors caught in the financial panic of 1819.

As Professor G. Edward White has correctly observed, the thrust of the Marshall Court's constitutional decisions was not directed toward consolidation of power in the federal government.[51] The Court's emphatic rejection of the compact theory of Union—that is, that the federal government was created by state action—marked it as a force for national unity. However, the justices also recognized the need to make federal judicial power coterminous with the broad construction of federal legislative power given Congress by the Constitution's first article. On the other hand, the Marshall Court justices never conceived that plenary federal power would be as pervasive as it has become in twentieth-century America.[52] While some caution may be advisable in accepting White's interpretation of the Court's alleged expansion of federal judicial power to match congressional authority,[53] he is quite correct in holding that Marshall and his colleagues should not be termed "nationalists."[54] Their service to the "Union" consisted of

---

48. 4 Wheaton 316–437.
49. 4 Wheaton 518–715.
50. 4 Wheaton 122–208.
51. White, *Marshall Court,* 485–487, 494.
52. *Ibid.,* 494.
53. There is a strong argument that the Supreme Court's narrow and restrictive construction of its powers under Article III were the basis upon which it built its foundations of power up to, and perhaps after, 1815. See Haskins and Johnson, *Foundations,* especially 612–613.
54. White, *Marshall Court,* 486–487.

restraining state power as it encroached upon the authority constitutionally granted to the federal government.

All three cases in the 1819 term, *M'Culloch, Dartmouth College,* and *Sturges,* represent sharp checks to states' efforts to impose burdens upon the federal government's exercise of its powers or to prevent states from violating provisions of the Federal Constitution. Predictably, *M'Culloch* attracted the greatest public attention because it dealt with the sensitive issue of intergovernmental tax immunity as well as the hot political question of centralized versus local banking. Because of this, *M'Culloch* became the case over which Chief Justice Marshall was willing to engage in political battle and join issue in a series of pseudonymous essays replying to newspaper attacks on the Court's reasoning. With his sensitivity to the political mood of Virginia, Marshall anticipated the journalistic attack before it occurred. He wrote to Judge Story, "Our opinion in the bank case has roused the sleeping spirit of Virginia—if indeed it ever sleeps. It will I understand be attacked in the papers with some asperity; as those who favor it never write for the publick it will remain undefended & of course be considered as *damnably heretical.*"[55]

Uncomfortable with the prospect of leaving the *M'Culloch* decision undefended, Marshall was also concerned lest the members of the Court be "condemned as a pack of consolidating aristocratics."[56] His alarm was accentuated by the realization that bank supporters in the administration and Congress would not speak out in the Court's favor; although they wanted the Court to legitimize the bank, they sought an obsequious, unreasoned opinion from the justices. Despite Marshall's foreboding, it appears that only after publication of the "Amphictyon" letters in the *Richmond Enquirer* (March 30–April 2, 1819) was he spurred to prepare essays to defend the bank case's outcome. To assure some degree of anonymity, he sent his essays to Judge Washington, then in Philadelphia, for publication in the *Philadelphia Union* (April 24–28), but they were so garbled in typesetting that he begged Washington to have them published a second time in the *Alexandria Gazette* (May 15–19).[57] Uncomfortable in the role of a political essayist, he instructed that the manuscripts be destroyed once the essays were set in type. He also refused to permit Court reporter Henry Wheaton

---

55. Warren, *Supreme Court,* vol. 1, 503, 515; White notes that the practice of newspaper commentary arose as a result of the 1819 decisions (*Marshall Court,* 930); March 24, 1819, Marshall to Story, Story Papers, Massachusetts Historical Society; see also *John Marshall's Defense of McCulloch v. Maryland,* Gerald Gunther, ed. (Stanford: Stanford University Press, 1969), 11, 12.

56. Marshall to Bushrod Washington, March 27, 1819, Marshall Papers, College of William and Mary.

57. See generally Gunther, ed., *John Marshall's Defense,* 11–17; all of these essays and those of Marshall's opponents are conveniently reprinted in Professor Gunther's book.

to republish the essays lest the author's identity be compromised. In forwarding his "Friend of the Constitution" essays to Washington, Marshall wanted the pseudonym changed to avoid identification with his earlier "Friend of the Union" publication. Apparently Judge Washington, or the editor of the *Alexandria Gazette,* thought the better of this suggestion. The "Friend of the Constitution" essays, ultimately nine in number, appeared in the *Alexandria Gazette* for June 30–July 15, 1819.[58]

By August 3 the Chief Justice suspected the identity of his opponent in the press. The "Amphictyon" letters were written by Judge William Brockenbrough, and the "Hampden" letters were authored by Spencer Roane, a judge of the Virginia Court of Appeals. Marshall's essays went to great length to refute the claims of his antagonists, pointing out that the Court was not consolidationist and that adopting the states' rights position of his opponents would lead to disunion. Repeating the view of constitutional construction voiced in *M'Culloch,* he emphasized that a constitution had to be written to be adaptable to future times and that the essence of American constitutional government was that both state and federal courts must protect the fundamental law against legislative infractions.[59] A persuasive and well-crafted defense, Marshall's essays fell on deaf ears, and the Virginia legislature duly passed a resolution condemning the Court's decision and recommending the creation of a new federal tribunal that would adjudicate issues of federal-state power.[60] Having declared its belligerency to *M'Culloch,* Virginia permitted its resentment to smolder, with occasional newspaper essays advocating the creation of an "impartial tribunal" to determine issues arising between the federal government and the states.[61]

THE LOTTERY CASE AND REPEAL
OF SECTION 25 OF THE JUDICIARY ACT

Two years after *M'Culloch,* Virginia's hackles were again raised by a Supreme Court opinion delivered on an appeal from a Virginia state court. In this instance the trial court was the Hustings Court of Norfolk, from

58. Marshall to Washington, June 28, 1819, Marshall Papers, Library of Congress; for refusal to permit Wheaton to print the essays see Marshall to Joseph Story, July 13, 1819, Story Papers, Massachusetts Historical Society.

59. Marshall to Bushrod Washington, August 3, 1819, Marshall Papers, Library of Congress; the arguments are at Gunther, ed., *John Marshall's Defense,* 158, 170–171, 187, 214.

60. Warren, *Supreme Court,* vol. 1, 519; Warren subsequently suggests that the strong Southern antipathy to the opinion in *M'Culloch* was due to the fear that a broad construction of the necessary and proper clause would permit the federal government to interfere with the states on the issue of slavery, which was then becoming critical in national politics. *Ibid.,* 514, 542.

61. For example, an open letter from Publicola to the Virginia General Assembly appeared in the *Richmond Enquirer,* January 30, 1821.

which no appeal was provided by state procedure. The partnership of P. J. and M. J. Cohen was convicted on an indictment for selling District of Columbia lottery tickets in Norfolk, contrary to Virginia criminal law. On appeal, they asserted that the supremacy clause of the Federal Constitution applied to the congressional statute establishing the lottery. Thus, they contended, the Virginia state law was invalid in its application to them. Ultimately the Supreme Court, in a brief section of the *Cohens* opinion by Chief Justice Marshall, rejected this appeal, pointing out that in passing laws for the District of Columbia, the federal Congress had no object beyond government of the District. Absent any expression of legislative intention that the act apply beyond the capital district, it was inappropriate to apply the supremacy clause to it. Furthermore, "to interfere with the penal laws of a state, where they are not leveled against the legitimate powers of the Union, but have for their sole object, the internal government of the country, is a very serious matter, which Congress cannot be supposed to adopt lightly, or inconsiderately."[62]

Like *Marbury*, the *Cohens* case was self-executing since it denied relief to the moving party. Like that of *Marbury*, its significance was that the Supreme Court ruled upon its own jurisdiction. Like *Marbury*, it vexed Jefferson and his party and goaded them to extreme measures.

The jurisdictional issue was among the most critical ever decided by the Supreme Court. It raised still again the question of Supreme Court review of state court decisions involving federal questions; this had been litigated in *Martin v. Hunter's Lessee*, which the Virginia bench and bar treated with contempt. Nevertheless, Marshall felt obligated to defend once more the Court's appellate jurisdiction over state court determinations which involved the Federal Constitution, treaties negotiated under the authority of the United States and federal statutes enacted pursuant to the Constitution. This "federal question" jurisdiction was an effective and indispensable instrument for securing the supremacy granted to the federal government under Article VI. Once more, as in *Marbury*, the Supreme Court asserted its jurisdiction but denied relief.

Predictably, the *Cohens* case generated a new outburst of protest from the Richmond junto. Justice Spencer Roane, using the pseudonym Algernon Sidney, launched a battery of essays criticizing the *Cohens* decision. From Thomas Jefferson's viewpoint, Roane had "pulverized" Marshall's opinion in these essays,[63] and even Marshall acknowledged that serious damage had been done by Roane's attack. To Justice Story the Chief Justice observed that "for coarseness and malignity of invective, Algernon Sidney

---

62. *Cohens v. Virginia*, 6 Wheaton 264, at 442 (1821).
63. White, *Marshall Court*, 340.

surpassed all party writers who have ever made pretensions to any decency of character."[64] He identified Thomas Jefferson—the "great Lama of the mountains," he called him—as the true source of the attack and attributed the elder statesman's animosity to the Batture controversy in 1813.[65] This case involved litigation over tidal land in the Mississippi River delta. President Jefferson had been accused of improperly ordering United States marshals to seize the property to which Edward Livingston claimed title. The controversy dragged on for years, and in retirement Jefferson printed a book-length brief defending his position on it.[66]

Rather than springing to the defense of the *Cohens* decision, Marshall elected to ignore the Algernon Sidney letters, resting content with letting Henry Wheaton do so while, at the same time, successfully preventing the Sidney essays from being published in a widely circulated Philadelphia legal periodical.[67]

As the Chief Justice anticipated, the Virginia legislature considered a resolution urging repeal of Section 25 of the Judiciary Act of 1789 but rejected that resolution. Public opinion, even in the South, remained divided over the wisdom of such a measure, but it would remain an issue of public concern over the next decade.[68] However, Marshall and his colleagues could not overlook the fact that the junto and its supporters had shifted their strategy. Earlier they had demanded that a new arbitral tribunal be established, a step that would have required elaborate procedures of constitutional amendment. The new strategy involved simply passing a statute that eliminated the Supreme Court's appellate jurisdiction over federal questions. Federal-question jurisdiction is based upon congressional action, and it gives the Supreme Court the authority to review cases in which the highest courts of the states have decided against claims based upon the Constitution, statutes, and treaties of the United States. Without the Supreme Court's right to hear such appeals from the states, each state would have the final say concerning what the Constitution of the United States meant in that state. As Judge Story had pointed out in *Martin,* this would result in a multifaceted array of opinions concerning what the Constitution meant.[69]

---

64. To Joseph Story, June 15 and July 13, 1821, quoted in Warren, *Supreme Court,* vol. 1, 560–561.

65. Marshall to Story, September 18, 1821, Story Papers, Massachusetts Historical Society.

66. *Livingston v. Dorgenois,* 7 Cranch 577–589 (1813); for discussions of the case see Edward Dumbauld, *Thomas Jefferson and the Law* (Norman: University of Oklahoma Press, 1978), 36–74; George Dargo, *Jefferson's Louisiana: Politics and the Clash of Legal Traditions* (Cambridge: Harvard University Press, 1975), 74–101; see Warren, *Supreme Court,* vol. 1, 562, for Marshall's conclusion concerning Jefferson.

67. White, *Marshall Court,* 521–524.

68. Warren, *Supreme Court,* vol. 1, 555, 559–560, 562.

69. *Martin v. Hunter's Lessee,* 1 Wheaton 304, at 347–348 (1816).

GREEN V. BIDDLE AND KENTUCKY DISCONTENT

The Court's decision in *Cohens* rekindled the smoldering fire of states' rights throughout the Union. As Charles Warren points out, by 1825 the Supreme Court had invalidated one or more laws passed by each of ten states—Georgia, Virginia, New Hampshire, New Jersey, Vermont, Maryland, New York, Pennsylvania, Ohio, and Kentucky.[70] Many of these were matters of considerable interest, including a New York insolvency law and its monopoly grant to insure the success of steamboat navigation and an Ohio law imposing a tax on the Bank of the United States and regulating banking.[71] Yet *Green v. Biddle*,[72] involving the "occupying claimant" laws of Kentucky, was unique both in the amount of criticism it generated and in its demonstration that states' rights forces opposed to the Court were most vitally concerned with advancing their own provincial interests and only moderately concerned about the Constitution of the federal Union.

The *Green* case presented the Supreme Court with a dispute arising under the land laws of Kentucky and was complicated by the 1792 compact between Virginia and her daughter state stipulating that titles arising under Virginia grants would be preserved inviolate by the new state's government. Chief Justice Marshall was no stranger to these matters. For himself and for his family he had dealt extensively in Kentucky land grants, relying upon Kentucky relatives to make the necessary entries and to secure surveys as appropriate. After Kentucky independence, Marshall and his family were protected by the 1792 compact to protect titles still held by them and to preclude warranty claims made by their grantees. As a consequence, Marshall did not participate in the decision of the case, the first opinion having been delivered by Judge Story (1821) and the second by Judge Washington (1823).[73]

The occupying claimant legislation passed by the Kentucky legislature in 1797 and 1812 provided relief to individuals who, under mistaken claim to title, made improvements upon realty actually owned by an absentee. In these circumstances the common law awarded the land to the legal owner, and no compensation was paid for improvements even though the occupant was liable for rent and for any waste to the land during his possession.

---

70. Warren, *Supreme Court*, vol. 1, 653.

71. *Sturges v. Crowninshield*, 4 Wheaton 122 (1819); *Gibbons v. Ogden*, 9 Wheaton 1 (1824); *Osborn v. Bank of the United States*, 9 Wheaton 738 (1824).

72. 8 Wheaton 1 (1823).

73. 8 Wheaton 1, at 3–11 (1823); Judge Story's 1821 opinion for the Court held the Kentucky statutes unconstitutional. *Ibid.*, 11–18. Senator Henry Clay's motion to reargue was granted, and the case was reargued at the 1823 term, when the Court, by Judge Washington, confirmed the earlier decision. *Ibid.*, 69–94.

The Kentucky statutory scheme permitted the occupant to recover for the value of the improvements and endeavored to adjust the interests of both parties in such a way that the occupant would not be inequitably penalized. Under certain circumstances an occupying claimant might acquire title when the improvements exceeded the value of the land involved.

Because of the large number of conflicting land grants in Kentucky before statehood, most Kentuckians held land as occupying claimants. Once Kentucky entered the Union, they brought pressure upon the legislature to alter the common-law rule concerning improvements. However, the Virginia-Kentucky compact, implicitly approved by Congress when Kentucky was admitted to the Union, was held in *Green* to be a contract subject to the obligation of contract clause of the Federal Constitution. Broadly read, the Supreme Court rule prevented Kentucky from passing remedial laws concerning civil procedures for the recovery of Virginia-granted land at any time subsequent to the 1792 compact. Viewed in this light, it constituted a serious limitation upon the legislative sovereignty of the state.[74] Thus it triggered strong reactions from Kentuckians.

Judge Story's 1821 opinion was rendered after the Court's first hearing of the case, during which no representative of the occupying claimants appeared. Discomfort at this situation, coupled with a plea for reargument lodged by Senator Henry Clay, moved the Court to allow reargument in 1822. In the intervening time, the Story opinion was denounced by the Kentucky legislature as incompatible with the state's constitutional powers. However, reargument of *Green* created even more difficulties for the Court. Justice Todd was absent from the 1822 sittings; Brockholst Livingston was languishing in terminal illness, which would claim his life before the opinion was delivered in 1823. Bushrod Washington was sick and absent. The Chief Justice, though present, was indisposed and weak and in any event may have disqualified himself because of interest. Historian Charles Warren correctly points out that the absent judges had concurred in the 1821 opinion, and thus there was a substantial majority in favor of the disposition. Be that as it may, the Court's opponents claimed that the 1823 opinion was supported by less than a majority of the members of the Supreme Court. As a consequence, both Senator Martin Van Buren (New York) and Senator Richard M. Johnson (Kentucky) introduced resolutions designed to require that a substantial number of members of the Supreme Court be present and voting affirmatively before a federal or State statute could be declared unconstitutional.[75] Although the resolutions failed, thereafter the Court seems to have insisted that at least five justices be present and vote in favor of the decision in constitutional cases.

---

74. This is essentially the argument of Judge Johnson's dissenting opinion. *Ibid.*, 94–107.

75. Warren, *Supreme Court*, 637–638; Beveridge, *Marshall*, vol. 4, 379–380.

Although proposals for judicial reform caused considerable concern among members of the Supreme Court bench, three factors contributed to a diminution of the threat over the subsequent three years. *Green v. Biddle* demonstrated the divided loyalties of the anti-Court party, if such a loose coalition might even be termed a party. While the same issues of state sovereignty were present in *Green* as in *Cohens,* Virginia heartily endorsed the *Green* opinion, which was favorable to those claiming under Virginia titles. Pecuniary interest rather than firm convictions concerning the balance of the federal system dominated the diverse concerns of the states' rights group, diluting their credibility among those Americans whose devotion to the Union was firmly based upon constitutional theory and political consistency.

Second, the Supreme Court's decision in favor of congressional power over interstate commerce, enunciated in the 1824 decision of *Gibbons v. Ogden,* not only guaranteed landlocked states river access to international trade routes but also provided a powerful argument for federal authority over the commercial prosperity of the nation. Significantly, Chief Justice Marshall's opinion refrained from vesting an exclusive commerce power in Congress, thus permitting states a role in shaping not only economic policy but also the conditions under which interstate and foreign commerce might be conducted.[76] The almost universal popularity of the *Gibbons* decision also quieted public clamor for the "reformation" of the Supreme Court's power to review state court holdings in regard to federal questions.

Third, Thomas Jefferson's death on July 4, 1826, removed from the political scene the most implacable enemy of federal judicial power. While others would arise to occupy an anti-Court position, none would have the personal influence wielded by the former president. The major attacks upon Marshall's Court had been triggered by his incitement of essay writers and partisan legislators into a series of denunciations and jurisdictional attacks. At the same time, Jefferson had made a concerted effort to undermine the seeming unanimity of Supreme Court decisions by urging Republican-appointed justices to revert to the older practice of delivering opinions seriatim.[77]

These were the reasons for diminished external pressure after 1823, but within the Court itself, divergent philosophical positions developed among the justices. As subsequent chapters will suggest, Marshall, perhaps drawing upon the natural-law learning of Joseph Story, adopted a natural-law posi-

---

76. Felix Frankfurter, *The Commerce Clause under Marshall, Taney and Waite* (Chapel Hill: University of North Carolina Press, 1937; reprint, Quadrangle Books, Chicago, 1964), 25–27.

77. Morgan, *Johnson,* 168–169.

tion in the field of contract law that eventually would lead to his landmark dissent in *Ogden v. Saunders* (1827). Story, on his part, made continuing efforts to extend the scope of federal crimes and reestablish federal common-law crimes through congressional legislative action.[78] In this he was opposed by William Johnson, who earlier had challenged Story's expansive concept of federal admiralty jurisdiction.[79]

Increasingly under the need to adapt to the opinions of his fellow justices, Marshall began the slow and begrudging process of limiting some of his earlier general pronouncements. This can be seen in the new balance between the federal commerce power and state police power marked by the 1829 case *Willson v. Black Bird Creek Marsh Company*. Similarly, in *Providence Bank v. Billings* (1830) Marshall held that state corporation charters did not carry exemption from taxation unless such a privilege was expressly granted, thereby limiting the applicability of the Federal Constitution's contract clause and the potential scope of the Dartmouth College case. These moderate changes of emphasis suggest that from 1825 through 1831 the justices were involved in intramural discussions that were but slightly impacted by external political pressure. That temporary calm would once again be disturbed by the Cherokee cases of 1831–32.[80]

THE CHEROKEE CASES AND
RENEWED PROPOSALS TO ALTER SECTION 25

The state of Georgia was sparsely settled in 1801, but the westward expansion of plantation agriculture raised legal and moral questions concerning treatment of the Cherokee tribe that remained within the boundaries of that state. Gradually the Indians were forced into the more mountainous areas of Georgia, where, a few years later, the discovery of gold again made their lands the object of white settlement. Unlike other tribes, the Cherokee adapted well to the white man's world—through becoming agriculturalists, by evolving a written language, and by preparing a constitution for their settlement that goaded the Georgia government into repressive actions to assert state authority. After obtaining legal opinions from a number of prominent American lawyers, the Cherokee brought a petition for injunction in the U.S. Supreme Court, invoking the Court's original jurisdiction on the premise that the Cherokee Nation had always been treated as a sovereign nation. They asked that the Court declare in-

---

78. *Ogden v. Saunders*, 12 Wheaton 213 (1827); Newmyer, *Story*, 408, n. 10.

79. For the discussion of Judges Story and Johnson, see chapter 1, 34, chapter 7, 197–199, and chapter 8, 231.

80. The *Willson* case is at 2 Peters 245 (1829); the *Providence Bank* case is at 4 Peters 514 (1830).

valid those laws of Georgia that purported to repeal the constitution and laws adopted by the tribe and to impose penal sanctions upon any Cherokee officials who acted contrary to Georgia law. A series of treaties with the former royal government of Georgia, the state government, and the United States government was identified in the bill as forming the constitutional basis for their request. A supplemental bill informed the Supreme Court that on the return date of the original bill, the Georgia authorities had hanged an Indian named Corn Tassel, who had been arrested in Cherokee territory. However, no answer was made by the Georgia officials served with the Supreme Court's writ, and no counsel appeared to argue the case on their behalf.[81]

Delivering the Court's opinion, Chief Justice Marshall focused upon the Court's jurisdiction. While he conceded that the Cherokee constituted a state, he denied that they might be a foreign state since their lands were within the territorial limits of the United States. The tribe was a "domestic dependent nation" under the protection of the United States, but it certainly was not a foreign state for purposes of giving the Court jurisdiction to restrain the Georgia legislature's enactment of laws for its state.[82] In effect, the Cherokee Nation as such had no standing to invoke the U.S. Supreme Court's original jurisdiction. It was not an independent sovereign nation, nor was it a state of the Union. Lacking those qualifications, it failed to meet the constitutional requirements. Individual members of the Cherokee Nation would be precluded from bringing action, either on the principles of sovereign immunity or because they fell within the prohibitions of the Eleventh Amendment. The only way the Cherokee Nation might have its status adjudicated by the Supreme Court would be in an action brought by a third party that collaterally raised the issue of the tribe's sovereignty.

At the 1832 term such a case arose, and the clash between state authority and federal treaty rights had to be faced head-on. Section 7 of an 1830 act of the Georgia legislature prohibited any white person not licensed by Georgia to reside on Cherokee lands after March 1, 1831. Samuel Worcester and Elizur Butler, among others, were indicted for violating this criminal statute by continuing to serve as missionaries to the Cherokee after the effective date of the statute. In their defense they pleaded the tribe's treaty rights under federal treaties. They were convicted and sentenced to serve four years at hard labor. Although duly served with a writ of error from the U.S. Supreme Court, the Georgia authorities did not appear, nor were they defended by counsel.[83]

---

81. *Cherokee Nation v. Georgia*, 5 Peters 1–80, at 3–13 (1831).
82. *Ibid.*, 15–20.
83. *Worcester v. Georgia*, 6 Peters 515, at 521–535 (1832).

Reviewing the text of treaties between the United States and the Cherokee tribe, Chief Justice Marshall for the majority found that these were guarantees of tribal independence and evidenced negotiations between equals rather than Indian submission to United States authority. The supremacy clause of the Federal Constitution made those treaties the supreme law of the land, binding upon Georgia and so recognized by that state until 1828. The Cherokee "had always been considered as distinct, independent political communities, retaining their original natural rights, as the undisputed possessors of the soil from time immemorial," and the Georgia statutes taking Cherokee lands, imposing Georgia law on the inhabitants, and prohibiting unlicensed residence by Worcester and Butler "interfere forcibly with the relations established between the United States and the Cherokee Nation." As such they were void and unconstitutional, and the two missionaries were entitled to have their convictions reversed.[84]

In his concurring opinion, Justice John McLean, appointed to the Supreme Court by President Jackson in 1829, agreed that the Court had jurisdiction of the case since the validity of treaties and acts of Congress was in issue. However, he pointed out that under the terms of the 1802 Georgia cession of the Yazoo lands to the United States, the federal government had agreed to extinguish Indian titles to lands within Georgia. In spite of repeated remonstrances, the United States government had failed to do this, and thus Georgia was justified in acting to protect her sovereignty against Cherokee claims of independence. Worcester, however, was acting in accordance with the statutes and treaties entered into by the United States, and hence he was improperly convicted under the Georgia statutes.[85]

In dissent Justice Henry Baldwin raised technical objections to the record before the Court. Concerning his view of the merits, he reaffirmed his position in *Cherokee Nation* and did not submit an opinion for publication.[86]

The *Worcester* opinion drew defiance from the Georgia legislature that met in November 1832, and President Jackson, writing to Samuel Worcester's employer, the American Board of Foreign Missions, expressed the opinion that Georgia had the power to extend its laws to all residing within its territory.[87] However, these were busy times, and public attention focused on other matters. The Second Bank of the United States was due for rechartering in 1832, a presidential election campaign was in progress, and South Carolina was on the road to the nullification crisis. On November

---

84. *Ibid.*, 542–560, quotations at 559, 561.
85. *Ibid.*, 583–595.
86. *Ibid.*, 597.
87. Warren, *Supreme Court*, vol. 1, 768–769.

24, 1832, the Nullification Ordinance was passed, and the president was forced to defend the Union despite abuse in the press that accused him of self-contradiction in his reactions to *Worcester* on one hand and South Carolina's defiance on the other. The net result was that as 1832 drew to a close, Andrew Jackson found himself allied with the nationalist views of the Supreme Court concerning the most pressing political issue of the day. Marshall and Story found themselves invited to the White House, and to Story's amazement, Old Hickory took pains to have a private drink with him.[88]

With the Union experiencing its most serious test to date, the *Worcester* case faded into relative insignificance. A year before, Congress had rejected still another effort to repeal Section 25 of the Judiciary Act, but the South's opposition to the Supreme Court and national supremacy continued unabated.[89] The press noted that as the Chief Justice read the Court's opinion in *Worcester*, his voice was feeble. Well it might have been, for his beloved Polly had died just four months earlier, and Marshall was still recuperating from surgery the previous autumn. A time of transition was at hand, not only for Marshall but for his Court. In the January 1834 term, Justices Johnson and Duvall were frequent absentees because of illness, and the alignment of Justices Thompson, McLean, and Baldwin against Marshall and Story usually precluded a four-judge majority. This deadlock resulted in the postponement of the *Charles River Bridge Case* and *New York v. Miln*, among several others, until the term following Marshall's death.[90] Events conspired to silence political criticism of the Court, but the precarious state of the Union left the justices little room for complacency.

---

88. *Ibid.*, 774–777.
89. Beveridge, *Marshall,* vol. 4, 515–517.
90. Warren, *Supreme Court,* vol. 1, 756, 789. Writing to Henry Clay to decline a speaking engagement, Marshall mentioned the weakness of his voice. Letter of February 10, 1832, Marshall Papers #3536, RG 128, National Archives. See also Beveridge, *Marshall,* vol. 4, 583.

FIAT JUSTITIA

Chief Justice John Marshall. Oil by Rembrandt Peale, 1825. Collection of the Supreme Court of the United States.

    This portrait of Marshall in his sixtieth year depicts him just after the decision in *Gibbons v. Ogden* (1824) and prior to his landmark dissent in *Ogden v. Saunders* (1827). It was presented to Chief Justice Salmon P. Chase by the Association of the Bar of the City of New York and bequeathed to the Supreme Court at Chase's death.

Justice William Johnson. Reproduced from the Collections of the Library of Congress, Neg. LC–USZ–6–915.

As President Jefferson's first Supreme Court appointee in 1804, Judge Johnson brought a new political viewpoint to the Supreme Court bench but disappointed Jefferson because he failed to dissent more frequently.

Justice John McLean. Reproduced from the Collections of the Library of Congress, Neg. LC–USZ62–9416.

After ten years' service as postmaster general, Judge McLean was appointed to the Court by President Jackson in 1829. Because his family was already settled in Washington, he did not join the other members of the Court in their boardinghouse. This weakened the collegial atmosphere that earlier may have enhanced Marshall's persuasive abilities among his associate justices.

Justice Joseph Story. Reproduced from the Collections of the Library of Congress, Neg. LC–USZ62–10382.

Judge Story was the closest associate of Chief Justice Marshall and also the leading intellect of the Court. In the latter part of Marshall's chief justiceship, Story took up additional duties as the first Dane Professor of Law at Harvard and published a number of treatises on the law.

Associate Justice Henry Baldwin. Oil by Thomas Sully, ca. 1830. Collection of the Supreme Court of the United States.

Appointed by President Andrew Jackson in 1830, Baldwin soon became a frequent dissenter on the Supreme Court. Plagued with periods of mental illness, he nevertheless made substantial contributions to the work of the Court. Despite jurisprudential differences with Marshall, the two became close friends, and Baldwin attended the Chief Justice during the course of his last illness at Philadelphia in 1835.

Henry Wheaton, Court reporter. Portrait by Robert Hinckley, Collection of the
Supreme Court of the United States.

　　After Wheaton ceased to be the Supreme Court's reporter he sued his successor, Richard Peters, asserting a copyright in the Court opinions that he published. Ultimately the Supreme Court held that there could be no copyright
in its opinions.

The Old Supreme Court Chamber in the Capitol Building. Photograph in the Collection of the Architect of the Capitol.

This representation of the courtroom shows the chamber as it was refurbished and redecorated in 1819, with some additions made subsequent to the Marshall period. The Court occupied this room continuously until its current building became available in 1937.

Chief Justice John Marshall. Oil by Henry Inman, 1831. Collection of the Philadelphia Bar Association, on loan and on display in the Diplomatic Reception Room of the Department of State, Washington, D.C.

Painted in the fall of 1831 while Marshall was awaiting bladder stone surgery in Philadelphia, this portrait depicts him at about the time of his seventy-sixth birthday and four months before the death of his wife.

III

MARSHALL AT THE MATRIX OF COURT LEADERSHIP

Vigilant protection of the Supreme Court from political attacks upon its jurisdiction or personnel was an important test, though not the primary test, of John Marshall's leadership. Professor Robert Steamer, in a comparative study of all the chief justices except William Rehnquist, points out that the main function of a chief justice is to lead the Court in deciding cases. Therefore the conference of the Court, at which the judges discuss their views of the cases before them, is the "matrix of leadership of the Court." It is there that the chief justice must use his personal and intellectual talents to minimize conflict, insure social cohesion, and move the Court's work to completion. He points out that while we do not know the precise way Marshall dealt with his colleagues, we can appreciate that those personal characteristics discussed in chapter 1 were major factors in his success. Interestingly, there are a number of traits that Marshall seems to have shared with Charles Evans Hughes and Earl Warren, the two other chief justices Steamer considers to be the most successful leaders, along with Marshall. They include possession of a commanding physical appearance and a natural dignity; robust health and capacity for hard work; a strong sense of self-discipline; a serious demeanor, but refusal to take themselves seriously; an exemplary sense of patriotism and concern for national welfare; and a conservative outlook coupled with willingness to stretch judging to accommodate their convictions.[1] Steamer views this leadership ability as innate. Marshall, Hughes, and Warren, in his view, "were supremely fitted to the office, not because they reflected the prevailing views of their time, but because they pursued their inner voices, their instincts, that aggregate of the innate and the attitudes acquired over the years from family, teachers, associates and books."[2] Of the three, Chief Justice Marshall is the most

---

1. Robert J. Steamer, *Chief Justice: Leadership and the Supreme Court* (Columbia: University of South Carolina Press, 1986), 24, 27, 37.
2. *Ibid.*, 89.

remote, both in time and in available evidence. For the most part, we must find information in details to be gleaned from the record of the Court's business. This is a task that must be, to a considerable degree, conjectural.

Traditionally the justices and other officials of the Court have been quite circumspect concerning the manner in which decisions are made, and relatively little is known about personal interrelationships. Public archival materials contain a bare minimum of information, and collections of personal papers are few and meager in detail concerning the Marshall Court's activities. Statistical materials on the Court, supplemented by corroborating documentary evidence, yield better insight into the business of the Court than might be expected.[3]

THE FOUR PHASES OF THE MARSHALL COURT

For purposes of analysis, it is helpful to divide the history of the Marshall Court into four phases. While this periodization is based in part on the frequency of John Marshall's delivery of opinions of the Court, other factors support the selection of these time segments. These are both internal to the Court in terms of its personnel and caseload and external to it in terms of the general history of the United States and the interplay between the states, the two other branches of the federal government, and the Supreme Court. The periods that emerge are as follows:

(1) The period when Marshall exercised considerable control over the Court and its decision-making process (1801–12);
(2) the period when internal conflicts over the law of war erupted, generating dissents and concurring opinions (1813–18);
(3) the "golden years" of the Court, when there were monumental constitutional decisions emphasizing federal powers, during which the Chief Justice seems to have regained substantial control over opinion delivery (1819–22); and
(4) the years of Marshall's declining authority over Court business, marked by the compromise of some golden years decisions and by Marshall's only dissent in a constitutional law case (1823–35).

---

3. A modern summary treatment is provided by *The Supreme Court at Work*, Elder Witt, ed. (Washington: Congressional Quarterly, 1990), 65–81. However, there is need to exercise caution in reading current practice and procedure "backward" into the Marshall era. Felix Frankfurter and James M. Landis, *The Business of the Supreme Court: A Study in the Federal Judicial System* (New York: Macmillan, 1928) remains a valuable source. This chapter also draws upon the microfilmed minutes of the Supreme Court, the docket entries, and the published opinions of the Court. Beginning in 1968 these materials have been assembled in machine-readable form to provide an index for research purposes and a database for some limited quantification.

Other schedules of periodization have been suggested by Donald G. Morgan, R. Kent Newmyer, and Albert Broderick, each proceeding from a slightly different perspective of the Marshall Court. Professor Morgan's analysis may rely too heavily upon the political affiliation of the justices. Professor Newmyer agrees with the fourth period, marking it as a time when Marshall began a strategic retreat from his earlier decisions. He suggests that this was when the Chief Justice was engaged in protecting the Court from its enemies. Because Newmyer pays more attention to the jurisprudential positions of the justices, he avoids giving undue emphasis to the *Gibbons v. Ogden* decision in 1824 or the advent of Jacksonian appointees in 1829. Professor Broderick divides the Court's history into three segments, the first being a struggle for survival (1801–18); the second, the time of expounding major doctrines (1819–23); and the third being years of "brake and decline" (1829–35).[4]

The predominance of Chief Justice John Marshall in delivering the Supreme Court's constitutional law decisions is responsible for the scholarly myth that he dominated his colleagues throughout the course of his chief justiceship. As table 1 and figure 1 indicate,[5] Marshall's predominance in opinion delivery was relatively short-lived, existing from his appointment in 1801 to the end of the 1810 term.[6] From 1813 through 1818 Marshall's participation in opinion delivery declined to less than half of all opinions by the Court.[7] The 1812 term, during which the Chief Justice delivered 57.7 percent of the opinions of the Court, was the term in which Judge

---

4. Donald G. Morgan, "Marshall, the Marshall Court, and the Constitution," in W. Melville Jones, ed., *Chief Justice John Marshall: A Reappraisal* (Ithaca: Cornell University Press, 1956; reprint, New York: Da Capo, 1970), 171, 172, 174, 177, 180–181; R. Kent Newmyer, *Supreme Court Justice Joseph Story: Statesman of the Old Republic* (Chapel Hill: University of North Carolina Press, 1985), 204–205; Albert Broderick, "From Constitutional Politics to Constitutional Law: The Supreme Court's First Fifty Years," 65 *North Carolina Law Review* 945, at 947–948 (1987).

5. The table and figure are derived from a 1969 study of 965 opinions of the Marshall Court, Herbert A. Johnson, "A Statistical Analysis of Marshall Court Opinions," a paper delivered at the 25th annual meeting of the Southern Historical Association, Washington, D.C., October 30, 1969, 43, 54–55.

6. During this period Marshall delivered all of the majority opinions of the Court in 1805 and 1806 and over 90 percent of the opinions of the Court in 1803 through 1808. In the aggregate, from 1801 through the end of the 1810 term the Chief Justice delivered 124 out of 141 opinions of the Court, for a rate of 87.9 percent. Not included in these figures are any per curiam or seriatim opinions. See figure 1. Robert G. Seddig indicates that Marshall began sharing opinion-writing tasks after 1812 but that the Court remained an ideological monolith in regard to national power until 1823. "John Marshall and the Origins of Supreme Court Leadership," 36 *University of Pittsburgh Law Review* 785–828, at 813, 822.

7. Of 211 opinions of the Court in this period Marshall delivered 82, for a rate of 38.9 percent. Again per curiam and seriatim opinions are not included.

TABLE 1

Number of Opinions Annually of the Court by Justices, 1801–1835

	Marshall	Cushing	Paterson	Chase	Washington	Johnson	Livingston	Todd	Duvall	Story	Total Opinions
1801	4										4
1803	10		1								11
1804	8	1									9
1805	16										16
1806	15										15
1807	9					1					10
1808	15	1		1		1					18
1809	28	2			1		1				32
1810	19				2	2	3				26
1812	15				4	3	1	1	1	1	26
1813	14				4	4	5		1	7	35
1814	14				6	6	4	1	2	10	43
1815	17				3	3	5			8	36
1816	12				3	6	1	3		9	34
1817	11				6	7			1	8	33
1818	14				3	4	4	2	1	2	30
1819	11				2	3			1	5	22

TABLE 1 (con't)

Opinions of the Court by Justices, 1801–1835

	Marshall	Washington	Johnson	Livingston	Todd	Duvall	Story	Thompson	Trimble	McLean	Baldwin	Wayne	Total Opinions
1820	11	2	3	3	1		3						23
1821	12	1	7	6	1		5						31
1822	13	1	2	1	1		4						22
1823	5	1	5	1		1	8						21
1824	13	5	3		1	1	8	3					34
1825	9	2	5				6	2					24
1826	10	3	3			1	6	4					27
1827	12	2	6				9	4	8				41
1828	21	1	6			2	7	5	7				49
1829	17	6	5			1	11	2					42
1830	15		6				8	5		6	6		46
1831	13		5				7	4		7	4		40
1832	14						13	9		8	1		45
1833	11		2				7	6		6			32
1834	23						13	6		10			52
1835	12						10	5		7	1	1	36
Total													965

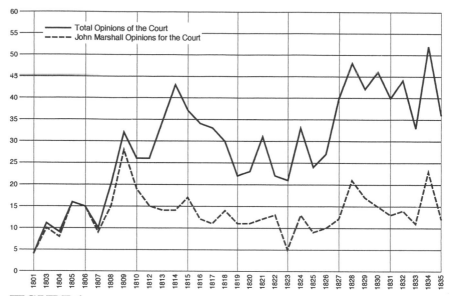

FIGURE 1

Story joined the Court. Marshall delivered 48 percent of the opinions of the Court in the four-year period 1819–22; these have traditionally been considered the "golden years" of the Marshall Court. It is important to recall that no justices joined the Court after the seating of Story and Duvall in 1812 until Smith Thompson began a new wave of appointees in 1823. In the 1823 term the Chief Justice's opinion-delivery rate dropped to an all-time low of 23.8 percent and fluctuated no higher than 44.2 percent until the end of his career. From 1823 to 1835 Chief Justice Marshall delivered 175 out of 489 opinions of the Court for a yearly average of only 35.8 percent.

Unquestionably Marshall's control over decisions announced as majority opinions, also termed opinions of the Court, declined markedly after his first decade on the bench. Judge Story's arrival in 1812 accelerated the decline already begun in 1810, but the six yearly terms that followed indicated remarkable lack of unity among the Supreme Court justices. These were wartime years and the immediate postwar period when prize case appeals dominated the docket. Differing interpretations of the law of war, particularly those that divided Marshall and Story, caused a significant rise in dissenting and concurring opinions, as shown by figure 2.[8]

---

8. Like the preceding table and figure, figure 2 is derived from the 1969 study. Johnson, "Statistical Analysis," 48. In his study of dissent, Percival Jackson does not identify the

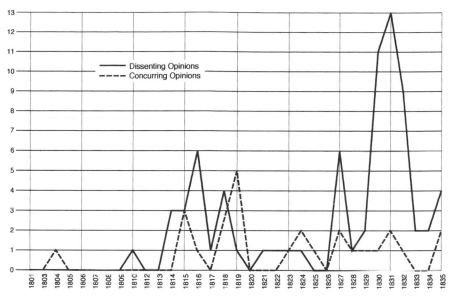

FIGURE 2

Toward the end of the 1813–18 period a case occurred that would set the tone for the remainder of Marshall's term as chief justice. This was *Martin v. Hunter's Lessee,* with the majority opinion by Judge Story because Marshall was financially interested in the litigation and did not take part in its decision.[9] *Martin* dealt with the entangled legalities of the Fairfax lands controversy in Virginia. More specifically, it represented the Supreme Court's insistence that the Virginia Court of Appeals comply with the British treaties negotiated in 1783 and 1794. Signaling renewed clashes between the Court and the rising spirit of state sovereignty, *Martin* anticipated a new and more focused nationalism on the part of the justices. As we have seen in the previous chapter, *Martin* also shifted the grounds of engagement between the Court and state sovereignty. Dating from 1793, the original jurisdiction of the Supreme Court had been most productive of conflict. After the 1816 *Martin* decision the Supreme Court's appellate review of federal questions in the state courts became central to its operations and the focal point of federal-state judicial confrontation.

Martin has also raised some interesting speculation concerning Judge

---

prize cases as a particular area of disagreement. *Dissent in the Supreme Court: A Chronology* (Norman: University of Oklahoma Press, 1969), 20–40. His emphasis upon Judge Johnson as a dissenter tends to obscure the stronger dissenting voices of Judges Thompson and Baldwin in the later years of Marshall's chief justiceship.

9. 1 Wheaton 304–379 (1816).

Story's influence upon opinion writing. Professor David Currie suggests that in its length and its attention to detail, *Martin* represents something of a watershed in the Marshall Court's craftsmanship. However, as Currie indicates, this new format for opinions had been anticipated in Marshall's contract clause opinions of the years after 1810. Neither Story nor Marshall used the form consistently, as Currie demonstrates with numerous examples of overly brief and unsupported conclusory statements. On Marshall's part, undoubtedly his most encyclopedic opinion is that delivered in *Gibbons v. Ogden* (1824).[10] This would suggest that although the Chief Justice may have adopted a more vigorous approach to judicial reasoning in his opinions, it was the presence of Judge Story (and to a lesser degree the influence of Judges Johnson, Livingston, and Thompson) that may have influenced this change in style and presentation.

The golden years, beginning with the momentous decisions of the 1819 term, *M'Culloch v. Maryland* and *Dartmouth College v. Woodward*,[11] marked the most creative period of the Marshall Court's history. *M'Culloch* sustained the constitutionality of the Second Bank of the United States and liberally construed the "necessary and proper" clause to permit federal incorporation of banking institutions. *Dartmouth College* built upon foundations laid earlier in *Fletcher v. Peck* and expanded the scope of the contract clause to include corporate charters. The decision in both cases centered upon the Chief Justice's opinion for the Court, supplemented in *Dartmouth College* by concurring opinions of Judges Washington and Story and a one-word dissent by Judge Duvall.

In 1821 Marshall's majority opinion in *Cohens v. Virginia*[12] elaborated upon the Supreme Court's right to hear appeals from state court decisions when the Federal Constitution, treaties, or Congressional statutes were brought into question. *Cohens* also disposed of uncertainty interjected into appellate process by the Eleventh Amendment. Some of Marshall's contemporaries believed that the amendment prohibited appeals when the state was a party. In sustaining the Supreme Court's appellate jurisdiction, *Cohens* was a major building block in the edifice of judicial review. The *Cohens* case was decided in the same term that witnessed the initial appear-

---

10. David P. Currie, *The Constitution and the Supreme Court: The First Hundred Years, 1789–1888* (Chicago: University of Chicago Press, 1985), 95–96, 114. *Gibbons* is reported at 9 Wheaton 1–241; Marshall's opinion for the Court is thirty-six pages long. Comparing the work of Story and Marshall, Seddig comments that Story seems to have assumed a specialized type of intellectual leadership after he joined the Court in 1812. "John Marshall," 815.

11. 4 Wheaton 316–437 and 4 Wheaton 518–712. Also of widespread impact in its partial validation of state insolvency laws was *Sturges v. Crowninshield*, 4 Wheaton 122–204.

12. 6 Wheaton 264 (1821).

ance of *Gibbons v. Ogden* (1824) before the Supreme Court.[13] This controversy over New York's grant of the Hudson River steamboat monopoly provided Marshall with the occasion to deliver an encyclopedic exposition of the federal commerce power.

Beginning with the appointment of Judge Smith Thompson in 1823, the Court divided over issues of legislative power, property rights, and the allocation of sovereignty between the federal government and the states. These conflicting views emerged most clearly in *Ogden v. Saunders,* the 1827 case notable for containing John Marshall's only dissenting opinion in a constitutional case.[14] *Ogden* involved the validity of state insolvency laws. Although Congress had not yet enacted a uniform bankruptcy act, it was argued that state insolvency laws impaired obligations of contract and were unconstitutional. In his dissent Marshall took the position that a contract arises from the agreement of the parties and that it is entitled to be enforced in accordance with its terms, supplemented by the law in existence at the time of agreement.[15] The majority justices, writing seriatim opinions, were willing to grant state legislatures more power to alter contractual remedies retrospectively through insolvency law changes.

Ogden v. Saunders, in its limitation of the contract clause potentialities of *Fletcher v. Peck* and *Dartmouth College,* is typical of Marshall Court development from 1823 to 1835. With the single exception of *Gibbons v. Ogden,* most major constitutional decisions in the last twelve years of Marshall's chief justiceship limited the nationalism of early years. The commerce clause was limited in its application by *Brown v. Maryland* (1827) and *Willson v. Blackbird Creek Marsh Company* (1829).[16] Both of these decisions recognized residual state police powers to act concurrently in regard to some aspects of interstate commerce. In *Providence Bank v. Billings* (1830), Chief Justice Marshall held that state incorporation of a bank did not, in the absence of express provisions, exempt that bank from the payment of state taxes.[17] Finally, in *Barron v. Baltimore* Marshall delivered the Court's opinion that the federal Bill of Rights did not protect private property against state

---

13. The earlier Gibbons case held that refusal to dissolve an injunction is not a final order or decree and hence is not appealable to the U.S. Supreme Court. 6 Wheaton 448 (1821). Marshall's 1824 landmark opinion is at 9 Wheaton 1, 186–222; Judge Johnson's concurrence is at *ibid.,* 222–239.

14. 12 Wheaton 213.

15. Marshall's position here seems similar to that of Judge Story, as characterized by Professor Newmyer, in that Story considered contract the organizing principle of a free-will society and held that the rights of contract were based on a tripartite foundation of moral law, universal law, and the laws of society. Newmyer, *Story,* 151.

16. *Brown* is reported at 12 Wheaton 419; *Willson* is at 2 Peters 245.

17. 4 Peters 514 (1830).

appropriation.[18] Precedents that once sharply restricted state initiatives were thus limited in favor of more flexible resort to state power, laying a foundation for the rapid expansion of state authority that would occur under the Taney Court.

To the degree that Marshall's dissent in *Ogden v. Saunders* was based upon natural-law theories, it also anticipated the Supreme Court's action in the Cherokee cases, beginning in 1831. The state of Georgia, anxious to exercise control over the rich alluvial lands possessed by the civilized Cherokee tribe, gradually asserted criminal and civil jurisdiction over those territories. In 1831 the Cherokees' attempt to bring the issue before the Court as an original jurisdiction case was defeated by Marshall's ruling that the Cherokee tribe was a separate but dependent nation. Thus it could not be a foreign nation, and it was not a state. Consequently, original jurisdiction was not authorized by the Constitution. These procedural complications were eliminated in a criminal case heard at the next term of Court in which two missionaries were convicted of living among the Cherokee without first obtaining a Georgia license. For the Court, Marshall reversed the conviction, holding that Georgia had no right under the Federal Constitution to interfere with the residents in the disputed territory.[19] The Supreme Court's mandate was ignored, the matter was not pursued by Worcester's counsel, and ultimately it was settled privately through a negotiated pardon for Worcester.

Recognizing the hazards of countering President Jackson's policy for the relocation of Indian tribes in the West, Chief Justice Marshall in *Cherokee v. Georgia* availed himself of a jurisdictional technicality to avoid conflict with Congress and the president. When that obstacle was removed, he and the Court took the high ground of natural law, coupled with respect for treaty rights, to extend a modicum of protection to the Cherokees.[20] In terms of power politics, even if Jackson had wished to protect the Cherokee, it would have been virtually impossible to do so, given the size of the federal army and the determination of the government and people of Georgia. The Cherokees began their march on the Trail of Tears, and the attention of the nation switched to the nullification crisis brewing in South Carolina.[21]

---

18. 7 Peters 243 (1833).

19. *Cherokee Nation v. Georgia*, 5 Peters 1 (1831); *Worcester v. Georgia*, 6 Peters 515 (1832).

20. See the discussion in chapter 8, 248–255.

21. G. Edward White, *The Marshall Court and Cultural Change, 1815–35*, vols. 3 and 4, *History of the Supreme Court of the United States*, 10 vols. to date (New York: Macmillan Publishing Company, 1988), 736–739; on the nullification controversy see William W. Freehling, *Prelude to Civil War: The Nullification Controversy in South Carolina, 1816–1836* (New York: Harper & Row, 1966), especially 260–297 in regard to the constitutional maneuvering of President Jackson in defeating nullification without the use of Unionist-oriented militia from South Carolina.

Although the Marshall Court did not deal directly with the domestic institution of slavery, an 1825 case reviewing forfeitures under the acts prohibiting the slave trade provides further insight into the Court's use of natural-law principles. In *The Antelope,* a vessel hovering off the American coast laden with over 250 African slaves was seized and brought in for condemnation. The evidence indicated that the slaves were captured earlier from vessels of American, Spanish, and Portuguese nationality. Spain and Portugal had not outlawed the international slave trade, but the United States had done so by statute and constitutional mandate. Writing for the Court, Marshall held that slavery was contrary to natural law and the law of nations. However, no valid seizure could occur before the slave trade was illegal under the municipal law of the culprit's nation. Since Spain and Portugal had not condemned the international slave trade, those slaves who had originally been in the possession of Spanish or Portuguese subjects would be returned to slavery. Those originally held by Americans were to be set free and, in accordance with the statutory mandate, transported to Africa.[22]

By refusing to condemn the international slave trade on broad international law grounds, the Court weakened American executive efforts to eliminate this inhumane activity. At the same time, it deftly avoided involvement in heated sectional debate over the legality and morality of slavery. In effect it "localized" the question of the international slave trade by tying the law of nations to the municipal law of each individual nation. To this extent it anticipated later decisions of the Taney Court that would treat slavery as a domestic institution in each American state.[23] *The Antelope* decision also undermined the impact of natural-law thinking upon American constitutional law.[24]

This fourth phase of the Marshall's Court's history thus evidenced gradual adjustments of federal jurisprudence to the demands of resurgent states' rights political theory. Even before the election of Andrew Jackson, the Republican appointees had made substantial inroads into the nationalism of earlier Marshall Court opinions. The Chief Justice turned to natural-law positions in defending both property rights and the status and independence of the Cherokees. The first fell victim to contrary majority opinions in his Court; the latter succumbed to adverse political pressure.

---

22. *The Antelope,* 10 Wheaton 66, at 113–130 (1825).
23. William M. Wiecek argues that the Philadelphia Convention and all other political efforts were directed toward making slavery a local, state-determined institution. *The Sources of Antislavery Constitutionalism in America, 1760–1848* (Ithaca: Cornell University Press, 1977), 76–83, 94–97, 105, 124–125, 138–139, 160, 169. The leading case is *Dred Scott v. Sandford,* 19 Howard 393, at 405–406 (Taney) and 536–538 (McLean in dissent) (1857).
24. This issue is discussed at length at White, *Marshall Court,* 674–703.

This was a time for cautious refinement of prior case law, usually in the direction of greater state autonomy. Marshall's control of Court business decreased markedly, with a correlative increase in concurring and dissenting opinions. His absence from the bench because of ill health breathed new life into the seriatim opinion system, which had long lain dormant.

UNANIMITY AND DISSENT IN THE MARSHALL COURT

Having placed the business of the Court in chronological perspective, we may consider those factors that favored Chief Justice Marshall's apparent influence in the early decades of his chief justiceship as well as those events and forces that generated its decline. Professor Donald Roper, following the lead of Donald Morgan, suggested that it would be helpful to look at the philosophical differences that existed between the justices of the Marshall Court. When supported by searching intellectual biographies of each judge, these variations would become more apparent and facilitate explanations of the internal dynamics of decision in the Marshall Court. Unfortunately, while a few good biographical studies have appeared in the intervening quarter-century, much remains to be done before the Marshall Court's prosopography is complete. However, Roper's initial study presents a persuasive argument that considerable unanimity was present because of the similarity in the justices' socioeconomic and constitutional views. Each had a strong sense of nationalism and a concern for private property rights; each accepted traditional dogmas and principles dear to the legal profession. Although he rejects Roper's interpretation that Marshall dominated the Supreme Court, Professor Robert Seddig finds Marshall's use of persuasion and "internal democracy" to have been an effective use of small- group dynamics in Court leadership. To Marshall's achievements in constitutional law, Seddig would add his establishment of a precedent of effective Supreme Court leadership.[25]

The selection of Supreme Court justices from the legal profession was probably one of the major reasons for the Marshall Court's unity. Within the memory of Marshall's generation, local judges and independent juries had been strong defenders of colonial rights against overly diligent and oppressive officers of the Crown. This direct experience supplemented a long and treasured seventeenth-century tradition of common-law courts embattled as the first line of defense against the royal prerogative. Raised on the writings of Sir Edward Coke, the revolutionary generation of attor-

---

25. Donald M. Roper, "Judicial Unanimity and the Marshall Court—A Road to Reappraisal," 9 *American Journal of Legal History* 118, at 128–132 (1964); Seddig, "John Marshall," 793, 801.

neys bred conservatism and constitutionalism into their young charges who would sit on the United States Supreme Court. With few exceptions, lawyers of Marshall's generation considered property ownership to be the sure foundation of a well-governed society. They shared a mutual dream of a great nation that would prosper through internal trade and economic diversification and earn international respect through strict adherence to treaty obligations. They shared an appreciation for the value of separation of powers, although they differed over the priority to be accorded to legislative authority. In short, the very process of appointing Supreme Court justices from the ranks of practicing lawyers produced a commonality of views that generated unanimity on the Court.

Upon receiving senatorial confirmation, each new justice acquired political independence. With the exception of Judges McLean and Thompson, Marshall and his colleagues abandoned political ambition when they donned judicial robes, thereby isolating themselves from partisan and popular pressure. This relative freedom from direct political manipulation by their own or another party allowed individual judges to be free agents in shaping the law and the constitution. Some, like Judge Johnson, would try to remain on friendly terms with the president who secured their confirmation. Others, like Story, found it liberating to join with judges of opposite political origins and to expound a new legal system for a changing and rapidly developing nation.

Supplementing these unifying influences in the Marshall Court was the manner in which the Court conducted its business. Formal sessions of the Court were held in a cramped, dimly lit basement room of the Capitol situated below the Senate Chamber. But the work of reaching agreement on cases was accomplished in the congenial informality of the boardinghouse at which virtually all of the justices resided.[26] There they gathered for meals and for discussion of the events of the day and the cases pending before them. When Judge Story arrived on the Court in 1812, he found the conferences "a pleasant and animated exchange of legal acumen" leading to a quick decision in a matter of hours.[27] From time to time the boardinghouse selection changed, but the Court members moved from one hotel or boardinghouse to another until 1828.[28]

---

26. Newmyer, *Story*, 76; Robert J. Steamer, *Chief Justice: Leadership and the Supreme Court* (Columbia: University of South Carolina Press, 1986), 18, 19, 52–53; the influence of the boardinghouse arrangement is discussed in G. Edward White, "The Working Life of the Marshall Court, 1815–1835," 70 *Virginia Law Review* 1, at 32, 40 (1984), and in Seddig, "John Marshall," 829 (1975).

27. Newmyer, *Story*, 78.

28. Charles Warren, *The Story-Marshall Correspondence (1819–1831)*, Anglo-American Legal History Series, series 1, no. 7 (New York: New York University School of Law, 1942), 25, lists the boardinghouses utilized by the justices.

It was in this hospitable but austere social atmosphere that the charm and warmth of Chief Justice Marshall was particularly effective in influencing decision. Living together protected the individual judges from the isolation that would have overwhelmed them in Jeffersonian Washington, for they rarely participated in state dinners or parties during Jefferson's presidency. Their quarantine from Washington society was relieved somewhat in the next administration, Judge Thomas Todd having successfully courted a niece of Dolly Madison. Thereafter the judges had an active social life away from their boardinghouse, but their habit of residing together continued until 1830, presumably because it was such an efficient and pleasant way to expedite Court business.

In the February 1828 term Judge Story's wife accompanied him to Washington, and Marshall, resigning himself to the inevitable, wrote that he expected they could find accommodations for her at Mrs. Rapine's boarding house. Graciously he added that he hoped that Sarah Story would be tempted to join their table "to shed the humanizing influence of the sex over a circle which has sometimes felt the want of it."[29] However, he hoped that she would not "monopolize" Story. Apparently both Storys took the hint, and Sarah Story found the male camaraderie of Supreme Court justices a little tedious, given the long hours of open court argument followed by conferences. Wisely she did not repeat the extended Washington visit during succeeding Supreme Court terms.

In May 1831 Story proposed that he and Marshall stay together during the next Court term and that Judge Thompson join them if he attended the session without his wife. A year earlier the Chief Justice had written to Polly Marshall that Judges Johnson and McLean did not board with the rest of the Court. Johnson's isolation was probably for political reasons, but McLean, a resident in Washington when he was appointed to the bench, understandably elected to remain at home. From Marshall's point of view, the boardinghouse situation was getting out of hand by the summer of 1831, and he unburdened himself to Story: "If the Judges scatter ad libitum, the docket I fear will remain quite compact, losing very few of its causes; and the few it may lose, will probably be carried off by seriatim opinion. Old men however are timid, and I hope my fears may be unfounded." He continued to bewail "the revolutionary spirit which displayed itself in our circle" and the uncertainty as to whether Judge Henry Baldwin had made suitable arrangements for the February 1832 term. As late as November 1831 the matter was apparently still unsettled, having

---

29. Marshall to Story, December 30, 1827, Clemens Library, University of Michigan, Ann Arbor; Gerald T. Dunne, *Justice Joseph Story and the Rise of the Supreme Court* (New York: Simon and Schuster, 1970), 271.

been delayed by one of Judge Baldwin's attacks of mental instability, but Marshall was reassured by the likelihood that five of the justices would board together, even though the location remained uncertain.[30]

While some of Marshall's concern can be attributed to the fussiness of old age and perhaps irritability due to pain from his bladder stones (to be removed by surgery in November 1831), it is apparent that living arrangements were very important to him. They provided an easy way for him to maintain close personal contact with the associate justices and gave him and Story ample opportunity to express their views. The breakdown of the boardinghouse routine further undermined the Chief Justice's ability to influence the decisions of the Court. Marshall could do little about it, given Judge Johnson's petulance and Judge McLean's understandable determination to live at home. He could fret about it, however, and the events of the 1828 term, with Sarah Story waiting in the wings for the conferences to cease, convinced Story that the demands of Supreme Court duties did not mix well with marital responsibilities.

Outright dissent from majority opinions was rare in the Marshall Court before 1830, when Judge Henry Baldwin took his place on the bench.[31] The first outbreak of dissents and concurring opinions occurred in prize cases from the War of 1812, and many of those individual opinions came from the energetic newcomer Joseph Story. Prize and admiralty issues continued to occupy the Court and generate dissent into the 1820s, when newly independent South American republics fought for self-determination. After former President Jefferson chided Judge Johnson about not writing individual opinions, Johnson began to exert himself in that direction, writing nine concurring and eighteen dissenting opinions during his last nine years on the Court. Judge Smith Thompson, who joined the Court in 1823, was active in stating his personal views, as was Judge McLean, appointed in 1829. The net result was a large number of concurring and dissenting opinions in 1827, 1830, and 1831.[32] These were also the years in which Judges Johnson and Story clashed over the proper limits of admiralty jurisdiction and Story began his efforts to install a federal common law in American jurisprudence.[33]

---

30. Story to Marshall, May 29, 1831, Marshall Papers, Swem Library, College of William and Mary, printed in part at Warren, *Story-Marshall Correspondence,* 26; Marshall to Mary W. Marshall, January 31, 1830, McGregor Collection, Alderman Library, University of Virginia (quotation from this source); May 3, 1831, Story Papers, Massachusetts Historical Society, extracted in Warren, *Story-Marshall Correspondence,* 25–26.

31. Baldwin dissented twelve times in his first three terms on the Court. Donald M. Roper, *Mr. Justice Thompson and the Constitution* (New York: Garland Publishing Co., 1987), 106. Figure 2 provides a graphic analysis of dissenting and concurring opinions.

32. See table 2.

33. Dunne, *Story,* 263–265.

SENIORITY AND MAJORITY OPINIONS

At no time was the Supreme Court more under siege than during the eight years of Jefferson's presidency. This situation produced cohesiveness and endurance, but it also generated fear in those either too elderly or too sick to fight back. When Chief Justice Marshall took his place on the bench, only Judge Chase was willing (perhaps unwisely) to fight the repeal of the 1801 Judiciary Act by refusing to hold circuit courts. Judges Cushing and Paterson were old and in declining health. Chase and Paterson were targets for conviction on impeachment charges based on their partisan behavior in trying Sedition Act defendants. Seizing upon the Ellsworth Court's use of the *per curiam* opinion, Marshall introduced the "opinion of the Court" device in his first term and used it effectively to protect individual members from identification with unpopular decisions. We know too little about the "opinion of the Court" to do other than speculate concerning its origin, but it is possible to suggest something of its inception from the surrounding circumstances. The Court opinion's sudden establishment in 1801 ties it to Marshall's becoming chief justice, and the vulnerable position of his associate justices suggests that political circumstances encouraged their acceptance of this innovation. Some textual evidence, corroborated by statistical information concerning the first decade of the Marshall Court, suggests that seniority determined which judge would deliver an opinion of the Court. In the 1803 case of *Stuart v. Laird,* reporter William Cranch began with the prefatory notation "March 2d. The Chief Justice, having tried the cause in the court below, declined giving an opinion. Paterson, J. (Judge Cushing being absent on account of ill health) delivered the opinion of the court."[34] Chief Justice Marshall, by virtue of his commission, was senior to all of the associate justices. Next, by virtue of having the earliest appointment, were Judge Cushing (1789) and Judge Paterson (1793). Cranch's labored effort to explain the seniority of the judges present when the opinion was delivered suggests that seniority was the way in which opinion delivery chores were assigned. In a later session of the Supreme Court, Judge Cushing, the senior associate justice present in the absence of the Chief Justice, delivered a lengthy and erudite opinion on the law of treason and alienage. It is unlikely that Judge Cushing could have written such an opinion at any age, even before ill health and approaching senility sapped his intellectual powers.[35]

Seniority as a mode of determining who would deliver an opinion of the Court is supported by a study of the reports from 1801 through 1810. If

---

34. 1 Cranch 299, at 307; see figure 3. for the applicability of the seniority rule in the Marshall Court.

35. *M'Ilvaine v. Coxe's Lessee,* 4 Cranch 209 (1808).

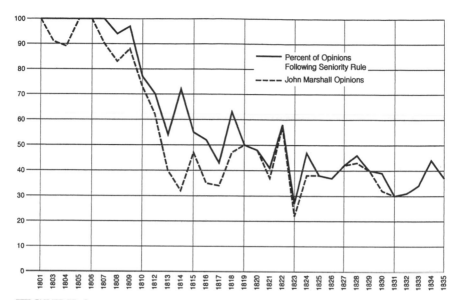

FIGURE 3

the justices are ranked by seniority, beginning with Marshall followed by
the senior associate justice, and those disqualified from participation are
eliminated along with those not physically present on the date the opinion
was announced, we can make some conclusions concerning the seniority
rule for a given case. Before 1810 seniority seems to have been the determining factor in who would deliver the opinion. Prior to 1807 every reported opinion of the Court conforms to the seniority rule. From 1807 to
1812, 70 percent of these opinions were delivered by the senior justice
present on the decision date.

The strongest proof of the seniority rule comes not from Chief Justice
Marshall's record but rather from those situations in which associate justices delivered opinions when Marshall was absent or disqualified. Aside
from the first decade, in which the Chief Justice delivered virtually all of
the Court's opinions, the 1814 term is most probative. Although Marshall
delivered only one-third of the majority opinions in that term, 70 percent
of all opinions for the Court conform to the seniority rule. We may conclude that the seniority principle applied even when only associate justices
were involved in opinion delivery. After 1819 the seniority principle seems
no longer to have applied to opinion delivery.[36]

Except for a scattered collection of manuscript opinions after 1830, no

---

36. Johnson, "A Statistical Analysis," 14–16, summarized in figure 3.

original appellate opinions survive in the archival records of the Marshall Court. The manuscript opinions after 1831 are "fair copies"; that is, they are written in the hand of the justice who delivered them, and there are no insertions or corrections. In this form the Court's decisions were delivered to the reporter, who in earlier days destroyed them but after 1831 preserved them for return to the Court's records. The original jurisdiction files for the Marshall period were badly burned when British troops burned the capitol in 1814.

Given the evidence, it is plausible that Chief Justice Marshall delivered an overwhelming number of opinions in the first decade of his chief justiceship not because he wrote, or entirely agreed with, those opinions but rather because it was his responsibility to announce them on decision day. The actual production of the opinions may have been a joint effort of all members of the Court, with the exception of those who chose to dissent from or concur with the Court majority. On the other hand, Professor White suggests that the speed with which the Court issued opinions after argument was completed indicates that opinions were not shared in advance with other members of the Court. That may well have been true in the first decade of Marshall's chief justiceship, but some consultation seems to have been the rule after 1820.[37]

CONFERENCE PROCEDURES AND OPINION DRAFTING

Among the correspondence of the justices there is some evidence that many of them prepared their separate opinions on a case before it was discussed by the entire Court. Marshall wrote Story, in regard to the 1820 opinion in *Houston v. Moore,* that since the case was assigned to Story, he had not intended to prepare an opinion. However, he wrote, "I shall just sketch my ideas for the purpose of examining them more closely, but shall not prepare a regular opinion."[38] One of Story's biographers suggests that Judge Story wished to reverse the state court's opinion upholding conviction by a militia court-martial, having concerns for federal prerogatives in the matter and also humanitarian objections to double jeopardy.[39] Interestingly, the Court opinion was delivered and presumably written by Judge Washington, who upheld the Pennsylvania Supreme Court's affirmance of the court-martial judgment. Judge Johnson and one other justice (uniden-

37. G. Edward White, "The Working Life of the Marshall Court 1815–1835," 70 *Virginia Law Review* 1, at 30–31 (1984); see discussion below concerning authorship and consultation.
38. July 13, 1819, Story Papers, Massachusetts Historical Society, referring to *Houston v. Moore,* reported at 5 Wheaton 1 (1820).
39. Dunne, *Story,* 199.

tified in the report but presumed to be Story) dissented, declaring the state law conferring jurisdiction on the court-martial repugnant to the Federal Constitution.[40] This correspondence and the ultimate alignment of justices in the *Houston* case suggest that each judge may have prepared either a full-length draft opinion or a summary of his thoughts before coming to the Court's conference.

Even with such careful preparation on the part of each individual justice, boardinghouse associations provided ample opportunity for two or more judges to confer informally before the conference meeting. In such discussions Chief Justice Marshall would have had a distinct advantage in bringing some of the justices over to his view of the case. When the conference convened, it was the Chief Justice who stated the case, an activity in which Judge Story claimed that Marshall excelled.[41]

Presumably the Court's review of the case involved some joint review and comparison of the various drafts. In the course of subsequent discussion, a justice might concede one or more points contained in his draft to be inaccurate or unwise or might insist that his view was correct. Perhaps the best example of this compromise is what purportedly occurred in *Sturges v. Crowninshield*. In that case Judges Livingston and Johnson acquiesced in the majority opinion in exchange for the reluctant agreement of Marshall, Washington, and Story to the proposition that prospective state insolvency laws were valid.[42] From this process an alignment of justices would evolve, and the opinion writing and delivery tasks would be assigned. When the Chief Justice formed a part of the majority, he or his designee would write the Court's opinion.

Participation in the conference meeting depended upon being present for argument, and attendance at the conference was a prerequisite for subsequent involvement in the writing or delivery of an opinion. In an 1831 letter Marshall advised an attorney that since he was not present at argument or at the conference concerning the case, he would not intervene in

40. 5 Wheaton 1 (18 U.S.), 1, at 32, 73.

41. Steamer, *Chief Justice*, 52.

42. Roper, *Thompson*, 99; Herbert A. Johnson, "Federal Union, Property, and the Contract Clause", in Thomas C. Shevory, ed., *John Marshall's Achievement: Law, Politics and Constitutional Interpretation* (Westport: Greenwood Press, 1989), 40–41. Roper states that Washington, Marshall, and Story tended to remain silent even when they disagreed with the Court decision, but Judge Thompson never hesitated to express his opposing views. Roper, *Thompson*, 94–95, 99. In a letter to William Gaston (December 11, 1818, Southern Historical Collection, University of North Carolina at Chapel Hill), Marshall wrote that the other justices disagreed with him concerning a purported interstate compact, but since Marshall's view would have perpetuated conflict, he was glad that the others prevailed. Judge Story acquiesced silently in cases denying that there was a federal common law of crime. Dunne, *Story*, 240.

the Court's subsequent action concerning the matter. Rather he referred the lawyer's request to Judge Johnson, who, as the senior associate justice, had presided over oral argument.[43]

After 1812, the rapidly increasing size of the docket forced the Court to limit oral argument to two attorneys for each litigant, and by the end of Marshall's chief justiceship a number of cases were submitted on briefs without oral argument. However, attendance at oral argument provided a justice with the opportunity to question counsel and to formulate a better understanding of the issues involved. Likewise, during the conference, the justices had an opportunity to compare their notes on the printed record of each case, and in the 1820s the Court issued detailed requirements that certain information be included in record.[44]

The submission of written briefs or summaries of points of law became more common and more formal during the Marshall Court period. At the outset a 1795 court rule required counsel to submit a statement of material points to be argued. By 1818 the Court followed the contemporary practice of the New York Court of Impeachment and Errors and required that a statement of the case be submitted before argument. Three years later the requirements were expanded to include the substance of material pleadings as well as a statement of the facts and copies of any pertinent documents. The 1821 rule also required the submission of all points of fact and points of law that would be relied upon in oral argument. Unfortunately, no party briefs survive in the Court's appellate case files.[45]

To the extent possible, each justice participating in the decision was given ample opportunity to become acquainted with the subject matter of the litigation prior to attending the conference of the Court. Even after the Court reached its decision and the opinion was read, there was time for consultation. The *Dartmouth College Case* opinion by Marshall was announced when the Court convened on February 3, 1819. Nearly three months later the Chief Justice wrote Judge Story to thank him for correcting an inaccurate statement Marshall had included concerning separation of powers.[46] Editorial work on a Court opinion continued until the volume of reports was printed, and care was taken to protect the final version from error.

---

43. Marshall to John H. Patton, March 2, 1831, Collection of Herbert A. Friedlich, Chicago, Illinois.

44. Johnson, "Statistical Analysis," 4–5, citing 1 Peters vii, 7 Peters ii, and Rules 28 and 30, 1 Peters viii; R. Kirkland Cozine, "The Emergence of Written Appellate Briefs in the Nineteenth-Century United States," 38 *American Journal of Legal History* 482, at 486.

45. Cozine, "Emergence of Written Briefs," 486, 488, 492, 514–517, 523.

46. Warren, *Supreme Court*, vol. 1, 483; April 28, 1819, Berg Collection, New York Public Library, New York, N.Y.

After 1823, perhaps as the result of a misunderstanding concerning the opinion in *Green v. Biddle,* the Supreme Court began to apply a four-judge rule, which required that all constitutional decisions be made by the affirmative vote of four judges of the Court regardless of the lesser number present at argument and decision date. In regard to *Green,* Senator Henry Clay of Kentucky, acting as attorney for one of the parties, believed that only four judges participated in the decision, and one had dissented. Actually Judge Johnson's opinion was a concurring opinion, and Judge Livingston, absent because of his last illness, reportedly favored the reasoning advanced by Judge Washington in the Court opinion.[47]

The controversial nature of the second *Green* decision awakened renewed criticism of the way the Supreme Court conducted its constitutional adjudications. *Fairfax v. Hunter,* the 1813 case concerning Virginia's forfeiture of the Fairfax proprietary lands, was decided by a Court opinion representing only three judges—Story, Livingston and Duvall. Marshall and Washington disqualified themselves, presumably because both had economic interests in the outcome of the decision. Judge Todd from Kentucky also did not sit in the proceedings on the case, and Judge Johnson filed a concurring opinion that differed markedly from Story's Court opinion. Enforcement of the *Fairfax* decree involved the Court in the controversial mandate in *Martin v. Hunter's Lessee.*[48]

Fairfax, Martin, and *Green* all involved appellate review of state court decisions, and by 1823 debates over the Union cast doubt upon the wisdom of committing such appellate power to the United States Supreme Court. However, in the wake of *Green,* Chief Justice Marshall adopted a four-judge rule for constitutional cases. Writing to Judge Todd in March 1823, Judge Story commented that both the Chief Justice and Judge Washington were sick but were recovering. With Judge Livingston critically ill with peripneumonia, he noted, "We have been a crippled Court. Nevertheless, we have had a great deal of business to do, and, as you will see by the Reports, tough business. We wanted your firm vote on many occasions."[49] A Story biographer suggested that although the four-judge rule was not formally announced until 1835, it had been applied in practice since 1824, when New York attorney Thomas Addis Emmett suggested it to Story. At a time when the Court was once again undergoing a personnel change and sharp differences of opinion had developed on constitutional issues, it was a wise step toward protecting the Court. It blunted the congressional effort to

---

47. White, *Marshall Court,* 643–645.
48. Dunne, *Story,* 116–148. Charles Warren incorrectly identified the Johnson concurring opinion as a dissent. *Supreme Court,* vol. 1, 466. See discussion at chapter 2, 71.
49. March 14, 1823, *Story Letters,* vol. 1, 422–423.

revoke the Supreme Court's appellate power in state cases involving the Federal Constitution, and it avoided embarrassment from uncertain precedents in constitutional law cases. Of course it also resulted in delayed constitutional litigation, which occurred in regard to *Ogden v. Saunders* and perhaps other controversial appeals on the docket.[50]

RULES, TERM TIMES, AND GROWING DOCKETS

For the Marshall Court, the Judiciary Act of 1789 and the Process Act of 1789, which supplemented it, formed the mainstay of procedure in both the Supreme Court and the circuit and district courts. Some early adjustments were made to facilitate circuit riding and conserve the time of the justices. For example, the Judiciary Act of 1793 provided that only one Supreme Court justice was required in a circuit court, although the Supreme Court in its discretion might assign two judges to one circuit court. The act of April 29, 1802, permitted the Court to allot circuit duties among the justices and also reduced the Washington en banc sittings of the Court to one term to commence on the first Monday in February. The 1802 act also provided a procedure for the certification of questions from a circuit court to the Supreme Court when the two judges on the circuit court were divided in opinion.[51]

This provision for certification of questions gives evidence of the growing power of district court judges in circuit court proceedings. When District Judge John Tyler resigned his commission in 1813 after being elected governor of Virginia, Chief Justice Marshall refused to sit in the Virginia circuit court until a new district judge (St. George Tucker) was appointed. As Marshall explained to attorney Littleton Waller Tazewell, the statutes permitted a Supreme Court justice to hold circuit court during the indisposition of a district judge but made no provision for the vacancy of the judgeship. If Timothy Pickering's later comment about Tyler is correct, the Chief Justice may have been gratified at the vacancy even if it halted the work of the court. In 1826 Pickering wrote Marshall that he understood Tyler was condemned on the floor of the U.S. House of Representatives as "the

---

50. Dunne, *Story,* 256, citing *Briscoe v. Commonwealth's Bank of Kentucky,* 9 Peters 85, at 85 (1835). Actually the *Briscoe* version is not clearly a four-judge rule but rather Marshall's statement that until there was a full Court (that is, until Duvall's successor was appointed), no constitutional cases would be heard.
51. Judiciary Act of September 24, 1789, 1 Stat. 73–93. Process Act of September 29, 1789, 1 Stat. 93–94. The two statutes are discussed at length in Julius Goebel, Jr., *Antecedents and Beginnings to 1801,* vol. 1, *History of the Supreme Court of the United States,* 10 vols to date (New York: Macmillan, 1971), 457–551. Judiciary Act of 1793, 1 Stat. 333 *et seq.;* Judiciary Act of 1802, 2 Stat. 156 *et seq.*

damndest fool that ever sat on a bench of justice." The New Englander continued that he had heard that Tyler was elected governor of Virginia only after twenty lawyers joined political forces to get him off the district court bench.[52]

Marshall's reference to statutory provisions governing circuit court business demonstrates that Congress and the Court shared the task of regulating procedure before the inferior federal courts as well as the Supreme Court. Terms of the circuit courts were fixed by statute, and as the volume of business grew in the larger and more populated districts, the state-aligned federal districts were divided. However, the Supreme Court justices continued to sit with the district judge in the original district and there heard appeals from the other circuit courts for that state. As dockets grew, it became necessary to establish longer terms for all of the federal courts. The Supreme Court's term was extended by three weeks in 1827, Congress having authorized the winter term to begin on the second Monday in January.[53]

In addition to responding to legislative alterations in its calendars, the Supreme Court made rules for the conduct of cases before it. At its initial 1789 term in New York City, the Court established the design of its own seal and that of the circuit courts. It announced admissions standards for attorneys and counselors and provided an oath of office for those admitted. In 1795 the Court insisted that counsel supply a statement of material points in the case to be argued and that motions to discharge prisoners on bail should be by deposition and not by oral submission of evidence. Control of records on file with the Court became a matter of concern in 1797 when the Court ordered that no record be removed from the clerk's office without the consent of the Court.[54]

By 1812 it became necessary to order that only two counsel be permitted to argue for plaintiffs and two for defendants, and the Court was adamant that only two appearances by counsel would be permitted, no matter how many issues or parties were present in a case. By 1821 the Court required that printed briefs or abstracts of the case be filed before oral argument, and in 1823 a complete record was required before an appeal could be argued.[55] Rule 40, approved in 1833, permitted counsel to submit cases upon printed briefs without oral argument.

---

52. Marshall to Tazewell, January 18, 1813, Marshall Papers, Swem Library, College of William and Mary; Pickering to Marshall, January 24, 1826, *ibid.*
53. Rule 40, 7 Peters i (1833). For the new convening date of the 1827 term see 3 Stat. 160 (1826).
54. See rules reported at 2 Dallas 399–400, 3 Dallas 120, and *ibid.*, 374; a composite list of rules appears in 1 Wheaton ix–xix (1816) and at 1 Peters v–xi (1828).
55. Rule 23, 1 Wheaton x, and colloquy of February 10, 1812, 7 Cranch 1; Rule 30, 6 Wheaton v (1821); Rule of Court, 8 Wheaton vi (1823).

After the Supreme Court petitioned President James Monroe for a law library in 1824, there was need for some control over the collection of books. Rule 39 authorized the clerk to lend not more than three books to counsel engaged in cases before the Court and imposed a dollar-a-day fine for late return. Understandably, the rule allowed unlimited borrowing privileges to the justices, to be regulated no doubt by their sense of communal responsibility to their colleagues.[56]

As late as 1810 the Supreme Court's room in the Capitol was still being furnished. Capitol architect Benjamin H. Latrobe wrote to Marshall informing him that it was necessary to go into debt to furnish the Supreme Court Chamber and requesting authorization to expend from the Contingent Fund for the Judiciary for that purpose. Latrobe's letter suggests that the Supreme Court Chamber was constructed to provide support for the Senate Chamber immediately above. However, Professor Haskins pointed out that at this time the Senate was also located on the ground floor. He claimed that Latrobe's drawings prove that from 1801 to 1808 the Court met in what had been designated Committee Room 2, with windows facing west.[57] Quarters were always cramped and inconvenient. From 1830 to 1833 the Court dealt with proposals that heavy draperies in the arches behind the judges' bench be eliminated so that light could enter the chamber. On the other hand, glare from the windows would have to be controlled by curtains in the windows. The Chief Justice agreed that these improvements would make the chamber more comfortable for the bar, but he reported that unfortunately they had not been authorized by Congress. A year later, Congress rather belatedly voted to commission a marble bust of Chief Justice Ellsworth to adorn the chamber.[58] It is likely that Marshall did not live to see this decoration to the Supreme Court Chamber, but he may have wondered whether some more practical use—such as curtains—might have been made of the $800 appropriated.

OPINION REPORTING AND *WHEATON V. PETERS*

The indefatigable William Cranch, chief judge of the District of Columbia circuit court, edited nine volumes of the Supreme Court's opinions before he relinquished those duties to Henry Wheaton of New York. It was

56. Supreme Court Justices to Monroe, February 4, 1824, RG 59, National Archives, Washington, D.C.; Rule 39, 7 Peters i (1833).

57. Latrobe to Marshall, June 5, 1810; Haskins and Johnson, *Foundations*, 79–82. Subsequently the Court moved to a somewhat larger room facing east, possibly after reconstruction of the capitol after its burning by British troops in the War of 1812.

58. Alexander J. Davis to Justices, ca. 1830, RG 267, National Archives, Washington, D.C.; May 4, 1833, Marshall to Richard Peters, Library of the U.S. Supreme Court, Washington, D.C.; the Ellsworth bust is authorized in the act of June 30, 1834, 3 Stat. 717.

Judge Cranch who began the practice of printing appendices to the reports that contained essays on legal subjects as well as obituaries and reprints of opinions delivered in the United States circuit courts.[59] The practice was continued by Wheaton, aided and assisted by Judge Story, and the appendices to the Supreme Court reports began to achieve remarkable length and variety. In his first volume Wheaton published essays on the claimant's law in Kentucky (upon which *Green v. Biddle* was based), the practice of prize courts, and the rule of the war of 1756 (dealing with neutral shipping rights). Wheaton's interest in prize law continued with publication of essays on prize causes and the standing instructions to private armed vessels, which appeared in his second Supreme Court volume. Prize law continued to dominate the appendix materials, but other essays dealt with patent law and charitable bequests.[60] Richard Peters, who succeeded Wheaton as reporter in 1828, used the appendix to his reports to print arguments of counsel and judicial opinions below that otherwise would not have been readily available.[61]

Marshall took care to see that the reported opinions were correct and free from error. He was determined that they provide a correct statement of the Supreme Court's reasoning to all federal courts and also serve as persuasive precedent for state tribunals.[62] When the final draft of an opinion was marked up with interlineations and changes, the Chief Justice was concerned that printers would be likely to commit errors of transcription. In those instances he referred other potential publishers to reporter Henry Wheaton for an authoritative copy. In regard to the *Cherokee Nation* opinion, Marshall urged reporter Richard Peters to print it in its entirety and was concerned that Judge Thompson's dissenting opinion be complete because it examined the subjects at greater length than his own. As space and the expense of two volumes per term became concerns, Marshall was quick to give Peters permission to expand his printed volumes as necessary to include arguments of counsel.[63]

---

59. See 1 Cranch 367–461 (on promissory notes); *ibid.*, 462–466 (on actions of debt on promissory notes); and 4 Cranch 3–12 (Richard Peters's essay on prize jurisdiction of federal district courts).

60. See 1 Wheaton 489; *ibid.*, 494; *ibid.*, 507; 2 Wheaton Ap. 1; *ibid.*, Ap. 80; 3 Wheaton Ap. 1; *ibid.*, Ap. 12; 4 Wheaton Ap. 3; *ibid.*, Ap. 23; 5 Wheaton Ap. 3; *ibid.*, Ap. 32; *ibid.*, Ap. 52, *ibid.*, Ap. 149; *ibid.*, Ap. 151; 6 Wheaton Ap. 3; *ibid.*, Ap. 59; 8 Wheaton Ap. 3; *ibid.*, Ap. 17.

61. See 2 Peters Ap. 681–686; 3 Peters 481, 7 Peters 553; 8 Peters 705; 9 Peters 765.

62. Marshall to Henry Wheaton, October 27, 1816, Wheaton Papers, Pierpont Morgan Library, New York, N.Y.; Marshall to Dudley Chase, February 7, 1817, RG 46, National Archives, Washington, D.C.

63. March 3, 1824, Marshall to Gales & Seaton, Collection of Henry N. Ess III, New York. N.Y.; May 19, 1831, Marshall to Richard Peters, Peters Papers, Historical Society of Pennsyl-

The transition from one reporter had been without incident when Henry Wheaton took over the duties of William Cranch. By way of contrast, Richard Peters's appointment to replace Henry Wheaton generated strife, acrimony, and much discomfort for the Court. In September 1826 Peters wrote to Marshall concerning rumors that Wheaton might be nominated to the district court for New York. In that event Peters asked that he be considered for the reporter's position. The judgeship did not materialize, but on July 1, 1827, Wheaton accepted a diplomatic post as ambassador to Denmark, and the path was clear for Peters to succeed him.[64]

The new reporter, son of the U.S. district judge of Pennsylvania by the same name, benefited from the sponsorship of Judge Bushrod Washington, who died a year after Peters was appointed. Washington had secured the acquiescence of Marshall and Story, but Judge Smith Thompson would not commit himself to Peters's candidacy. This discontent present at Peters's appointment was encouraged by reviews critical of the quality of his headnotes to the reports. Beset by periodic bouts of mental illness, Judge Henry Baldwin took offense at Peters's failure to publish his dissenting opinions, and an ongoing quarrel erupted between the two men, with the Chief Justice mustering his fading energies to arbitrate between them.[65]

To increase his income as reporter, Peters hit upon the scheme of issuing all prior reports in a "condensed edition" that would be cheaper than the reports still being marketed by Wheaton's representatives. In fact Peters's condensation was a reprinting of the entire text of the reports. Wheaton and his publisher sued, claiming violation of their copyright in the reports. In the United States circuit court for the Eastern District of Pennsylvania, District Judge Joseph Hopkinson held that Henry Wheaton had failed to comply with the filing and publication requirements of the copyright acts of 1790 and 1802. Replying to Wheaton's argument that the copyright existed as a matter of common law, Judge Hopkinson denied that copyright was ever a part of the common law of the American colonies, and he asserted that in any event, such a common law would be superseded by the acts of Congress.[66]

On appeal to the Supreme Court in 1834, Judge McLean remanded the

---

vania, Philadelphia; March 20–22, 1830, Richard Peters to Marshall, Marshall to Peters, 3 Peters vi, and the manuscript letter of March 22 at Rutgers University Library, New Brunswick, N.J.

64. September 30, 1826, Peters to Marshall, Cadwalader Collection, Historical Society of Pennsylvania; Marshall to Wheaton, June 21, 1827, Wheaton Papers, Pierpont Morgan Library.

65. The intricacies of the appointment and subsequent troubles are set forth in White, *Marshall Court*, 384–415.

66. 8 Peters 725–741 (E. Dist. Pa., 1832); 29 Fed. Cas. (No. 17,486) 862–872 (1832).

case to the circuit court for a jury to determine whether or not Wheaton had in fact omitted compliance with the statutory requirements. In addition, McLean observed that "the court are unanimously of opinion that no reporter has or can have any copyright in the written opinions delivered by this court; and that the judges thereof cannot confer on any reporter any such right." The majority opinion called into question the existence of a common-law copyright in England after the 1710 statute was passed and in any event found no evidence that, if there was such a rule in English law, it applied in Pennsylvania or any other American colony.[67] Judge Smith Thompson dissented, finding that the federal copyright statutes merely provided additional remedies to those available at common law. He argued that the language of the statutes left no doubt that a preexisting right was made more enforceable by their enactments. Thus even if Wheaton failed to meet the formal requirements of the statutes, his common-law rights persisted. Ironically, given Judge Baldwin's quarrels with reporter Richard Peters, the Justice's dissent is noted, but no opinion follows.[68]

CONCLUSION

The clash of personalities, both on and off the Court, that marked *Wheaton v. Peters* contrasts sharply with the seeming harmony and unanimity of the Marshall Court before 1812. In part this was due to frequent absences of Chief Justice Marshall because of illness, but the appointment of new justices led to the introduction of strong personalities that could be controlled only with difficulty. The alignment of Marshall, Story, and Washington persisted in the matter of the Peters appointment. However, Judge Thompson seems to have been outside of that block that supported Peters, and Judge Baldwin upon his appointment in 1830 quickly turned hostile to the reporter's interests. Significantly, *Wheaton v. Peters* was decided in the circuit court for the Eastern District of Pennsylvania when Judge Baldwin was ill, having been stalled by a disagreement between Baldwin and Hopkinson.[69]

Abandonment of the boardinghouse living arrangements for the justices, due in part to Republican pressure and in part to the newly appointed Jacksonian justices' having established residences in Washington, also undermined Supreme Court unanimity. An ever- extending docket, longer court sessions, and greater formality in relationships accentuated these developments. If the Supreme Court had ever been "Marshall's Court," it no longer deserved that appellation after 1827.

---

67. *Wheaton v. Peters,* 8 Peters 591–669 (1834), with quotation at *ibid.,* 668.
68. Thompson's dissent is at *ibid.,* 668–698; the notation of Baldwin's dissent is at *ibid.,* 698.
69. White, *Marshall Court,* 415.

IV

THE CIRCUIT COURTS
AND THE PROJECTION OF
FEDERAL POWER

Had there been no circuit-riding duties for members of the Supreme
Court, John Marshall might never have been offered the chief justiceship
of the United States. Former Chief Justice John Jay was President Adams's
first choice, but he declined appointment because of his reluctance to resume the grueling burden of riding the circuits. Ultimately the circuit-riding requirement not only discouraged many individuals from accepting a
Supreme Court appointment but also created what might be termed "circuit seats" on the Supreme Court. The political result was that senatorial
delegations from the circuit's states gained an enhanced veto power over
nominees for that seat.[1]

While Jay was chief justice, and under the leadership of his successor
Oliver Ellsworth, the Court spent much effort to obtain legislative relief
from this obligation.[2] When the lame duck Federalist Congress eliminated
circuit-riding duties in the Judiciary Act of 1801, the Supreme Court judges
enjoyed only a brief respite from riding the circuits. The newly elected
Republican majority promptly repealed the Federalist-sponsored 1801 legislation, canceling the provision for independently appointed circuit
judges. It was then left for the Marshall Court to accept the inevitable,
uphold the constitutionality of the 1802 repealing act, and set out once
more to ride their circuits. By its decision in *Stuart v. Laird* (1803) the
Supreme Court abandoned any constitutional scruples it may have enter-

---

1. Paul A. Freund, "Appointment of Justices: Some Historical Perspectives," 101 *Harvard
Law Review* 1146, at 1148 (1988). For a description of the circuit system see Julius Goebel,
Jr., *Antecedents and Beginnings to 1801*, vol. 1, *History of the Supreme Court of the United States*,
10 vols. to date (New York: Macmillan, 1971), 471–493, 554–589.
2. William R. Casto, *The Supreme Court in the Early Republic: The Chief Justiceships of John Jay
and Oliver Ellsworth* (Columbia: University of South Carolina Press, 1995), 55, 250.

tained concerning the justices' continuing to ride circuit.[3] Not until the passage of the Evarts Act in 1891 were the Supreme Court justices relieved of these trial duties.[4]

Circuit courts were the principal federal trial courts established by the Judiciary Act of 1789. Each of the states had at least one federal district with a United States district judge for that district. However, the district court functioned mainly in admiralty matters and had a limited jurisdiction in civil and criminal cases. Several districts were combined into a circuit, and the assigned Supreme Court justice presided over all circuit courts held for districts within his circuit. The district judge joined the Supreme Court circuit justice to hold the circuit court for his district. This remarkably flexible system of riding circuit was an integral part of each Supreme Court justice's duties, and it represented a vitally important institution for the administration of justice throughout the nation. Of course no system can be better than its component parts, and advanced age or ill health of a district judge or Supreme Court justice could result in substantial delays. That proved to be the case when Judge Cushing was unable to hold court for several terms prior to his death in 1810. As a consequence, Massachusetts federal court dockets were badly behind when Judge Story began his duties in 1812.

During Marshall's chief justiceship, circuit duties involved Court members in a number of controversial and highly political matters. It will be recalled that Judge Chase was impeached on charges that grew out of his conduct of circuit court trials before Marshall's appointment, particularly those criminal trials in which Jeffersonian Republican newspaper editors were convicted of sedition. It was in the circuit court for South Carolina that Judge William Johnson issued an opinion challenging presidential micromanagement of the 1807–9 embargo of transatlantic trade. Chief Justice Marshall presided over the colorful and bitterly contested treason trial of former vice president Aaron Burr. Judge Johnson's 1823 South Carolina circuit court decision courageously upholding international law and national supremacy against the state's punitive Negro Seamen's Act ultimately led to his ostracism and a self-imposed exile from his native state.

The circuit courts, as the general federal trial courts, were important in their own right, but as shown by figure 4, a substantial portion of the Marshall Court's appellate cases originated in the United States circuit courts. Among the federal circuit courts, the District of Columbia circuit was by

---

3. 1 Cranch 299.

4. Circuit Court of Appeals Act of 1891, March 3, 1891, 26 Stat. 826–830; see discussion at James W. Ely, Jr., *The Chief Justiceship of Melville W. Fuller, 1888–1910* (Columbia, University of South Carolina Press, 1995), 42–44.

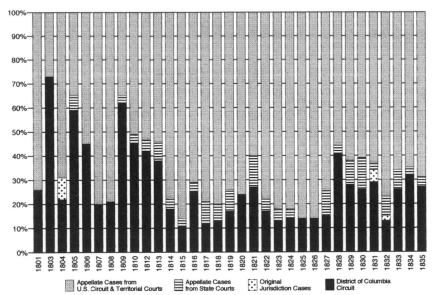

FIGURE 4: Sources of Supreme Court Cases, 1801–1835

far the most productive in cases appealed to the Supreme Court, but that circuit's proportion of the total appellate caseload declined during the Marshall era. The remaining circuit courts as a general rule supplied more than 50 percent of the Supreme Court's appellate caseload.[5] This large number of appeals within the federal system meant that fewer cases involved appellate review of State court decisions in regard to federal questions.

However, the volume and importance of appellate cases originating in the lower federal courts raises questions concerning the degree to which riding the circuit influenced the decision of appeals in the Supreme Court. Did the justices return to Washington intent upon upholding their own decisions in the court below? The data represented in figure 5 suggests that while there were a certain number of appeals decided by the Supreme Court judge who decided the matter below, this never exceeded 25 percent of the total opinions of the Supreme Court for that term.

THE CONTOURS OF CIRCUIT COURT BUSINESS

Although we do not have a consistent body of information concerning the work of the circuit courts in the Marshall era, there is more than enough material from which to draw some general conclusions on the busi-

---

5. See figure 4 for a graphic representation of the sources of appellate cases.

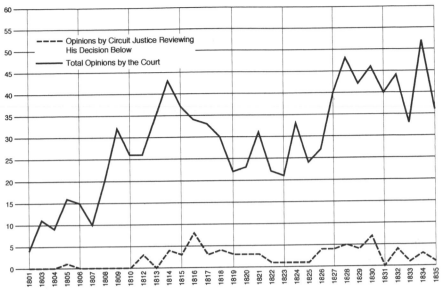

FIGURE 5

ness conducted in most circuit courts. Of the 3,636 cases reprinted in *Federal Cases* for the Marshall chief justiceship, 3,620 can be classified by date of decision, court of origin, judge delivering opinion, and points of law involved in the case. Given the presiding role of the Supreme Court circuit justice, it was usually he who delivered circuit court opinions, with the associated district judge occasionally filing dissenting or concurring opinions.[6]

Analysis of circuit court business is complicated by variances in the case-reporting practices in each circuit court. For some districts there are no reported cases for all or a part of the Marshall Court era. These districts include South Carolina, Tennessee, Kentucky, Ohio, Indiana, Illinois, Missouri, Alabama, Mississippi, and Louisiana. Of course the *Federal Cases* series contains individual cases from these jurisdictions extracted from a variety of original sources. In contrast, William Cranch was indefatigable in reporting cases from the District of Columbia circuit, and his reports constitute an exhaustive guide to the minutiae of practice and pleading in the nation's capital. Given this uneven coverage among various circuit courts, even in the same federal circuit, it is impossible to judge the quantity of

---

6. The district courts for the states of Kentucky, Tennessee, and Ohio were constituted independent districts by sections 16 and 17 of the Act of April 29, 1802, 2 Stat. 156, at 165. As such they functioned as circuit courts until the formal establishment of the seventh circuit on February 24, 1807. 2 Stat. 420–421.

litigation in each district or the volume of work that faced each Supreme Court justice on circuit.

It is possible, however, to classify the points of law decided in each reported circuit court case and to calculate what percentage of a justice's circuit time was devoted to such matters. For this purpose the various points of law have been grouped into twenty-four broad categories for purposes of comparison. Table 2 suggests that commercial law matters (bills and notes, debtor-creditor transactions, and insurance) were common to all of the circuits, as were admiralty cases (prize, maritime liens, salvage, and shipping). However, Chief Justice Marshall's circuit, which covered Virginia and North Carolina, was not rich in admiralty matters but shared with the Massachusetts circuit an emphasis upon business organizations (corporations, partnerships, banks, joint ventures, and the like).

A comparison of the amount of work each justice did in the circuit courts and the Supreme Court opinions delivered by that justice suggests the way circuit duties shaped Supreme Court business. Of the nine justices listed in table 3, six were most occupied with commercial law matters, mirroring a similar concentration of cases in the circuit courts over which they presided. Admiralty was the predominant form of business in the circuit courts for New York and Connecticut, served by Judges Livingston and Thompson. Admiralty law was the second most important category in Livingston's Supreme Court opinions but is not predominant in Thompson's Supreme Court opinions. The Massachusetts, Rhode Island, and New Hampshire circuits also provided a large number of admiralty and maritime cases. This field comprised a significant part of Judge Story's contributions to Supreme Court opinions.[7] From correspondence between the justices we know that Marshall sought advice in admiralty matters from Judges Story and Washington, reflecting the dearth of admiralty cases in Virginia and North Carolina.

Table 2 indicates that taxation matters (customs duties, internal revenue, and taxation) terminated at the circuit court level and formed a more considerable part of lower court business than they occupied in the Supreme Court. At the same time, the legal topics dealing with court procedure and jurisdiction (certiorari, mandamus, quo warranto, venue, and so on) occur with greater frequency in Supreme Court work than in the circuit courts. This would suggest that, to the extent that it was possible, in making rules for their circuits, Supreme Court justices preferred to seek guidance from the Supreme Court en banc. This could be done by the simple expedient of dividing on the question. That is, the district judge

---

7. For graphic presentations of the type of cases in each judge's circuit and his decisions in the Supreme Court, see appendix B.

TABLE 2

Number of Legal Categories in Opinions by Justices, 1801–1835

	Marshall	Cushing	Paterson	Chase	Washington	Johnson	Livingston	Todd	Duvall	Story	Thompson	Trimble	McLean	Baldwin	Wayne	Seriatim	Totals
Constitutional Law	44	1	2		8	8				16	6			3		4	92
Admiralty Law	45			2	8	21	6			62	3		1	1			149
International Law	11				1	3				4	3			1			23
Courts	129		1		9	16		3		38	11	6	14	6		2	235
Business Organization	44				3	8		1		34	4	1	7	1			103
Commercial Law	119				15	29	23			50	15	5	4	1		2	263
Real Property	33				1	3		5	3	29	5	3	10	11		1	104
Public Lands	97				1	11		7		13	5	6	16	12			168
Status of Persons	32	2			15	7	1		4	24	9	1	1		4		99
Contracts	37				14	9				11	15	1	13	3			103
Security Instruments	35				9	3	1			10	2	3		1			64
Patents	6				2					12			3				23

TABLE 3

Law Points in Supreme Court and Circuit Courts (by Percentages of Total Law Points in Those Courts)

Justice	Law Points	Supreme Court	Circuit Court
Marshall[a]	Commercial Law	13.5	7.0
	Courts	9.0	
	Appeals	6.0	
	Real Property	4.0	
	Criminal Law		6.0
	Civil Procedure		5.8
	Business Organizations		4.1
Washington[b]	Commercial Law	10.6	14.8
	Contracts	7.3	
	Appeals	5.7	
	Equity	5.3	
	Admiralty		7.3
	Real Property		5.8
	Civil Procedure		5.7
Johnson[c]	Commercial Law	16.9	
	Courts	6.0	Not
	Admiralty	5.6	Reported
	Business Organizations	5.6	
Livingston[d]	Commercial Law	25.6	6.5
	Admiralty	7.5	9.7
	Taxation	4.5	4.3
	Appeals	4.5	
	Courts		7.5

[a]On Marshall Court 1801–35; 1,962 Supreme Court points of law, 243 circuit court points of law.

[b]On Marshall Court 1801–29; 245 Supreme Court points of law, 909 circuit court points of law.

[c]On Marshall Court 1804–34; 414 Supreme Court points of law.

[d]On Marshall Court 1806–23; 133 Supreme Court points of law, 93 circuit court points of law.

Justice	Law Points	Supreme Court	Circuit Court
Story[e]	Commercial Law	8.9	8.6
	Admiralty	7.3	17.1
	Real Property	6.7	
	Courts	4.9	
	Taxation		5.1
	Business Organizations		3.8
Thompson[f]	Commercial Law	11.6	6.6
	Civil Procedure	7.8	
	Equity	7.2	
	Contracts	5.8	
	Admiralty		13.2
	Courts		9.5
	Taxation		4.4
Trimble[g]	Courts	10.2	
	Commercial Law	9.0	Not
	Equity	7.7	Reported
	Appeals	7.7	
	Government Officers	7.7	
McLean[h]	Real Property	12.7	
	Contracts	7.6	Not
	Commercial Law	7.6	Reported
	Courts	7.2	
Baldwin[i]	Real Property	21.0	4.3
	Courts	9.2	
	Contracts	5.3	
	Constitutional Law	3.9	4.3
	Commercial Law	3.9	
	Civil Procedure		10.6
	Criminal Law		6.4
	Equity		4.3

[e]On Marshall Court 1812–35; 976 Supreme Court points of law; 865 circuit court points of law.

[f]On Marshall Court 1823–35; 293 Supreme Court points of law, 136 circuit court points of law.

[g]On Marshall Court 1826–28; 78 Supreme Court points of law.

[h]On Marshall Court 1829–35; 251 Supreme Court points of law.

[i]On Marshall Court 1830–35; 76 Supreme Court points of law, 94 circuit court points of law.

would vote contrary to the vote of the Supreme Court justice. Such a contrived tie vote permitted the matter to be brought to the Supreme Court as a certified question.

Constitutional law issues occur in high percentages only for Judge Henry Baldwin, a relatively late appointee to the Marshall Court and a Jacksonian who felt impelled to deliver separate opinions in the Supreme Court. The striking aspect of this small amount of constitutional law work is that while constitutional law cases, and public law generally, have attracted the most attention of contemporaries and historians alike, the bulk of Marshall era circuit court caseload was in nonconstitutional litigation. Most specifically, the judges on circuit were developing a commercial law for the United States and secondarily administering admiralty and prize jurisdiction. An earlier study of the Marshall Court before 1815 identified both of these emphases in the work of the Court, and those trends persisted until Marshall's death.[8]

During Marshall's chief justiceship, the circuits were arranged into the configuration they would have throughout Marshall's chief justiceship. The Act of April 29, 1802, established six circuits. The First Circuit consisted of the states of New Hampshire, Massachusetts, and Rhode Island, joined by Maine upon its 1820 admission to the Union. Judge William Cushing presided in these circuit courts until his death in 1810, and he was succeeded by Judge Story, who presided until his death in 1845. The Second Circuit, containing the districts of Connecticut, New York, and Vermont, had William Paterson as its circuit justice until 1806. At his death Paterson was succeeded by Judge Brockholst Livingston, who served until 1823, followed by Judge Smith Thompson. The Third Circuit, consisting of New Jersey and Pennsylvania, had Judge Bushrod Washington as its circuit justice. Judge Henry Baldwin succeeded Washington in 1830. Judge Samuel Chase served in the Fourth Circuit (Maryland and Delaware) until his death in 1810, when he was followed in office by Judge Gabriel Duvall. Chief Justice Marshall was circuit court justice for the Fifth Circuit, consisting of Virginia and North Carolina. The Sixth Circuit (South Carolina and Georgia) was assigned to Judge Alfred Moore and then successively to Judge William Johnson (1804–34) and Judge James Moore Wayne (1835–63). In 1807 the Seventh Circuit was formed to consist of the districts of Ohio, Kentucky, and Tennessee. A new associate justice was authorized by

---

8. George L. Haskins and Herbert A. Johnson, *Foundations of Power: John Marshall, 1801–15*, vol. 2, *History of the Supreme Court of the United States*, 10 vols to date (New York: Macmillan Publishing Company, 1981), 407–492, 560–566; G. Edward White, *The Marshall Court and Cultural Change, 1815–35*, vols. 3 and 4, *History of the Supreme Court of the United States*, 10 vols. to date (New York: Macmillan Publishing Company, 1988), 810–829.

the same legislative act, and Thomas Todd was appointed. He served until 1826, after which he was succeeded briefly by Judge Robert Trimble (1826–28), who was followed by Judge John McLean (1829–61). Prior to 1807 the Ohio, Kentucky, and Tennessee district courts were authorized to exercise circuit court jurisdiction without the presence of a circuit justice. A similar arrangement was used for the districts of Indiana, Illinois, Missouri, Alabama, Mississippi, and Louisiana upon the admission of those states to the Union.[9] The assignment of circuit justice duties generally conformed to the residence of the Supreme Court justice selected. In the case of Judge Washington, not only was his residence at Mount Vernon fairly close to his circuit, but he had received his legal training in Philadelphia under the former associate justice James Wilson. The District of Columbia circuit court was erected in 1802 with a separate staff of judges and without the assignment of a circuit justice.[10] Circuit courts in the states met twice a year; those for the District of Columbia met four times a year, but the Supreme Court justices did not sit in the District of Columbia circuit.[11]

Professor White correctly observes that life on the circuits was strenuous, and a Supreme Court judge for a "comparatively paltry salary" had to leave family and home to travel for extended periods of time through largely undeveloped country. On the other hand, at a time when the Supreme Court had relatively little control over cases coming before it, the judges on circuit could channel some of the most important political and constitutional questions to the Supreme Court's docket. In regard to federal-question appeals from the highest courts of the states, the Supreme Court judge presiding in the circuit court was required to sign the writ of error to the Supreme Court. After 1802 the Supreme Court judge might agree with the district judge to differ concerning the case, thereby expediting consideration of the matter by way of certified questions.[12]

During Marshall's chief justiceship, the federal courts' diversity jurisdiction was limited by the Court's demand for "complete diversity" of citizenship. Diversity jurisdiction arises when a citizen of one state or a foreign nation is involved in litigation with a citizen of another American state. Originally federal courts could entertain such cases when the amount in controversy exceeded $500. However, when corporations were parties to the case, jurisdiction would be lost if one shareholder of the corporation

9. A list of circuit court alignments and circuit justices appears in *Federal Cases*, vol. 1, x–xvi; see also Section 4, Act of April 29, 1802, 2 Stat. 156, 157.

10. Sections 3–6, Act of February 27, 1802, 2 Stat. 103, 105–106

11. Section 4, Act of April 29, 1802, 2 Stat. 156, 157; Section 4, Act of February 27, 1802, 2 Stat. 103, 106.

12. G. Edward White, "The Working Life of the Marshall Court," 70 *Virginia Law Review* 1, at 9 (1984).

shared citizenship with the opposing party. The same restrictions applied to applications to transfer a case from the state courts to a federal court. As we shall see, in the case of the Bank of the United States, Congress enacted a statute giving federal courts jurisdiction in all cases brought or defended by the Bank. With this single exception, the complete diversity precedents served to isolate corporate enterprises from federal court adjudication.[13]

CIRCUIT APPEALS IN THE SUPREME COURT

How did Supreme Court justices react when one of their cases was appealed from the circuits? Excluding the District of Columbia circuit cases, there are a hundred appealed cases identifiable in both the Supreme Court and circuit court for which printed opinions in both courts are available. Chief Justice Marshall and Judges Johnson, Livingston, Story, Thompson, and McLean account for most of the opinions affirming or reversing circuit court opinions. Neither Marshall nor Johnson wrote a Supreme Court opinion concerning appeals from their circuit courts. Judge Washington, although rarely delivering opinions of the Court in the fields represented, delivered the Supreme Court's majority opinion affirming two of his own circuit court cases. Judge Thompson did the same in regard to one of his lower court cases. By way of contrast, Judge Story wrote affirming opinions for the Supreme Court in four cases he decided in his circuit court. Judge McLean wrote four Supreme Court opinions affirming his decisions and rather remarkably wrote a Supreme Court opinion *reversing* one of his own circuit court decisions. While the pattern is ambiguous, it would appear that it was unusual for the circuit justice to deliver an affirming or dissenting opinion in a matter on appeal from his decision below. However, forceful judges like Story and McLean did not hesitate to do so.

The assignment of opinion writing in these matters seems to have been done with attention to the sensibilities of the Supreme Court justice who decided the case below. Given the intellectual differences and personality conflicts that marked the relationship of Johnson and Story, it comes as little surprise that they rarely were permitted to review each other's circuit court opinions. Normally the judges who sat in admiralty-heavy circuit courts were called upon to write Supreme Court opinions on the admiralty appeals. Livingston was frequently called upon to perform this task when

---

13. *Strawbridge v. Curtiss*, 3 Cranch 267–268 (1806); *Bank of the United States v. Deveaux*, 5 Cranch 61–90 (1809); Edward Hartnett, "A New Trick from an Old and Abused Dog: Section 1441 (c) Lives and Now Permits the Remand of Federal Question Cases," 63 *Fordham Law Review* 1099, at 1108–1113 (1995). On the exception for the Bank of the United States see chapter 5, 157–159.

either a Johnson or Story case was before the Supreme Court. Despite this deft avoidance of personality conflict, some of the passion generated by these reviews can be sensed in the Supreme Court's reports. In 1832 Judge McLean was somewhat heavy-handed in reversing Judge Henry Baldwin's Pennsylvania circuit court decision in *Barclay v. Howell's Lessee:* "Upon a deliberate consideration of the points involved in the case, this court are clearly of the opinion that the judgment of the Circuit Court was erroneous."[14] Judge Baldwin remained silent under the rebuke but availed himself of a dissenting opinion in *Harrison v. Nixon* when his decision below was reversed by a Story opinion for the Court. Baldwin's extended attack upon the reversing order asserted that the Court had improperly overstepped its boundaries as an appellate court.[15] Affirming his own opinion in the Massachusetts circuit court, Judge Story made short shrift of appellate arguments: "The grounds upon which a decree of condemnation was pronounced in the Circuit Court fully appear in the opinion of that court which accompanies this record. That opinion has been submitted to my brethren, and a majority of them concur in the decree of condemnation, upon the reasons and principles therein stated. It is not thought necessary to repeat those reasons and principles in a more formal manner."[16] To make certain that the reasons were publicized, the Supreme Court reports contain the affirmed circuit court opinion.[17]

Before 1820 a major portion of the cases appealed from United States circuit courts concerned admiralty or marine insurance. Given the predominance of prize and illegal trade litigation generated by the advent and conduct of the War of 1812, it is not surprising that these were exceptional years. An additional but smaller increase in appeals from the circuit courts occurred in 1829 through 1835, when land cases became the predominant subject of appeal, supplemented with an number of equity cases and scattered cases in bankruptcy, insolvency, copyright, and patents.

Counsel before the circuit courts may well have been discouraged by the fact that among the cases taken on appeal, fifty-four were affirmed by the Supreme Court, but only twenty-three were reversed in whole or in part. Given the close relationships between the justices and their endeavor to maintain cordiality in the conduct of Supreme Court business, the predominance of affirmances is not surprising. On the other hand, the possibility of reversal made appeal worthwhile in matters involving substantial value

---

14. 6 Peters 498, at 512 (1832).

15. 9 Peters 483, at 505, 538 (1835).

16. *The Julia,* 8 Cranch 183, at 190 (1814); Story used the same words in *The Octavia,* 1 Wheaton 20, at 23 (1816).

17. *The Julia,* 8 Cranch, 190–203.

or major constitutional issues. Among the circuit justices, Joseph Story and Bushrod Washington accounted for the bulk of cases appealed. Of Story's twenty-two circuit court decisions, fourteen were affirmed and eight were reversed. Washington was affirmed in sixteen cases and reversed in seven. Both justices had circuits with heavy admiralty business as well as large and litigious populations.

THE BURR CONSPIRACY CASES

Unquestionably the most sensational trial held in the United States circuit courts in the Marshall era was that of former vice president Aaron Burr of New York. Shortly after he left office, Burr left Washington and made his way through the Ohio and Mississippi River Valleys, gaining support and adulation from the population. Among those he contacted was Brigadier James Wilkinson, commander of American armies in the West, who had long been a secret agent of the Spanish Crown. Burr also had a series of meetings with Tennessee's militia general, Andrew Jackson. He reached New Orleans on June 25, 1805. There he met with leading members of the Mexican Association, a filibustering group, and with prominent Catholic clergy who were united by common hopes of invading and liberating Mexico from Spanish rule.

After this, Burr returned to Washington, where he renewed contacts with British and Spanish diplomats and alarmed American naval and military officers with comments concerning war with Spain and the possibility of conquering Mexico. By August 1806 Burr was back in the West at Pittsburgh, launching flatboats into the Ohio River, accompanied by young men who spoke vaguely of settling a tract of western land. At this time General Wilkinson provided the President with copies of Burr's dispatches, and Jefferson in turn issued a proclamation for Burr's arrest (November 27, 1806).[18]

Two of Burr's companions, Erick Bollman and Samuel Swarthout, were arrested around the same time as Burr and sent under guard to Washington. There the United States Supreme Court issued a habeas corpus for their release, declaring its jurisdiction in the matter by a three (Marshall, Washington and Livingston) to two (Johnson and Chase) vote. On February 21, 1807, the Chief Justice issued the Court's opinion concerning the validity of the two men's arrest. He held that actual resistance to federal authority need not take place before treason occurs; rather an assemblage of men with the intention of opposing the government was sufficient.[19]

---

18. Beveridge, *Marshall,* vol. 3, 274–342.
19. The documentary record is at *The Papers of John Marshall,* Herbert A. Johnson, Charles

Examining the evidence, Marshall found it ambiguous concerning Burr's intentions and vague in alleging the nature of the supposed treasonable activity. He also noted that any trial of Bollman and Swarthout, if it did occur, should take place in New Orleans rather than in Washington, where no offense was alleged to have taken place.[20]

The Republican administration followed with interest the progress of the Bollman and Swarthout cases and attempted to revoke the Supreme Court's habeas corpus jurisdiction before the Court could take action. Jefferson's floor leader in the Senate, William Branch Giles of Virginia, introduced a bill for that purpose on January 23, 1807. It was promptly passed by the Senate, only to be rejected overwhelmingly by a 113–19 vote in the House.[21] Subsequently both houses were incensed at General Wilkinson's superseding civil authority in New Orleans, and Congressman John Randolph charged the administration with breaking the Constitution.[22]

Meanwhile Burr had been arrested in the Mississippi Territory but released by a grand jury that found no evidence of criminal or treasonable activity. As he headed east, he was overtaken by Wilkinson's soldiers and placed under military arrest. In accordance with President Jefferson's instructions he was taken to Richmond, Virginia, to await trial at the United States circuit court to be held there by John Marshall in April 1807.

From March 30 to April 1 the Chief Justice held commitment hearings, first at the Eagle Tavern and then in the House of Delegates chamber in the Virginia capitol, where the actual trial would take place. Burr was ordered jailed until a grand jury could be assembled. Initially he was incarcerated in the dark and dank Richmond City jail, but within a short time he was transferred to a suite of rooms in the newly constructed Virginia State penitentiary.[23]

The circuit court convened on May 22, and District Judge Cyrus Griffin joined the Chief Justice on the bench. While awaiting the arrival of Briga-

---

T. Cullen, William C. Stinchcombe, Charles F. Hobson, et al., editors, 8 vols. to date (Chapel Hill: University of North Carolina Press, 1974–date), vol. 6, 477–497; Haskins and Johnson, *Foundations,* 248–262; Albert J. Beveridge, *The Life of John Marshall,* 4 vols. (New York: Houghton Mifflin Company, 1916–19, vol. 3, 343–346, 350–351; *Ex Parte Bollman and Ex Parte Swartwout,* 4 Cranch 75–137, at 126 (1807).

20. Beveridge, *Marshall,* vol. 3, 354–357.

21. Haskins and Johnson, *Foundations,* 256. Beveridge comments that party discipline was lost as the House indignantly rejected the Senate's urgings to act promptly to revoke the right of recourse to habeas corpus. *Marshall,* vol. 3, 346–348.

22. Haskins and Johnson, *Foundations,* 217–219.

23. *Political Correspondence and Public Papers of Aaron Burr,* Mary-Jo Kline and Joanne Wood Ryan, eds., 2 vols. (Princeton: Princeton University Press, 1983), vol. 2, 1025–1029; Thomas P. Abernethy, *The Burr Conspiracy* (New York: Oxford University Press, 1954; reprint, Gloucester, Mass.: Peter Smith, 1968), 211–226, 229–236.

dier General James Wilkinson, the government's principal witness, Burr's attorneys moved before the Court for the issuance of a subpoena *duces tecum,* requesting production of one of the general's letters to President Jefferson. After two days of acrimonious argument by counsel, Marshall authorized the subpoena. He found precedent for taking this step before grand jury indictment, both in Virginia state practice and in the Sixth Amendment to the Federal Constitution. Brushing aside the prosecution's assertion that there was matter in the letter that ought not be disclosed, Marshall rejected the government's argument that issuance of a subpoena was disrespectful to the chief executive. The subpoena was issued, and in due course President Jefferson provided a copy of the letter.[24]

A number of other pretrial motions occupied Marshall's time while the circuit court and the nation awaited Wilkinson's arrival from New Orleans to give testimony before the grand jury. On June 15 the general strode into Court; according to newspaper reporter Washington Irving, he "stood for a moment swelling like to turkey cock" in a splendid full uniform. Since Wilkinson had long been a secret pensionary of the Spanish king, it is quite possible that his martial magnificence was itself a product of treachery. In the grand jury proceedings and the subsequent trial, he and the prosecution witnesses provided a tangled and confusing bundle of testimonial and documentary evidence that was followed avidly by the press and the public.[25] After Wilkinson narrowly escaped indictment for self-contradictory statements, the grand jury, on June 24, 1807, returned a true bill charging Aaron Burr with treason against the United States.[26]

The treason indictment was based upon the claim that Burr and his partisans intended to foment rebellion in the western states and territory of the United States. Had they succeeded, they allegedly planned to set up a separate national state with the assistance of Spain or Britain. The misdemeanor charges involved the assertion that the assemblage of men and equipment was preliminary to an invasion of Spanish possessions west and south of the Louisiana Purchase.[27] Because Blennerhassett's Island (in the Ohio River), where the gathering had taken place, was in Virginia's territory, President Jefferson and his advisors directed that Aaron Burr be taken to Richmond for trial at the United States circuit court for Virginia. However, for purposes of venue, it would prove significant that the former

---

24. *Marshall Papers,* vol. 7, 37–50; a photograph of the subpoena is reproduced on 38.
25. Abernethy, *Burr Conspiracy,* 238–240.
26. Beveridge, *Marshall,* vol. 3, 381; Haskins and Johnson, *Foundations,* 266–268, 272–276.
27. An invasion of the territory of a friendly power was punishable by a fine of three thousand dollars or imprisonment for not more than three years. Act of June 5, 1794, 1 Stat. 381, 384.

vice president was not present at Blennerhassett's Island at the time of the assembly.

The treason trial reached its climax in a motion by Burr's attorneys to prevent the admission of evidence of events both before and after December 10, 1806, that occurred elsewhere than on Blennerhassett's Island. In deciding this issue, Chief Justice Marshall set forth the restrictive definition of treason that would govern the determination of the case. Turning to the Constitution, he noted that treason was levying war against the United States. Although actual violence was not essential, it was not true under the *Bollman and Swarthout* rule that any assembly for a treasonable purpose was an act of war. In addition, since the conduct of war involved a variety of tasks, both logistical and combative, all those who perform these tasks fell within the definition of those who levy war.

However, some use of violence or force in advancement of the treasonable purpose was necessary to establish treason; there was a clear distinction between levying war and a conspiracy to levy war.[28] Traveling to an assembly point for the purpose of levying war might be a treasonable act, but it was also an equivocal act. To constitute treason, it would have to be unequivocal and have a warlike appearance. To be valid, an indictment must allege acts at a particular place, and the Constitution required that trial be held in the state and district where the act allegedly took place. It was inadequate to charge generally that the accused levied war against the United States without specifying particular overt acts that constituted levying war.[29]

The critical issue was whether Aaron Burr might be considered constructively present at the Blennerhassett Island assemblage point on December 10, 1806. If Burr was not present and did not intend to join the assembly, then distinct overt acts elsewhere had to be alleged and established by the evidence of two witnesses. Although not entirely rejecting the historical English concept of constructive presence, Marshall followed a very narrow view of what it meant to be present legally or constructively. The individual charged had to be closely connected to the warlike assembly and had to have performed some overt act either instigating the assembly or supporting it. That act also needed proof by the testimony of two witnesses. Any different doctrine would make a person levying war in one state constructively present in all other states where similar actions were taking place, even if he had absolutely no role in those other overt actions. If, as in the case of Burr, the charge was the procurement of a warlike assembly, both procurement and assembly are component parts of the overt act, and both

28. Opinion of August 31, 1807, *Marshall Papers*, vol. 7, 78, 80–81, 86–88.
29. *Ibid.*, vol. 7, 91, 96.

must be proved by two witnesses. Furthermore, procurement of an assembly without taking part in the assemblage, however remotely, is more in the nature of a conspiracy to commit treason rather than an overt act of treason.[30]

If Burr had been the instigator of the Blennerhassett Island gathering, he would have been an accessory to that treason, if treason it was. Since the guilt of the principal must be established before the accessory can be tried, Marshall reasoned that Burr's trial was premature. In addition, no overt act by Burr had been proved by two witnesses to have taken place at Blennerhassett Island or in support of the assembly there. What had been offered was merely corroborative evidence, not the constitutionally required testimony of two witnesses to the same overt act. After Marshall's statement of the law, the prosecution announced that no further evidence would be presented. On September 1 the jury returned a verdict that the defendant had not been proven guilty under the indictment, and the Court entered "not guilty" on the record as the verdict and judgment.[31]

After the treason trial, the remaining misdemeanor charges against Burr failed to form the basis of a conviction. The misdemeanor charges, based upon allegations of making war upon a friendly foreign power, were tried in Richmond before Chief Justice Marshall's circuit court. From September 3 to September 15 fifty witnesses were examined, and the jury returned a verdict of not guilty. The following day the circuit court began preliminary hearings concerning the treason and misdemeanor trials to be conducted either in Ohio or in Kentucky, and on October 20 Marshall dismissed charges of treason but ordered Burr, Harman Blennerhassett, and Major Israel Smith to be held on the misdemeanor charges for trial at Chillicothe, Ohio. Harman Blennerhassett synopsized Marshall's opinion dismissing the treason charges thus: "He cannot commit any of us for treason; not because we had none in our hearts, but because we did none with our hands." The Ohio case came on for trial in the first week of January 1808, but it was never prosecuted. The Burr affair finally drew to a close, leaving the former vice president to deal with his debts and his plan for exile in Europe.[32]

The Chief Justice's correspondence leaves no doubt that the conduct of these trials was both challenging and exhausting. Writing to U.S. District Judge Richard Peters a month after the acquittals, he described the prosecution as "the most unpleasant case which has ever been brought before a Judge in this or perhaps in any other country which affected to be gov-

30. *Ibid.*, 94, 97, 101–103, 107, 109–110.
31. *Ibid.*, 110–112, 114–116, and 118–119, n. 68.
32. Abernethy, *Burr Conspiracy,* 248–249, 259–260; quotation at 259.

erned by laws."[33] In addition to the difficult legal questions and the intense public interest in the prosecutions, Marshall undoubtedly was conscious of the danger he faced from the Jeffersonian administration. The novelist Gore Vidal has suggested, albeit without any firm evidence, that Jefferson hoped public opinion would be outraged at Burr's acquittal and that Marshall's impeachment might be facilitated by his participation in the Burr trials.[34] Realistically that threat could not have escaped Marshall's attention, and we have clear evidence that the Chief Justice took care to exercise caution in his conduct of the trial and in his rulings on the law.

Early in the treason trial Marshall wrote to Judge Cushing, and perhaps to the other justices as well, asking advice on whether or not there should be two witnesses to the same overt act before an indictment of treason could be returned. He also asked whether constructive treason formed a part of American law and whether the Supreme Court's earlier decision in *Bollman and Swarthout* might have gone too far in adopting that English doctrine. Finally, he wondered about the degree to which double jeopardy operated to prevent multiple prosecutions in Virginia and in other venues through which Burr and/or his colleagues traveled while allegedly committing treasonable or criminal acts.[35]

In spite of his precautions, Marshall inadvertently provided Thomas Jefferson with grist for an editorial partisan attack upon the Court, with special focus upon its chief justice. One of Burr's attorneys, John Wickham, was a close friend and next-door neighbor of the Marshalls. Periodically "lawyers' dinners" were held at Wickham's home, and the Chief Justice was regular in his attendance. Marshall arrived for such a dinner scheduled during the grand jury proceedings involving Burr and was shocked to find Burr, released on bail, as one of the guests. Reluctant to embarrass Wickham and wanting not to attract attention to the awkward situation, he decided to remain for the meal. Thereafter the dinner party was widely cited as evidence of Marshall's favoritism to the defense.[36] During the course of final arguments in the Burr treason case, Marshall was threatened with impeachment, and President Jefferson in his seventh annual message to Congress suggested that the Chief Justice deserved impeachment for his role in trying Aaron Burr.[37]

33. *Marshall Papers*, vol. 7, 165.
34. See Haskins and Johnson, *Foundations*, 264, n. 125. Vidal's speculations upon Jefferson's motives are obviously based on more than a novelist's "hunch"; his historical research was extensive, and his work benefitted from editorial review by knowledgeable students of Burr's career.
35. *Marshall Papers*, vol. 7, 60–62.
36. Beveridge, *Marshall*, vol. 3, 395.
37. *Ibid.*, 500, 530–531.

Leading as it did to a restrictive constitutional definition of treason, the Burr trial has attracted scholarly attention and disputation. Professor Edward S. Corwin considered the "one serious blemish in his [John Marshall's] judicial record" and concluded that the opinion defining treason was given far more weight in 1919 than it had been in Marshall's lifetime. Essentially Corwin viewed the trial as a continuum with the political and personal antagonism marking the relationship between the Chief Justice and President Jefferson. By way of contrast, Professor Faulkner insisted that the Burr case differed factually from the situation that gave rise to Marshall's dicta defining treason in *Ex Parte Bollman* and *Ex Parte Swarthout*. Thus the Chief Justice's seemingly conflicting opinions did not in fact exist. Faulkner relied upon the detailed studies by Willard Hurst and Bradley Chapin, not available to Corwin, to argue that English precedent should not control American definitions of treason. The Framing Fathers' intention, according to Faulkner, was that there should be a more limited scope for treason than existed in England, and Marshall was correct in applying a narrow constitutional definition. In addition, Faulkner defended the Chief Justice against Corwin's charge of partisanship in trying the Burr case.[38]

Despite the growing literature on the Burr trial, it still remains, as Professor Corwin termed it, an "unsolved enigma."[39] However, when it is set in the context of American legal and constitutional developments of the period, the resolution of the cases begins to lose much of the partisanship Corwin attributed to John Marshall. These were years when a federal common law of crime was undergoing strenuous attack; the doctrine would be declared contrary to the Constitution in 1812, necessitating that thereafter all federal offenses should be set forth in statutory form.[40] In demanding that the prosecution comply with the precise terms of the Constitution, Marshall was in accord with prevalent Jeffersonian attitudes toward federal

38. Edward S. Corwin, *John Marshall and the Constitution: A Chronicle of the Supreme Court* (New Haven: Yale University Press, 1919), 90–91, 95–96, 109, 111; Robert K. Faulkner, *The Jurisprudence of John Marshall* (Princeton: Princeton University Press, 1970), 269–285. The articles by Willard Hurst are "English Sources of the American Law of Treason," 1945 *Wisconsin Law Review* 315–356; "The Historic Background of the Treason Clause of the United States Constitution," 6 *Federal Bar Journal* 305–313 (1945); and "Treason in the United States," 58 *Harvard Law Review* 226–272, 395–444, 806–857 (1944–45). Bradley Chapin's work is *The American Law of Treason: Revolutionary and Early National Origins* (Seattle: University of Washington Press, 1964).

39. Corwin, *Marshall*, 86.

40. *United States v. Hudson & Goodwin*, 7 Cranch 32; see discussion at Haskins and Johnson, *Foundations*, 633–646, and also Kathryn Preyer, "Jurisdiction to Punish: Federal Authority, Federalism and the Common Law of Crimes in the Early Republic," 4 *Law and History Review* 223–265 (1986); Robert C. Palmer, "The Federal Common Law of Crime," *ibid.*, 267–323; and Stephen B. Presser, "The Supra-Constitution, the Courts, and the Federal Common Law of Crimes: Some Comments on Palmer and Preyer," *ibid.*, 325–335.

common-law crime. The Burr cases were instituted without regard for venue requirements in criminal cases, which the Constitution required to be tried by jury in the state and district where the offense was committed.[41] Although the Chief Justice dwelt upon the venue requirements in his opinion, they seem to have escaped scholarly attention even though they were vital to the treason case and the other matters heard at Richmond. Since Kentucky and Ohio, as well as Virginia, were locales where offenses were alleged to have occurred, all three jurisdictions were involved in a complex venue situation. Aaron Burr was in Kentucky when the December 10, 1806, rendezvous took place at Blennerhassett Island. Presumably he should have been tried in Kentucky, but how could that court have jurisdiction if the contention was that he was "legally present" at the island in Virginia? In other words, venue demands further limited the government's discretion by requiring it to allege and prove an overt act that took place within one state and federal court district. All of these limits upon prosecution discretion were designed to insure that treason indictments were not used for political purposes and to insure a rule of law and not of men.[42]

ELKISON V. DELIESSELINE, THE NEGRO SEAMAN'S ACT CASE

In the aftermath of the Denmark Vesey slave uprising (June–July 1822), the South Carolina legislature enacted a comprehensive law to restrict the access of free blacks to South Carolina slaves. Among the groups included in this legislation were black seamen on board ships that entered South Carolina ports. The statute required a black seaman be imprisoned and released to his ship's captain upon its departure. Should the captain fail to pay the expense of the seaman while he was in jail and to cooperate with the authorities, he might be fined and imprisoned. Any black seaman left in prison after his ship sailed was to be sold into slavery. Following protests by foreign consuls and intervention by President John Quincy Adams and Joel Poinsett, the South Carolina authorities delayed implementing the punitive provisions of the statute, but public pressure demanded its enforcement.[43]

---

41. Constitution, Article III, § 2, and Amendment VI.

42. Haskins and Johnson, *Foundations,* 260, 286.

43. The statute is summarized in *Elkison v. Deliesseline,* 8 Fed. Cas. (No. 4,366) 493; see also Donald G. Morgan, *Justice William Johnson, the First Dissenter: The Career and Constitutional Philosophy of a Jeffersonian Judge* (Columbia: University of South Carolina Press, 1954), 192–193. It has been argued that *Elkison* might have been resolved by a partial invalidation of Section 11 of the Judiciary Act of 1789, which limited the availability of federal habeas corpus in cases of imprisonment under state process. Rather than examine this possibility suggested by counsel, Judge Johnson utilized the commerce clause. W. Howard Mann, "The Marshall Court: Nationalization of Private Rights and Personal Liberty from the Authority of the Commerce Clause," 38 *Indiana Law Journal* 117, at 131–149 (1963).

The arrival of Henry Elkison, a black seaman who was a British subject, began the sequence of events that would lead to Judge William Johnson's declaring the South Carolina statute unconstitutional. The sheriff of Charleston removed Elkison from his ship and jailed him in accordance with the statute. Elkison's attorney petitioned the United States circuit court for a writ of habeas corpus or a writ *de homine replegiando* in an attempt to obtain Elkison's release. Prevented by restrictive provisions in the Judiciary Act of 1789 from issuing a habeas corpus writ, Johnson found adequate grounds to utilize *de homine replegiando,* which was available against private individuals who held another person in prison.[44]

In deciding the case, Judge Johnson was called upon to consider the South Carolina act in the light of the Federal Constitution's provision vesting the regulation of interstate and foreign commerce in the federal Congress. Counsel for the sheriff argued that in joining the Union, South Carolina had not surrendered a right of vital importance—in this case, the power to legislate in the interest of public safety. Despite this strong states' rights submission, Johnson went on to point out the broad scope of the statute. It might be construed to authorize the seizure of Nantucket Indians, also persons of color, who were the best sailors on Massachusetts ships, and they might all become slaves as a consequence. The British could not employ seamen of color on their vessels, and they had subjects of all colors throughout the world.

But ultimately the South Carolina law clashed with the federal government's right to regulate commerce among the states and with foreign nations. This was a "paramount and exclusive right," and the very words of the constitutional grant "sweep away the whole subject and leave nothing for the states to act upon."[45] Furthermore, the state statute was in conflict with the United States–British commercial convention of 1815, which in turn rested upon the supremacy clause of the Constitution. For a state to pass such a law was to embroil the nation in diplomatic difficulties, for the passage of such a law contrary to treaty-based agreements was tantamount to a declaration of war. Even more dangerous to contemplate was the possibility that the South Carolina provision should be applied to sailors from warships, either American or foreign. Would the crews of those vessels tamely submit to having one of their members impressed by state officials?

---

44. 8 Fed Cas. 493, at 496–498.

45. *Ibid.,* at 494–495; the quotations are at 495. It has been suggested that despite Johnson's broad assertion of federal power over foreign and interstate commerce in *Elkison,* he nevertheless conceded to the states a generous amount of power to regulate access to their harbors, based upon long-established common law and statutory usages. Albert S. Abel, "Commerce Regulation before Gibbons v. Ogden: Interstate Transportation Enterprise," 18 *Mississippi Law Review* 335, at 376–377 (1947).

Based upon these considerations, Johnson declared that the South Carolina Negro Seaman's Act was unconstitutional.[46]

Judge Johnson had rushed in where Marshall had feared to tread. As the Chief Justice wrote to Judge Story, "Our brother Johnson, I perceive, has hung himself on a democratic snag in a hedge composed entirely of thorny states rights in South Carolina, and will find some difficulty, I fear, in getting off into smooth open ground." Noting the existence of similar cases in Massachusetts and Virginia, Marshall confided to Story that in his Virginia case he had chosen to avoid the constitutionality issue since "I am not fond of butting against a wall in sport."[47] Unfortunately for Johnson, Marshall's prediction proved correct. Exclusivity of the commerce power was an unpopular position in 1823, and it would continue to be so despite Judge Johnson's concurring opinion in *Gibbons v. Ogden* the following year. Accompanied by the fear of slave insurrection that gripped Charleston in 1823, Johnson's opinion in *Elkison* placed him within range of withering attacks in the public press. He wrote defensive essays, some of them published anonymously, but thereafter his nationalist convictions alienated him from most of his South Carolina friends and neighbors.[48]

South Carolina's growing states' rights position was in marked contrast to the nationalism of William Johnson, the Palmetto State's resident Supreme Court justice. As a Unionist in the nullification controversy, Johnson became painfully aware of his unpopularity, and in 1833 he took up residence in Brooklyn, New York, to avoid the unpleasantness of living in nullifying Charleston.[49] There he spent the last summer before his death in 1834. His experience in the *Elkison* case paralleled that of Chief Justice Marshall following the Burr trials: Marshall was burned in effigy by a Baltimore mob after Burr's 1807 acquittals. It required courage and strongly held constitutional convictions for Supreme Court judges on circuit to face popular contempt, ridicule in the media, and mob violence that could threaten life and limb.

Riding the circuits placed Supreme Court justices in the front lines of the political struggles concerning the Union. They brought federal justice to all parts of the nation, but they carried back to Washington a well delineated understanding of the public's attitude toward the central government and federal justice. Such a chastening experience had an impact upon their approach to constitutional issues before the Supreme Court. Al-

---

46. 8 Fed. Cas. 493, at 495–496.

47. Marshall to Story, September 26, 1823, Story Papers, Massachusetts Historical Society.

48. Morgan, *Johnson*, 196–200; see also Oliver Schroeder, Jr., "The Life and Judicial Work of Justice William Johnson, Jr.," 95 *University of Pennsylvania Law Review* 344, at 364–366 (1946–47).

49. Morgan, *Johnson*, 277–278.

though the Court was not subject to the political process of election and rejection by the voters, it nevertheless bore scars from its opposition to the popular will. In good measure the Marshall Court's circumspection in politically charged situations may have been a product of circuit riding.

We may also suspect that the justices' circuit duties affected their Supreme Court decision making. If Joseph Story's nationalism found some basis in his circuit court experience with illegal trade before and during the War of 1812, so also might William Johnson's nationalism, emerging in *Gibbons,* have found its origins in his opposition to the extreme states' rights positions advocated by South Carolina in *Elkison* and similar cases.

THE SUPREME COURT JUSTICES ON CIRCUIT

Difficulties of travel and coordination of calendars made the circuit riding task irksome for many, but Chief Justice Marshall seems to have taken both in stride. On an 1803 ride into the North Carolina circuit, Marshall managed to lose $15 through a hole in his pocket, and this disaster was followed by the discovery that his formal breeches were left at home in Richmond. He wrapped himself in his judicial robe, covering the trousers he was compelled to wear, and had "the extreme mortification to pass the whole term without that important article of dress." Cases tried on circuit brought the Supreme Court justices down to earth—the earthy quality of the litigation insuring a modicum of sympathy with state trial court judges. In 1826 Marshall wrote Judge Story about a double bastardy case he tried in North Carolina. He was asked "to try the legitimacy of two children of a woman residing in North Carolina in the free indulgence of her natural appetites,—whose husband resided in Virginia with another woman whom he married between the two births."[50] Apparently in Marshall's circuit (the Fifth, which included Virginia and North Carolina), diversity jurisdiction had acquired a broad meaning.

Presiding in circuit courts, the Chief Justice developed an effective technique for bringing pending cases to trial. With a six-month interval between court sittings, Marshall's method was guaranteed to get results. As he wrote to District Judge St. George Tucker, "The lawyers had as usual been unprepared in every thing till I spoke of adjourning when they brought in so much business that my attention was wholly taken up with my official duty."[51]

---

50. The loss of clothing incident, reported to Marshall's wife, is recounted in full at *Marshall Papers,* vol. 6, 145–146; the quotation is from a letter to Story, May 31, 1826, Story Papers, Massachusetts Historical Society.

51. Marshall to Tucker, June 2, 1820, Tucker-Coleman Papers, Swem Library, College of William and Mary.

Perhaps at least part of Marshall's good humor can be attributed to his relatively light circuit court assignment. He presided over the Virginia circuit court while in residence at Richmond, and riding the North Carolina circuit carried him to Raleigh for about a week.[52] By way of contrast, Judge William Johnson, a Charleston resident, rode the Sixth Circuit, which included both South Carolina and Georgia and hence took him on long journeys across the virtually uninhabited sections of those two states. The newly admitted states—Kentucky, Tennessee, and Ohio—were constituted separate districts where the United States district courts were authorized to exercise circuit court jurisdiction. This meant that the Supreme Court justices were not required to attend those courts. As additional states entered the Union, the independent district arrangement kept the Supreme Court circuits manageable, but in 1807 Congress increased the Court's membership to seven. The new justice, Thomas Todd, was a resident of Kentucky, and he subsequently presided over circuit courts for that state as well as Ohio and Tennessee.[53]

CONSULTATIONS WHILE ON CIRCUIT

Although Marshall's surviving correspondence is fragmentary, it shows that he relied upon his associate justices for guidance and support in his circuit court work. This was particularly true in admiralty cases. He admitted to Judge Washington that "having much less of Admiralty business in my circuit than there is in any other circuit on the Atlantic I am always inclined when an admiralty question of some intricacy occurs to consult my brethren upon it."[54] He seems to have followed this procedure with great regularity, as his letters to Washington and Judge Story attest. In 1813 he sought advice concerning the disqualifying interest of a witness in a prize case as well as the need for a chain of custody regarding ships' papers. He readily accepted Washington's argument that piracy was an offense that fell within the civil jurisdiction of admiralty rather than prize court authority. Prize courts were international law tribunals that applied the law of war to determine the claims of privateers and other vessels of war to captured merchant ships and cargoes. Piracy, on the other hand, was an offense against the custom of the seas. It involved criminal sanctions for preying upon merchant vessels without a letter of marque issued by a warring nation. Thus piracy was part of the civil, or instance, jurisdiction of an admi-

---

52. *Marshall Papers*, vol. 6, 128–128,* 142–144.
53. See chronological table at 1 Federal Cases x–xvii.
54. Marshall to Washington, May 25, 1813, Marshall Papers, Swem Library, College of William and Mary.

ralty court. Marshall's difficulty apparently involved a variance in evidence rules between prize cases and instance litigation.

A three-way correspondence developed among Marshall and Judges Washington and Story in a case concerning hypothecation of a vessel for repairs. This admiralty doctrine permitted a ship and her fittings to be pledged as loan collateral to secure emergency repairs. Marshall's question was whether the doctrine applied only when the ship was away from her home port. Although the full correspondence does not survive, it would appear that Judge Story favored adoption of the European admiralty rule, which permitted the master to hypothecate whenever repairs were needed, even in the home port where the owner was located. By way of contrast, the English rule permitted such a financing arrangement only when the ship was repaired in a foreign port.[55]

A letter from the Chief Justice to Judge Washington concerning the latter's decision of *Golden v. Prince* (1814) in the circuit court for Pennsylvania throws some light on Marshall's attitude toward state bankruptcy laws.[56] Previously he had considered the bankruptcy power to remain in the states, at least until Congress enacted a uniform bankruptcy law as authorized by the Constitution. He viewed the constitutional phrase as being prospective; in other words, it did not invalidate existing state bankruptcy laws. On the other hand, a state bankruptcy law might attach to contracts made within the state without violating the obligation of contract clause. Such a contract would be made with knowledge that such a state law might act upon the contract, but the state bankruptcy law could not be given extraterritorial effect, and hence the rule would not apply to contractual obligations enforced outside the state where the contract was made. This letter shows that circuit court cases provided the Supreme Court justices with an opportunity to consider issues well before they reached the highest court. Thus this 1814 correspondence between Marshall and Washington was a precursor of the issues they would face in *Sturges v. Crowninshield* (1819).[57]

These informal consultations between the Supreme Court judges on circuit permitted them to accord their views on areas of the law in which the circuits might otherwise differ. When cases lacked a jurisdictional amount

---

55. *Ibid,;* Marshall to Washington, September 10, 1816, Marshall Papers, Swem Library, College of William and Mary; Marshall to Story, May 27, 1819, Story Papers, Massachusetts Historical Society. Other correspondence concerning piracy, salvage, and attachment of vessels can be found in Marshall to Washington, October 31, 1819, Marshall Papers, Library of Congress; Marshall to Story, December 9, 1823, and May 23, 1831, Story Papers, Massachusetts Historical Society.

56. 3 Wash. C.C. 313, 10 Fed. Cas. 542 (No. 5,509) (Pa. Cir Ct., 1814); the letter is dated April 19, 1814, and is in the Marshall Papers, Swem Library, College of William and Mary.

57. 4 Wheaton 122 (1819); see discussion at chapters 6, 181–184, and 7, 210–213.

or were otherwise ineligible for appeal to the Supreme Court,[58] such consultation became important to the impartial administration of justice in the federal system. Equally important was the opportunity these consultations afforded judges to increase their acquaintance with hitherto little-known fields of law. In this sense the circuit courts were training grounds for Supreme Court justices.

CONCLUSION

Riding their circuits, the justices of the Supreme Court came face to face with some of the pressing legal controversies of their day. Unlike other generations, they were personally present to administer federal law in the localities where offenses occurred and where civil controversies were tried. Politically charged cases like *Burr* and *Elkison* demanded that the justices involved exercise care and discretion; they also required of the judges a double measure of courage to face public opprobrium in their home states. Not only did circuit duty bring the judges into contact with the grass roots of American life, but it also gave insight into the difficulties facing trial judges throughout the federal system. Because of their work on the circuits, Supreme Court justices were constantly revising their understanding of local law and conditions.

---

58. Marshall to Story, July 13, 1819, Story Papers, Massachusetts Historical Society. In a criminal case, an application for a foreign jury was the subject of a division between Marshall and the Virginia federal district judge. Although the case was not subject to appeal, Marshall told Story he would bring the issue to the Supreme Court's attention at its next meeting. November 24, 1823, Story Papers, Massachusetts Historical Society.

V

FEDERAL SUPREMACY
AND JUDICIAL POWER

When John Marshall became Chief Justice of the United States, his predecessors in office had already made substantial contributions in the fields of international law and admiralty.[1] These areas of law had been matters of embarrassment under the Articles of Confederation,[2] and in addition the Constitution and the Judiciary Act of 1789 had singled them out as topics of preeminent concern to the newly constituted federal courts.[3] Of necessity these matters drew the earlier Supreme Court into consideration of treaties, and *Ware v. Hylton* (1796) represented a forceful stand by the Court against Virginia's efforts to frustrate solemn national commitments contained in the 1783 peace treaty.[4] However, *Ware* involved only commercial debts payable to British merchants, and it was left to the Marshall Court to resolve the more controversial issues of land confiscation and treason forfeiture imposed under state law during the course of the Revolution.[5] Chief Justice Marshall, as an attorney and as an investor, was directly involved in these matters. He had argued *Ware* on behalf of his clients, the

1. For a thorough coverage of the chief justiceships of John Jay and Oliver Ellsworth, see William R. Casto, *The Supreme Court in the Early Republic: the Chief Justiceships of John Jay and Oliver Ellsworth* (Columbia: University of South Carolina Press, 1995).

2. This was particularly true of the *De Longchamps* case (1784), in which a Pennsylvania court refused to convict a citizen of an assault and battery upon the person of the French consul in Philadelphia. For a discussion of these difficulties see Herbert A. Johnson, "Toward a Reappraisal of the 'Federal' Government, 1783–1789," 8 *American Journal of Legal History* 314–325 (1964). In addition, the Court of Appeals in Cases of Prize and Capture experienced difficulties in having its decrees enforced in the state courts of admiralty. See the background of *United States v. Peters,* 5 Cranch 115, at 115–135 (1809), involving Pennsylvania's refusal to enforce the mandate of the federal court.

3. These topics are designated the "first tier" of federal jurisdiction in a perceptive analysis by Akhil Reed Akmar, "Jurisdiction Stripping and the Judiciary Act of 1789," in *Origins of the Federal Judiciary: Essays on the Judiciary Act of 1789,* Maeva Marcus, ed. (New York: Oxford University Press, 1992), 40–65.

4. 3 Dallas 199–285.

5. See discussion at chapter 8, 228–233.

Virginia debtors, and he served as attorney for the Fairfax estate interests as they were litigated in both Virginia and federal courts. Since February 1793 he and other members of his family had composed a syndicate that purchased certain manor lands from Lord Fairfax's devisee. Marshall was well aware that several troublesome international law issues awaited him and the Court in the years beyond 1801.[6]

In the constitutional law area, by way of contrast, the Jay-Ellsworth Courts left a legacy of confusion and doubt concerning federal-state relations. Perhaps unwisely, the Jay Court had permitted itself to be drawn into adjudging an original jurisdiction case brought against the state of Georgia by a citizen of South Carolina. *Chisholm v. Georgia* (1793) revealed significant differences between the justices concerning the relationship of the states to the United States government, and the decision rendered for the plaintiff, Chisholm, sparked the enactment and ratification of the Eleventh Amendment.[7] Designed to eliminate the jurisdiction of the Supreme Court in similar cases, the amendment gave rise to conflicting interpretations concerning the sovereign immunity of state governments and their new-found insulation against federal judicial power. These ambiguities were partially resolved during the course of Marshall's chief justiceship, but the field is not without its uncertainties even today.

At least one domestic aspect of federalism was well established before Marshall's confirmation. This was the development of national familiarity with the operation of the federal district and circuit courts. The routine exercise of admiralty and prize jurisdiction, particularly during the Quasi-War with France, made the presence of federal judges a common and accepted incident of national power.[8] Indeed, the manifestation of federal authority through Supreme Court justices riding the circuits, however fatiguing it may have been to them, demonstrated the new government's determination to function at the grassroots level as well as at the seat of government.

SOVEREIGNTY, SUPREMACY AND SEPARATION OF POWERS

Twenty years after Cornwallis surrendered at Yorktown, the United States had not resolved to its own satisfaction the basic constitutional questions of sovereignty, supremacy, and separation of powers. Each state

6. For discussion of Marshall's professional and financial interests see *The Papers of John Marshall*, Herbert A. Johnson, Charles T. Cullen, William C. Stinchcombe, Charles F. Hobson, et al., editors, 8 vols. to date (Chapel Hill: University of North Carolina Press, 1974–date), vol. 2, 140–149, and vol. 3, 4–6; see also Albert J. Beveridge, *The Life of John Marshall*, 4 vols. (New York: Houghton Mifflin Company, 1916–19), vol. 2, 186–198, asserting that Marshall's advocacy brought him to public attention at the national level.

7. Dallas 419–479; see also Casto, *Supreme Court in the Early Republic*, chapter 7, 188–202.

8. See Casto, *Supreme Court in the Early Republic*, chapter 5, 130–141.

emerged from the Revolution with a strong sense of its own identity; throughout Marshall's lifetime he and his fellow Virginians called the state their "country." Localism had been accentuated by the colonial need to withstand the power of the British Privy Council and the impositions of Parliament. As a consequence, the new Federal Constitution was drawn to divide sovereignty between the states and federal government, but with federal power sharply circumscribed by enumeration of federal powers and the reservation of all other powers to the states or to the people. Among the most critical provisions of the Constitution was the supremacy clause in Article VI, making the Constitution, all statutes enacted by Congress pursuant to the Constitution, and all treaties of the United States the "law of the land." It subordinated state constitutions and statutes to that overarching supremacy. Yet the central government's primacy was only in what might be called federal matters, those powers granted the federal government by express constitutional enumeration, by necessary implication, or by virtue of the still ambiguous "necessary and proper" clause.

Supplementing the enumerated legislative powers was a rich mixture of English and American legal and political tradition concerning the nature of "executive power" and "judicial power," enhancing the potential authority of those two branches of government while at the same time providing ample opportunity for constitutional debate. American application and adaptation of Montesquieu's theory of separation of powers demanded that the functions and limitations of all three federal branches should be more clearly delineated than they had been within the Federal Constitution's text. By deciding cases touching upon these matters, the Marshall Court shaped constitutional government in antebellum America.

FOUNDATIONS OF POWER, 1801–19

The outstanding Marshall Court opinion defining federal-state relationships is *M'Culloch v. Maryland* (1819),[9] which clearly asserted federal supremacy over conflicting state legislation, adopted a loose construction of the "necessary and proper" clause, held the Bank of the United States constitutional, and approved its exemption from certain forms of state taxation. Why were two decades of Marshall Court jurisprudence a precondition for such a declaration of federalism and national supremacy? Possibly the vagaries of the Court's docket failed to present an appropriate case for decision at an earlier date. On the other hand, it is clear that several decisions from 1801 through the end of the 1818 term formed necessary building blocks in the *M'Culloch* foundation.

---

9. 4 Wheaton 316–437.

Marbury v. Madison affirmed the doctrine of judicial review at the Supreme Court level and formed a critical part of federal supremacy and the rule of law.[10] It began the procedural development by which the Court enhanced federal judicial authority and power through jurisdictional decisions. While the Marshall Court accepted limitations on its power in *Marbury* and other cases, it managed to enhance its authority in those situations where its jurisdiction was at least subject to doubt.[11] In regard to appellate review of state court decisions, Judge Story's landmark opinion in *Martin v. Hunter's Lessee* set forth both the constitutional basis and the practical need for Supreme Court review of state court decisions involving federal questions.[12] As the federal courts gained power, it became clear not only that matters constitutionally assigned to the federal government were preeminent over state concerns but also that it was the federal judiciary that would determine issues of supremacy as they arose.

Abandonment of the Federalist doctrine of federal common-law crime through the decision in *United States v. Hudson and Goodwin* in 1812 decreased conflict over this issue,[13] which involved both separation of powers concerns as well as federal-state allocations of power. The brevity of the opinion obscures its constitutional significance. In effect, it swept aside a number of lower federal court precedents and reversed a general acceptance of the prosecution of common-law crimes in federal courts. Before 1812 most federal statutory crimes dealt with offenses by federal officers or employees or with crimes committed on the high seas. Enforcement of the embargo after 1807 and suppression of illegal trade during the War of 1812 dominated the work of federal prosecutors.[14]

Hudson and Goodwin also subordinated common law to constitutional principle, imposing the rule that substantive criminal law in federal courts was to be statutory rather than a creation of judicial decision. Jeffersonians, taught to mistrust the concept of common-law crime by the Sedition Act prosecutions, rested secure in the assurance that political repression through federal criminal trials was a thing of the past.[15] At the same time,

10. 1 Cranch 137–180 (1803), considered earlier at chapter 2, 57–59.
11. For a detailed discussion of these matters see George L. Haskins and Herbert A. Johnson, *Foundations of Power: John Marshall, 1801–15*, vol. 2, *History of the Supreme Court of the United States*, 10 vols. to date (New York: Macmillan Publishing Company, 1981), 612–628.
12. 1 Wheaton 304–282 (1816). Earlier the Court had held that before Section 25 jurisdiction was asserted, the state court decision involved must deny the asserted federal right. *Gordon v. Caldcleugh*, 3 Cranch 268 (1806).
13. *United States v. Hudson & Goodwin*, 7 Cranch 32–34 (1812).
14. Dwight F. Henderson, *Congress, Courts, and Criminals: The Development of Federal Criminal Law, 1801–1829* (Westport: Greenwood Press, 1985).
15. 7 Cranch 32, at 34; Gary D. Rowe, "The Sound of Silence: United States v. Hudson & Goodwin, the Jeffersonian Ascendancy and the Abolition of the Federal Common Law of

Hudson and Goodwin insured that powers reserved to the states were no longer subject to erosion by judicial creation of federal common-law crimes.

Unfortunately, aversion to domestic nonstatutory crime spilled over into international law with *United States v. Coolidge* (1816). As circuit judge for the New England circuits, Joseph Story was acutely aware of the disaffection of New England during the embargo and the War of 1812, and his decision applied federal common-law crime in maritime matters. However, when the case came up to the Supreme Court, the justices chose to apply the rule in *Hudson and Goodwin* to maritime crimes, thereby creating the need for treaty or statutory provisions delineating and providing sanctions for criminal behavior on the high seas.[16] Ultimately this sequence of cases led to an increase in statutorily proscribed federal crimes and to confusion concerning the ability of the United States to prosecute maritime crimes, especially piracy, in the absence of statutory authorization.

Before deciding *M'Culloch*, Marshall's Court also dealt with the question of property rights that conflicted with international legal custom. *The Exchange v. M'Faddon* involved ownership of a vessel seized by the French for trading with Spain during the Peninsula War. After the *Exchange* was condemned as prize in a French admiralty court, she was refitted as a warship and commissioned in the French Navy. It was in this status that she entered the port of Philadelphia, where her former owner attempted to assert his claim. Chief Justice Marshall, writing for the Court, held that by international law a public vessel of a foreign sovereign was exempt from judicial action in the United States. M'Faddon's claim could therefore not be entertained by the federal courts. The case demonstrated the Court's respect for international law even in those cases in which the legitimate property claims of an American citizen might be denied.[17]

M'CULLOCH AND THE DEBATE OVER THE NATURE OF THE UNION

Marshall's exposition of the Court's opinion in *M'Culloch* drew heavily upon the briefs of counsel for the Bank of the United States. He adopted many of the principles advocated by Daniel Webster but avoided going to

---

Crimes," 101 *Yale Law Journal* 919, at 928, 931, 943–947; Leonard W. Levy, *Jefferson and Civil Liberties: The Darker Side* (Cambridge: Harvard University Press, 1963).

16. 1 Wheaton 415–417 (1816). Story's opinion in the Massachusetts federal circuit court is at 25 Fed. Cas. 619 (No. 14,857) (Cir. Ct. Mass., 1813); Professor Rowe suggests that Story's concurrence in *Hudson & Goodwin* was based upon his expectation of legislative action to create common-law crime jurisdiction in the federal courts. He also asserts that Story's decision below may well have been intended to bring up a reconsideration of *Hudson & Goodwin*. "Sound of Silence," 931.

17. 7 Cranch 116–145 (1812), discussed more fully at chapter 8, 226–227.

the extreme of denying the state's power to tax in all cases whatsoever. Many of the most famous quotations in Marshall's opinion originate in the argument of William Pinkney, who reportedly made the most extensive and most eloquent plea for the bank. During the three days devoted to oral argument of the case, the Court also heard a very creditable and conflicting view advanced by Joseph Hopkinson on behalf of Maryland.[18]

Hopkinson's presentation is revealing. It clearly shows the degree to which many political leaders wished to make federal sovereignty coequal with that of the states. Acknowledging the persuasive points made in Alexander Hamilton's 1791 opinion upholding the bank's constitutionality, Hopkinson argued that while a national bank might then have been a necessity, the national situation had changed markedly by 1819. An adequate number of state banks were available to handle federal revenue and fiscal requirements. Federal powers based upon necessity should not survive that need, and thus they fluctuate with the passage of time.

In addition, Hopkinson stressed the private nature of the bank and questioned its status as a public federal instrumentality. Should such a private entity be permitted to establish branches in the various states, generate profits for its private shareholders, and enjoy immunity from the laws and sovereignty of the states in which the branches were located?

Even if the bank were a federal instrumentality, he continued, the law was clear that a sovereign might not place his property in the territory of another sovereign without subjecting it to the revenue demands of the receiving sovereign. Indeed, the Constitution had provided expressly that certain federal activities might be conducted within state boundaries, but even in those cases, it required that the state's consent be obtained. This was particularly so in regard to state taxation, for no provision in the Constitution prohibited states from imposing taxation upon activities of the federal government. Hopkinson cited *The Federalist Papers* as representative of preratification promises that the new Constitution would not in any way undermine the taxing powers of the states except as they related to imports and exports. He concluded that whatever taxing authority the federal government might exercise over state banks might also be exercised by a state government over a federally chartered bank, since it was clear that the taxation power was concurrent in the states and the federal government.

Hopkinson's argument for Maryland was grounded on the proposition that since there was a concurrence of powers in regard to taxation, there also was a concurrence of sovereignty. Under this doctrine, every state in

---

18. The arguments synopsized in the following text are at 4 Wheaton 316, 330–353 (1819); for a good summary see Maurice G. Baxter, *Daniel Webster and the Supreme Court* (Amherst: University of Massachusetts Press, 1966), 170–181.

the Union possessed equality of sovereignty with the United States and might, except in matters exclusively federal, refuse the federal authorities the right to act within its boundaries.

What matters were exclusively federal? We must assume that they included the enumerated powers in Article I that were made exclusive by an express denial of those powers to the states. In addition, exclusively federal powers would include matters of international law, including the conduct of warfare and diplomacy. Coupled with a strict construction of the "necessary and proper" clause, such a concurrent approach to sovereignty would largely nullify the supremacy provisions of Article VI and leave the federal government at the mercy of the states in the conduct of most domestic affairs. The Jefferson administration's difficulties in enforcing the embargo by state action would alone seem sufficient to cast doubt upon this constitutional theory. That Hopkinson's proposition was seriously advanced in argument before the Court in 1819 evidences the persistence of state-sovereignty doctrines in the early American republic.

Supporting Hopkinson's presentation for Maryland, Walter Jones referred to the Federal Constitution as "a compact between the states" and noted that "all the powers which are not expressly relinquished by it are reserved to the states." Jones said further that "the exercise of the one sovereign power cannot be controlled by the exercise of the other" and admitted this to be an anomaly and perhaps an imperfection in the constitution of government; but since the system was created by a compact, he held, neither the Congress nor the U.S. Supreme Court could rectify it.[19]

Not surprisingly, it was this compact theory of the Federal Constitution that was emphatically rejected in the first portion of Chief Justice Marshall's opinion for the Court. He pointed out that while the process of ratification was accomplished through state conventions, it was the people of the United States acting in those conventions who adopted the new form of government. When so ratified, the Constitution "was of complete obligation, and bound the state sovereignties."[20] The Chief Justice drove home the point by adopting phraseology suggested in Daniel Webster's argument "that the government of the Union, though limited in its powers, is supreme within its sphere of action."[21] Webster had applied similar language to legislative powers of Congress, but Marshall broadened its scope to include all federal governmental powers. He also specifically incorporated in

19. 4 Wheaton 316, 363. In his last appearance as counsel before the Supreme Court, Luther Martin supported the dual sovereignty argument submitted by Hopkinson. William L. Reynolds III, "Luther Martin, Maryland and the Constitution," 47 *Maryland Law Review* 291, at 317–320 (1987).

20. 4 Wheaton 316, at 402–404, quotation at 404.

21. *Ibid.*, 405.

his opinion a doctrine of supremacy that was lacking in Webster's brief. These principles were submitted by William Wirt, the attorney general of the United States, and William Pinkney, arguing on behalf of the bank.[22]

Moving on to the specific question of the constitutionality of Congressional action establishing a corporation, Marshall injected a point apparently not argued by counsel—that the Constitution could not include all of the means that Congress might use to effectuate its powers, for doing so would make the Constitution as prolix as a legal code. Only its great outlines and important objects needed to be designated. Not only is the creation of a corporation a function of sovereignty, but it also might be one of those means selected by Congress to carry out its "ample powers, on the due execution of which the happiness and prosperity of the nation so vitally . . . [depend]."[23] Marshall thus accepted the arguments of the bank's counsel that the incidental power to incorporate was inherent in sovereign government.[24]

On the other hand, the framers of the Constitution had not left congressional authority to rest upon inherent powers of government. They inserted among the enumerated powers the power of Congress to make all laws necessary and proper for executing the previously enumerated powers. The Chief Justice expressly rejected Maryland's arguments that this clause was merely a general authority to legislate under the enumerated powers and likewise found unpersuasive the contention that it restricted the methods Congress might select to effectuate its purposes. Perhaps the rhetoric of bank counsel struck home, for William Pinkney had argued that "it is the duty of the court to construe the constitutional powers of the national government liberally, and to mould them so as to effectuate its great objects."[25] Mindful of Attorney General Wirt's historical reference to the difficulties of conducting the War of 1812 without a national bank, Marshall readily adopted a broad construction of the necessary and proper clause: "Let the end be legitimate, let it be within the scope of the constitution, and all means which are appropriate, which are plainly adapted to

---

22. *Ibid.*, 360–362, 377–378; see Baxter, *Daniel Webster,* 169–181.

23. The quotation is as follows:

"But it may with great reason be contended, that a government, entrusted with such ample powers, on the due execution of which the happiness and prosperity of the nation so vitally depends, must also. . ."

The depend/depends clause, to my mind at least, seems to modify "powers" rather than "government." Marshall was probably a much better lawyer than grammarian, and here I think he was wrong.

24. 4 Wheaton 406–411, quotation at 408; Professor Currie comments that in this discussion Marshall is his most persuasive, but that many of the points touched upon had been resolved in *United States v. Fisher,* 2 Cranch 358 (1805). *Constitution,* 160–164.

25. Constitution, Art. I, § 8; the quotation is at 4 Wheaton 386.

that end, which are not prohibited, but consist with the letter and spirit of the constitution, are constitutional."[26]

Turning to the question of state taxation and the bank's operations, the Chief Justice took pains to restate the governing influence of the supremacy clause upon the issue. A neat syllogism demonstrated the repugnance of a state taxing power to federal supremacy: "1st. that a power to create implies a power to preserve. 2d. That a power to destroy if wielded by a different hand, is hostile to, and incompatible with these powers to create and preserve. 3d. That where this repugnancy exists, that authority which is supreme must control, not yield to that over which it is supreme."[27] While he admitted that both state and federal governments possessed the power to tax, he pointed out that the only practical limit on those powers was the structure of government. Subsequently this reason was supplemented by the observation that state taxation powers were given by the people of each state, just as those of the federal government were granted by all of the people of the Union. However, he held that when a state attempts to tax the federal government, it acts upon those powers given not by the people of a single state but by those of the entire nation. This view of sovereignty, both at the state and federal level, provided safety and security for both individual states and the United States.[28]

There remained only the question of how far federal exemption from state taxation would extend. Marshall noted that the opinion did not apply to real-property taxes assessed by state authorities in common with all other realty in the state. Nor did it restrict the ability of the states to tax dividends on Bank of the United States shares held by citizens of the states. On the other hand, no state might by taxation or otherwise impede, retard, burden, or control the operation of the constitutional laws enacted by Congress. As Professor Currie quite correctly notes, Marshall neglected to point out that the Maryland tax considered in M'Culloch was a discriminatory tax against the Bank of the United States, perhaps the strongest reasons for holding it unconstitutional but one that was ignored by Marshall.[29]

---

26. 4 Wheaton 316, at 421; Pinckney's comment is reported at ibid., 386. Currie correctly points out that Marshall did not prove the way the bank was necessary to the effectuation of enumerated powers. David P. Currie, The Constitution and the Supreme Court: The First Hundred Years, 1789–1888 (Chicago: University of Chicago Press, 1985), 164–165. Perhaps the wartime experience, fresh in the minds of Marshall's contemporaries, rendered explanation unnecessary.

27. Marshall's treatment of the taxation issue in M'Culloch is at 4 Wheaton 425–437; the quotation is at 426.

28. Ibid., 428–430. Marshall returns to the point and carefully rephrases his argument to deal with contentions that portions of the Federalist Papers supported the position that no state powers of taxation were to be revoked by ratification of the Constitution. Ibid., 431–436.

29. 4 Wheaton 316, at 436–437; Currie, Constitution, 167–168.

The Court's opinion in *M'Culloch* did not end the debate over federal supremacy and national sovereignty either in the courts or in political discourse. Goaded by newspaper attacks on the *M'Culloch* decision, Marshall took up the essayist's pen to write a series of anonymous vindications of his opinion.[30] Even then the issue of state sovereignty remained the constitutional paradigm about which the slavery question would be debated by subsequent generations. However, *M'Culloch* engrafted the concept of federal supremacy upon the constitutional law of the United States, and it continues to serve as the fundamental enunciation of that principle.

State Sovereignty in a Federal Union

Despite the Marshall Court's endeavor to establish supremacy as a keystone in the American constitutional arch, constitutional theory predicated upon state sovereignty continued to threaten the federal Union. Those political and sectional forces that established the Articles of Confederation and contributed to its ineffectual scheme of government persisted in the United States throughout Chief Justice Marshall's thirty-four years on the Court. The Court was called upon to deal with two categories of cases: challenges to federal court authority based upon the provisions of the Eleventh Amendment and cases questioning and obstructing the U.S. Supreme Court's authority to hear appeals from the decisions of the highest courts of the states when federal questions were involved. These lines of decision ultimately converged in the Court's opinion in *Cohens v. Virginia* (1821).[31]

THE ELEVENTH AMENDMENT NEMESIS

Throughout Marshall's chief justiceship, the Court was faced with construing the Eleventh Amendment and assessing its impact upon the jurisdiction of the Supreme Court and, to a lesser degree, upon the lower federal courts. The first among these cases was *United States v. Peters* (1809), which involved the enforcement of a prize case award as modified by the decree of the Court of Appeals in Cases of Prize and Capture, the latter court having been established under the Articles of Confederation. Since the Pennsylvania Court of Admiralty had refused to accept the decision of the federal tribunal, the prize money was transferred to David Rittenhouse

---

30. On December 1, 1819, the Kentucky Court of Appeals held that the capital of a Bank of the United States branch in Kentucky was subject to state taxation; the justices divided over the issue of state sovereignty and whether *M'Culloch* controlled their decision. *Commonwealth v. Morrison*, 9 Ky. (2 Marshall) 75–101 (1819). Marshall's journalistic defense of the Court's opinion is discussed at chapter 2, 73–75.

31. 6 Wheaton 264–444.

as a stakeholder. Rittenhouse was the state treasurer at the time the funds were assigned to his care. Although he died before the successful claimants brought suit to collect in the federal circuit court for Pennsylvania, his executrices found within his papers a memorandum indicating that the funds would belong to the state once a bond he had posted in the case was revoked.[32]

After the action for the prize money was filed in the United States circuit court, the Pennsylvania legislature passed a statute asserting its title to the prize money and instructing the attorney general to commence action to reduce the fund to the state's possession. Faced with a potential conflict between state and federal authority, District Judge Richard Peters refused to make any further order in the case. The claimants then sought a mandamus in the U.S. States Supreme Court. It was awarded in *United States v. Peters* despite Pennsylvania's contention that it was not subject to jurisdiction because of the Eleventh Amendment. Referring to the precedent established in *Penhallow v. Doane's Executor* (1795),[33] Chief Justice Marshall considered the appellate jurisdiction of the court of appeals well established. In regard to the Eleventh Amendment, he observed that the funds were held by Rittenhouse in his individual capacity rather than as treasurer. The state of Pennsylvania could not, by legislation or otherwise, declare itself the owner of the prize money. Therefore it was not a party defendant in the case, and the Eleventh Amendment did not apply.[34] By insisting that the state be a party of record, Marshall sharply limited the application of the Eleventh Amendment. Generally the Amendment did not apply to cases in which state officials were defendants unless they were sued *ex officio*. Much later, in *Ex Parte Juan Madrazzo*, Marshall applied this rule when the governor of Georgia was sued by the title of his office, rather than in his personal name, for the recovery of slaves imported illegally into the United States. For the Court, Marshall pointed out that such an action was not within the Court's original jurisdiction.[35]

It is difficult in retrospect to understand the consternation caused by the ratification of the Eleventh Amendment. As a lawyer who had defended the Fairfax estate's land interests in the Northern Neck of Virginia, Marshall was well aware of its potential threat both to the Union and to prop-

32. *United States v. Peters*, 5 Cranch 115, at 138–140.

33. 3 Dallas 54–120.

34. 5 Cranch 115, at 139–140. For more detailed discussion of the case, see Clyde E. Jacobs, *The Eleventh Amendment and Sovereign Immunity* (Westport: Greenwood Press, 1972), 77–80; Haskins and Johnson, *Foundations*, 322–331, 626–628.

35. 7 Peters 627–632 (1833); see also discussion at Jacobs, *Eleventh Amendment*, 103–105; and John V. Orth, *The Judicial Power of the United States: The Eleventh Amendment in American History* (New York: Oxford University Press, 1987), 41.

erty interests. Most of those questions would reach the U.S. Supreme Court in *Fairfax v. Hunter*,[36] but earlier in this protracted litigation he had filed an action in the U.S. District Court for Virginia challenging the validity of an inquest of office proceeding brought by the Commonwealth of Virginia. The inquest was to escheat the Fairfax manor lands and destroy all titles obtained from the Fairfax family. Since the state was directly involved in this proceeding, he feared that ratification of the Eleventh Amendment would preempt the Fairfax interests from appealing to the U.S. Supreme Court.[37] His concern in 1794 was twofold: that his action in federal court might be barred by ratification of the Amendment and that judicial construction of the Amendment might pose a serious threat to appeals under Section 25 of the Judiciary Act of 1789. The second alternative would leave Virginia's Court of Appeals the last resort in which to defend a right arising under the provisions of the Peace Treaty of 1783.

Section 25 Jurisdiction

Beginning with the 1813 decision in *Fairfax v. Hunter*, opponents of the Marshall Court jurisprudence focused their political and legislative attacks upon amending or repealing Section 25 of the Judiciary Act of 1789. This was the provision that gave the Supreme Court appellate jurisdiction over cases raising federal questions that had been decided in the highest courts of the states having jurisdiction in them. Since federal questions were those that involved the construction of the Federal Constitution, statutes enacted pursuant to the Constitution, and treaties entered into by the United States, these cases would involve federal supremacy and international relations in a direct way. Section 25 appeals were designed to enforce supremacy in the Union and to render uniform state court interpretations of the Federal Constitution.

The landmark case setting forth the rationale for Section 25 jurisdiction is *Martin v. Hunter's Lessee,* the case that represented a critical stage in Marshall's long professional and financial involvement with this land litigation.[38] Because of his prior connection with the Fairfax land controversy, the Chief Justice absented himself from argument in *Martin* as well as in its predecessor case, *Fairfax's Devisee v. Hunter's Lessee* (1813).[39] He assigned Judge Story to prepare the Court's opinion in both cases.

---

36. 7 Cranch 603–632 (1813).

37. See editorial note on the Fairfax lands in *Marshall Papers*, vol. 2, 140.

38. 1 Wheaton 304–382 (1816), discussed above at chapter 2, 68–72. See also Charles Warren, "Legislative and Judicial Attacks on the Supreme Court of the United States—A History of the Twenty-fifth Section of the Judiciary Act," 47 *American Law Review* 1, at 6–17 (1913).

39. 7 Cranch 603–632 (1813).

When *Fairfax's Devisee* was before the Supreme Court, counsels' arguments centered upon the 1783 and 1794 treaties with Britain, the primary issue at law being whether the Fairfax title was valid and existing when the 1783 treaty was signed. By the treaty terms, no future confiscations of British-held lands were to occur within the United States. Since the case involved private parties, neither side relied upon the Eleventh Amendment or discussed its relevance. The critical point in Judge Story's opinion for the Court was that the inquest of office proceeding, required at common law to vest title of escheated lands in the Crown (or the state), had not been accomplished by the time the treaty was signed in 1783. Therefore the Fairfax title was good, and the Virginia Court of Appeals erred in denying its validity.[40]

When the court of appeals received the Supreme Court's mandate issued in *Fairfax's Devisee,* it refused to obey the order. The result was a writ of error from the Supreme Court, bringing the litigation once more before the Court under the title *Martin v. Hunter's Lessee.*[41] Again the Eleventh Amendment was not available as to those claiming title through the state, but a sharp challenge was mounted to the exercise of Supreme Court review under Section 25.

Tasked with establishing the constitutionality of Section 25, Story focused upon the terms of Article III of the Constitution. He noted that by its terms judicial power was "vested in one Supreme Court, and in such other inferior courts as the Congress may . . . ordain and establish." Noting that the judicial power of the United States was more extensive than the authority specifically bestowed upon the Supreme Court, he concluded that Congress was under a positive duty to vest all judicial power conferred by the Constitution and thus required to establish inferior federal courts.[42]

Did the Constitution limit the Supreme Court's appellate jurisdiction to those cases pending in federal courts? The supremacy clause in Article VI clearly indicated that state judges should be bound by the provisions of the Constitution, statutes, and treaties of the United States. When cases involving federal questions arose in state courts, the judicial power of the United States extended to them by the exercise of the Supreme Court's appellate power. There were cogent reasons why the final decision in such matters should rest with federal courts, for "the constitution has presumed . . .

---

40. *Ibid.,* 612–618, 622–623, 627. Judge Johnson dissented, asserting that the state's grant to Hunter divested the alien title held by Fairfax and that no prior inquest of office was necessary to confer title upon the state. *Ibid.,* 628–632.

41. 1 Wheaton 304–382 (1816).

42. *Ibid.,* 324–330. *Martin* involved international law, a subject Akmar assigns to the first and most important tier of federal court jurisdiction. "The Two-tiered Structure of the Judiciary Act of 1789," 138 *University of Pennsylvania Law Review* 1499 (1990).

that state attachments, state prejudices, state jealousies, and state interests, might sometimes obstruct, or control, or be supposed to obstruct or control, the regular administration of justice." These considerations supported both the appellate review available under Section 25 and the power of the federal courts to remove cases from state courts. Without such control over federal questions, the laws, the treaties, and the Constitution itself would be subject to different constructions in different states and this could not have been the intention of the Philadelphia Convention or those state conventions that ratified the document.[43]

Contrary to *Martin,* the Virginia Court of Appeals and its supporters believed that Supreme Court appellate review should apply only to cases in the lower federal courts. Should a matter of federal law arise in the state courts, according to their view it should be transferred to the appropriate federal court from which review might occur. As Professor Wechsler has noted, this system would probably have been more intrusive than direct appeal from the highest state court to the U.S. Supreme Court.[44]

Finally, Judge Story dealt in *Martin* with the contention that the scope of appellate review was limited only to construction of treaty terms. He rejected that restriction, pointing out that title of the Fairfax interests depended upon the treaty, but to determine its validity in light of the treaty, the Court would first have to make preliminary inquiry into the existence and structure of the title. While that was a matter of state common law, the Supreme Court was entitled to make its own determination. He pointed out that in *Smith v. Maryland,* a case involving another state seizure of British lands, the Supreme Court held that under Maryland law the plaintiff no longer held title when the treaty was signed, and hence its provisions could not apply.[45] Following its procedures in *Smith,* the Court considered any title error in the Fairfax litigation to be subject to Section 25 appellate review. The *Martin* and *Smith* practice clearly is essential to federal supremacy. Denying the Supreme Court's authority to make independent thresh-

---

43. 1 Wheaton 304, at 339–342, 347–351, quotation at 347. H. Jefferson Powell asserts that Story's nationalism consisted of seeing the Federal Constitution as depriving the states of some of their sovereign powers and regulating them in the use of their remaining powers. "The Oldest Question of Constitutional Law," 79 *Virginia Law Review* 633, at 680–681 (1993).

44. Herbert Wechsler, "The Appellate Jurisdiction of the Supreme Court: Reflections on the Law and the Logistics of Direct Review," 34 *Washington and Lee Law Review* 1043, at 1047 (1977).

45. 6 Cranch 286–305 (1810), opinion by Judge Bushrod Washington. Judge William Johnson dissented from the Court's opinion, being persuaded that the Fairfax title had been extinguished before 1783 and that an inquest of office was no longer needed under Virginia procedures. See discussion at Haskins and Johnson, *Foundations,* 553–557, and Wechsler, "Appellate Jurisdiction," 1052.

old determinations of state common law in federal-question cases would have neutralized this powerful judicial tool for regularizing construction of the Constitution, federal statutes, and treaties.[46]

COHENS V. VIRGINIA

Section 25 appellate review and Eleventh Amendment issues converged in the argument and decision of *Cohens v. Virginia* (1821), which triggered still another series of newspaper attacks upon the Court and political efforts to repeal Section 25. It has been suggested that the case may have been expedited to resolve questions concerning Virginia's antilottery law as well as to raise once more the question of Section 25 review.[47] As in *Marbury*, the Court's decision in *Cohens* gave the decision on the merits in favor of the most politically popular party—in *Marbury* for Secretary of State Madison and in *Cohens* for the Commonwealth of Virginia in its efforts to prohibit lotteries. Jurisdictionally, *Cohens* followed *Martin* in upholding Section 25 appellate review, and it rejected the contention that the Eleventh Amendment prohibited Supreme Court procedures by which a state might be involuntarily brought before the Court as an appellee.

The decision on the merits, although relatively straightforward, should not be overlooked, for it raised an important issue of federal supremacy. The Cohens firm sold District of Columbia lottery tickets in the City of Norfolk, and their defense involved the claim that the federal statute that established the lottery was the supreme law of the land in accordance with Article VI of the Federal Constitution. In his opinion for the Court, Marshall rejected this defense, pointing out that the District of Columbia statute was enacted for purely local purposes and, in the absence of a clear contrary Congressional intent, could not be given extraterritorial effect.[48]

The jurisdictional issues raised earlier did not lend themselves to such a

46. Haskins and Johnson, *Foundations,* 553–554.
47. 6 Wheaton 264–448 (1821); see discussion at chapter 2, 75–77; see also W. Ray Luce, *Cohens v. Virginia (1821): The Supreme Court and State Rights, a Reevaluation of Influences and Impacts* (New York: Garland, 1990); Orth, *Judicial Power,* 37–40; Warren, "Legislative and Judicial Attacks," 16–20; and Currie, *Constitution,* 96–102. Some valuable insight can be gained from Stewart A. Baker, "Federalism and the Eleventh Amendment," 48 *University of Colorado Law Review* 139, at 140–149 (1977); Martha A. Field, "The Eleventh Amendment and other Sovereign Immunity Doctrines," 126 *University of Pennsylvania Law Review* 515, at 518–519, 538–545 (1977); and William A. Fletcher, "A Historical Interpretation of the Eleventh Amendment: A Narrow Construction on an Affirmative Grant of Jurisdiction Rather Than a Prohibition against Jurisdiction," 35 *Stanford Law Review* 1033, at 1078–1083 (1983); and John J. Gibbons, "The Eleventh Amendment and State Sovereign Immunity: A Reinterpretation," 83 *Columbia Law Review* 1889, at 1952–1959 (1983).
48. 6 Wheaton 264, at 440–449.

simple resolution. Chief Justice Marshall's opinion for the Court began by considering the two major divisions of "judicial power of the United States" as enunciated in Article III, Section 2. One division was cases over which the federal courts had jurisdiction because of the nature of the cause; this applied to those matters "arising under . . . [the] Constitution, the Laws of the United States, and Treaties made, or which shall be made, under their Authority." It was the very nature of the federal Union that some of the sovereignty of the states was surrendered to the federal government upon ratification of the Constitution, and the supremacy clause affirmed that relationship.[49]

The other division of federal judicial power consisted of cases in which the character of the parties conferred jurisdiction. Here Marshall readily admitted that there were many cases between a state and its own citizens in which the U.S. Supreme Court would not have jurisdiction. On the other hand, he pointed out that such a case as fell under the first division of federal judicial power—that is, one that "arose under the Constitution"— would not be excepted from Supreme Court appellate review by virtue of the fact that the state was a party.[50] It was true that in *Marbury* there was a clear distinction between the Supreme Court's original and appellate jurisdiction. However, Marshall found the issue in *Marbury* distinguishable from that in *Cohens* because in the case before him the Supreme Court's appellate jurisdiction was based on the federal question involved and not upon the character of the parties. In a case such as *Cohens* the Supreme Court might not exercise original jurisdiction even though a state was involved as a party. He concluded that "as the constitution originally stood, the appellate jurisdiction of this court, in all cases arising under the constitution, laws, or treaties of the United States, was not arrested by the circumstance that a state was a party." Had the ratification of the Eleventh Amendment altered this situation?[51]

Noting that the Amendment had left untouched the jurisdiction of the U.S. Supreme Court over actions between two or more states or between states and foreign states, Marshall denied that its purpose was to protect the sovereignty of a state against federal judicial power. The express provisions of the Amendment dealt with suits brought in the United States courts by an individual advancing a claim against a state of the Union. To

---

49. *Ibid.*, 380-382.
50. *Ibid.*, 376–381, 389–395. The "functional bifurcation" of Article III, creating a distinction between "cases" that raised vital federal or national questions and "controversies" between two private parties entitled to sue in federal courts, is highlighted in Robert J. Pushaw, Jr., "Article III's Case/Controversy Distinction and the Dual Functions of Federal Courts," 69 *Notre Dame Law Review* 447, at 495–502.
51. 6 Wheaton 400–405; quotation at 405.

determine the applicability of the amendment, it was necessary to determine who brought the action. Appealing a state court judgment by writ of error does not make the state a party defendant if it was not a party at the commencement of the action. Counsel conceded that the great change from the Confederation government had been the ability of the United States to act directly upon individuals; should not such a policy apply as much for the protection of individuals as for their coercion?[52]

In regard to the validity of the Court's appellate review of state court decisions under Section 25 of the Judiciary Act of 1789, Marshall left no doubt that this was essential to the supremacy of the federal government. The very nature of the supremacy clause demanded such an authority. Uniformity of constitutional interpretation demanded that such an appellate control exist. It existed under the Confederation in regard to prize appeals. The *Federalist Papers* gave constitutional support to Section 25 review, and for purposes of administering federal law, "the national and state systems are to be regarded as one whole. The courts of the latter will of course be natural auxiliaries to the execution of the laws of the Union, and an appeal from them will as naturally lie to that tribunal which is destined to unite and assimilate the principles of natural justice, and the rules of national decision."[53] A government with thirteen or more interpretations of its fundamental law would be a virtual "hydra in government." Thus *Cohens* and *Worcester v. Georgia* (1832) made it clear that federal-question jurisdiction under Section 25 remained substantially undisturbed by the Eleventh Amendment.[54] On the other hand, the Chief Justice stopped short of asserting that states were subject to Section 25 appellate review in all situations where federal questions were involved, presumably leaving that question open for future consideration.[55]

BILLS OF CREDIT AND *CRAIG V. MISSOURI*

Despite Marshall's emphatic statement concerning Section 25 review in *Cohens,* the Supreme Court's appellate authority over State decisions concerning federal questions was challenged one more time in *Craig v. Missouri*

---

52. *Ibid.,* 388, 391, 405–412.

53. *Ibid.,* 413–423; quotation at 419–420. Earlier, in *United States v. More,* 3 Cranch 159 (1805), and *Durousseau v. United States,* 6 Cranch 307 (1810), Marshall stated the principle that the Court's appellate jurisdiction was given by the Constitution, subject to such limits Congress had made pursuant to the Judiciary Act of 1789. Ralph A. Rossum, "Congress, the Constitution, and Appellate Jurisdiction of the Supreme Court: The Letter and Spirit of the Exceptions Clause," 24 *William & Mary Law Review* 385, at 395–396 (1983).

54. *Worcester v. Georgia,* 6 Peters 515 (1832); Calvin R. Massey, "State Sovereignty and the Tenth and Eleventh Amendments," 56 *University of Chicago Law Review* 61, at 127 (1987).

55. Vicki C. Jackson, "The Supreme Court, the Eleventh Amendment, and State Sovereign Immunity," 98 *Yale Law Journal* 1, at 15 (1988); Massey argues that the Eleventh

(1830).[56] Within the first year of its admission to the Union, Missouri established loan offices and proceeded to issue $200,000 worth of certificates in small denominations. Hiram Craig executed a promissory note to pay for $199.99 in certificates and subsequently failed to pay the note on the due date. The state brought an action against him, and he defended by pleading the illegality or, more properly, unconstitutionality of the contract to purchase certificates. Citing the Federal Constitution's prohibition against states' issuing bills of credit, Craig asked the Missouri courts to hold the certificates violative of the Constitution and to rule the transaction void because of illegality. Failing to persuade Missouri's courts, he took a Section 25 appeal to the U.S. Supreme Court.

For the Court majority, the Chief Justice held that the only issue before the Missouri courts was the constitutionality of the loan act and the certificates issued in accordance with its provisions. Although the certificates admittedly were not termed bills of credit, Marshall refused to permit terminology to shelter the state action from Supreme Court review. Nor would the fact that the Missouri Supreme Court did not mention the federal question insulate the case from Section 25 review. The loan office legislation and the certificates authorized by the provision had been challenged as being repugnant to the Federal Constitution, and the statute had been upheld even if the federal question ostensibly was ignored.[57]

The major substantive issue before the Court was whether the Missouri certificates qualified as bills of credit and thus fell within the Federal Constitution's prohibition. Drawing upon American colonial and Confederation period history, Marshall traced the development of bills of credit from a 1690 Massachusetts issue to the extensive and destabilizing use of state bills of credit under the Confederation government. He pointed to convincing similarities between the Missouri certificates and eighteenth-century bills of credit: both were in denominations that facilitated their use in retail business; like bills of credit, the certificates were acceptable in payment of state taxes; and both were issued by the government. Rejecting arguments of counsel, he insisted that the Constitution prohibited issuing bills of credit on one hand and the emission of currency or coin that was legal tender on the other. Thus the fact that the Missouri bills were not granted legal tender status did not insulate them from illegality as bills of credit.[58]

Since the bills of credit were void because they were repugnant to the

---

Amendment should have barred the appeal in *Worcester v. Georgia* and that since the Cohens were Virginia citizens, the Eleventh Amendment did not apply to their case. "State Sovereignty," 127–128 (1989).

56. 4 Peters 410.

57. *Ibid.*, 425–429; see also Warren, "Legislative and Judicial Attacks," 161–166.

58. 4 Peters 410, at 429–436.

Constitution's prohibition, the contract between Craig and the loan office was unauthorized by law and his promissory note was also invalidated. Section 25 was once more utilized as a brake upon state checks to federal supremacy. However, 1830 was not 1821, and John Marshall was no longer able to carry the Court with him in the *Craig* opinion. Judge William Johnson dissented, being persuaded by history that the Framing Fathers meant to enjoin the issuance of paper money when they prohibited state emission of bills of credit. That construction was given weight by the fact that the same provision of the Constitution excluded anything but gold or silver as legal tender currency. Terming the certificates to be of "amphibious character," Johnson felt that such a doubtful case should be resolved in favor of state autonomy. Furthermore, if citizens needed protection from such state financial transactions, the contract clause was adequate security.[59]

The second dissenting justice, Smith Thompson, also centered his discussion on the definition of "bills of credit" and seems to have followed Judge Johnson's reasoning. In addition, he was much concerned about the inability of the states to obtain circulating currency. If a state could not issue loan office certificates, was it not just one step further to prohibit state-chartered banks from issuing bank notes? The Framing Fathers certainly did not intend to combat the evil of paper money through suppressing paper currency of every kind.[60]

Judge McLean, the third dissenter, reluctantly conceded Section 25 jurisdiction but complained about the lack of a clear federal-question issue on the record from the Missouri courts. Again the definition of a bill of credit was the central focus of his opinion, and he was reluctant to afford the term such a broad meaning that virtually all fiscal operations of state governments would be impeded. The loan office certificates appeared to be a means by which the state facilitated payment by its debtors, but they were not recognized as legal tender, nor was any creditor other than the state bound to accept them in payment. McLean, like Johnson, felt that doubts concerning the certificates should be resolved in favor of Missouri's sovereignty.[61]

The majority in *Craig* was composed of Judges Story, Duvall, and Baldwin, who joined the Chief Justice in his opinion. Among the dissenters there was some concern about the validity of Section 25 jurisdiction, but what emerges most clearly is the suggestion that, in doubtful cases, it is wise to permit the states to have their way. Smith Thompson and John McLean,

59. *Ibid.*, 441–444.
60. *Ibid.*, 447–449.
61. *Ibid.*, 452–461.

the first a one-time presidential hopeful and the other still awaiting a draft, were men who were perhaps closer to the political pulse of the times than their senior colleagues and the Chief Justice. McLean, from the Midwest, and Johnson, from South Carolina, were from agrarian areas, but both had strong national feelings, and Johnson had been through the long Section 25 siege of the Court by congressional reformers. *Craig*, for whatever reason, represents a weak sequel to Judge Story's *Martin* opinion and the equally powerful Marshall opinion in *Cohens*.

THE *OSBORN* CASE AND CIRCUIT COURT JURISDICTION

Henry Wheaton's reports of the 1824 Supreme Court term ended with two more Bank of the United States cases. *Osborn v. Bank of the United States* and a companion case, *Bank of the United States v. Planter's Bank of Georgia*, challenged the statutory right of the national bank to sue in federal circuit courts.[62] Ohio and Georgia claimed that the Eleventh Amendment protected state officials from being sued by the bank even though the states themselves were not joined as parties in the pleadings.

In *Osborn* the Chief Justice delivered the Court's opinion sustaining the right of the bank to sue in federal circuit courts. He asserted that the bank existed by virtue of a federal statute, hence all of its actions, contractual and otherwise, arose under a law of the United States. Any challenge to the bank's operations raised a federal question, cognizable before the courts of the United States. In a dictum in *Cohens*, Marshall had conceded that in the absence of an express provision in Article III excluding state court jurisdiction, those tribunals and the federal courts had concurrent jurisdiction in all cases to which the judicial power extended.[63] Thus *Osborn* did not divest state court jurisdiction over the Bank of the United States, nor did it confer exclusive jurisdiction upon the federal courts. Rather, it conferred upon the bank a right to sue in federal courts that it otherwise might not have had.

---

62. *Osborn v. Bank of the United States*, 9 Wheaton 738–903 (1824); *Bank of the United States v. Planter's Bank of Georgia*, ibid., 904–914. The cases are discussed at greater length in G. Edward White, *The Marshall Court and Cultural Change, 1815–35*, vols. 3 and 4, *History of the Supreme Court of the United States*, 10 vols. to date (New York: Macmillan Publishing Company, 1988), 524–535. Beveridge attributes the Court's expansion of federal jurisdiction and its emphasis upon supremacy to the prevalence of state-based obstructions to federal authority. *Marshall*, vol. 4, 384–396.

63. 6 Wheaton 397–398. Professor Massey suggests that Marshall developed the "party of record" rule to avoid an Eleventh Amendment bar to the Court's consideration of *Osborn*. On the other hand, he argues that the need to develop such a rule indicates Marshall had doubts that *Cohens* made all federal question cases immune from the bar of the Eleventh Amendment. "State Sovereignty," 132–133.

Upon this jurisdictional point Judge William Johnson dissented vigor-ously, arguing that federal-question jurisdiction should be much more nar-rowly construed. Congress could not by virtue of the bank legislation confer federal-question jurisdiction upon federal circuit courts. In Judge Johnson's view, federal-question jurisdiction could be constitutionally exer-cised only by the Supreme Court and might not be conferred upon lower federal courts by congressional statute. Otherwise federal circuit court ju-risdiction conceivably could be expanded without limit by indirection; Congress might make each American citizen a corporation sole and confer upon that entity the right to sue in federal courts.[64]

The Court's problem in *Osborn* was the anomalous position of the Bank of the United States, which performed many functions of a central bank but was owned by private shareholders, among whom there were many foreigners. Marshall and the majority viewed the bank as an instrumentality of the federal government; indeed, at one point Marshall speculated upon the bank's similarity to and distinction from federal executive officials.[65] The United States unquestionably had the right to sue in federal circuit courts when its beneficial interests in a transaction were involved,[66] but did the Bank of the United States? Judge Johnson viewed the jurisdictional provision in the bank's charter as a "boot-strap" measure, designed to grab jurisdiction for the federal courts and to enhance the power of the bank.

Marshall's reasoning followed a rather dubious circuit: (1) a federal stat-ute created the bank; (2) whatever the bank does is as a result of federal law and therefore raises a federal question; and (3) the constitutional and statutory foundation of federal-question jurisdiction applies to the Bank of the United States.[67]

Two questions added to the Court's dilemma: Ohio and Georgia had claimed the actions were barred by the Eleventh Amendment; and the same supremacy issues that had been raised in *M'Culloch* were subject to reconsideration in *Osborn* and *Planter's Bank*. Chief Justice Marshall began his opinion by accepting counsel's argument that the judicial power of

---

64. 9 Wheaton 819–828, 871–903; 1 Stat. 73, at 85–86; Professor Barry Friedman shares some of Judge Johnson's apprehensions and characterizes the Supreme Court's jurisdic-tion as being "tenuous indeed." "A Different Dialogue: The Supreme Court, Congress and Federal Jurisdiction," 85 *Northwestern University Law Review* 1, at 21 (1990).

65. 9 Wheaton 819, at 866–868.

66. *Dugan v. United States,* 3 Wheaton 172–183 (1818), opinion by Judge Livingston.

67. Professor Massey points out that Marshall's construction of federal jurisdiction is "ex-treme by modern standards." "State Sovereignty," 131–132 (1989). In asserting jurisdic-tion in *Osborn,* Marshall developed the "party of record" exception to the Eleventh Amendment; that is, he refused to look beyond *Osborn,* an Ohio official, to hold that the case was against the state of Ohio. Stewart A. Baker, "Federalism and the Eleventh Amendment," 48 *University of Colorado Law Review* 139, at 155 (1977).

the United States was coextensive with the legislative and executive power because "all governments which are not extremely defective in their organization, must possess, within themselves, the means of expounding, as well as enforcing, their own laws. . . . [the] framers kept this great political principal [*sic*] in view."[68] Noting that the Constitution granted both original and appellate judicial power to the federal courts, he reasoned that judicial power mentioned in the Constitution as appellate might by Congressional action be conferred upon courts exercising original jurisdiction.[69] This represents an extremely broad interpretation of federal judicial power and one to which Judge Johnson made very cogent (and valid) objections. Apparently considerations of federal supremacy and a protective attitude toward the bank moved the majority to ignore Johnson's logical reservations about taking jurisdiction. In addition, *Osborn* represented something of a retreat from the *Marbury* practice of strictly construing federal court jurisdiction, for the Court had given Congress virtual carte blanche in its exercise of its power to bestow jurisdiction upon the lower federal courts.

In a practical sense a contrary decision in *Osborn* would have hampered the bank's ability to conduct business by restricting its litigation to state courts. Two earlier Marshall Court cases imposed a rule that would become known as the "complete diversity" principle. It held that since corporations were neither citizens of a state nor aliens, a corporation might not sue in federal courts under diversity grounds. On the other hand, the individual shareholders of the corporation might sue or be sued as long as *each* of the defendants held citizenship other than that of the suing shareholders. In other words an action would fail in federal court if any plaintiff shared citizenship with any defendant; in the case of corporations, a case would fail if any corporate shareholder shared citizenship with any corporate shareholder on the opposite side of the case.[70] Quite clearly the bank's extensive shareholder list would undoubtedly disqualify it from resort to federal courts on diversity grounds and subject its litigation to the parochialism of state court juries.

Since the difficulties of complete diversity were known well before the 1816 incorporation of the Second Bank of the United States, Congress expressly provided for the bank's access to federal courts. In *Bank of the United States v. Deveaux* (1809) counsel had argued unsuccessfully that the

---

68. 9 Wheaton 818–819.

69. *Ibid.*, 819–823.

70. *Strawbridge v. Curtiss*, 3 Cranch 267–268 (1806); *Bank of the United States v. Deveaux*, 5 Cranch 61, at 86, 90–91 (1809). There is a good detailed discussion in Currie, *Constitution*, 102–106.

bank's right to sue in federal courts should be implicit in its federal incor-poration.[71] Marshall denied the validity of that position, pointing out that concurrent jurisdiction of federal or state courts was expressly permitted should the bank be prosecuted for unlawful and excessive bank note issu-ance. This demonstrated Congress's acceptance of concurrent jurisdiction of federal and state courts; had it wished the bank to have access to federal courts, it would have specified this in the incorporation act.[72] Congress took the hint as it incorporated the Second Bank in 1816, and Marshall was badly situated to deny validity to the provision even if he had been so inclined.

The tension between Marshall's expansive view of federal judicial power and Judge Johnson's tendency to restrict jurisdictional extension is perhaps best illustrated by the Court's decision in *Houston v. Moore* (1820). A Penn-sylvania militiaman, having refused to answer the president's 1814 call into federal service, was court-martialed by a state military tribunal and fined. The defendant, a Pennsylvania deputy marshal, was sued for seizing prop-erty in settlement of the fine. The validity of the state court-martial jurisdic-tion was raised on writ of error issued by the Supreme Court. For the Court, Judge Bushrod Washington held that in the absence of express congres-sional intention to the contrary, the state court-martial had concurrent ju-risdiction with national courts-martial. Judge Johnson, focusing upon the fact that the militiaman was not in the service of the United States, refused to believe that he was subject to national court-martial jurisdiction but, on the other hand, felt that there was unquestionable jurisdiction in the state court. In his dissent, probably joined by the Chief Justice, Judge Story viewed the comprehensive nature of the federal militia law as an indication that calling out the militia and employing it in national service were exclu-sively federal activities. Hence the national courts-martial were the only tribunals that would have jurisdiction, and the state law providing for state courts-martial jurisdiction was unconstitutional. Concerning Johnson's dis-cussion of whether the militiaman was in federal service, Story expostu-lated, "We do not sit here to fritter away the constitution upon metaphysical subtleties."[73]

---

71. 5 Cranch 61, at 84–86.

72. *Ibid.*, 84–86; the provision concerning excessive bank note issue is Section 9, An Act to Incorporate the Subscribers to the Bank of the United States, February 25, 1792, 1 Stat. 191, at 194. The section was reenacted as to the second bank as Section 11, cl. 8, An Act to Incorporate the Subscribers to the Bank of the United States, April 10, 1816, 3 Stat. 266, at 272. Section 7 of the same statute gives state courts concurrent jurisdiction with federal courts in any litigation brought by the bank. *Ibid.*, 269.

73. 5 Wheaton 1–76, Story quotation at 64; the suggestion that Marshall joined silently in Story's dissent is made in White, *Marshall Court*, 537.

Houston and *Osborn* suggest that there was a lively debate over the concurrency of federal and state judicial power after the 1819 *M'Culloch* decision. Marshall and Story were inclined to construe congressional action in favor of expanded federal court jurisdiction. Although their colleagues were willing to permit Congress to have its way in regard to the Bank of the United States, they were reluctant to find exclusive federal court jurisdiction when faced with vague insinuations of congressional intention. These alignments within the Court would again surface in its consideration of the commerce clause.

CONCLUSION

Without doubt, defining the nature and scope of federal supremacy was the major constitutional achievement of Chief Justice Marshall and his associate justices. Supplementing that effort was their work in shaping federal court jurisdiction. As a consequence, the Supreme Court became the focal point for resolving federalism issues, and the lower federal courts flourished as a consequence of what may be considered an excessively broad definition of federal judicial power. These political contributions should not detract from the Marshall Court's substantial contribution to the future economic prosperity of the United States. To this aspect of the Court's work we now may turn our attention.

VI

THE AMERICAN COMMON MARKET AND PROPERTY RIGHTS

There is some irony in the fact that John Marshall as a Virginian was responsible for laying the foundations of commercial and industrial development throughout the United States. Most Virginians found themselves attached to the agrarian ideal and sought to preserve the status quo in American economic life. Marshall looked forward to a changed world in which the American states, bound together in a strong common market, would become independent of European-manufactured goods and self-sufficient for all other necessities. This was part of the national vision held by many delegates to the Philadelphia Convention and the state ratifying conventions, and it seems to have impressed upon the Chief Justice the need to establish legal and constitutional foundations for such a new American nation. Indeed, behind most of his constitutional opinions touching upon economic matters there was the tacit assumption that for America to grow, the economy must be diversified to include commercial activity and industrial development. To achieve those goals, Marshall and many of his contemporaries saw the need to encourage foreign investment and to protect interstate commercial activity from the baneful effects of incipient state mercantilism.

Yet Marshall's innate caution did not make him an advocate of industrialization at all costs and in all haste. Quite the contrary, he was aware that the economic changes he anticipated might well produce hardship and dislocation for many citizens. This was a matter of regret and concern. However, he believed that this economic growth was inevitable and that it was unwise to attempt to restrain it. For these reasons his approach to economic matters tended to be rather pragmatic and tentative. Like many of his fellow Americans, he preferred to face questions and problems as they arose, and it is characteristic that in *Gibbons v. Ogden* he was willing to leave the scope of the commerce power open to future Supreme Court consideration.

The unhampered flow of trade among the American states was essential to their political and business connectedness; it also built national strength and prestige in world markets. That activity, as well as foreign trade, depended upon safety and predictability in commercial and contractual arrangements. It required a system of impartial federal courts to adjudicate disputes and to define and secure property rights. Transfer of funds demanded solidity and reliability in banking institutions, and the risks of commercial activity needed to be lessened by an effective system of insolvency and bankruptcy laws. Obviously the ideal common market has never been created, but Marshall and his colleagues went a long way toward creating such an economic system within the Union.

THE STEAMBOAT CASE AND THE FEDERAL COMMERCE POWER

No constitutional law case in American history has a more colorful background than *Gibbons v. Ogden* (1824).[1] It began in a New York State monopoly grant to Robert Fulton that, among other things, provided injunctive relief against any individuals who attempted to navigate New York State waters by steamboat. Fulton's interests were ultimately transferred through the Livingston family to a number of licensees, including Colonel Aaron Ogden, who was granted authority to navigate the Hudson River, New York Bay, and the tidal waters separating Staten Island from New Jersey. Other entrepreneurs were assigned the Fulton-Livingston rights to navigate Long Island Sound. Business competition and personal animosity marked the relationship of Thomas Gibbons and Colonel Ogden. Before their case was brought to trial in New York State chancery courts, Gibbons had experimented with transferring passengers in midstream to avoid the charge that he navigated in New York waters. New York's chancery court enjoined Gibbons from continued operation of his steamships, and at Gibbons's request, the New Jersey legislature enacted a statute permitting operators damaged by Ogden's monopoly to recover monetary damages in that state.

---

1. 9 Wheaton 1–240. Maurice G. Baxter, *The Steamboat Monopoly: Gibbons v. Ogden, 1824* (New York: Alfred A. Knopf, 1972), and George L. Haskins, "John Marshall and the Commerce Clause of the Constitution," 104 *University of Pennsylvania Law Review* 23–27 (1955), provide good introductions to the case and an evaluation of its impact upon American law and economics. State regulatory activity prior to *Gibbons* is analyzed in Albert S. Abel, "Commerce Regulation before Gibbons v. Ogden: Interstate Transportation Enterprise," 18 *Mississippi Law Journal,* 335–380 (1947). Herbert Hovenkamp has suggested that the Livingston-Fulton monopoly artificially restricted the availability of steamship navigation in New York waters; once *Gibbons* was decided, the number of New York's operating steamships rose from six to forty-three. "Technology, Politics, and Regulated Monopoly: An American Historical Perspective," 60 *Texas Law Review* 1263, at 1268–1269, 1273–1275, 1284–1286 (1984).

Similar clashes between New York and Connecticut complicated the political situation, but they are not necessary to an understanding of the *Gibbons* case.[2] The significant point is that the case, either directly or indirectly, involved three contiguous states in which judicial and legislative conflict might soon erupt into violent confrontations. Since the Confederation period, this was as close to interstate warfare as the United States had come.

The case also focused national attention upon the riparian sovereignty of individual states and the efficacy of the commerce power as a congressional instrument to insure national free trade. The litigation involved the Hudson River, but the economic impact of the Supreme Court's decision would fall upon the vast stretch of the Ohio-Missouri-Mississippi Rivers network. Should any one state exercise sovereignty over that transportation route, it would hold most of the Union in an economic stranglehold.

Gibbons came to a Supreme Court that had already taken a federal supremacy position in regard to the Bank of the United States and its right to sue in federal circuit courts. Judge Washington, normally closely aligned with the Chief Justice, wrote for the Court majority in *Houston*. That decision indicated, at the least, a limited receptivity to the concurrent-powers arguments advanced by Joseph Hopkinson's brief in *M'Culloch*. Within Marshall's *M'Culloch* opinion there was express acceptance of the view that concurrency in the taxing power could result in situations in which the federal government might be constitutionally required to pay taxes to the states. Without any significant Court pronouncements on the commerce power, there was ample room to classify that constitutional grant of authority as being either exclusive or concurrent.

Daniel Webster and Attorney General William Wirt made eloquent and persuasive presentations focused on the need for an extensive (but not necessarily exclusive) commerce power in the United States government. Webster conceded that the concept of commerce was so vast that all aspects of its regulation could not be exclusive in Congress; on the other hand, historically the Constitution was framed to eliminate economic competition and rivalry between the states in this very field of endeavor. Monopolies of trade and navigation were among those things that had to belong

---

2. The progress of the litigation in state courts is detailed in Herbert A. Johnson, "Gibbons v. Ogden before Marshall," in Leo Hershkowitz and Milton M. Klein, eds., *Courts and Law in Early New York: Selected Essays* (Port Washington: Kennikat Press, 1978), 105–113, 147–148, and W. Howard Mann, "The Marshall Court: Nationalization of Private Rights and Personal Liberty from the Authority of the Commerce Clause," 38 *Indiana Law Journal*, 117, at 149–193 (1963). A valuable summary and comparison of the views of Chancellor Kent and Chief Justice Marshall are available in Thomas P. Campbell, "Chancellor Kent, Chief Justice Marshall and the Steamboat Cases," 25 *Syracuse Law Review*, 497–534 (1974).

exclusively to Congress. Rejecting the doctrine of concurrent powers, he went on to point out that even in the case of concurrency, when Congress acts, the supremacy clause subordinates repugnant state legislation to the enactments of Congress. Attorney General Wirt agreed that the commerce power was so vast and multifarious that some of its branches might be exclusively vested in Congress while others might be regulated by the states without interfering with Congress's authority.[3]

For the appellee, Colonel Ogden, counsel argued the historical sequence of events leading to the ratification of the Constitution. At the time they declared independence, the states were independent sovereigns, and they remained so in the Confederation period. Ratification of the Constitution conferred only enumerated powers upon the new federal government, and the Ninth and Tenth Amendments guaranteed that the central government would have no implied powers to the exclusion of the states. Thomas Oakley defined exclusive powers as

(1) those granted by express constitutional provision,
(2) those granted to the United States and specifically prohibited to the states, and
(3) those that are exclusive in their nature.

He went on to say that those exclusive in their nature were limited to those that did not exist before the Constitution and had their origin in the Constitution—what he termed strictly national powers—and those that, when exercised by a state, would have an extraterritorial effect. Finally, all powers should be construed to be concurrent unless such a view so would violate the plain letter of the Constitution. Through well-crafted definitions and rules of construction, the argument cloaked a renewed appeal to the compact theory of government and the strict construction of congressional power.

Building upon Oakley's arguments, Thomas Addis Emmett elected to enlarge upon his co-counsel's distinction between commerce as consisting of the sale or exchange of goods, and the function of transporting passengers for hire. Furthermore, Emmett challenged the right of Congress to regulate navigation except when that regulation pertained directly to commerce—that is, the sale or exchange of goods.[4]

The broad and far-reaching arguments of counsel on both sides pre-

---

3. 9 Wheaton 1, at 165–166. There is a useful critique of Webster's argument in Mann, "The Marshall Court," at 193–213.

4. 9 Wheaton 1, at 88–91. For a more detailed account of these arguments see Mann, "The Marshall Court," at 214–221, which traces some of the concurrent sovereignty arguments to the writings of St. George Tucker.

sented the Supreme Court with a series of well-reasoned positions on all of the issues. Characteristically, Chief Justice Marshall, writing for the Court, first dealt with questions of sovereignty and federal supremacy. As far as appellee's historical argument was concerned, he pointed out that the ratification of the Constitution radically altered federal-state relationships. Strict construction of federal authority was not acceptable when such a narrow construction would cripple the government and make it ineffectual. Furthermore, even in the case of a concurrent power, when a federal law came into conflict with a state law on the same subject, supremacy demanded that the federal law prevail.[5]

Having well established the majority's opposition to the compact theory, strict construction, and the purported equality of federal and state governments, Marshall began a careful textual analysis of the commerce clause. Commerce could not be limited to trade in merchandise, as appellee contended; quite the contrary, it dealt with commercial intercourse in all of its branches, including navigation. The word "among" had the special meaning of permitting Congress to regulate commerce within the boundaries of a state and was not limited to extraterritorial regulation as counsel had urged. On the other hand, regulation within a state's boundaries was predicated upon the commerce's being "among" two or more states and hence not intrastate in character.[6]

Was the commerce power exclusive, or was it concurrent? Answering this question, the Chief Justice seems to have adopted the appellee's suggestion that the nature of a power determines which government is entitled to its exercise. In regard to taxation, he pointed out that both states and the federal government might impose taxes. Furthermore, neither form of government could exist without the power to tax. On the other hand, when a state presumes to regulate interstate commerce, it does the very thing Congress is authorized to do.[7]

Many state regulations based on the constitutional authority of the states might impact upon the United States government's regulation of interstate commerce. These included inspection laws, laws governing turnpikes and ferries, and regulations of the internal commerce of the state. Far from being regulations evidencing concurrent power with the federal government, they rather showed that under the Federal Constitution, the states retained broad legislative powers. The question in all such cases was whether these regulations conflict with (or are repugnant to) the federal commerce power. As scholars have pointed out, this was a strange answer

5. 9 Wheaton 1, at 187–189, 208–210.

6. *Ibid.*, 189–190, 193–195, 217–218.

7. *Ibid.*, 189–202.

to the exclusivity question; it left to the Supreme Court the authority to determine which state laws or regulations conflicted with the commerce power and thus were null and void.[8]

In deciding *Gibbons v. Ogden,* Chief Justice Marshall felt relieved from the necessity of discussing the dormant commerce clause because, as he pointed out, the 1793 Federal Coasting Licensing Act demonstrated the intention of Congress to confer privileges of interstate commerce upon Gibbons's steamships, and the New York monopoly granted to Ogden conflicted with that federal right. However, a valuable accumulation of dicta made the *Gibbons* opinion a gold mine for future litigants. Also, there was no need to resolve the question whether the patent granted to the Livingston-Fulton enterprise violated an exclusive federal power to grant copyrights and patents. Since the conflict between the commerce clause, supplemented by the licensing act, and the New York monopoly disposed of the case, the Court declined to discuss this second issue even though it had been extensively debated by counsel.[9]

Judge William Johnson concurred in the decision of the majority but challenged the Court's reliance upon the Federal Coasting Licensing Act. Because the power to regulate foreign commerce was linked in the same clause with the interstate commerce power, he concluded that since the first power was exclusive, the second was also. This was supplemented by the fact that in the law of nations, the power to regulate commerce was an attribute of sovereignty. Such a power must be exclusive, for it could reside only in one sovereign, and in the case of the United States that sovereign was the federal government. Even if there had never been a Federal Coasting Licensing Act, the Court's conclusion would be the same. He agreed that the exercise of valid state powers might collide with Congress's actions under the commerce clause, but a frank and candid cooperation would serve as an adequate remedy in such cases.[10]

It is hazardous to speculate concerning the motivations that underlay Johnson's concurrence in the absence of direct evidence from his pen. Clearly he was persuaded by the more sweeping claims for exclusivity advanced by Webster and Wirt. His opening paragraph suggests that some

---

8. *Ibid.,* 195–211; Felix Frankfurter, *The Commerce Clause under Marshall, Taney and Waite* (Chapel Hill: University of North Carolina Press, 1937), 14, 18, 25–27; David P. Currie, *The Constitution and the Supreme Court: The First Hundred Years, 1789–1888* (Chicago: University of Chicago Press, 1985), 173–176.

9. 9 Wheaton 1, at 200, 212–216, 221; Professor Currie points out that the licensing acts were not such an exercise of the commerce power as to justify Marshall's position and that indeed in *Willson v. Black Bird Creek Marsh Company* (1829) a party holding such a license failed to prevail against an assertion of the state's police power. *Constitution,* 171–172, 175.

10. *Ibid.,* 223, 227, 231–232, 238.

part of his motivation was derived from his 1822 correspondence with former president Jefferson, urging him to set forth his opinions at length so that his positions would be clearly established. In that opening paragraph Judge Johnson observed that "in questions of great importance and great delicacy, I feel my duty to the public best discharged by an effort to maintain my opinions in my own way."[11] Yet Johnson's disagreement on the merits of the case seems to be more semantic than substantive; he objected to Marshall's unwillingness to characterize the commerce power as being exclusive. Perhaps more to the point, while presiding in his circuit court for South Carolina, Judge Johnson had ruled that state's Negro Seaman's Act to be an unconstitutional infringement upon Congress's power over foreign commerce. For this he had been ridiculed and verbally attacked by his South Carolina neighbors, and his advocacy of nationalist views ultimately drove him to resettle in New York City shortly before his death in 1834.[12] His growing insistence upon filing separate concurrences and dissents irked his less assertive Supreme Court colleagues, but they certainly provided little comfort to states' rights Jeffersonians. Outlining the holding in *Gibbons* does not exhaust the value of the case, which is undoubtedly one of the most encyclopedic decisions rendered by Chief Justice Marshall in his thirty-four years on the bench. The Court's opinion literally bristles with dicta, most of which would reappear in constitutional discourse and be read into law in subsequent Supreme Court terms. There are rules for constitutional construction in this decision that possess validity to the present day. For example, the observation that the objects for which the commerce power was given should be evidence of the construction attached to the power.[13] Somewhat later the Chief Justice observed that exceptions to the commerce power are useful instruments to be applied in determining the scope of the power.[14]

Dealing with inspection laws, quarantine regulations, and other commercial rules, Marshall freely admitted that Congress might, in regulating interstate and foreign commerce, resort to methods used by the states in regulating their intrastate commerce. However, those measures would flow from distinct powers and hence not be identical.[15] Finally, the fact that Congress had in a number of cases adopted earlier state commercial regu-

---

11. *Ibid.*, 223.
12. The circuit court case was *Elkison v. Delisseline*, 8 Fed. Cas. (Cir. Ct., S.C., 1823) (No. 4,366) 493; see discussion in Herbert A. Johnson, "The Constitutional Thought of William Johnson," 89 *South Carolina Historical Magazine* 132, at 136–138 (1988).
13. 9 Wheaton 1, at 188–189.
14. *Ibid.*, 191.
15. *Ibid.*, 203–209.

lation as its own did not mean that the states were granted authority to intrude upon Congress's right to legislate on that subject.[16]

THE COMMERCE POWER
IN *BROWN* AND *WILLSON*

The Court was far from finished with commerce clause considerations when it decided *Gibbons*. Indeed, the very fact that the Court in *Gibbons* failed to adopt an exclusive interpretation of the commerce clause made renewed litigation inevitable. In something of a replay of *M'Culloch*, the state of Maryland once more invoked its taxing power in *Brown v. Maryland* to impose a tax upon an importer's sale of foreign goods consigned to him. This renewed assault upon federal supremacy also involved constitutional limitations upon state power to impede international and interstate commerce with local tax burdens. An express provision in the Constitution prohibited state customs duties upon foreign imports unless Congress permitted those taxes. Even in cases where permission was given, which was not true in *Brown*, the revenues generated were payable into the United States Treasury and not to the state involved.[17] However, federal dominance in international trade regulation did not answer all of the issues raised in *Brown*. Once cargo arrived in an American state, continued federal legislative authority depended upon either its continuance in foreign trade, or upon its entry into interstate commerce. When did foreign trade cease, when did interstate movement begin, and what authority did the state have to tax in the interim?

Writing for the Court majority, Chief Justice Marshall left no question that the decision in *M'Culloch* applied to *Brown*, wasting few words on the supremacy issue and even fewer on the question of federal government immunity from certain forms of state taxation. He first directed attention to the prohibition against state taxes upon imports and exports, asserting that a tax upon imports was not merely a tax on the act of importation but also extended to duties imposed after the imported articles entered the United States. The framers of the Constitution were aware of the economic disruption and diplomatic embarrassments that arose in the Confederation period because of state taxes upon imported goods. The fact that laws for inspection were excepted from the prohibition against state action also proved that post-entry taxation otherwise was included within the prohibition. On the other hand, there was a need to delineate when importation ceased and the state's power to tax began. That point was when the im-

---

16. *Ibid.*, 208–209.
17. 12 Wheaton 419 (1827); Article I, §10, al.2.

ported thing had "lost its distinctive character as an import" and "become incorporated and mixed up with the mass of property in the country." While goods remained the importer's property, held in his warehouse or shipped in the original form or package in which they were brought into the United States, they could not be subjected to state taxation. This gave rise to the original package doctrine applicable to foreign imports, and, by Marshall's dictum, also to domestic goods moving in interstate commerce.[18]

The state of Maryland also contended that the tax was imposed upon the sale of foreign goods, not their importation, and that in any event the tax was for a license issued to the importer and consequently was a tax regulating an occupation. Marshall brushed aside these distinctions, pointing out that whether the tax was upon importation or upon sale, it still increased the price of the article. He summarily rejected the occupational tax argument, observing that "it is impossible to conceal from ourselves that this is varying the form, without varying the substance. . . . a tax on the occupation of an importer is . . . a tax on importation."[19] Moving on to the commerce clause aspects of the case, Marshall relied upon *Gibbons* for doctrinal support that sale of imported goods was an integral part of the federal right to import. Congress had the power to authorize importation and thus also could empower the importer to sell. What foreign power negotiating commercial arrangements with the United States would think to the contrary?

Understandably, the one dissenting opinion came from Judge Smith Thompson, whose 1812 opinion concerning the steamboat monopoly, rendered in the New York Court of Errors and Impeachments, had been reversed by *Gibbons*.[20] Pointing to Marshall's *Gibbons* distinction between interstate and intrastate commerce, Thompson asserted that importation was complete as soon as the importer introduced the goods into the state with the intention of selling them there. The state tax fell upon importers and other wholesalers equally, and the Federal Constitution provided no protection for an importer against a valid tax imposed by the state in which he conducted business. The Maryland tax might increase the price of

---

18. 12 Wheaton 419, at 437–442, 448–449, quotation at 441–442. At the end of his opinion the Chief Justice commented, "We suppose the principles laid down in this case, to apply equally to importations from a sister state." *Ibid.*, 449.

19. *Ibid.*, 437–440, 444, quotation at 444.

20. See Gerald T. Dunne, "Smith Thompson," *Justices of the United States Supreme Court, 1789–1969*, Leon Friedman and Fred L. Israel, editors, 4 vols. (New York: Chelsea House, 1969), vol. 1, 477. Thompson had been appointed to the Supreme Court in 1823, but having missed the argument in *Gibbons* the following year, he did not participate in the decision of that case. *Ibid.*, 482–483.

goods indirectly, but it in no way impeded importation as the bank note tax in *M'Culloch* inhibited the operations of the federal government. Smith Thompson's strong states' right stance would become even more obvious when he became the determining vote in *Ogden v. Saunders* during the same 1827 term of the Supreme Court.[21]

Willson v. Black Bird Creek Marsh Company may well be the shortest constitutional opinion written by Chief Justice Marshall for the Court majority. It involved a brackish tidal creek in the state of Delaware that the appellee had dammed in accordance with an act of the state legislature. The appellant broke the dam to permit navigation of the creek by his vessel and asserted as a defense that the state statute was unconstitutional because it was repugnant to the commerce power conferred upon the United States Congress. Marshall rejected a challenge to the Supreme Court's jurisdiction that asserted that neither the Federal Constitution nor the statutes and treaties made under the Constitution were at issue in the state courts that convicted Willson, hence federal-question jurisdiction was absent. He then held that since Congress had not legislated concerning the creek, the commerce power was dormant. In such a case, state legislation was not in conflict with the unexercised power of Congress.[22]

The case seems to have been resolved by balancing the benefits to be obtained under the state legislation and how those benefits were offset by navigation rights to the creek. Damming the creek redounded to the advantage of riparian property owners, who then might drain water from the marsh. This resulted in improved health for the inhabitants. This initial weighing of advantages might easily have led the Chief Justice to uphold the dam construction. However, the determining factor would appear to have been the fact that Congress had not seen fit to legislate concerning the waters of Black Bird Creek. Given the size of the creek today and its probable size in Marshall's day, it is implausible that it would have attracted such national legislative attention.

Even though Marshall refrained from deciding the case by a balancing analysis, it is most likely that he considered that Delaware's police powers were exercised so beneficially that it would be unwise to invalidate the statute. But were private rights involved in his reluctance to uphold the dormant commerce power against such legislation? Presumably no such rights existed in individuals absent an act of Congress concerning either this creek in particular or navigable creeks in general. Between the state and federal governments, the state legislation was valid because there was no conflict with congressional action to regulate commerce.

---

21. 12 Wheaton 419, at 449–459; see discussion at chapter 3, 93–94.
22. *Willson v. Black Bird Creek Marsh Company*, 2 Peters 245–252 (1829).

As we have seen, the development of interstate commerce doctrine took place at a time when there were strong political and legal tendencies toward concurrency of federal and state power. Perhaps an earlier explication of the clause might have led to a more forthright nationalist position, but as matters stood at the end of Marshall's chief justiceship, it was unclear how far the states might legislate under their police powers without violating Congress's authority to legislate. In the other area where constitutional law touched economics—the exposition of vested rights and the scope of the contract clause—the parameters of decision were much more precise.

PROPERTY RIGHTS IN THE FEDERAL UNION

As the Court noted in discussing the commerce clause cases, the framers of the Constitution wished to create a Union in which there would be free trade between the states, and the federal government would control international trade and commercial relationships with the Indian tribes. This arrangement served both economic and political purposes. By trading within its borders, the United States could minimize its dependence upon European imports and thus escape its former colonial role as a supplier of cheap raw materials and a consumer of expensive manufactured products. Vestiges of the mercantilist system, tying sections of the United States to foreign trading partners, threatened to divide the Union into distinct spheres of European influence. As a major impetus to disunion and economic conflict, state mercantilism had to be eliminated from the American landscape.

Another goal of the framers found its roots deep in the political thought of Britain and the American colonies. This was the need to insure that the new governments, either state or federal, could not undermine the sanctity of private property. At the commencement of Marshall's chief justiceship, the electoral franchise in all of the states was contingent on ownership of real property or some significant amount of personal property. The prevalent political theory justified this requirement as a guarantee that voters had a financial stake in the political unit. Thus private property was a critical constitutional component of the eighteenth-century polity, and suitable safeguards had to be inserted in the Constitution to insure the security of private property itself.[23] A series of debtor protection laws in some states,

---

23. For colonial and early national views see James W. Ely, Jr., *The Guardian of Every Other Right: A Constitutional History of Property Rights* (New York: Oxford University Press, 1992), 10–58. William B. Scott, *In Pursuit of Happiness: American Conceptions of Property from the Seventeenth to the Twentieth Century* (Bloomington: Indiana University Press, 1977) gives a useful survey of American property views. Jennifer Nedelsky, in *Private Property and the Limits of American Constitutionalism: The Madisonian Framework and its Legacy* (Chicago: Uni-

particularly Rhode Island, graphically demonstrated the need for federally imposed guarantees of property rights.[24]

Equally important were the economic benefits of secure property rights throughout the Union. As a developing nation, the United States was heavily dependent upon foreign capital to finance a developing industrial system and fund construction of an adequate transportation system. Foreign investors justifiably demanded more security for their investments than was attainable in light of the irresponsible and confiscatory policies of some state legislatures. In terms of the American common market, or free trade area, interstate trade was jeopardized by local laws favoring state residents over the claims of nonresident merchants.[25] For these reasons the Federal Constitution enhanced property protection through its "obligation of contract" clause; at the federal level the Fifth Amendment provided due process protection and compensation for the federal government's taking of property by eminent domain.[26] Supplementing these provisions, there was a body of Supreme Court case law, beginning with *Calder v. Bull* (1798),[27] advocating the natural-law principle that vested property rights should not be disturbed by governmental action.

Vested Property Rights in the Marshall Court

Late in the Marshall era the Supreme Court, speaking through Judge Washington, denied that any federal remedy was available in the case of property rights divested by a state statute. In effect it linked federal protection of vested rights to the existence of a contract clause violation.[28] The

versity of Chicago Press, 1990), suggests that the emphasis upon property rights in American constitutionalism has obscured some variations among the Founding Fathers. Also of value is the work of Stuart Bruchey, which places Marshall in a Lockean political and economic pattern. "The Impact of Concern for the Security of Property Rights in the Legal System of the Early American Republic," 1980 *Wisconsin Law Review* 1135–1158. Marshall's economic and political views are discussed at chapter 1, 13–15.

24. Peter J. Coleman, *Debtors and Creditors in America: Insolvency, Imprisonment for Debt, and Bankruptcy, 1607–1900* (Madison: State Historical Society of Wisconsin, 1974), 6–22, 31–38, 86–101.

25. The years 1815–18 and 1832–39 were times of significant foreign borrowings by United States business interests, coinciding with acceleration of economic growth during 1823–39. A surge of immigration took place in 1816–18, and from 1828 to 1835 the aggregate foreign investment in the United States increased by about 50 percent. Douglas C. North, *The Economic Growth of the United States, 1790–1860* (New York: Norton, 1966), 82, 83, 86, 96, 189, 194.

26. Article I, § 10; Amendment V.

27. 3 Dallas 386; see discussion at William R. Casto, *The Supreme Court in the Early Republic: The Chief Justiceships of John Jay and Oliver Ellsworth* (Columbia, University of South Carolina Press, 1995), 227–234.

28. *Satterlee v. Matthewson*, 2 Peters 380, at 412 (1829).

case simply enunciated a rule that long represented the practice of the Supreme Court. In *Fletcher v. Peck* (1810) Chief Justice Marshall discussed the nature of vested property rights, stressing that the Georgia legislature was not immune "from those rules of property common to all the citizens of the United States, and from those principles of equity which are acknowledged in all our courts."[29] On the other hand, he based the Court's jurisdiction upon a contract clause violation, not upon the sanctity of vested property rights. The following year Marshall delivered the Court's opinion upholding the continued validity of a tax exemption granted by the New Jersey colonial legislature to the Delaware Indians. Again vested property rights were involved, but the contract clause served as the basis for Supreme Court jurisdiction.[30] In 1815 Judge Story dealt with glebe lands purportedly granted by the colonial authorities in Virginia and New Hampshire.[31] For the Court, he held that the state of Virginia could not by statute divest such a title since it succeeded to the Crown's interests and was bound by the contract clause. Mere change of government did not alter private rights earlier vested, and, Story further explained, "We think ourselves standing upon the principles of natural justice, upon the fundamental laws of every free government, upon the spirit and the letter of the constitution of the United States, and upon the decisions of the most respected judicial tribunals, in resisting such a doctrine."[32] Again the principle of vested rights received endorsement by the Court, but the authority to enforce property rights upon the states depended upon a contract obligation's being impaired by state action.

The Contract Clause

State debtor relief laws passed during the Confederation period are the background against which the framers included the obligation of contract clause in our Federal Constitution. Based upon what we know of the economic and commercial situation of the time, we can assume that the Philadelphia Convention's primary concern was undoubtedly about commercial transactions. On the other hand, as Professor Boyd has suggested, the contract clause meant different things to various individuals, and it was unclear whether public as well as private contracts were within its ambit. The fact

---

29. 6 Cranch 87, at 134.

30. *New Jersey v. Wilson*, 7 Cranch 164–167 (1812).

31. *Terrett v. Taylor*, 9 Cranch 43–55 (1815); *Town of Pawlet v. Clarke*, 9 Cranch 292–338 (1815). In the second case the grant was held invalid since there was no church body in existence at the time of the grant, which failed for lack of a grantee. 9 Cranch 292, at 330, 335.

32. *Terrett v. Taylor*, 9 Cranch 43, at 52.

that the contract clause was first introduced into the draft constitution after the Philadelphia Convention rejected federal legislative review of state statutes would indicate that the balance of federal-state power in the commercial arena was certainly a consideration. The Marshall Court was responsible for broadening the scope of the term "contract" in such a way that the obligation of contract clause became the major judicial instrument for protection of private-property rights against state seizure. Such a broad definition of contract was possible because the private-law concept was then in the process of formulation. Contract as we know it today did not mature in definition until the nineteenth century.[33]

The first opportunity for the Marshall Court to consider the contract clause arose in the famous case of *Fletcher v. Peck* (1810), which involved an effort by Georgia to rescind fraudulent land grants made by a corrupt state legislature. The action was brought in the Massachusetts federal circuit court on diversity grounds. Neither the defendant grantor nor the grantee testing title was party to the bribery. For the Court, Marshall readily found that absolute property rights in the vast and fertile Yazoo tract vested in the grantees by virtue of the legislative grant. The subsequently elected legislature's attempt to repeal the statutory grant was ineffective even though the traditional rule was that no legislative body could bind the actions of its successor. Rights vested under the fraudulently induced grant were protected by the contract clause of the Federal Constitution.[34]

In his concurring opinion, Judge Johnson objected to the Court's characterizing the legislative act as an executed contract. He claimed that unextinguished Indian titles cast a cloud over the title purportedly conveyed by

33. Stephen R. Boyd, "The Contract Clause and the Evolution of American Federalism, 1789–1815," 44 *William and Mary Quarterly*, 3d series, 529, at 530–533 (1987); on the commercial origins of the clause, see Barton H. Thompson, Jr., "The History of the Judicial Impairment 'Doctrine' and Its Lessons for the Contract Clause," 44 *Stanford Law Review* 1373, at 1380–1388 (1992); Nathan Isaacs provided a variety of explanations for his conclusion that Marshall drew upon eighteenth-century conceptions contract but claimed that one of Marshall's unique contributions was to apply the idea of contract to corporations. "John Marshall on Contracts, A Study in Early American Juristic Theory," 7 *Virginia Law Review* 413, at 425, 427 (1921). Currie's discussion of Marshall's expansion of the scope of the contract clause, at *Constitution*, 130–141, is well balanced and helpful.

34. 6 Cranch 87, at 132–137. For more extended discussion of the case see George L. Haskins and Herbert A. Johnson, *Foundations of Power: John Marshall, 1801–15*, vol. 2, *History of the Supreme Court of the United States*, 10 vols. to date (New York: Macmillan Publishing Company, 1981), 336–353, 579–581, 595–597; and C. Peter McGrath, *Yazoo: Law and Politics in the Early Republic, The Case of Fletcher v. Peck* (New York: Norton, 1967). Wallace Mendelson suggested that the exceptional protection of private property rights incorporated in *Fletcher* and *Dartmouth College* prevented the New York legislature from dissolving the Fulton-Livingston monopoly before the Supreme Court's decision in *Gibbons*. "New Light on Fletcher v. Peck and Gibbons v. Ogden," 58 *Yale Law Journal* 567–573 (1949).

the legislature. Finally, he implied that, except for his confidence in the integrity of counsel, he would be inclined to consider the case to be feigned—in today's terminology, collusive.[35]

The Marshall Court revisited the contract clause during its eventful 1819 term, handing down what may be the most important Supreme Court opinion concerning the clause and the nature of property rights in the United States. In *Dartmouth College v. Woodward* Chief Justice Marshall applied the contract clause to an attempt by the New Hampshire legislature to revoke Dartmouth's colonial charter. The case was argued in the 1818 term of the Supreme Court, with Daniel Webster and Joseph Hopkinson representing the college. John Holmes and the newly appointed attorney general of the United States, William Wirt, presented the case for the state. According to Senator Beveridge, Webster and Hopkinson overwhelmed their opponents in argument.[36] Immediately before concluding his oral argument, Webster is reported to have declaimed, "Sir, you may destroy this little Institution; it is weak; it is in your hands! I know it is one of the lesser lights in the literary horizon of our country. You may put it out. But if you do so, you must carry through your work! You must extinguish, one after another, all those great lights of science which, for more than a century, have thrown their radiance over our land! It is, Sir, as I have said, a small College. And yet, *there are those who love it.*"[37] At this point, as he professed his love for his alma mater, Webster's eyes filled with tears and he broke down. According to a witness, Chief Justice Marshall bent forward in his chair, and he too became teary. The other members of the Court sat with their attention fixed upon Webster, who recovered his composure and finished his argument shortly thereafter.[38]

Two decades before, Marshall had served as attorney for the board of visitors of the College of William and Mary, and thus he was familiar with the legal aspects of colonial college establishment and operations. How-

---

35. 6 Cranch 87, at 144–148. The comment is interesting in light of the future relationship between Johnson and Joseph Story, who was of counsel for the defendant in error, but Professor R. Kent Newmyer apparently found no reference to it while writing Story's biography. See *Story, passim.* Earlier works by Beveridge and Morgan differ on whether there was a political motive for Johnson's comment. See Donald G. Morgan, *Justice William Johnson, the First Dissenter: The Career and Constitutional Philosophy of a Jeffersonaian Judge* (Columbia: University of South Carolina Press, 1954), 213–214.

36. Albert J. Beveridge, *The Life of John Marshall,* 4 vols. (New York: Houghton Mifflin Company, 1916–19), vol. 4, 236–255.

37. *Ibid.,* 248–249.

38. *Ibid.,* 249–250. Professor G. Edward White casts some doubt upon this colorful story, especially Webster's expression of love for the college. *The Marshall Court and Cultural Change, 1815–35,* vols. 3 and 4, *History of the Supreme Court of the United States,* 10 vols. to date (New York: Macmillan Publishing Company, 1988), 615–618.

ever, that case, *Bracken v. College of William and Mary,* arrayed the trustees against the faculty over the power to dismiss faculty members and only indirectly touched upon William and Mary's charter rights.[39] While it is unlikely that these past professional activities made Marshall unduly receptive to Webster's argument, they may have alerted him to the dangers inherent in such a state seizure. After the 1818 oral argument it was generally believed that Judges Story and Washington supported the Chief Justice's position in favor of Dartmouth. Judges Gabriel Duvall and Thomas Todd reportedly would vote against the college, and Judges Livingston and Johnson were considered to be undecided. Webster returned home feeling that the case had been lost and awaiting the arrival of such an opinion. Instead the matter was held over until the 1819 term.[40]

Although William Pinkney was retained to reargue the case for the New Hampshire state interests in 1819, Marshall, at the first opportunity on the opening day of the term, announced that the Court had reached a decision and began to read his opinion for the Court.[41] In the intervening months, Judges Story and Washington had composed their own opinions. Although they concurred in Marshall's decision and followed most of his reasoning, Judge Story was reluctant to limit the operation of the contract clause to private corporations and transactions. Rather he noted that municipal and other public corporations might on grounds of public policy and equity be accorded protection by the contract clause. Judge William Johnson concurred silently in the Chief Justice's opinion, and Judge Livingston concurred, without opinion, with all three reasoned opinions. Because of illness, Judge Todd was absent from the 1819 term.[42]

Marshall's opinion began with a consideration of what types of activities fell within the protection of the Federal Constitution's contract clause. He accepted the argument that relationships between a government and its citizens might be within the term contract, although he was clear that the marriage contract was not within its scope. The contract clause applied to property interests only. Furthermore, if a state legislature conferred political power on a civil institution by an act of incorporation, the contract

---

39. *Bracken v. College of William and Mary,* 3 Call's Reports 573–599 (1790) is discussed at *The Papers of John Marshall,* Herbert A. Johnson, Charles T. Cullen, William C. Stinchcombe, Charles F. Hobson, et al., editors, 8 vols. to date (Chapel Hill: University of North Carolina Press, 1974–date), vol. 2, 67–72; the two cases are contrasted and compared in Florian Bartosic, "With John Marshall from William and Mary to Dartmouth College," 7 *William and Mary Law Review* 259–266 (1966).

40. Beveridge, *Marshall,* vol. 4, 255.

41. *Ibid.,* 259–260.

42. See discussion at White, *Marshall Court,* 618–628. During the months between terms the justices also took the opportunity to consult with leading jurists, including Chancellor James Kent, concerning the case. *Ibid.*

clause would not apply. However, the incorporation of a private eleemosynary institution (one sustained by donations from persons anticipating a given use of their gifts) did fall within contract clause protection.[43] Having traced the history of Dartmouth College, he concluded that its charter rights fell within the scope of the contract clause. Furthermore, the donors' interests were represented not by their heirs or estates but by the college trustees appointed under the charter. The Crown's obligations, on the other hand, devolved upon the state of New Hampshire since even a revolutionary change of government would not alter private common-law relationships. In addition to his close examination of the charter's terms, Marshall suggested that the gifts made by donors were predicated upon their belief that they would be immutably dedicated to the uses specified in the charter. This suggestion of an estoppel against state action confirmed his feeling that the revoking legislation was unconstitutional.[44]

One comment in Marshall's opinion deserves some attention for the light it sheds upon his views of the Union before and after the Constitution's ratification. In two widely separated sections he compared the power of the British Parliament to annul charter privileges, the authority of the states to do so under the Articles of Confederation, and finally the situation following adoption of the Federal Constitution. He agreed that Parliament could have changed such rights and the trustees would have had no recourse since the decision could not be reviewed. Among the states before the Constitution went into effect, the only limitation upon state authority was to be sought in the states' constitutions; otherwise legislative power could not be questioned. It was the ratification of the Constitution with its prohibition against states' impairing the obligation of contracts that provided federal recourse against such an action.[45]

However, whether considered by the British Parliament or an indepen-

---

43. 4 Wheaton 518, at 627–630. James Kainen suggests that corporate charters were the least vested form of property rights that were considered by the Marshall Court. "Nineteenth Century Interpretations of the Federal Contract Clause: The Transformation from Vested to Substantive Rights against the State," 31 *Buffalo Law Review* 381, at 463–467 (1982).

44. 4 Wheaton 518, at 642, 644, 647, 651. It has been suggested that Marshall's personal experiences and observation of Virginia legislative and judicial interference with corporate rights were formative influences in the *Dartmouth College* decision. Bruce A. Campbell, "John Marshall, the Virginia Political Economy, and the Dartmouth College Decision," 19 *American Journal of Legal History* 40–65 (1975).

45. 4 Wheaton 518, at 643, 651–652. Professor Currie questions the logic of this reasoning, pointing out that there was no consideration for the Crown's issuance of the Dartmouth charter. He argues that the distinction between *Fletcher*, in which rights arose under state government action, and *Dartmouth*, in which royal authority was involved, made the outcome in *Dartmouth* far from certain. *Constitution*, 143–145.

dent American state legislature under the Articles of Confederation, the contract nevertheless would have been deemed sacred. Revocation by legislative enactment would have been an "extraordinary and unprecedented act of power."[46] In terms of devolution of sovereignty from the British empire, Marshall clearly felt that all of the power, prerogatives, and obligations of the colonial governments devolved upon the American states except as they were circumscribed by subsequently adopted state constitutional provisions. Did the states delegate part of their power to the new government under the Constitution, or did the United States government's authority come from the people? Unfortunately, Marshall's *Dartmouth College* opinion fails to deal with this question. We must find his rejection of the compact theory in his more expansive treatment in *M'Culloch*, decided at the same term of Court. There he argued persuasively that the people of the United States, acting as a sovereign body, adopted the new Constitution by their separate constitutive action.[47] It would appear that the Chief Justice did not feel the need to fully explore the sovereignty implications of his comments in *Dartmouth College*. Why did he venture this dictum? Perhaps he felt the need to defend the charter contract on natural-law grounds rather than simply relying upon the contract clause. Thus he condemned legislative disregard of property rights, even in situations where existing constitutional law afforded no remedy against legislative excess. As early as 1819 Marshall felt that property rights, especially those based in contract, had both natural-law and constitutional underpinnings. In *Ogden v. Saunders* (1827) this view would become manifested in his only constitutional dissenting opinion.[48]

Judge Bushrod Washington's concurring opinion is relatively short by comparison with the submissions by Marshall and Story. Washington's opinion points to *Fletcher v. Peck* as controlling precedent for the principle that a state's land grant is a contract, subject to protection under the Federal Constitution. In like manner, a corporate charter is a contract, but the right of the legislature to alter the terms of the charter depends upon whether the corporation is a public institution or one of private functions. Closely following Marshall's argument in *Bracken* before the Virginia Court of Appeals, Judge Washington found that Dartmouth was a private corporation. Therefore any state alteration of the charter would breach the obligation of contract and violate the Federal Constitution.[49]

---

46. 4 Wheaton 518, at 651–652.

47. See discussion at chapter 5, 144.

48. 12 Wheaton 213 (1827), discussed at chapter 6, 211–213.

49. 4 Wheaton 518, at 654–666; compare Washington's analysis, *ibid.*, 659–663, with Marshall's argument in *Bracken, Marshall Papers*, vol. 2, 72–76, or 3 Call 573, at 579–580, 591–596 (1790).

As might be anticipated, Judge Story's lengthy and erudite opinion followed the general outlines of those rendered by Marshall and Washington. His citation to English authorities far exceeded Washington's effort, and Marshall's opinion is virtually devoid of citations.[50] The major contribution of Story's opinion was its effort to expand contract clause protection well beyond the public land grants and corporate charters. He was reluctant to agree that legislatures might alter the law of divorce or grant legislative divorces. After all, he observed, "a man has just as good a right to his wife as to the property acquired under the marriage contract." But leaving that matter unresolved, Story moved on to point out that various other rights should also receive constitutional protection. These included franchises for profit, such as rights to fish, to operate a ferry, to establish a market or fair or bank, to operate a toll road, or to build a bridge. He challenged Marshall's dictum that legislatures might alter the charters of municipal or other public corporations, pointing out that funds held by such corporations might also be kept in trust for certain private uses. By enumerating these additional forms of property within contract clause protection, Story pointed the way for an expansion of the federal judicial power far beyond that realized by his successors. Perhaps the most sweeping dictum of all was his observation that the terms in a grant by the Crown or state should be construed in favor of the grantee; any power not expressly reserved in the grant or charter could not thereafter be made to alter or amend the grant without the grantee's consent.[51] Ironically, this comment alerted states to include such reservations in their future issuance of corporate charters. Of course the strict construction of corporate charters in favor of grantees and against the state was specifically negatived in Chief Justice Taney's opinion for the Court in *Charles River Bridge v. Warren Bridge* (1837), from which Judge Story dissented.[52]

In passing, we should note that there is a wealth of contract-law analysis in Story's opinion. He was concerned with the impact of the concept of consideration, as then understood, upon Dartmouth's charter and ultimately held that a completed gift was irrevocable, even without consider-

---

50. Not content with the space devoted to his opinion in the case report, Story wrote an article on charitable bequests that Henry Wheaton published in the volume of his reports containing the *Dartmouth College* case. 4 Wheaton, appendix 1–23.

51. 4 Wheaton 518, at 697, 699–702; Story's comment about the state reserving powers by express terms in corporate charters occurs at *ibid.*, 675.

52. 11 Peters 420, at 547–549. Story's dissent, an impassioned legal and economic argument for stability of contractual commitments, which was joined by Judge Smith Thompson, is at *ibid.*, 583–650. However, it should be appreciated that the Marshall Court had also refused to read into the charter of a bank the presumption that the new corporation would be exempt from any future taxing legislation. *Providence Bank v. Billings,* 4 Peters 514, at 560–565 (1830).

ation. Upon acceptance of the grant or charter, the grantee implicitly promised to deal with property in accordance with the charitable objects of the charter or grant, and the Crown or state implicitly contracted with the donors that their money would be administered under the terms of the charter.[53]

The Insolvency-Bankruptcy Act Issue

In addition to its classic decisions in *M'Culloch* and *Dartmouth College*, the Court in its 1819 term began an extended consideration of state insolvency laws, their relationship to the contract clause, and the seemingly exclusive but dormant power of Congress to enact a uniform bankruptcy law. For a brief period early in Marshall's chief justiceship there was a uniform bankruptcy law; enacted in 1800, it was repealed in 1803 and generated only one Supreme Court case involving the federal government's right to priority as a claimant.[54] Thereafter neither the normal course of business failure nor the financial panic that climaxed in 1819 generated sufficient support for federal bankruptcy legislation.

There was a twofold need for a uniform federal law on the subject. First and foremost, it was important that one proceeding settle all creditors' claims throughout the United States. State procedures provided limited relief from debts beyond territorial borders and were usually in the nature of insolvency laws that released the debtor from prison without discharging the debt. Second, each state had discretion in the administration of its insolvency statute to encourage or discourage interstate trade and financial transactions. Bankruptcy and insolvency issues were at the confluence of the two constitutional rivers—the commerce clause and the contract clause. It is not surprising that the intersection of these vital constitutional and economic concerns caused eddies and turbulence within the Supreme Court's jurisprudence and ruptured any semblance of unanimity.

Sturges v. Crowninshield involved the constitutionality of an 1811 New York insolvency statute that, in addition to releasing a debtor from prison, relieved him from the responsibility for paying his debts.[55] Although insolvency laws providing for the collection of a debtor's assets by a trustee and proportional payment to creditors were part of the law of most American

---

53. 4 Wheaton 518, at 682–683, 688–690. It is interesting that the matter of privity of contract is not mentioned.

54. *United States v. Fisher*, 2 Cranch 358 (1804); see discussion at Haskins and Johnson, *Foundations*, 582–587; the history of the 1800 act is covered in Charles Jordan Tabb, "The Historical Evolution of the Bankruptcy Discharge," 65 *American Bankruptcy Law Journal* 325, at 344–349 (1991).

55. 4 Wheaton 422 (1819).

colonies, bankruptcy relief was not available before 1811. This situation persisted until the economic fluctuations caused by the embargo triggered New York's 1811 attempt to provide discharge relief to those in economic distress. The insolvency statute, pleaded in defense against a debt collection action, was the focal point of the *Sturges* case. For the first time, the Court considered, first, whether the Constitution's bankruptcy clause vested exclusive power in Congress and, if so, whether Congress's failure to enact a bankruptcy statute permitted states to legislate until Congress did so. Second, since the New York legislation purportedly discharged debtors from obligations incurred before its effective date, did it impair the obligation of contracts and thus violate the contract clause?

Apparently the first question so divided the Court that a resolution could not be reached on the exclusivity issue. As Judge Johnson observed in 1827, there had been a compromise rather than a decision.

> The court was . . . greatly divided in their views of the doctrine [of exclusivity], and the judgment partakes as much of a compromise, as of a legal adjudication. The minority thought it better to yield something than risk the whole. And although their course of reasoning led them to the general maintenance of the state power over the subject [of bankruptcy and insolvency] . . . yet, as denying the power to act upon anterior contracts, could do no harm, but, in fact, imposed a restriction conceived in the true spirit of the constitution, they were satisfied to acquiesce in it, provided the decision were so guarded as to secure the power over posterior contracts, as well from the positive terms of the adjudication, as from inferences deductible from the reasoning of the court.[56]

From the justices' alignment in *Ogden,* and based upon Johnson's unusual revelation of conference deliberation, we are justified in concluding that Judges Story, Duvall, and Washington supported the Chief Justice in his opinion that the federal bankruptcy power was exclusive and that state legislation providing bankruptcy relief would be unconstitutional whether or not Congress had acted. The minority, composed of Judges Johnson and Livingston, were committed to a concurrent interpretation of federal bankruptcy power.[57]

---

56. Quoted from *Ogden v. Saunders,* 12 Wheaton 213, at 272–273 (1827).

57. See discussion at Herbert A. Johnson, "Federal Union, Property, and the Contract Clause," in *John Marshall's Achievement: Law, Politics, and Constitutional Interpretation,* Thomas C. Shevory, editor (Westport: Greenwood Press, 1989) 33, at 40–41. It should be noted that Judge Thomas Todd, the seventh member of the Court, was absent throughout the 1819 term. The standard work on debtor relief is Peter J. Coleman, *Debtors and Creditors in America: Insolvency, Imprisonment for Debt, and Bankruptcy, 1607–1900* (Madison: State

Chief Justice Marshall began writing his "compromise" *Sturges* opinion with the observation that bankruptcy and insolvency laws were not easily separated into distinct categories. The enactment and subsequent repeal of the federal bankruptcy act of 1800 provided no evidence of future Congressional intention, nor did a dormant bankruptcy power in Congress preclude nonconflicting state bankruptcy legislation that did not violate the contract clause. Therefore it was unnecessary to decide whether the 1811 New York statute was a bankruptcy or insolvency statute since the applicable tests applied to either category of state legislation. On the other hand, the New York law discharged debts and thus impaired the contract obligation. In addition, immunizing the debtor's future property acquisitions from satisfaction of the debt also impaired the contract's obligation, contrary to the Federal Constitution.[58]

Marshall went on to distinguish between the contract obligation and the remedies states provided for the enforcement of that obligation. While the obligation was accorded constitutional protection, the remedy was a matter for state legislative action. State statutes providing remedies would be constitutional unless they impaired contractual obligations in existence prior to their enactment. For example, imposing a statute of limitations upon a contract executed when there was no limit upon its enforcement would violate the Federal Constitution's contract clause. Marshall concluded by expressly limiting the holding of the case to the specific factual pattern before the Court.[59]

At the 1819 term *M'Millan v. M'Neill* threw some additional light upon the question of bankruptcy and insolvency.[60] *M'Millan* involved a contract entered into at Charleston, South Carolina, by a debtor who subsequently moved to Louisiana, where he obtained a discharge from that state's courts. Around the same time he and his English partner obtained a dis-

---

Historical Society of Wisconsin, 1974); also useful are S. Lawrence Shaiman, "The History of Imprisonment for Debt and Insolvency Laws in Pennsylvania, as they Evolved from the Common Law," 5 *American Journal of Legal History* 205–225 (1960), and Kurt H. Nadelmann, "On the Origin of the Bankruptcy Clause," 1 *American Journal of Legal History* 215–228 (1957). Professor Currie points out that Judge Washington and possibly Judge Story had issued circuit court opinions based upon an exclusive view of the bankruptcy clause. *Constitution,* 148.

58. 4 Wheaton 122, at 193–198.

59. *Ibid.,* 200, 206–208. Professor Steven R. Boyd provides evidence that the obligation-remedy distinction was perhaps recognized when the Philadelphia Convention approved the contract clause in its present form. "The Contract Clause and the Evolution of American Federalism, 1789–1815," 44 *William and Mary Quarterly,* 3d series, 546 (1987); but Currie suggests that the right-remedy distinction runs contrary to Marshall's statements in *Marbury. Constitution,* 147, 153–154.

60. 4 Wheaton 209–213 (1819).

charge from an English bankruptcy court. These two discharges were pleaded in bar to M'Millan's collection action, but the United States District Court for Louisiana (exercising circuit court powers) refused to accept the discharges. Chief Justice Marshall wrote a short opinion for the Supreme Court affirming the decision below and stating that a discharge obtained in a jurisdiction foreign to the place of contracting was ineffective to bar actions on the debt.

Consideration of the bankruptcy-insolvency issue languished for eight years beclouded by the irksome *Sturges* compromise. American states provided what relief they could to those debtors caught in the 1819 panic and the instability that followed. Predictably, the questions raised but left unanswered in *Sturges* returned for argument before the Court in *Ogden v. Saunders* (1827).[61] *Ogden* involved bills of exchange drawn upon a New York City merchant by a resident of Kentucky. They were accepted in New York and after being negotiated to Saunders were dishonored and protested for nonpayment. The plaintiff, a Louisiana resident, sued in the United States District Court for Louisiana, and the defendant pleaded his New York discharge as a bar. As it had in *M'Millan,* the district court, sitting in its capacity as a circuit court, rejected the discharge as a defense, and the case came to the Supreme Court on writ of error.

Since Chief Justice Marshall was in the minority, he was not in the position to assign the case to a justice for writing and delivery. Presumably the choice fell to Judge Washington, the senior judge voting with the majority. However, all four judges voting with the majority wrote their own opinions. Contrary to the practice followed in the Jay-Ellsworth Courts, the separate opinions were delivered in order of seniority. Judge Washington (appointed in 1798) began with his opinion, followed by those of Judges Johnson (1804), Thompson (1823), and Trimble (1826). Traditionally the junior justice began the presentation of seriatim opinions.[62] Since several common themes run through all of these majority opinions, it is unclear why each judge elected to write a separate opinion. Possibly Judge Johnson, recalling his promise to the recently deceased Thomas Jefferson, insisted

61. 12 Wheaton 213 (1827). Robert L. Hale provides a thorough comparison of Marshall's views with those of his colleagues in "The Supreme Court and the Contract Clause," 57 *Harvard Law Review* 512, at 519–541 (1944).

62. In *Chisholm v. Georgia,* 2 Dallas 419 (1793), the opinions were delivered in reverse order of seniority: Iredell (1790), Blair (1789), Wilson (1789), Jay (Chief Justice); in *Ware v. Hylton,* 3 Dallas 199 (1796), the same order applied: Chase (1796), Paterson (1793), Iredell (1790), Wilson (1789), and Cushing (1789). The order continued in the Ellsworth Court; see *Bas v. Tingy,* 4 Dallas 37 (1800), with opinions by Moore (1799), Washington (1798), and Chase (1796). Of the judges sitting in *Ogden v. Saunders,* only Judge Washington had experience on these earlier courts.

upon doing so and persuaded his colleagues also to submit separate opinions.[63] For the dissent, consisting of Marshall himself, Judge Duvall, and Judge Story, Marshall wrote a unitary opinion.

The majority opinions contain three common points made by the four judges that led them to reverse the decision below and extend extraterritorial validity to the New York discharge:

(1) They made a distinction between a contract and the "obligation of contract" mentioned in the Federal Constitution. They held that while the parties might enter into a contract, the enforcement of its terms and the availability of remedies were the essence of its obligation, and these were provided by the municipal law.[64]

(2) They also agreed that the contract incorporated the law of the place of its making, and Judge Thompson went further to insist that the agreement of the parties could not alter the existing law of the state in which the contract was made.[65]

(3) Based in greater or lesser degree upon the *Sturges* precedent, they decided that the bankruptcy power was not exclusive but that the states had residual powers to legislate in the area even if Congress at some future date enacted a uniform law.[66]

In addition to these holdings, each of the four majority judges found it necessary to deal with the impact of natural law principles upon contract law. Judge Washington acknowledged that some contracts, especially those involving the several states and independent nations, were governed by the "universal law of all civilized nations." He insisted that municipal law controlled obligations other than those entered into in a deserted area of the world. Judge Johnson saw the rights and obligations of persons in society to be governed by a combination of moral law, universal (natural) law, and the laws of society (municipal law). Judge Thompson emphasized the origin of contract rights in the law of the place where the contract was executed and denied the relevance of natural law to the act of contracting. While Judge Trimble was willing to accept some natural-law elements in the formation of a contract, he pointed out that municipal law was the governing ingredient in determining contract rights. Otherwise the states

---

63. Morgan, *Johnson*, 168–170.

64. Washington, 12 Wheaton 213, at 259; Johnson, *ibid.*, at 283; Thompson, *ibid.*, at 297, 302; Trimble, *ibid.*, at 317.

65. Washington, *ibid.*, at 259; Johnson, *ibid.*, at 282; Thompson, *ibid.*, at 297–299; Trimble, *ibid.*, at 320–321.

66. Washington reluctantly accepted the majority view on this point, *ibid.*, at 263–264; Johnson, *ibid.*, at 274; Thompson, *ibid.*, at 310–312; Trimble, *ibid.*, at 314.

would have no control over contracts.[67] Together the majority laid down the rule that the law of the place of contracting determined the availability of remedies and also provided bankruptcy or insolvency procedures that under rules of comity would be valid throughout the United States.[68]

Marshall's opinion for the dissenting justices represents a significant change in his former approach to the contract clause. Indeed, it also suggests a sharp departure from his normal approach to decision making. Writing as well for Judges Story and Duvall, he denied that the New York insolvency statute was available as a bar to the Louisiana collection action. According to Marshall, a contract arises from the acts of the parties, and it originates in the natural right of individuals to agree upon their obligations. Thus contracts do not depend upon state (municipal) law for the creation of obligations. Absent express stipulations by the parties, municipal law principles would not be included in the agreement and should not be implied or in any way treated as conditioning the express contractual terms. The obligation of a contract depended entirely upon the will of the parties. On the other hand, the states could provide remedies for the enforcement of contract obligations, subject to restrictions imposed by the Federal Constitution's contract clause. Even if a contracting party found himself precluded from, or without, a state-supplied remedy, the obligation of the contract nevertheless subsisted. Should the breaching party be found within the jurisdiction of another state that afforded a remedy, the obligation might be enforced.[69]

Chief Justice Marshall rejected the majority's reliance upon *Sturges,* which in turn had been based upon the unconstitutional aspects of a retroactive insolvency statute. He assembled both logical argument and historical analysis to support his position that the Philadelphia Convention intended the contract clause to prohibit *both* retrospective and prospective state action that impaired the obligation of contracts. Given the circumstances prevalent in 1787, it was clear that the framers eschewed such a distinction.[70]

Marshall's dissenting opinion is notable for its extension of natural-law protection to contractual agreements. This adoption of what may be con-

---

67. Washington, *Ibid.,* at 258–259; Johnson, *ibid.,* at 282–284; Thompson, *ibid.,* at 297–300; Trimble, *ibid.,* at 318–320.

68. Washington, *Ibid.,* at 259–260; Johnson, *ibid.,* at 281. Smith Thompson went further and declared that the agreement of the parties could not negate the application of the law of the place of execution. *Ibid.,* 299–302. For Judge Trimble see *ibid.,* 320–321.

69. *Ibid.,* 345–356.

70. *Ibid.,* 356–357. The use of extratextual arguments in early constitutional adjudication is discussed at H. Jefferson Powell, "The Political Grammar of Early Constitutional Law," 71 *North Carolina Law Review* 949, at 964–971 (1993).

sidered an extremely theoretical view of contractual rights may well be what caused Judge Washington to vote with the majority, partially repudiating his position in *Sturges*. Unquestionably Judges Story and Duvall were receptive to natural-law arguments, although their views are better articulated in litigation dealing with the international slave trade and status of chattel slavery in natural law.[71] Unfortunately, we have no evidence to indicate what role, if any, Joseph Story played in the preparation of the dissenting opinion. In structure and content the opinion gives every evidence of the Chief Justice's authorship, but the expanded discussion of natural-law principles may well have been based upon suggestions made by Story.

With this dissent Marshall's expansion of the contract clause seems to have received a permanent check. The growing strength of the concept of concurrent powers succeeded in eroding the broad scope of the contract clause which had become a hallmark of Marshall's jurisprudence. As we have seen, the commerce clause was undergoing a similar metamorphosis with the 1827 decision of *Brown v. Maryland* and the acceptance of a balancing state police power in *Willson v. Blackbird Creek Marsh Company* (1829).

Interstate Compacts and the Contract Clause

Contract clause cases necessarily involved state actions that impaired the obligation of contracts, and in *Fletcher* and *Dartmouth College,* grants made by state legislatures that transferred property rights to private owners were held to be within the scope of the contract clause. However, it was not until *Green v. Biddle* (1823) that the Marshall Court applied contract clause protection to compacts entered into between two states.[72] Argued first at the 1821 term of the Supreme Court, the *Green* case arose on certified questions from the Circuit Court for Kentucky, the first of which involved the constitutionality of the Kentucky "occupying claimant law." These two statutes, enacted in 1797 and revised in 1812, provided relief to occupants of land who had made improvements thereon but were subsequently dispossessed by proof of a prior valid title. The Kentucky statutes relieved the occupier of the need to account for mesne profits and also provided substantial compensation for improvements made prior to the title's being challenged. These alterations in normal common-law rules were alleged to violate the 1789 Virginia-Kentucky compact authorizing the admission of

71. See R. Kent Newmyer, *Supreme Court Justice Joseph Story: Statesman of the Old Republic* (Chapel Hill: University of North Carolina Press, 1985), 347–350; see also White, *Marshall Court,* 674–682.

72. 8 Wheaton 1–108; the case is discussed at chapter 2, 78–79.

Kentucky into the Union. That compact stipulated that interests in land arising under Virginia law prior to the transfer of sovereignty would not be abridged by Kentucky.[73] The heirs of John Green, claimants under the Virginia prior title, were represented before the Supreme Court in 1821, and after argument of their attorneys, Judge Story delivered an opinion holding that the Kentucky statutes were repugnant to the contract clause of the Federal Constitution. However, since the opposing parties' interests were not presented to the Court, reargument was ordered upon the motion of Henry Clay.[74] The matter was reargued in the 1823 term before a five-member Supreme Court, with the Court's opinion being delivered by Judge Washington.[75] After a consideration of the common law, statutes, and equity rules of both Virginia and England, Washington held that no relief such as that contained in the Kentucky acts was available in either jurisdiction. Any deviation in the conditions attaching to the demanding party's title that diminished the demandant's rights, including changes in remedies, would impair the obligation of the contract between the two states. Judge Washington brushed aside the fact that the United States Congress had not approved the Kentucky-Virginia compact, finding that by admitting Kentucky to the Union, it had taken under consideration and approved the terms of the 1789 compact.[76] He also dismissed objections to the Supreme Court's jurisdiction, pointing out that such matters could not be left to the discretion of the two states involved and that "a state has no more power to impair an obligation into which she herself has entered, than she can the contracts of individuals."[77] The Supreme Court's jurisdiction was also questioned since an issue of Kentucky constitutional law was involved as well, a contention Washington rejected with the bold assertion that "our opinion is founded exclusively upon the constitution of the United States." This ignored the facts that the Kentucky-Virginia compact formed a part of the constitutional law of Kentucky and that such a question was distinct from the impact of the federal contract clause upon the obligations incurred by the two states under the compact.

Judge William Johnson dissented on the ground that such a construc-

---

73. The two acts are summarized in Judge Story's 1821 opinion, at *ibid.*, 13–15.

74. *Ibid.*, 18.

75. The five justices present were the Chief Justice and Judges Washington, Johnson, Duvall, and Story. Since Marshall had been involved in Kentucky land grants and patenting, he probably disqualified himself. Judge Todd, who had not participated in the 1821 decision, although he was sitting in that term, was absent in 1823 because of illness, as was Judge Livingston. Judge Story dissented. See Minutes of the Supreme Court of the United States, vol. C, 191–192, 380–381, Microcopy No. M215, National Archives, Washington, D.C.

76. *Ibid.*, 81, 84, 86–87.

77. *Ibid.*, 92.

tion of the Kentucky-Virginia compact restricted the right of a sovereign state to exercise jurisdiction over its own territory. He referred to the peculiar nature of land titles while the territory was under Virginia jurisdiction. They were "floating over" the future state of Kentucky. "Land they were not, and yet all the attributes of real estate were extended to them."[78] Johnson admitted that he was "groping [his] . . . way through a labyrinth" in outlining his objections, but it is readily apparent in his dissent that he objected to the limits the Court's opinion placed upon the legislative authority of Kentucky. He felt that the compact provisions concerning land titles were at best precatory and certainly not operative to restrict future state legislation concerning Virginia land grants.[79]

Judge Washington's majority opinion has much to commend it. It recognized the need for the Supreme Court to enforce agreements entered into between the several states. This was a matter of securing federal tranquility, and even before the Constitution, it had been recognized that conflicting land grants issued by different states were a matter of federal concern. That concern was evident in the Supreme Court's having original jurisdiction of controversies between states of the Union. In *Green* neither state was a party, but federal adjudication was available through the United States circuit court proceeding in keeping with the spirit of Article III. *Green* may thus be seen as a logical increment in federal court jurisdiction.

On the other hand, the contract clause was perhaps stretched to its logical limit in applying it to an agreement between two states. At the level of state admission to the Union, and the requisite agreements between the petitioning territory and the state acquiescing in the petition, it would seem that the law of nations, or at least the principles of natural law, should be the determining factor. The political heat generated by *Green v. Biddle* was undoubtedly more attributable to its implications for state sovereignty than for its contract clause holding, but perceptive advocates of states' rights cannot have missed the threat inherent in such an expanded contract clause.

---

78. *Ibid.*, 100.
79. See *ibid.*, 101–107, quotation at 101.

VII

FINE-TUNING THE FEDERAL COMMON MARKET

PRIVATE LAW IN THE SUPREME COURT

The Supreme Court's preeminent responsibilities in areas of public law tend to obscure the fact that it is both the highest court in a self-contained system of federal law and a regulator of those areas of state private law that raise federal questions. During John Marshall's chief justiceship, Supreme Court private law activity fluctuated in subject matter but remained steady in its need to fashion federal law to advance national requirements and to accommodate special situations in the federal territories. Growing commercial activity in the District of Columbia, which then included the ports of Alexandria and Georgetown, generated a veritable torrent of commercial-law litigation, particularly in regard to negotiable instruments. Over this and other federal territories the Supreme Court exercised the authority of a state supreme court. During the Marshall era, new federal territories were carved out of the geographical areas of the Louisiana Purchase (1803) and the Florida cession (1819). As a consequence, the Court's appellate docket not only grew in size but expanded in subject matter because of an increasing number of cases tried within the territorial court systems. These territorial cases supplemented the well-established flow of appellate business from federal circuit courts and the independent federal district courts. Admiralty and maritime cases formed a consistently high proportion of all United States court business. Even Chief Justice Marshall, who often found himself overwhelmed by complicated admiralty cases, played a reluctant role in the development of maritime law. The circuit courts sitting in New England, New York, Philadelphia, and Charleston supplied Supreme Court judges on circuit with large admiralty dockets. The expertise Judges Story and Johnson gained on circuit marked them as major contributors of admiralty and maritime opinions. Judge Bushrod Washington, circuit justice for the Pennsylvania circuit, also made major contributions to this field. In the second half of Marshall's chief justiceship, Judges

Brockholst Livingston and Smith Thompson, who successively presided over burgeoning admiralty litigation in New York City, were regularly recruited as authors of Supreme Court admiralty opinions.

The law of marine insurance was closely related to admiralty and illegal trade litigation, and a considerable amount of Supreme Court time was devoted to this subject. Although marine insurance fell outside the modern jurisdiction of English admiralty courts and hence was outside federal admiralty jurisdiction, the very nature of underwriting practices stamped marine insurance with an interstate character. Rarely was the same state the place in which a marine insurance contract was made as well as the place where it was performed, and in most instances a multitude of American states and foreign nations were involved. As a consequence, diversity jurisdiction, predicated upon differing citizenship of the parties, served as the foundation for federal court prominence in development of this lucrative and litigious branch of insurance law.

The rapid commercial development of the United States was accelerated by its emergence as the leading neutral oceanic carrier during the Napoleonic Wars. Both foreign and interstate trade generated litigation within the federal court system, providing additional opportunities for the judges of the Court to develop rules of private law. As Britain and France struggled for control of Atlantic trade routes, American merchantmen were subjected to seizure by both belligerents, and President Jefferson resorted to trade restrictions that inflicted some economic pressure upon the warring nations. Those restrictions, incorporated in the Non-Importation Act of 1806 and a series of embargo statutes (1807–9), gave the Supreme Court and federal circuit courts a unique opportunity to evolve rules of admiralty and criminal law. In terms of economic development, these restrictions on oceanic trade altered American investment patterns. Thereafter industrial capitalism became more attractive than the risks of transatlantic mercantile activity. Although most of the development of corporate law was left within state judicial control, the Marshall Court subsequently found it necessary to deal with the nature of corporations and their status in federal courts.

ILLEGAL TRADE

Thirty-two per cent of the cases heard by the Marshall Court from 1801 to 1815 dealt with illegal trade or prize cases. To a degree this represented a continuum from the colonial period of American history, when illegal trade in violation of the British navigation laws was something of a national pastime.[1] On the other hand, the peculiar international situation from

---

1. See George L. Haskins and Herbert A. Johnson, *Foundations of Power: John Marshall,*

1798 to 1815 generated a constant flow of federal legislation involving illegal trade and increased federal prosecution for violation of trade laws. Prior to Marshall's appointment as chief justice, three nonintercourse acts enacted during the Quasi-War with France prohibited American trade to the French Republic and its overseas territories and colonies. After the third act became effective on February 27, 1800, the prohibition also included trade from France and her possessions. These Quasi-War cases established the principle that American citizenship or nationality was to be the basis for trade regulation. *Little v. Barreme* (1804) established the rule that Congressional enactments may limit presidential discretion in dealing with emergency situations.[2] In this, Marshall anticipated Judge Tom Clark's concurring opinion in the *Youngstown Sheet and Tube Company* case.[3]

After a short respite, the Napoleonic Wars resumed with renewed depredations upon American commerce. President Jefferson was determined to uphold the commercial rights of neutral nations; as a means of exerting economic coercion upon the belligerents and limiting the possibility of conflict on the high seas, he adopted new schemes of trade restriction. The Non-Importation Act of 1806 was quickly replaced by the more sweeping controls over oceanic commerce later to be denominated by the embargo. This embargo was established by a series of federal statutes passed between December 1807 and January 1809. Each amendment and supplement to the enforcement provisions tightened loopholes in earlier statutes; usually it fell to the federal courts to play a role in pointing out these defects. The embargo sharply restricted American imports of British goods, but despite earnest state and federal enforcement efforts, the goal of altering the diplomatic situation through economic sanctions was not achieved.[4] However, the cases appealed to the Supreme Court, and some decided by the justices on circuit, made important contributions to federal law.

1801–15, vol. 2, *History of the Supreme Court of the United States*, 10 vols. to date (New York: Macmillan Publishing Company, 1981), 407; except where otherwise indicated, materials in this section have been extracted from that source, 407–437.

2. 2 Cranch 170–179.

3. 343 U.S. 579, at 660–662 (1951). Judge Robert Jackson's concurring opinion, which does not cite *Little v. Barreme*, sets forth a tripartite classification concerning emergency presidential powers that draws heavily upon the same analysis made by Marshall. *Ibid.*, 635–638.

4. A good discussion of the embargo and its impact is found in Walter W. Jennings, *The American Embargo, 1807–1809* (Iowa City: University of Iowa, 1931). The Jeffersonian effort to implement the embargo drew upon the combined authority of federal and state governments and was one of the most extensive law enforcement activities of the antebellum period. See Louis M. Sears, *Jefferson and the Embargo* (Durham: Duke University Press, 1927); and Leonard D. White, *The Jeffersonians: A Study in Administrative History* (New York: Free Press, 1951).

In *The Active v. United States* the Supreme Court held that a mere intention to violate the embargo laws was not actionable; only an attempt to clear port illegally subjected a vessel and its cargo to forfeiture. Similarly, otherwise innocent activity would not give rise to liability unless the government could establish a connection to some other action prohibited by law.[5] Although these rules appear to favor defendants, the Court also insisted upon convincing evidence when defendants claimed exceptions to the embargo laws. Claims of being driven to a foreign port by necessity or bad weather or being carried there as a prize were considered excuses and viewed with skepticism. The Supreme Court established high standards of proof to be met in claiming these exceptional circumstances. In addition, once a vessel cleared an American port in violation of the law, it remained subject to seizure even upon its return voyage.[6]

Although the embargo was a highly controversial measure in American political life, the Supreme Court and the justices on circuit were even-handed in their administration of the law. It is notable that it was Jefferson's appointee Judge William Johnson who held that the president might not control a subordinate's exercise of discretion vested in the junior official by the Congressional statute. This holding in *Gilchrist v. Collector of Charleston* (1808)[7] weakened centralized control of the embargo mechanism and caused the administration to attack Johnson in the public press. However, given the fact that the New England states were staunchly opposed to trade restrictions, it is even more remarkable that Federalist-appointed District Judge John Davis upheld the constitutionality of the embargo in his Massachusetts court.[8]

Closely related to the illegal trade cases was the series of federal prosecutions of American captains and vessels for accepting letters of marque and reprisal from South American republics. These bogus commissions permitted them to prey upon Spanish commercial shipping. The federal courts played a major role in policing this piratical activity, which will be discussed at greater length in chapter 8.

The revolt of colonies in the Spanish empire placed the United States in the position of controlling the mercantile activities of its oceanic shippers that violated Spain's laws against unauthorized trade with South

---

5. *The Active v. United States,* 9 Cranch 55; *The Schooner Paulina's Cargo v. United States,* 7 Cranch 52.

6. *United States v. Hall & Worth,* 6 Cranch 171 (1810), and *The Brig James Wells v. United States,* 7 Cranch 22 (1812); *The Brig Short Staple and Cargo v. United States,* 9 Cranch 55 (1815); *United States v. The Brig Eliza,* 7 Cranch 113 (1812).

7. 10 Fed. Cas. (C. C. D. S. C. 1808) (No. 5,420) 202; see discussion at chapter 2, 67.

8. *United States v. The William,* 28 Fed. Cas. (C. C. D. Mass. 1808) (No. 16,700) 47; see discussion at chapter 2, 67–68.

America. The 1831 case of *Sheppard v. Taylor* provides a good overview of the enforcement difficulties, and it also illustrates the Supreme Court's use of admiralty law principles to advance the diplomatic neutrality embraced by the executive department of government.[9] The ship *Warren*, armed with twenty-two guns and entered for a voyage to Canton, China, left Baltimore in 1806. While she was at sea, a second set of owners' instructions was opened, and thereafter she sailed for the western coast of South America with a destination on the coast of Chile. Officers and crew protested the change in instructions, and eventually the original captain of the vessel became deranged and committed suicide. The first mate succeeded to command and, following the direction of the owner's agent (a supercargo named Pollock), hovered about the entrance to the harbor at Talcahuana, Chile. After some negotiations between the Spanish authorities and Pollock, the *Warren* entered the harbor only to have her officers and crew removed and imprisoned for illegal trade. Under condemnation by an admiralty court, the vessel and cargo were sold, and the owners petitioned the king of Spain for a restoration of the proceeds. Their petition was granted in 1815, but no payment was made even after the ratification of the Treaty of Washington (1819), which guaranteed payment of debts owed by the Spanish government to American citizens.[10]

The commissioners under the 1819 Spanish treaty awarded the *Warren* sale proceeds to a trustee on April 24, 1824, and the seamen filed a claim for their back wages by a libel in the United States District Court for Maryland. The district court decree dismissing the libel was affirmed pro forma in the circuit court, and an appeal was taken to the Supreme Court. Judge Joseph Story wrote the Court's opinion in litigation he characterized as "this protracted suit; in its duration almost unparalleled in the annals of the admiralty,"[11] pointing out that the seamen were victims of an illicit voyage in which they participated involuntarily and for which they did not contract when shipping on board the *Warren*. Since the owners were insolvent, it was necessary to determine whether the seamen had a lien against the proceeds from the vessel and cargo. Story held that since they originally had a right to libel the ship and cargo, they might also file a claim against the proceeds of the sale. The seamen also had a claim against the freight payable to the owners since there was at admiralty an intimate relationship between freight payable for the voyage and the wages of seamen.[12] The

---

9. 5 Peters 675 (1831).

10. The facts and the order of restitution are at *ibid.*, 676–686.

11. *Ibid.*, 681–686; the Story comment is at *ibid.*, 709.

12. *Ibid.*, 710–712. Story held that the Spanish restitution order did not render the voyage legal for purposes of deciding the seamen's claim, and he also upheld admiralty jurisdiction in contract actions based upon seamen's wage claims. *Ibid.*, 710, 712–713.

Sheppard case represents an exception to the general rule that American seamen who participated in illegal trade were not entitled to recover their wages in a United States admiralty court.[13]

After January 1, 1808, the United States embarked on an ambitious program to stop the transatlantic slave trade into the American states. Pursuant to the Federal Constitution, Congress enacted a comprehensive law that provided a graded list of sanctions against captains and others who participated in the slave trade or assisted those who carried on the trade. The act applied to American citizens, and seizures might be made upon the high seas if American citizens or residents were involved. A system of duplicate manifests was instituted to insure that coastal transportation of slaves and individuals held to indentured servitude would not be utilized as cover for conduct of the international slave trade.[14] The statute was amended in 1818 to utilize longer prison terms as sanctions to supplement fines earlier stipulated. Section 8 shifted the burden of proof to defendants, requiring them to prove by way of defense that the slave had arrived in the United States five years prior to commencement of the prosecution, thus placing the case beyond the statute of limitations applicable under the 1818 enactment.[15] In 1819 Congress abandoned the *qui tam* system adopted in the 1807 statute and instead authorized division of forfeited ships and goods among the officers and crews of United States Navy ships making the seizures. In addition, the naval officers and crews were to receive a bounty of $25 for each slave seized for importation in violation of the statute.[16] The following year legislation was passed penalizing as a pirate any American citizen found engaging in the slave trade. The penalty for piracy was death, and it also applied to the crew of any American-owned vessel, regardless of citizenship.[17]

Besides the *La Josefa Segunda* and *The Antelope,* discussed in chapter 8, three additional cases evidence the Marshall Court's role in suppressing illegal commerce in slaves. In *The Emily and the Caroline* (1824), two vessels were seized in the port of Charleston, South Carolina, upon the claim that they were being fitted for the slave trade. Judge Smith Thompson, for the

---

13. *The St. Jago de Cuba,* 9 Wheaton 409.

14. An Act to prohibit the importation of slaves into any port or place within the jurisdiction of the United States. . . , March 2, 1807, 2 Stat. 426–430, enacted in accordance with Constitution, Art. I, § 9, clause 1.

15. An Act in addition to "An act to prohibit the introduction (importation) of slaves. . . ," April 20, 1818, 3 Stat. 450–453, especially §§ 3, 4, 8, and 9.

16. An Act in addition to the acts prohibiting the slave trade, March 3, 1819, 3 Stat. 532–534. A *qui tam* action is one in which the informer is awarded half of the forfeited property or fine and the other half belongs to the government.

17. An Act to continue in force "An Act to protect the commerce of the United States. . . ," May 15, 1820, 3 Stat. 600–601.

Court, upheld forfeiture. He found it unnecessary that the prohibited equipage be finished or that the ships be stopped in the course of leaving port for the offense to be complete. The testimony of the ship's carpenter that the fitting was being accomplished so that the vessel could be used in the slave trade was sufficient to prove the offense.[18] *The Merino, The Constitution and The Louisa* involved vessels carrying slaves from Havana to Pensacola, the latter port being under temporary American military occupation in 1818. The Court, in an opinion by Judge Washington, held that while American vessels engaged in the slave trade might be condemned by any United States district court to which they were carried, nevertheless Congress did not intend to interfere with transportation of slaves within a foreign nation.[19]

The appeal concerning *The St. Jago de Cuba* (1819)[20] involved both the wages of seamen and the claims of materialmen asserted against a ship forfeited for breach of the 1818 slave trade statute. Originally of United States registry, the ship was directed to Cuba, where, after sale, she departed upon a slaving voyage to Africa. At the time *The St. Jago de Cuba* was seized off the coast of Africa, she was fitted out for the slave trade. The seamen's wage claims were dismissed, with Judge Johnson, for the Court, pointing out that no one could have boarded the vessel without gaining perfect knowledge of her character and destination. He stated that "the general policy of the law is, to discountenance every contribution, even of the minutest kind, to this traffic in our ports; and the act of engaging seamen is an unequivocal preparatory measure for such an enterprise." The materialmen's claims, on the other hand, were determined by the maritime rules concerning contracts and loan security. They were dismissed upon Johnson's finding that when the funds were advanced, the vessel was already under arrest in the admiralty court and the creditors could have ascertained that she was alleged to be a United States-registered ship.

The Marshall Court's skepticism in dealing with slave trade cases mirrors a similar approach to that taken in other illegal trade cases under the non-intercourse and embargo acts. The justices were alert to fraudulent practices of carrying duplicate sets of papers and sailing instructions. Suspicious behavior had to be explained by the clearest and most convincing proof, and burdens of proof were assigned to those advancing claims that were either unusual or unlikely. When American national interests were involved and diplomatic complications threatened, the Court was careful to follow the lead of the political branches of government. In the interest of

---

18. 9 Wheaton 381–390.
19. 9 Wheaton 391–408.
20. 9 Wheaton 409.

diplomatic harmony, technical violations of trade regulations were over-looked in appropriate cases. However, in the Supreme Court and on the circuits, the justices were aware of the prevalence of illegal commerce and stood ready to employ federal judicial power for its suppression.

ADMIRALTY INSTANCE CASES

Article III of the Federal Constitution confers jurisdiction in admiralty and maritime cases upon the judiciary of the United States. However, prior to the ratification of the Constitution, state admiralty courts had been active in the post-Revolutionary era, and this raised some question about the continued exercise of some maritime jurisdiction in state tribunals.[21] In the salvage case of *Peisch v. Ware* (1808) the parties had submitted the case to arbitrators as required by a 1786 Delaware statute. The award and the arbitrators' computation of salvage award was affirmed by the United States circuit court. On appeal, the Supreme Court, by Chief Justice Marshall, held that the state arbitration award was valid and binding upon the parties. Although Marshall declined to say whether the award was valid because of the consent of the parties or by virtue of the Delaware statute, the Supreme Court divided upon the issue. Two justices felt the award to be binding because of the parties' submission to arbitration. Two other Supreme Court justices accepted the award computation because it was entered after careful consideration of evidence, and it had been accepted by the lower federal courts. Three dissenting justices voted to disregard the arbitral award and were willing to consider the salvage amount de novo. Although the Court divided in its opinion, the majority of four justices accepted the Delaware arbitral procedure as a valid exercise of state fact-finding authority. Thus a residuum of maritime authority could be said to remain with the states despite the vesting of admiralty jurisdiction in federal courts.[22]

In the sixteenth and seventeenth centuries the jurisdictional boundaries of English admiralty courts had been a matter of great concern, primarily because of the civil-law procedures that eliminated the need for jury trial. Judges Story and Johnson perpetuated aspects of this ancient confrontation in the Marshall Court, with Story pressing to expand admiralty and maritime jurisdiction as far as possible. The Chief Justice and most mem-

---

21. Art. III, § 2, Federal Constitution; proceedings of the New York State Court of Admiralty are printed in Charles M. Hough, *Reports of Cases in the Vice Admiralty of the Province of New York and in the Court of Admiralty of the State of New York, 1715–1788* (New Haven: Yale University Press, 1925).

22. 4 Cranch 347, at 348, 366; see discussion at Haskins and Johnson, *Foundations*, 478–480.

bers of the Court seem to have favored a narrowing of admiralty's jurisdiction. In *United States v. Bevans* Marshall wrote the Court's opinion, reversing a murder conviction in federal courts. The crime took place in Boston Harbor, and Marshall held that the federal circuit court lacked jurisdiction under the Constitution's admiralty provisions since the crime did not occur on the high seas.[23]

The Story-Johnson disagreement over civil jurisdiction in admiralty also touched upon jurisdiction of contract matters. In *The General Smith* (1819) Judge Story in the Court's opinion applied English admiralty precedents concerning maritime liens and their inapplicability to materialmen who supplied vessels in their home port. However, in passing he acknowledged a "general jurisdiction" of admiralty courts in such contractual matters, as William Pinkney had argued on behalf of a ship chandler. Pinkney had asserted that admiralty courts might exercise both in personam and in rem jurisdiction in such cases. Since the *General Smith* case was resolved by the fact that no lien had been established, there was no need to examine the availability of in personam jurisdiction. Subsequently, in *Ramsay v. Allegre* (1827) the libelant who asked for in rem enforcement of a maritime lien was shown to have accepted a negotiable promissory note in satisfaction of the debt. On this basis Chief Justice Marshall affirmed the circuit court's dismissal of the admiralty libel. In a lengthy concurring opinion, Judge Johnson struck out against any in personam contract jurisdiction in American admiralty courts. He expressed the belief that it was "high time to check this silent and stealing progress of the admiralty in acquiring jurisdiction to which it has no pretensions. Unfounded doctrines ought at once to be met and put down; and dicta, as well as decisions, that cannot bear examination, ought not to be evaded and permitted to remain on the books."[24] Pointing to English legal history, Johnson proved that no in personam jurisdiction in contract matters remained to English admiralty courts, with the single exception of actions for seamen's wages. However, despite distinguished authority he cited for this point, "loose obiter dicta" had "cast some doubt upon these doctrines in modern times." Among those federal courts misled by these comments was the District Court for Maryland, which, in its decision in *Stevens v. The Sandwich,* produced a "tissue of errors" because of its reliance upon Continental rather than English precedents. Johnson concluded: "I am fortifying a weak point in the wall

---

23. *United States v. Bevans,* 3 Wheaton 336, at 387–391. In *The Steamboat Thomas Jefferson* the Supreme Court held that admiralty jurisdiction did not apply to vessels navigating the Missouri River. 10 Wheaton 429, opinion by Judge Story.

24. *The General Smith,* 4 Wheaton 438, at 443–444; *Ramsay v. Allegre,* 12 Wheaton 611, at 613–643, with quotation at 614. The dictum in *The General Smith* discussing jurisdiction was adopted by the Supreme Court in *Peyroux v. Howard,* 7 Peters 324, at 341 (1833).

of the constitution. Every advance of the admiralty is a victory over the common law; a conquest gained upon the trial by jury. . . . Congress has indeed given a power to issue prohibitions to a district court, when transcending the limits of the admiralty jurisdiction. But who is to issue a prohibition to us, if we should ever be affected with a partiality for that jurisdiction?"[25] What Judge Johnson did not note in his *Ramsay* concurring opinion was the impact of an expanded admiralty jurisdiction upon the federal system. The federal courts already had an extensive maritime jurisdiction, and further extension would erode the business of state courts. Joseph Story's commitment to a broad civil jurisdiction of federal admiralty courts was part and parcel of his desire to establish uniform rules in maritime and commercial law.[26] In Johnson's eyes, regularization of commercial and maritime precedents was not worth sacrificing jury trial on one hand and preeminence of common-law courts on the other.

Maritime Liens

Prize and illegal trade cases familiarized the Marshall Court with maritime liens, which for the most part were exotic areas of the law for common-law practitioners and judges. To facilitate completion of a voyage, masters of vessels were authorized to pledge the ship as security for loans, repairs, and materials provided while away from the ship's home port. The liens so created attached in reverse order of priority; the last lien was superior to all earlier liens, contrary to common-law rules concerning real-property mortgages and other security instruments. In addition, a bottomry bond executed after a vessel became forfeited under the sanctions of prize or illegal-trade law was also superior to the United States' interest through forfeiture. Unlike mortgages or other liens at common law, the bottomry bond did not attach to the vessel until it was declared by an admiralty court.[27] In an early Marshall Court decision, Judge Samuel Chase held that

---

25. *Ramsay v. Allegre*, 12 Wheaton 619–620, 625–627, 638–640, with quotation at 640. James Winchester was the district judge whose decision in *Stevens v. The Sandwich*, 23 Fed. Cas. (No. 13,409) 29–31 (1801), drew the sharpest attack from Johnson. Henry Wheaton, retiring as reporter for the Supreme Court, took pains in a footnote to exonerate William Pinkney from Johnson's inference that he had misled the Court in *The General Smith* and *Ramsay v. Allegre*. *Ibid.*, 640–643. However, in the case of a maritime trespass where the district court established jurisdiction but the vessel was absent, the court might order the action to proceed in personam with attachment against goods of the defendant. *Manro v. Almeida*, 10 Wheaton 473 (1823), majority opinion by Judge Johnson.
26. On Story see Newmyer, *Story*, 123–125; Morgan, *Johnson*, 80–82.
27. Grant Gilmore and Charles L. Black, Jr., *The Law of Admiralty*, 2d ed. (Mineola, N. Y.: Foundation Press, 1975), 587–589; on the lien's not attaching until declaration by an admiralty court see *Blaine v. The Charles Carter*, 4 Cranch 332 (1808).

maritime liens pertaining to a vessel upon account of one voyage were voided by her departure from home port on a subsequent voyage before the liens were foreclosed. In addition, Chase stated the rule that a bottomry bond would not be effective in the ship's home port because there the owner could execute a mortgage on the vessel or otherwise obtain an extension of credit.[28]

In delivering the Court's opinion in *The St. Jago de Cuba* (1824), Judge William Johnson set forth the above rules concerning bottomry bonds. Normally an earlier forfeiture would not take precedence over sums advanced to a captain for necessary equipment and repairs away from the vessel's home port. However, here the sums were advanced while the vessel was in her home port, and hence a lien by way of bottomry would not arise. Although the *St. Jago de Cuba*'s American registry was unknown to them, they were aware that the ship was under arrest by the admiralty court. Examination of the filed libel would have revealed that she was being proceeded against as an American vessel and should have alerted them to her home port.[29]

The Supreme Court's elucidation of bottomry bond law is best illustrated by the 1834 opinion of Judge Story in *The Virgin v. Vyfhuis*.[30] After the ship left Baltimore on a voyage to Amsterdam, her owner transferred a third of the ownership to one Frederick Graf, who held title to some of the cargo on board. The ship met with bad weather and needed repairs upon reaching Amsterdam, but the consignees of the cargo, having heard that the original owner had become insolvent, refused to advance funds to the captain. After a few days of negotiation, the captain obtained funds upon security of a bottomry bond to one Vyfhuis. The necessary repairs completed, he sailed the ship in ballast to Baltimore. The circuit court held the bottomry bond to be voided because it was for a larger amount than the repairs and because, among other things, returning in ballast was a deviation from the captain's instructions. On appeal, the Supreme Court rejected these arguments, asserting that there was no fraud or collusion in the execution of the bottomry bond and that the captain was justified in deviating because of the insolvency of the owner and lack of instructions from him. Finally the Court rejected the defense that more funding than required for repairs had been obtained through execution of the bond. For the Court, Judge Story left no doubt that the vessel was subject to a maritime lien because of the bottomry bond, "for it is notorious that in foreign countries supplies and advances for repairs and necessary expendi-

---

28. *Blaine v. The Charles Carter*, 432; see discussion at Haskins and Johnson, *Foundations*, 491–492.
29. 9 Wheaton 409, at 416–417.
30. 8 Peters 538 (1834).

tures of the ship constitute, by the general maritime law, a valid lien on the ship; a lien which might be enforced in rem . . . even if the bottomry bond were . . . void in toto."[31] To set aside a bottomry bond in the circumstances of the case would be to undermine the commercial community's confidence in bottomry bonds as security instruments.

Local state law created a maritime lien when a vessel was repaired in or near water that responded to the tides. General maritime law applied to ships needing repairs away from their home port, but local rules protected laborers and materialmen who contracted for services and repairs to domestic vessels. Absent any evidence that the contractors were willing to waive a lien, the ship would be subject to the charges made for repairs.[32] This broad spectrum of maritime liens available to ship captains needing to repair or refit their vessels insured that the financial needs of vessels and cargo in distress would be met promptly and with adequate security.

Another security device, the respondentia contract secured by a bond, was available to provide a lender with security in the cargo rather than the hull of the vessel. The nature of respondentia bonds was considered by the Marshall Court in regard to the United States government's priority in collecting obligations from judgment debtors. Writing for the Supreme Court in *Conard v. Atlantic Insurance Co. of New York* (1828), Judge Story held that goods subject to a respondentia contract could be assigned in state insolvency proceedings. If the loan transaction was bona fide, the United States government could not claim priority to the goods covered by the respondentia. The case also broadly construed the purpose of respondentia transactions. The proceeds of the loan might be used to pay a preceding obligation, and there was no requirement that the funds be utilized in support of the voyage involved in the loan arrangement. In outlining the continuing ownership interests of a shipper who executed a respondentia bond and then endorsed a bill of lading to the consignee, the Court once more emphasized the flexibility and security of such commercial loan arrangements. Had the United States government been permitted to assert priorities to the pledged cargo, this negotiability would have been sorely compromised.[33]

Salvage Cases

The first appellate case reported from Marshall's Supreme Court was that of *Talbot v. Seemen,* which involved a New York admiralty proceeding for military salvage. This was perhaps an omen of the Court's future preoc-

---

31. *Ibid.,* 550.

32. *Peyroux v. Howard,* 7 Peters 324 (1833), citing *The General Smith,* 4 Wheaton 438 (1819).

33. *Conard v. Atlantic Insurance Co. of New York,* 1 Peters 386 (1828), at 434–437, 439–440, 444–446, 449–450.

cupation with admiralty and maritime matters under the Virginian's presidency. Salvage represented a reward made to those ships and crews that extended assistance to vessels, crews, or cargo at risk of perishing at sea. The international rule set civil salvage at one-third the value of the vessel or cargo saved, but it might be adjusted according to the ease or difficulty of the salvager's exertions or the dangers inherent in the rescue. The U.S. Supreme Court took the position that American salvage awards should be subject to the rule of reciprocity. This limited a civil salvage award to what would have been made if the salvaged ship had been libeled in the home port of the vessel that rescued it. Military salvage was established by statute and was limited to situations in which ships taken as prize were recaptured before condemnation in the belligerent captor's prize courts.[34] Salvage gave rise to a maritime lien subject to recognition by an admiralty court having in rem jurisdiction of the vessel or cargo.

Since the first fifteen years of Marshall's chief justiceship were dominated by naval warfare against France and England, with intermittent periods of peace marked by illegal trade and the Haitian rebellion, most salvage cases fell into the military salvage category. *Talbot v. Seeman* (1801), one of Marshall's first cases, involved the recapture of a Hamburg-based merchant vessel by a French privateer during the Quasi-War with France (1798–1800). Since Prussia was neutral at the time, there should have been no danger of the *Amelia*'s being condemned in a French admiralty court. However, the French had altered the rules of neutral commerce, and condemnation was likely. Could the Supreme Court take notice of the French change in international law and award salvage to the officers and crew of the *U.S.S. Constitution,* who had recaptured the *Amelia?* For the Court, Marshall held that it was appropriate to take notice of such changes in international law, and when this new rule was applied, the *Amelia* was in jeopardy and military salvage was payable. When the French decree was repealed and the international law rules concerning neutrals were reinstated, salvage was denied in a similar situation.[35]

During the War of 1812 an American vessel carrying United States and French cargo was captured by a British warship, and then recaptured by an American privateer. Both Britain and France applied prize rules that worked a forfeiture of the vessel and cargo twenty-four hours after capture. Hence salvage was payable, but the parties differed on the amount as well as on the jurisdiction of the district court. Judge Story held that the statu-

---

34. See discussion at Haskins and Johnson, *Foundations,* 473–475, and see generally Gilmore and Black, *Law of Admiralty,* 532–585. The rule of reciprocity was applied in *Mason v. The Blaireau,* 2 Cranch 264 (1804).

35. 1 Cranch 1 (1801); salvage was denied in *Murray v. The Charming Betsey,* 2 Cranch 64 (1804).

tory limit of military salvage to one-sixth of the value of the goods was applicable in this case; the salvage of the vessel, which was armed at the time of recapture, was properly set at one-half its value in accordance with an 1800 statute regulating military salvage awards.[36] Dealing with the libelant's objection that a salvage claim had to be specially pleaded and was not cognizable in a prize case, Story indicated that liberal amendment of pleadings was customary in admiralty and that military salvage was an inherent part of prize jurisdiction.[37]

After the War of 1812, the focus of salvage litigation shifted to civil salvage. For the most part, the Supreme Court deferred to the discretion of the district and circuit courts of the United States, both of which exercised original and general jurisdiction in matters of civil salvage. In the exercise of appellate jurisdiction, the circuit courts exercising review functions and the Supreme Court were limited by the value of the subject matter in litigation. When conducting appellate review, the Supreme Court presumed the validity of the trial court's assessment of salvage. Should the goods saved be the property of several owners, each owner was responsible for paying that portion of the salvage award that was proportional to his property's value.[38]

Unquestionably the best known civil salvage case is that of *American and Ocean Insurance Company v. 356 Bales of Cotton (Canter, Claimant)* (1828). This litigation involved a salvage award made by a court consisting of a notary and five jurors, assembled in accordance with an act of the governor and legislative council of the newly acquired territory of Florida. The owner challenged the jurisdiction of the court, claiming that since the Federal Constitution vested all admiralty and maritime jurisdiction in the federal courts, the notary's court was unconstitutional and its decree null and void. For the Supreme Court, Chief Justice Marshall rejected this contention, pointing out that within the territory, the authority to make law was vested in Congress since that body had the constitutional power to make rules for the territories. The legislative action of the territorial government, under delegated authority from Congress, was adequate to constitute the notary's court and to give it jurisdiction in salvage matters.[39]

MARINE INSURANCE

The underwriting of insurance on vessels and cargoes formed an essential part of the commercial practice of spreading the risks of voyages upon the high seas, particularly in time of war or when trade restrictions limited

---

36. *The Adeline and Cargo,* 9 Cranch 244 (1815).

37. *Ibid.,* 284–285.

38. *The Sybil,* 4 Wheaton 98 (1819), opinion by Chief Justice Marshall; *Stratton v. Jarvis & Brown,* 8 Peters 4, at 11 (1828), opinion by Judge Story.

39. *The American and Ocean Insurance Company v. 356 Bales of Cotton (Carter, Claimant),* 1 Peters 511, at 545–546 (1828). The case is more fully discussed at chapter 8, 233–234.

the scope and profitability of maritime commerce. A substantial amount of American wealth was invested in the shipping industry, and thus the Supreme Court's adjudications concerning marine insurance were significant events for a large and influential portion of the populace.

Like many other fields in which the law touched upon commerce, the preparation and judicial construction of marine insurance policies was heavily influenced by mercantile practice. The policies stipulated the property to be insured—usually a vessel, the cargo, or both—and the extent and limits of the voyage covered by the policy. The time period encompassed by the policy depended upon custom as well as the intention of the parties. In the case of hull insurance, which covered the vessel, coverage lapsed at the termination of the voyage, assuming all of the other conditions of the policy had been met. A policy insuring cargo terminated at the time stipulated or at a time that appeared to be the intent of the parties. Underwriters distinguished between insurance on the vessel *for* the voyage and coverage of the vessel *and* the voyage, the latter phrase including profits that could have been made through successful completion of the trip. As the Marshall Court developed the American law of marine insurance, it drew heavily upon English precedents to define these terms and to reduce commercial practice to reliable legal precedents.[40]

Underwriters also employed exceptions to limit their liability if the insured failed to conduct the voyage in the manner stipulated in the policy or if some illegal behavior resulted in loss that the underwriter had not agreed to cover. Deviation from the route of the voyage was permissible only in cases of necessity, and failure to sail at the time stated also made possible the voiding of the policy. Excessive delays in port and unnecessarily prolonging the voyage were also the subject of exceptions. Finally, changing the cargo might alter the nature of the voyage to the extent that insurance coverage was denied. The ship *John,* cruising the African coast, was insured to carry "stock, such as hogs, goats and poultry." Her captain took on a group of jackasses, and the Supreme Court, in an opinion by Judge Johnson, agreed with the insurer that jackasses were not included within the term "stock." Johnson viewed the general term "stock" as being limited in the contract by the fact that hogs, goats, and poultry were smaller animals used for food.[41]

---

40. See Haskins and Johnson, *Foundations,* 454–457, 461–463, citing, among other cases, *Maryland Insurance Co. v. Woods,* 6 Cranch 45 (1810); *Head and Amory v. Providence Insurance Co.,* 7 Cranch 331 (1812); *Gracie v. Marine Insurance Co. of Baltimore,* 8 Cranch 75 (1814); and *Alexander v. Baltimore Marine Insurance Co.,* 4 Cranch 370 (1808). It was also possible to insure freight; see the discussion of *King v. Delaware Insurance Co.,* 6 Cranch 71 (1810), at Haskins and Johnson, *Foundations,* 462–463.

41. *Maryland Insurance Co. v. LeRoy,* 7 Cranch 26, at 31 (1812); see discussion at Haskins and Johnson, *Foundations,* 457–461.

The existence of war between France and Britain during the early years of the Marshall Court meant that marine insurance companies were anxious to limit their liability for any breaches of neutrality committed by their assureds. These involved both the carriage of goods owned by merchants of a belligerent nation and actions of a nonneutral character, such as attempting to break the blockade of a belligerent port. Policies usually carried warranties by the insured that they would not engage in such activities, and the coverage was canceled by breach of the warranty.[42]

The 1794 Jay Treaty provided some relief for American merchant vessels that were generally at risk of being seized and condemned for unneutral behavior, thus voiding their insurance coverage. One provision permitted the American merchantman to approach a blockaded port and be exempt from seizure by a British blockading squadron unless he attempted to enter the port after having been "warned off."[43] Marine insurance contracts written subsequent to the Jay Treaty frequently contained a provision that neutrality was to be construed by proofs made only to a United States court. Because the belligerents frequently altered their rules concerning blockade and their definition of unneutral conduct, American shippers might inadvertently violate a trade prohibition and be condemned by a foreign prize court. The provision for proof only in the United States permitted continued insurance after a foreign court declared the vessel or goods forfeit for unneutral actions.[44]

COMMERCIAL LAW: BILLS AND NOTES

Since the Federal Constitution originated in the need to encourage interstate commercial ties, it is not surprising that the federal courts were involved in the development of American negotiable instruments law. However, it was a matter of circumstances rather than the Philadelphia Convention's intention that John Marshall's Court was so closely involved with development of law in this area. When it was decided that the federal capital would straddle the banks of the Potomac and that the western half of the District of Columbia would continue to follow Virginia law, a complicated situation faced the Supreme Court of the United States. The Commonwealth of Virginia, through its Revolutionary War Reception Act, adopted only those English statutes that predated the settlement at James-

---

42. See discussion at Haskins and Johnson, *Foundations,* 465–469, citing *Church v. Hubbart,* 2 Cranch 187 (1804) and Henry Wheaton, *A Digest of the Law of Marine Captures and Prizes* (New York: R. M'Dermut & D. D. Arden, 1815), 190–209.

43. See Haskins and Johnson, *Foundations,* 456–457, 467, discussing *Croudson v. Leonard,* 4 Cranch 434 (1808).

44. Haskins and Johnson, *Foundations,* 467–468.

town in 1607. This legislation precluded the applicability of the English Promissory Note Act of 1704 to the newly independent state. Subsequently this result was ratified by the revisal of Virginia law completed in 1792. The revised compilation of statutory law failed to list the 1704 English act among those statutes applicable in Virginia. As a consequence, promissory notes, one of the most common forms of credit in early America, were not assignable by endorsement in Virginia. However, those instruments were transferable in Maryland and thus also negotiable in the Maryland side of the District of Columbia. Congress's failure to rectify this matter until 1812 placed the courts of the District of Columbia, and the Supreme Court as its highest tribunal, in the position of administering equitable relief to those holders of promissory notes disadvantaged by the disparity of rules applicable to the counties of Washington and Alexandria.[45]

Although the Marshall Court continued to apply Virginia law to Alexandria County, it held that recourse to equity was not contrary to Virginia law in these circumstances. In addition, it implied a contract between parties to a promissory note, guaranteeing the assignee of the note that the assignor would be liable for any loss the assignee might suffer through accepting the note. However, such a guarantee was not itself assignable to a subsequent assignee since it was based upon privity of contract between the original parties.[46] To broaden this limited ground for relief, the Chief Justice and his colleagues established a doctrine that subsequent assignees of a promissory note relied upon the credit of the assignor and that banking institutions might be held to rely upon commercial custom rather than the limitations of Virginia law in their receipt or transfer of promissory notes.[47]

Additionally, the Supreme Court utilized conflicts of law rules to provide relief to holders of Alexandria promissory notes. In *Slacum v. Pomeroy* it recognized the accepted principle that a promissory note is governed as to the original parties by the law of the place it was executed, and the legal implication of endorsement was determined by the place of endorsement. In a subsequent Marshall opinion for the Court, the fact that the note involved was negotiable at a Washington County bank was adopted as a foundation for attributing negotiability to the instrument. Since the original parties anticipated that the bank might extend credit in reliance upon negotiability, they were precluded from pleading defenses derived from the underlying transaction.[48]

---

45. For a detailed discussion see *ibid.*, 560–566.
46. *Riddle & Co. v. Mandeville & Jameson*, 5 Cranch 322 (1809); *Mandeville & Jameson v. Riddle & Co.*, 1 Cranch 290 (1803); *Violett v. Patton*, 5 Cranch 142 (1809).
47. *Yeaton v. Bank of Alexandria*, 5 Cranch 49 (1809); *Riddle & Co. v. Mandeville & Jameson; Lawrason v. Mason*, 3 Cranch 492 (1806).
48. 6 Cranch 221 (1810); *Mandeville v. Union Bank of Georgetown*, 9 Cranch 9 (1815).

Recognizing the commercial dangers inherent in the District of Columbia situation, the Supreme Court utilized its place as the highest tribunal of the District to rectify the maladjustment. Fortunately, Congress made Maryland negotiable-instruments law applicable to the county of Alexandria in 1812, ending the Court's self-appointed duties in this area.[49] However, both the Supreme Court and its justices, while riding circuit, were to continue their work with negotiable instruments in the years beyond 1812. Given the commercial activity within the District of Columbia, that jurisdiction continued to supply a substantial portion of the cases in this field decided by the Supreme Court.[50]

However, the 1812 congressional act concerning commercial paper in the District of Columbia did not terminate the Supreme Court's activity in the field. In regard to promissory notes, the Virginia rule of non-negotiability continued to generate commercial difficulty. Even at the end of Marshall's chief justiceship, the holder of a Virginia or Kentucky promissory note was still required to expend extraordinary efforts to collect from the maker. Only after the maker had been rendered insolvent through successive property executions on a judgment might the note holder sue the maker. In Maryland, on the contrary, the holder of a note did not have to issue executions after obtaining judgment against the maker, and simple notice of nonpayment or nonacceptance triggered the endorser's liability.[51]

A number of cases before the Supreme Court involved the holder's demand upon the maker or the notice that was required to charge an endorser with an obligation to pay. Primary was the requirement that the holder exercise due diligence in presenting the note to the maker as well as in giving notice of nonpayment or nonacceptance to the endorser. Presentment to the maker for payment might be made at the residence or the place of business of the maker, or, if the maker had moved away from the state, the demand might be left at his last place of residence.[52] However, in

---

49. 2 Stat. 755–756 (1812).

50. See the allocation of Supreme Court and circuit court cases decided by the justices in table 1, 88–89 and Appendices A and B, 265–291.

51. *Clark v. Young*, 1 Cranch 181 (1803), opinion by Marshall; *Bank of the United States v. Weisiger*, 2 Peters 331 (1829), opinion by Johnson; *Bank of the United States v. Tyler*, 4 Peters 366 (1830), opinion by Baldwin. In Virginia and presumably also in Kentucky, privity of contract limited the ability of a holder to sue anyone in the chain of endorsement other than the maker or his immediate endorser. *Harris v. Johnston*, 3 Cranch 31 (1806), opinion by Marshall. For a discussion of the distinction between assignability and negotiability see Joseph Story, *Commentaries on the Law of Bills and Exchange, Foreign and Inland. . . .* (Boston: Charles C. Little and James Brown, 1843), 18–20.

52. On diligence see *McDonald v. Magruder*, 3 Peters 470 (1830), opinion by Marshall, and *Magruder v. Union Bank of Georgetown*, 3 Peters 87 (1830), opinion by Marshall. Circum-

a situation in which a bank was the holder of a note made payable at the bank and the maker of the note had insufficient funds in his account to pay the amount due, the bank did not have to demand payment from the maker.[53]

After nonpayment or nonacceptance, the note holder could effectively notify the endorser by mailing a notice to the post office where the endorser normally received his mail. The notice might be left at the home of the endorser's neighbor, but leaving a notice in a retail store near the maker's former residence was inadequate. The actual receipt of notice would cure any defects in serving notice.[54] Statements by the endorser might be construed as waivers of notice or as undertakings to pay if the maker defaulted; these would eliminate the need for notice, and, in the case of a waiver of notice, the endorser was precluded from denying the waiver if the holder had relied upon it to his detriment.[55] No particular form of notice was required, but any wording adequate to inform the endorser of the note's dishonor was effective to charge him with liability.[56] In *French's Executor v. Bank of Columbia* (1807), Chief Justice Marshall indicated that "strict notice" would be required in situations where the endorsement was made for the accommodation of the maker and the endorser had not received payment for his endorsement. However, in all promissory note cases, the payment demand and notice rules applicable to bills of exchange would be applied to promissory note cases.[57]

Although most negotiable instruments cases dealt with promissory notes, Marshall's Court also had occasion to consider bills of exchange. These instruments had long been considered negotiable by the law merchant and were generally so accepted throughout the American colonies and states. Unlike the promissory note, which was a promise to pay at a given place and date, the bill of exchange was an order to pay the holder

---

stances constituting an adequate demand upon the maker are discussed in *M'Gruder v. Bank of Washington*, 9 Wheaton 598 (1824), opinion by Johnson; *Bank of United States v. Smith*, 11 Wheaton 171 (1826), opinion by Thompson; *Bank of Columbia v. Lawrence*, 1 Peters 578 (1828), opinion by Thompson.

53. *Bank of the United States v. Smith*, 11 Wheaton 171 (1826), opinion by Thompson.

54. Mailing, *Bank of the United States v. Carneal*, 2 Peters 543 (1829), opinion by Story; at neighbor's home, *Williams v. Bank of the United States*, 2 Peters 96 (1829), opinion by Washington; leaving at store inadequate, *Bank of United States v. Corcoran*, 2 Peters 121 (1829), opinion by Washington.

55. *Union Bank v. Hyde*, 6 Wheaton 572 (1821), opinion by Johnson; *Union Bank of Georgetown v. Magruder*, 7 Peters 287 (1833), opinion by Story; *Thornton v. Wynn*, 12 Wheaton 183 (1827), opinion by Washington.

56. *Mills v. Bank of the United States*, 11 Wheaton 431 (1826), opinion by Story.

57. 4 Cranch 141, at 160–161 (1807). On the other hand, a formal notarial protest was not required in the case of a promissory note. *Nicholls v. Webb*, 8 Wheaton 326 (1823), opinion by Story.

from the funds held by the drawee for the account of the drawer. The bill of exchange was a "substitute for the transfer of money by sea or land."[58]

Normally, external evidence was not admissible to alter the terms expressed upon the face of the bill of exchange. Assignment of a bill was no evidence that secured goods were also assigned as a consequence of the bill's issue. A promise to accept the bill— that is, to agree to pay when the bill came due—normally had to be reflected upon the bill itself. However, if third parties relied upon a letter written after the bill's issuance and promising to accept the bill, the letter might be evidence of such an acceptance or at least of an agreement to accept. Such a letter was required to clearly identify the bill of exchange that was intended.[59]

The extent to which the Marshall Court dealt with negotiable instruments illustrates the role that federal courts were destined to play in this field of law. Although the federal courts applied the laws of the various states, the cases reflect a genuine effort on the part of the Supreme Court to foster uniformity in the substantive law and to apply equitable solutions whenever possible. Conflicts rules were announced, making it easier to predict the jurisdiction whose law would govern. For example, in *Young v. Bryan* the Court decided that each endorsement constituted a separate contract for purposes of determining diversity of citizenship. Presumably it also became subject to the substantive law of the place of endorsement.[60] Subsequently Judge Story dealt with the problem of a promissory note executed in Kentucky that had been endorsed in Virginia. By Virginia law the instrument fell within the bar of the statute of limitations, and that law applied to the case. Story observed, "The general principle . . . is that the nature, validity and interpretation of contracts are to be governed by the law of the country where the contracts are made, or are to be performed. But the remedies are to be governed by the laws of the country where the suit is brought."[61] He acknowledged that an instrument might be negotiable in one state and not in another but asserted that remedies should depend upon the law of the state in which the case was heard.[62]

In deciding negotiable instruments cases the Marshall Court was careful to follow state law when it existed, but it frequently found that English cases, readily available in printed form, were the best evidence of commercial practice and mercantile law. Gradually American state cases and the

---

58. Judge Johnson, in *Parsons v. Armor,* 3 Peters 413 at 428 (1830).

59. *Coolidge v. Payson,* 2 Wheaton 66 (1817), opinion by Marshall; *Schimmelpennich v. Bayard,* 1 Peters 264 (1828), opinion by Marshall; *Townsley v. Sumrall,* 2 Peters 170 (1829), opinion by Story; *Boyce & Henry v. Edwards,* 4 Peters 111 (1830), opinion by Thompson.

60. *Young v. Bryan,* 6 Wheaton 146 (1821); *Kirkman v. Hamilton,* 6 Peters 20 (1832).

61. *Bank of the United States v. Donnally,* 8 Peters 361, at 372 (1834).

62. *Ibid.*

Supreme Court's own precedents began to replace English cases as sources for decisions in commercial law cases.

COMMERCIAL LAW: BANKRUPTCY AND STATE INSOLVENCY LAWS

During most of Marshall's chief justiceship there was no federal bankruptcy law, but a variety of state insolvency provisions kept the Court involved in this area of litigation.[63] The 1800 Bankruptcy Act remained on the statute books for three years and eight months and generated one major Supreme Court case.[64] This case, *United States v. Fisher* (1804), involved the federal government's right to a priority in the assets of a bankrupt under the act. For the Court, Chief Justice Marshall held that debts owed to the United States by all categories of debtors were entitled to a priority. He based his decision upon a reading of Section 62 of the Bankruptcy Act and its relationship to other statutes giving preference to the federal government. Congress was entitled to use such a preference for the efficient operation of its revenue- collection functions, and similar policies made the statutory priorities applicable to other business transactions of the United States. While it might be asserted that the legislative grant of a priority was not "indispensably necessary," this was not required by the necessary and proper clause of the Constitution. "Congress must possess the choice of means, and must be empowered to use any means which are in fact conducive to the exercise of a power granted by the constitution," Marshall asserted. That was true even if the preference interfered with the rights of state sovereigns in arranging the dignity of debts for collection.[65] In many ways this case anticipated the Chief Justice's more elaborate approach to federal supremacy and the necessary and proper clause in *M'Culloch v. Maryland* (1819).

---

63. Bankruptcy was a commercial law procedure by which a merchant who found that his debts exceeded his assets might obtain the protection of the courts and, upon pro rata payment to his creditors, be released from all claims and judgments against him. Insolvency in the colonial sense of the term was the surrender of any individual's assets to trustees. The property was held in trust for creditors, and the debtor was released from debtor's prison; however, all of the judgments and other obligations remained intact. There is a valuable general discussion of debt collection sanctions in Peter J. Coleman, *Debtors and Creditors in America: Insolvency, Imprisonment for Debt, and Bankruptcy, 1607–1900* (Madison: State Historical Society of Wisconsin, 1974), 247–293.

64. A minor construction of the uniform Bankruptcy Act occurred in *Wood v. Owings and Smith,* 2 Cranch 239 (1804), opinion by Marshall, in which the Court held that a deed signed, sealed, and delivered before the effective date of the Bankruptcy Act was not governed by its provisions.

65. 2 Cranch 358, at 385–397 (1804); the quotation is at 396. The statute is An Act to establish a Uniform System of Bankruptcy throughout the United States, April 4, 1800, 2 Stat. 19–36; Section 62 is located at 36.

Judge Washington dissented, finding in other portions of the Bankruptcy Act no legislative intention to include all debts to the United States. Rather he felt that the government's priority should be limited to debts owed by revenue officers or other officials. Since the *Fisher* case involved a negotiable bill of exchange, he was reluctant to uphold the government preference to the disadvantage of others in the chain of endorsement. No holder could be certain that some endorsement by an individual who did not appear on the face of the bill to be a government official might not by his act entitle the government to a hidden-priority claim. That would inhibit commercial transactions and reduce confidence among would-be creditors.[66]

The federal government's preference upheld in *Fisher* was sustained in *Harrison v. Sterry* (1809). A British firm trading in England and the United States was declared a bankrupt in England. In upholding the United States government's priority to the American assets, Chief Justice Marshall, for the Court, noted that there was no equitable reason to withhold the government's priority since there had been no reliance upon the nature of the firm's assets to the detriment of another creditor. In addition, he held that no transfer of firm assets by English courts could effect a title change in the American assets of the firm.[67]

The Supreme Court was relieved from further consideration of the Bankruptcy Act by its repeal in 1803, but the lack of a uniform federal bankruptcy law through the remainder of Marshall's tenure raised other problems. The Court was called upon to consider a variety of state insolvency acts in the light of their impact upon interstate commerce and the Union. As we have seen, the critical point in the Court's consideration of these matters occurred in *Sturges v. Crowninshield* (1819) and *Ogden v. Saunders* (1827). These decisions, in addition to their constitutional importance, established for a short time the principle that retroactive insolvency acts that discharged debts as well as the debtor from prison violated the Constitution's contract clause. After *Ogden v. Saunders* the prohibition of retroactive insolvency relief seemed to remain, but there was no doubt that the insolvency laws of the state where a contract was made provided relief to debtors who sought protection.[68] Thereafter state initiatives were paramount in affording relief to unfortunate debtors.

State insolvency statutes were valid within their states of enactment, and

---

66. *Ibid.*, 398–400, 402–403. A second Supreme Court case interpreting the Bankruptcy Act of 1800 is reported at 8 Cranch 84 (1804). *Richards v. Maryland Insurance Co.* provided that although the statute did not so stipulate, when an assignee in bankruptcy died, his duties devolved upon his executor.

67. 5 Cranch 289, at 299–302 (1809), opinion by Marshall.

68. See the discussion at chapter 6, 181–187.

contracts entered into while the parties were in those states were subject to the state insolvency law. Over the strong protest of Judge Bushrod Washington, the Court majority upheld the Rhode Island practice by which the legislature revived the 1756 insolvency law by private bill, affording a particular debtor release from prison.[69] However, the Rhode Island insolvency procedure was not permitted to negate federal government preferences against the debtor's assets. It did not discharge the judgment debt, nor might it be pleaded in bar to a debt that originated in a foreign country.[70]

Congress enacted an insolvency statute for the District of Columbia shortly after the repeal of the Bankruptcy Act of 1800. Very likely this legislative action was necessitated by the Supreme Court's decision in *Reily v. Lamar, Beall & Smith* (1804). For the Court, Marshall delivered an opinion concerning a resident of the newly formed District who attempted to take advantage of the Maryland insolvency act after Washington County was ceded by Maryland. The Chief Justice held that the Maryland insolvency act had no extraterritorial effect in Washington County after the first Monday of December 1800. Although the judgment debtor had not changed his residence, the law changed with the transfer of sovereignty. Therefore the Maryland courts could not provide relief to a District of Columbia judgment debtor even though judgment had been entered on the debt prior to the date of transfer.[71]

The second case from the District of Columbia courts emphasized the fact that the District statute was a true insolvency law. Again writing for the Court majority, Marshall pointed out that release of the debtor from prison was the only relief provided by the law. The judgment remained unsatisfied and thus might be the subject of additional proceedings other than imprisonment for debt.[72]

With the financial panic of 1819, the states began to enact insolvency laws containing provisions for the cancellation of obligations as well as for the release from prison. Because these statutes not only limited remedies available to creditors but also eliminated the debts, they not only came into conflict with the obligation of contracts clause but also raised questions concerning state bankruptcy laws.[73]

With the repeal of the federal Bankruptcy Act the evolution of debtor-

---

69. *Boyle v. Zacharie and Turner,* 6 Peters 635 (1832), opinion by Story; *Mason v. Haile,* 12 Wheaton 370 (1827), opinion by Thompson.

70. *Clark's Executor v. Van Riemsdyck,* 9 Cranch 153 (1815), opinion by Marshall; *Hunter v. United States,* 5 Peters 173 (1831), opinion by McLean.

71. 2 Cranch 344, at 356–357 (1804).

72. *King v. Riddle,* 7 Cranch 168, at 171 (1812).

73. This constitutional issue and the cases of *Sturges v. Crowninshield* and *Ogden v. Saunders* are discussed in chapter 6, 181–187.

creditor law became a primary responsibility of state legislatures and courts. Those matters that came before the U.S. Supreme Court were the result of diversity jurisdiction in the lower federal courts, appeals in insolvency cases from the District of Columbia, or federal-question matters raised by state insolvency or bankruptcy proceedings that were contrary to the provisions of the Constitution or federal statutes or treaties. The narrow scope of Supreme Court activity may perhaps cloak the decentralizing impact of Congress's failure to enact a uniform bankruptcy law.

Maintenance of a wide variety of state insolvency laws balkanized debt collection activity throughout the Union, providing opportunities for discrimination against out-of-state merchants. To the extent that this occurred, the free-trade aspects of the United States Constitution were undermined by Congress's inaction, and the Supreme Court was unable to alter the situation. Trade was also restricted by the limited territorial scope of relief afforded by state insolvency proceedings. Because judgments remained outstanding, merchants released from prison were hampered in reentering commerce, and even in the case of insolvency laws that discharged debts, sister states were not required to extend full faith and credit to those procedures. Merchants who had experienced insolvency relief in one state were thus subject to litigation or execution in a sister state.[74] Ironically, when the first recession hit the American economy in 1819 the United States was already moving toward a states' rights position that hindered enactment of a uniform federal law.

CORPORATIONS IN THE SUPREME COURT

In the first three decades of the nineteenth century, the corporate form began to predominate in American commercial and industrial activity. Part of the attraction of the corporate form of conducting business was its flexibility in operation and the potentiality of amassing substantial amounts of capital through the investment of shareholders who participated only indirectly in corporate management. For some time incorporation was available only by special enactment of the state legislatures or by congressional statute. However, in 1811 the states began to make the corporate form more generally available through general incorporation laws. The statutes made corporate organization available to all who filed the appro-

---

74. Some of the broader implications of the bankruptcy-insolvency problem before the Court, and its supposed resolution in *Ogden v. Saunders,* are explored in Herbert A. Johnson, "Federal Union, Property, and the Contract Clause: John Marshall's Thought in Light of *Sturges v. Crowninshield* and *Ogden v. Saunders,*" in Thomas C. Shevory, ed., *John Marshall's Achievement: Law, Politics and Constitutional Interpretation* (Westport: Greenwood Press, 1989), 47–49.

priate application and paid the required fees. Undoubtedly the Marshall Court's 1819 decision in the *Dartmouth College* case, applying contract clause protection to corporate charters, increased enthusiasm for this new form of business organization. However, even in the normal course of federal judicial business, the Chief Justice and his associates made their contribution to the development of corporate law.

There were initial difficulties concerning the nature and status of corporations that had to be resolved. For example, on a motion for new trial in a criminal case for destroying a vessel at sea to the prejudice of the underwriting insurance corporation, the defendant moved for a new trial based upon the assertion that the corporation was not a person, as mentioned in the act.[75] The judges hearing the trial in the circuit court for Virginia divided in their opinion, and the question was certified to the Supreme Court. Judge Story held that "corporations are, in law, for civil purposes, deemed persons." Referring to English authority, he demonstrated that for criminal purposes a corporation had long been treated as a person.[76] Similarly, in cases involving colonial land grants to an English corporation, subsequently revoked by the Vermont legislature, the Court extended treaty right protection to the corporation as if it were a natural person. The state statute specifically denied the capacity of a foreign corporation to hold title in Vermont after the Revolution, but the Court insisted that the political changes necessitated by the rebellion did not alter civil rights of individuals or corporations.[77]

The legal personality of a corporation was also upheld in two cases involving federal court jurisdiction and the Eleventh Amendment. In *Bank of the United States v. Planters' Bank of Georgia* the defendant claimed that state sovereign immunity under the Eleventh Amendment was involved since the state of Georgia was a shareholder of the bank. For the Supreme Court, Chief Justice Marshall observed that the Eleventh Amendment applied only if the state was a party of record. Furthermore, he continued, "when a government becomes a partner in any trading company it devests itself, so far as concerns the transactions of that company, of its sovereign character, and takes that of a private citizen. . . . As a member of a corporation a government never exercises its sovereignty. It merely acts as a corporator."[78] Subsequently the Court held to its earlier decision even though the

---

75. Section 2, An Act in addition to the act intituled "An act for the punishment of certain crimes against the United States," March 26, 1804, 2 Stat. 290, at 290.

76. *United States v. Amedy*, 11 Wheaton 392, at 412–413 (1826).

77. *Society for the Propagation of the Gospel in Foreign Parts v. Town of New Haven*, 8 Wheaton 464, at 482–484, 487 (1823), opinion by Judge Washington; *Society for the Propagation of the Gospel in Foreign Parts v. Town of Pawlet*, 4 Peters 480, at 502–503, opinion by Judge Story.

78. 9 Wheaton 904, at 906–907, quotation at 907–908 (1824).

sole shareholder in the defendant corporation was the state of Kentucky. Directly quoting *Planters' Bank,* Judge Johnson reaffirmed the Court's conviction that states that held corporate shares to that extent waived sovereign immunity under the Eleventh Amendment. He also noted that should the contrary position be taken, the bank's (that is, the state's) issuance of notes would be indistinguishable from the issuance of state bills of credit prohibited by the Federal Constitution.[79]

Given the Supreme Court's precedents in the foregoing cases, it is surprising that the justices were willing to pierce the corporate veil when considering the jurisdiction question in diversity of citizenship cases. Early in Marshall's chief justiceship the Court adopted the rule of complete diversity—that when parties had a joint interest, federal diversity jurisdiction could be invoked only if all of the parties had citizenship that was diverse from that of their opponents.[80] In *Bank of the United States v. Deveaux* Chief Justice Marshall dealt with the nature of the corporation as a litigant in a diversity case. First rejecting the plea that the bank had a right to sue in federal court by virtue of its charter, the Chief Justice moved on to deal with the question of the corporation's status under the judiciary acts. While an express statutory provision requiring that the corporation be treated as a person or citizen would be binding upon the Court, there was no such direction applicable to the case. Rather, the rule enunciated in *Mayor of London v. Wood* governed, and the alien or diverse status of the Bank of the United States would be determined by the citizenship of each of its shareholders.[81]

When the second Bank of the United States was incorporated by Congress in 1812, it was given authority to bring its lawsuits in federal circuit courts. On the other hand, the judiciary acts remained as they stood when *Deveaux* was decided. In 1824 the Bank of the United States brought an action on a promissory note in the federal circuit court of Georgia. The defense claimed that since at least one shareholder of the Bank of the United States was a citizen of Georgia, no diversity, and hence no jurisdiction, existed. The Supreme Court, in an opinion by Chief Justice Marshall, rejected the relevance of the diversity argument since the Bank of the United States had express statutory authority to sue in federal courts. Consequently the federal court's jurisdiction did not depend upon diversity of

---

79. *Bank of Kentucky v. Wister,* 2 Peters 318, at 323–324 (1829). The *Wister* case, in regard to bank note issue, may be seen as a predecessor to the "bills of credit" decision in *Craig v. Missouri* (1830). See the discussion of *Craig* in chapter 6, 154–157.

80. *Strawbridge v. Curtiss,* 3 Cranch 267 (1806).

81. 5 Cranch 61, at 85–92, citing *Mayor of London v. Wood,* 12 Modern 669, 88 English Reports (Full Reprint) 1592 (Exchequer, 1702).

citizenship.[82] In his dissenting opinion Judge Johnson criticized the Court for not adhering to its "canon" in *Bank of the United States v. Deveaux,* which required the Court to pierce the corporate veil when considering a litigant's citizenship. According to Johnson, the *Deveaux* rule required the Court to examine the citizenship of the corporation's shareholders. That included consideration of the status of those shareholders, and since the state of Georgia was a shareholder, the Bank was exempted from defending in federal courts by the provisions of the Eleventh Amendment.[83]

The Supreme Court also dealt with cases defining the rights and obligations of corporate shareholders. Where a banking corporation's certificate of incorporation provided that a shareholder indebted to a bank might not transfer his shares on the corporate books without paying the indebtedness, the attempted transfer was void.[84] Although the corporate charter of a bank stipulated the capital authorized, there was no reason for the bank to refrain from opening business until all of the shares were fully subscribed.[85]

In *Mechanic's Bank of Alexandria v. Seton,* Judge Thompson, for the Court, dealt with the refusal of a bank to transfer its corporate stock into the name of a trust beneficiary entitled to the shares.[86] Although Thompson conceded that the statute incorporating the bank provided that shares would not be transferred if a shareholder was indebted to the bank, he pointed out that in this case the board of directors knew of the fiduciary relationship when the shares were registered in the trustee's name. Furthermore, the bank did not lend to the trustee relying upon his being the beneficial owner, for no evidence in the case showed that the loan was made after the shares were registered in the trustee's name. For these reasons Judge Thompson held that the bank's position was "repugnant to the most obvious principles of justice and equity."[87]

Other cases involved the means by which corporations transacted business and the formalities required for those transactions. The Supreme Court early recognized that a corporation acted by its corporate officers and that charter provisions would in most situations determine whether an officer's acts bound the corporation.[88] However, when bank officers gave

82. *Bank of the United States v. Planter's Bank of Georgia,* 9 Wheaton 904, at 907–908, 909–910 (1824). See discussion of *Osborn v. Bank of the United States* in chapter 5, 157–160.

83. *Bank of the United States v. The Planter's Bank of Georgia,* 911–912.

84. *Union Bank of Georgetown v. Laird,* 2 Wheaton 390 (1817).

85. *Minor v. Mechanic's Bank of Alexandria,* 1 Peters 46, at 63–65 (1828).

86. 1 Peters 299, at 304–310 (1822).

87. *Ibid.,* 309.

88. *Bank of Columbia v. Patterson's Administrator,* 7 Cranch 299 (1813); *Mechanics Bank of Alexandria v. Bank of Columbia,* 5 Wheaton 326 (1820). When an officer or agent was authorized to act on a bank's behalf, he might do so by signature without affixing the corpo-

assurances that would release parties from their obligations or that tended to release the endorser to a note, the bank was not bound by those actions.[89]

Although most case law concerning corporations emerged from state courts, the Supreme Court did not lack familiarity with this rapidly developing area of the law. As circuit judges, the Court members were involved in diversity cases brought by or defended by corporations. In addition, some of these matters were raised on appeal from District of Columbia courts. Finally, the predominance of banking corporations among the litigants illustrates the degree to which commercial transactions in negotiable instruments brought corporate law questions before the Supreme Court.

REAL-PROPERTY LAW

The extent of Supreme Court involvement in deciding real-property cases appears unusual to the twentieth-century observer. Again it is important to recall that states had just begun to print the opinions of their highest courts, and United States circuit courts were frequently without guidance concerning the state law they should follow. The Judiciary Act of 1789 clearly mandated that except when federal questions were to be decided, the federal courts were to follow the laws of the several states.[90] That was particularly so when the case involved titles to real property located within the state, and the state's highest court had rendered an opinion on the question.[91] A federal circuit court that followed Supreme Court precedent on a state law real-property issue and ignored a subsequent and conflicting rule in the state courts was subject to reversal by the Supreme Court.[92] For these reasons the real-property decisions of the Marshall Court tended to follow local state law whenever it was available. At the same time, the Court was more directly involved when land grants from two states were at issue, when state boundaries were litigated, or when a federal question was raised in the state courts.

There was, of course, a constitutional roadblock in having resort to state law when the highest court of the state had rendered an opinion that precluded the Court from reaching a federal question. For example, in *Fair-*

---

rate seal. *Fleckner v. Bank of the United States,* 8 Wheaton 338 (1823), and *Chesapeake and Ohio Canal Co. v. Knapp,* 9 Peters 541 (1835).

89. *Bank of the Metropolis v. Jones,* 8 Peters 12 (1834); *Bank of the United States v. Dunn,* 6 Peters 51 (1832).

90. Section 34, Judiciary Act of 1789, 1 Stat. 73 at 92.

91. *Henderson v. Griffin,* 5 Peters 151, at 155–157 (1831).

92. *Green v. Neal,* 6 Peters 291, at 297–301.

fax's Devisee v. Hunter's Lessee (1813),[93] Judge Story was faced with a Virginia Court of Appeals decision that upheld the validity of legislative sequestration. Only after examining the Virginia precedents de novo could he conclude that Virginia had not completed the inquest necessary for a lawful escheat of alien lands. This situation involved a threshold question upon which the Court's jurisdiction depended. Federal supremacy demanded that in these circumstances state law be reconsidered by the Supreme Court and that the Court not be constrained by the state law precedent.[94]

The Pennsylvania and Maryland Proprietaries

At the eve of the American Revolution only two colonies, Pennsylvania and Maryland, remained proprietary in their constitutional form. Since both proprietors either never left England or returned to the mother country at the outbreak of hostilities, the independent states of Pennsylvania and Maryland took steps to adjust the proprietary rights held by both families. The political authority of the proprietors ended with the establishment of Revolutionary state governments.

In accordance with the Pennsylvania charter, the Penns were entitled to set off manors in their own name, and lands within those boundaries were sold by special agreement with purchasers. The state legislature passed a statute in 1779 that transferred proprietary rights to the state; however, it appeared that lands set aside in manors were excepted from that transfer. In *Kirk v. Smith ex dem. Penn* (1824) the Supreme Court reviewed by writ of error an ejectment action that the United States circuit court for Pennsylvania resolved in favor of a plaintiff who derived his title from the proprietary Penn family. Chief Justice Marshall wrote the opinion for the Court, affirming the decision below and upholding the Penn family's continued ownership interest in lands set aside as manors in the colonial period.[95]

Noting that there was no evidence of hostility between the Pennsylvania legislature and the proprietor, Marshall held that the manor lands were unaffected by the 1779 statute and that they continued in the proprietor's name until the purchasers completed payment on the agreed purchase price. He observed that it was usual for long periods of time to elapse before such purchases were complete but that in no case had the proprietors exercised their contractual right to reenter the lands for failure to complete payment within six months of the agreement.[96] Henry Clay and Dan-

---

93. 7 Cranch 603.
94. See Haskins and Johnson, *Foundations*, 597–599.
95. *Kirk v. Smith ex dem. Penn*, 9 Wheaton 241 (1824).
96. *Ibid.*, 261–262, 267–269, 275–276, 280, 293–294.

iel Webster had argued for the state grantee that the 1779 act transferred all property rights of the proprietor to the state and that it defeated the purpose of the act to construe it as excepting proprietor's interests remaining in the manors. In opposition it was asserted that the manor lands were private property of the Penn family and held by manorial and not proprietary title. It was only the latter form of ownership that was vested in the state of Pennsylvania by the 1779 legislation.[97]

Judge William Johnson dissented from the Court opinion, claiming that the manor creations were not geographical portions of the Pennsylvania proprietorship. The manors were estates or legal interests in lands designated as being within the manors. As such they were owned by the proprietor and hence subject to the operation of the 1779 Pennsylvania statute transferring title to the state.[98] In the case of those occupying manor lands for more than seven years, the colonial statute of limitations gave them good title. Hence the defendants in *Kirk* should have prevailed, in Johnson's view of the case.[99]

The litigation in *Kirk* reached the Court from the United States Circuit Court for Pennsylvania, not as a federal-question appeal from the highest court of a state having authority to hear the case. Rather the Supreme Court was involved in resolving a matter of state law allocating colonial proprietary rights among the Penn family, individual grantees, and the Commonwealth of Pennsylvania. Because of diversity jurisdiction, a number of land cases reached the Supreme Court during the Marshall era, expanding the scope of the Court's business and demanding a wide knowledge of state law and procedures.

Cassell v. Carroll (1826) involved quit rents payable to the Calvert family as proprietors of the province of Maryland. In 1780 the state legislature enacted legislation decreeing that the quit rent system be discontinued and that citizens were exonerated from paying any future quit rents. The two surviving daughters of the last Lord Baltimore entered into an agreement with the male relative mentioned as devisee in Lord Baltimore's will. By this agreement, arrears in quit rent payments that fell due prior to 1774 were assigned to Henry Harford, the devisee. Harford, a British subject, sued in the circuit court of the United States for Maryland to collect the sums due. On appeal by writ of error, Judge Story, writing for the Court, affirmed the circuit court judgment for Harford. Story observed that the sums due were those accumulated before the outbreak of the war and that the contract assigning the quit rents was valid under British law. All of the

97. *Ibid.*, 245–255.
98. *Ibid.*, 305, 308, 310–311.
99. *Ibid.*, 319–325.

parties were British subjects residing in England at the time the agreement was executed. Such an assignment and settlement of the affairs of the Maryland proprietary "ought, under the circumstances, to be recognized as valid in tribunals of every other country."[100]

The Florida Cession Lands

As a matter of international law and as a court deciding private rights, the Supreme Court was involved in interpreting the complexities of Spanish land grants in Florida. The leading case, *United States v. Arredondo* (1832),[101] involved a land grant of slightly less than three hundred thousand acres located about fifty miles west of St. Augustine. The purported owner had petitioned the Spanish authorities to make the grant based upon the assurance that he would settle two hundred Spanish families on the territory. Because of hostilities with the Seminole tribe and uncertainties introduced by the execution of the cession treaty in 1819, he failed to make the necessary settlement. Nevertheless, he petitioned the superior court of the Eastern District of Florida to confirm the validity of his grant. In opposition, the United States authorities claimed that the Spanish officials lacked authority to make the grant, that the petitioner had failed to fulfill the settlement condition, and that fraud was involved in the land grant. On a decree for the petitioner in the superior court, the United States took an appeal to the U.S. Supreme Court.

For the Court, Judge Baldwin affirmed the decree of the superior court. He pointed out that by international law the authority of a foreign government official was not subject to challenge and that the decisions of Spanish tribunals were entitled to comity in the United States courts. In addition, he said, fraud cannot be presumed but must be proven, and fraud must be shown present in the act complained of rather than by a series of fraudulent transactions. Finally he viewed the claimant as having received an estate in land equivalent to a fee simple subject to divestment in the event of nonsettlement. However, when a condition subsequent becomes impossible to perform, he decreed, the title becomes absolute.[102]

Judge Thompson dissented, based upon his analysis of diplomatic correspondence during the negotiation and ratification of the Florida cession treaty. He found there a clear intention upon the part of the signatories that no Florida land grants made after January 1818 would be valid. In any event, the signature of the treaty on February 22, 1819, should have been

---

100. *Cassell v. Carroll*, 11 Wheaton 134, with quotation at 153 (1826).
101. *United States v. Arredondo*, 6 Peters 691 (1832).
102. *Ibid.*, 711, 716, 727, 729–735, 745.

the final date for Florida land grants, but settlement of the Arredondo tract had not begun until September or November 1820.[103] Again it would appear that Thompson's view of the case was in part attributable to a greater sensitivity to the political consequences of upholding the grant, which covered a large portion of Seminole territory and threatened to involve the United States in an Indian uprising.

Baldwin and the Court, on the other hand, were reluctant to challenge the land grant or the Spanish authority to transfer such a large tract to a private individual. The opinion shows substantial deference to the bona fides of the Spanish intendant, and a rather strained analysis of the Spanish version of the treaty was used to circumvent the fact that no settlement of the lands had been made prior to the signature of the treaty.

KENTUCKY LAND GRANTS IN THE SUPREME COURT

A large part of the Supreme Court's activity in the field of real-property law involved land grants in the state of Kentucky. This constituted a quagmire of overlapping entries based upon treasury warrants and military warrants issued by Virginia immediately after the Revolution. It was a part of the law that Chief Justice Marshall knew from long experience. His father was a surveyor in Kentucky at the time Marshall was beginning his law practice. Between them they acquired a substantial number of Virginia land warrants and made entries in Kentucky, about half of which were surveyed and patented to one of the Marshall family members. By the time Marshall became chief justice, he seems to have shifted his investments from Kentucky to the Fairfax lands in northern Virginia. Consequently he was available to participate in the Court's labors untangling Kentucky's land system.[104]

In its decisions dealing with Kentucky real estate, the Court followed state precedents where they were available. This included accepting vague natural boundary marks and taking judicial notice of the unlettered status of many of the settlers. In *Wilson v. Mason* the Chief Justice decided that the nature and priority of the entry determined the equitable interests of rival claimants even though a survey was necessary before a land grant might issue.[105]

---

103. *Ibid.*, 749–759.

104. *The Papers of John Marshall*, Herbert A. Johnson, Charles T. Cullen, William C. Stinchcombe, Charles F. Hobson, et al., 8 vols. to date (Chapel Hill: University of North Carolina Press, 1974–date), vol. 1, 100–108. On the Fairfax lands transactions see *ibid.*, vol. 2, 140–149.

105. *Wilson v. Mason*, 1 Cranch 45 (1801); see discussion in Haskins and Johnson, *Foundations*, 601–603.

The Court was liberal in dealing with formal errors in Kentucky land patenting. In *Hunt v. Wickliffe* (1829) it permitted an entry made for "John Floyd's Heirs" to be amended to reflect the names of the individuals involved. In the same case Chief Justice Marshall for the Court held that the boundaries of a settlement entry could be established by measuring the land involved to be in a rectangular tract with the settlement in the center of the tract. Prior and publicly recognized entries might also be accepted as boundaries to an otherwise inadequately described tract. Finally, he applied the rule enunciated in *Green v. Liter,* that when a party with superior title succeeds in establishing his claim, an adverse possessor may retain as his property only that land which he has actually occupied for the required time period.[106]

THE OHIO MILITARY RESERVE CASES

Three real-property cases heard by the Marshall Court involve federal government grants within the Ohio military reserve. This territory was withheld from the Virginia cession of the northwest territory to the United States based upon the finding that lands reserved for military land grants in Kentucky were inadequate for that purpose. Unfortunately the western boundary of the reserved lands continued to be the subject of continuing discussion and resurveys until 1812. With the final determination of the boundary line it was argued that earlier grants made by the United States west of the line were invalid. In *Doddridge v. Thompson* the Supreme Court held that Congress did not intend to annul previously patented land grants at the time it negotiated the boundary line with the state of Virginia and that the patents issued prior to the fixing of the western boundary were valid.[107]

Five years later Chief Justice Marshall again dealt with the Ohio military reserve in delivering the Court's opinion in *Reynolds v. McArthur* (1829).[108] The case raised a number of additional challenges to the earliest land grants in the military reserve, predicated upon a variety of definitions of what constituted a river. The Chief Justice rejected the propositions that all rivers are navigable, that all rivers have water in their beds throughout the year, and that all rivers have flowing water throughout the year. Essentially the case denied any definition of a river that was based upon water volume or flow.[109]

---

106. *Hunt v. Wickliffe,* 2 Peters 201, at 208–209, 212 (1829); the rule in *Green v. Liter,* enunciated by Judge Story, is that if a man enter lands without title, his seizin is confined to the amount of land he has possessed, 8 Cranch 229, at 250 (1814).
107. 9 Wheaton 469, at 479–482 (1824), opinion by Marshall.
108. 2 Peters 417, at 423–441.
109. *Ibid.,* 437–440.

The third attack upon a title in the Ohio military reserve reached the Court in 1832, and Judge McLean delivered the opinion of the Court, with Judge Baldwin dissenting.[110] The occupying defendant's title was shown to be based upon a land warrant issued by Virginia for service in the state line rather than for continental service. In addition, the defendant's entry and survey were made upon a warrant issued by the state after 1784 when the territory north of the Ohio was ceded to the United States. Subsequent to that date, lands northwest of the Ohio River could be entered only by Virginia veterans of three years of service in the Continental Line. McLean pointed out that after 1784 all patents for land located northwest of the Ohio had to be issued by the federal government. Furthermore, under the Virginia land grant system, a survey could not cure a defective entry unless the survey was made the subject of a grant by a land patent. The invalidity of the defendant's warrant, coupled with the defendant's failure to obtain a patent on the basis of the survey, meant that he had no color of title. In any event, adverse possession could not run against the state. Although he recognized the great hardship caused by the decision, Judge McLean was compelled by these reasons to affirm the federal circuit court's decision for the plaintiff.

CONCLUSION

This brief sample of the private-law litigation before the Supreme Court illustrates the degree to which the justices gave the nation law in a large number of fields normally considered beyond the scope of federal judicial power. To the extent that its reports were more widely circulated than those of the states, the Supreme Court's decisions contributed to shaping the development of American jurisprudence in these areas. While cases in areas of commercial law seem to be the most significant, the Supreme Court also utilized its private-law jurisdiction to implement principles of international law and to reinforce points made more obviously in constitutional-law litigation. A more exhaustive survey of the private litigation in the Supreme Court and in the circuit courts is badly needed before any firm conclusions can be drawn concerning the influence of the federal courts in antebellum America.

---

110. *Lindsey v. Miller's Lessee*, 6 Peters 666, at 672–679 (1832).

VIII

THE UNITED STATES
IN THE FAMILY OF NATIONS

As a newcomer in the world of sovereign nations, the newly independent United States of America found itself almost immediately engaged in the conduct of diplomacy to avoid the threat of war. Ink on the 1783 peace treaty was barely dry before the Barbary states of North Africa declared war on the young republic. Previously the British government had paid the tribute required by these piratical potentates, but the Confederation Congress mistakenly assumed that Americans would be permitted to continue in the Mediterranean trade without annual payments to those petty vassals of the Ottoman Empire. Not until 1805 was the power of the Barbary pirates broken by American naval action, insuring peaceable trading conditions to all merchants in that littoral. As secretary of state, John Marshall had been closely involved with American arrangements to pay the annuities demanded by Algiers, Tripoli, and Tunis.[1] After his resistance to bribe requests from France as a member of the XYZ Mission, this humiliation from minor seafaring powers must have been especially galling.

American international relations were complicated by a succession of wars and revolutions that characterized virtually every year of Marshall's chief justiceship. The Napoleonic Wars forced the United States into the role of a neutral carrier of food and raw materials to belligerent groups headed by France on one hand and Britain on the other. Relying upon the 1778 US.-French treaty of amity, the French Directory expected American

---

1. *The Papers of John Marshall,* Herbert A. Johnson, Charles T. Cullen, William C. Stinchcombe, Charles F. Hobson, et al., editors, 8 vols. to date (Chapel Hill: University of North Carolina Press, 1974–date, vol. 6, 65–66, 511, 515, 519–520. A useful summary of Marshall's connection to international law throughout his career is given in Frances H. Rudko, *John Marshall and International Law: Statesman and Chief Justice* (Westport: Greenwood Press, 1991); however, the definitive monograph is still Benjamin M. Ziegler, *The International Law of John Marshall: A Study in First Principles* (Chapel Hill: University of North Carolina Press, 1939).

support in the worldwide struggle against Britain. Presidents Washington and Adams, without repudiating the treaty with France, steered a neutral path until French intransigence brought on a maritime confrontation called the Quasi-War. Although the hostilities, which began in 1798, were formally terminated in 1800 by the Ellsworth Mission's negotiation of the consular convention with France, the underlying problems of neutral status persisted. Ultimately the United States utilized nonimportation as a weapon against all belligerents who violated standards of conduct toward neutral shipping, first through the nonintercourse acts and finally through a succession of statutes that prohibited all American transatlantic shipping. Committed to upholding its neutral right on the oceans, the United States declared war upon Great Britain and fought the War of 1812.

Even as American attention focused upon commercial rights to trade with Europe, discontent with Spanish and Portuguese rule in Latin America precipitated a series of national revolutions beginning in 1808. As Napoleon's armies conquered Portugal and Spain, the already weak administrative ties between colonies and mother countries were broken, providing additional opportunity for colonial rebellions. Again the United States was cast in the role of a neutral commercial carrier, and once more American admiralty courts were challenged with a substantial caseload in illegal trade and prize litigation.

In 1807 the Federal Constitution's mandated end of the slave trade became effective. As the United States Navy began to enforce the prohibition, complicated issues concerning the nature of slavery and the definition of contraband were brought before the Supreme Court. Toward the end of Marshall's chief justiceship (in 1833), the British Parliament abolished slavery throughout the empire, raising anew the politically inflammatory moral issues of chattel slavery.

Against this complex and eventful background of world affairs the Marshall Court functioned as the principal court of international law within the federal republic. Its role in international law was enhanced by its extensive jurisdiction in admiralty and prize matters, based upon the Federal Constitution and the Judiciary Act of 1789.[2] It took good advantage of the

---

2. Constitution, Art. III, § 2 provides that the judicial power of the United States shall extend to "all cases of admiralty and maritime jurisdiction" that include proceedings for the condemnation of vessels taken as prize in wartime. Section 9 of the Judiciary Act of 1789 conferred exclusive original jurisdiction in all civil causes of admiralty and maritime jurisdiction upon district and circuit courts. It also conferred jurisdiction upon those federal courts in all criminal prosecutions for offenses on the high seas and in all illegal trade and customs violation cases. However, the Marshall Court early recognized that some residual civil jurisdiction in maritime matters remained with the states. *Peisch v. Ware,* 4 Cranch (8 U.S.) 347–366 (1808); see discussion at George L. Haskins and Herbert A. Johnson, *Foundations of Power: John Marshall, 1801–15,* vol. 2, *History of the Supreme Court of*

circumstances and made major contributions to American understanding and interpretations of the law of nations.

DIPLOMATIC AFFAIRS AND CONSTITUTIONAL PRINCIPLE

Although the Supreme Court is the judicial body responsible for applying the law of nations in the United States, the degree to which it would play an initiating role in that task was not clear until 1812. Intermittent prize litigation between Britain and France raised many issues concerning the legitimacy of condemnations, and many American vessels were involved in this uncertainty. The schooner *Exchange,* an American merchant vessel sailing from Baltimore to Spain in 1809, had been seized on the high seas and condemned as prize to her French captors. Subsequently the ship was refitted as a warship and commissioned as such in the French Navy. Under the press of necessity, the ship, now named the *Balaou,* was forced to take shelter at Philadelphia, where she was libeled by her former owners.[3]

Admitting the delicacy of the case, Chief Justice Marshall, for the Court, decided that the ownership rights of the American libelants had to be denied in favor of the exemption of a foreign public vessel in American ports. He began by observing that although every sovereign nation had complete power to act within its own territory, there were circumstances in which exceptions had to be made to that rule. When a sovereign entered the territory of a friendly power, he or she was exempt from arrest or detention. From this immunity was derived a second: the sanctity of the person of foreign ministers based upon the concept of extraterritoriality. A third waiver of sovereignty occurred when a nation permitted another to march troops through its territory; in such cases the sovereign commanding the troops exercises disciplinary control over them while they are in another nation's territory. This last rule concerning foreign armies was not applicable to public ships of a foreign nation, but absent notice that the ports of a neutral nation were closed to public vessels of another sovereign, they were presumed to be open. In the case of private citizens and privately owned vessels, entry into the territory of a sovereign nation imposes a temporary allegiance upon the entrant; the contrary is true of a public armed vessel, which cannot be interfered with without an affront to the power and dignity of her sovereign owner.[4]

---

the United States, 10 vols. to date (New York: Macmillan Publishing Company, 1981), 399, 478–490. Judge Edward Dumbauld pointed out that Marshall's Court delivered 62 constitutional law decisions compared to 192 opinions on international law. "John Marshall and the Law of Nations," 104 *University of Pennsylvania Law Review* 38, at 40 (1955).

3. *The Exchange v. M'Faddon,* 7 Cranch 116–147, at 117–118 (1812); see also Ziegler, *International Law,* 81–87.

4. *The Exchange v. M'Faddon,* 136–145.

Marshall concluded his opinion by noting that while the libelant had a just claim to ownership, the judicial power of the courts was unable to enforce such claims. Rather it was for the sovereign power of the United States to address those matters through diplomatic negotiation.[5] The Supreme Court's willingness to follow presidential and congressional decisions in diplomatic matters was affirmed at the next term of court in *Williams v. Armroyd*. This case involved the Milan Decree issued by Napoleon, by which neutral vessels that submitted to British inspection requirements were assumed to be British in nationality and subject to French seizure. In *Williams* goods belonging to an American had been captured by a French privateer and condemned as being destined for a British possession. They were sent to Philadelphia by the purchaser and there libeled by the original owner. In awarding the cargo to the purchaser under the French decree, Marshall noted that the United States Congress had condemned the Milan Decree as a violation of the law of nations. However, although it was free to do so, Congress did not limit the operation of the Milan Decree or declare void condemnations under its provisions. Therefore the decree of condemnation, issued by a competent court proceeding in rem, was binding upon American admiralty courts.[6]

Schooner Exchange and *Williams* established the primacy of the political arms of government—the president and Congress—in determining foreign policy matters. Beyond the limits established by the action of those branches of the federal government, the Supreme Court would not venture, even when private-property rights were involved. That deference, duplicated in the Marshall Court's reluctance to expand presidential war powers in the absence of congressional action, rested solidly upon the doctrine of separation of powers.[7]

Within the framework established by the political branches of government, the Supreme Court took care to advance the declared policies without trespassing upon the sovereign rights of foreign nations. This is well demonstrated in a case arising from the background of the Latin American revolutions, *The Santissima Trinidad and the St. Ander*.[8] The captor vessel had been built in Baltimore as a privateer during the War of 1812 and was refitted and sold to new owners who ordered her to sail to Buenos Aires with a cargo of munitions. The captain was a United States citizen who announced upon his arrival in Argentina that he had become a citizen of

5. *Ibid.*, 146–147.
6. *Williams v. Armroyd*, 7 Cranch 423, at 433–444 (1813).
7. See discussion of *Brown v. United States*, 8 Cranch 110–154 (1814), in Haskins and Johnson, *Foundations*, 543–545.
8. *The Santissima Trinidad and the St. Ander*, 7 Wheaton 283–355 (1822).

the rebelling republic of Rio de la Plata and was commissioned by that country's government to command the vessel as a public warship. The ship then sailed to raid along the coast of Spain, returning to Baltimore to recruit new members for her crew and to be repaired. While no additional guns were mounted on the vessel while it was in Baltimore, the captain managed to purchase a smaller privateer to serve as a tender and thus increased the fire power available to him. After a successful voyage plundering Spanish vessels, the two ships returned to Norfolk carrying goods seized on the high seas. The federal district court ordered restitution to the Spanish claimant-owners, and the circuit court affirmed the decree.

For the Supreme Court, Judge Story affirmed the circuit court. Despite his "suspicion of a lurking American interest" in the ship, he found valid the sale and transfer to Rio de la Plata national service. The settled practice in international law was to recognize transfers to public warship status. Had the ship and her captain violated American neutrality? The Court's precedents favored denying property captured through a violation of American neutrality, but the violation must, in such cases, be proved beyond all reasonable doubt. While the original commercial voyage to Buenos Aires was unobjectionable, the recruitment of new crew members at Baltimore upon the ship's return, coupled with the purchase of the ship that served as a tender, violated American neutrality.[9]

To the assertion that the public warship of a nation could not be subjected to forfeiture, Judge Story gave ready assent, but he then proceeded to point out that it was not the capturing vessel that was before the Court but rather the fruits gained through her captures and illegal fitting out in Baltimore. In defending United States neutrality by refusing to condone captures, the federal courts need make no distinction between privateers and public warships of a belligerent.[10]

TREATIES AND PROPERTY RIGHTS

When John Marshall became chief justice, there was only a bare outline of what would become American law concerning treaties. In 1796 the Ellsworth Court held, against Marshall's argument on behalf of Virginia debtors, that the 1783 peace treaty with Great Britain required that prerevolutionary creditors be paid despite state legislation that sequestered the debts as enemy property.[11] Although this decision clearly established

---

9. *Ibid.*, 334–344; see Ziegler, *International Law*, 191–194.

10. *The Santissima Trinidad and the St. Ander*, 350–352, 354.

11. *Ware v. Hylton*, 3 Dallas 199–285 (1796); on the formative influence of British debt cases on federal court structure see Wythe W. Holt, " 'To Establish Justice': Politics, The Judiciary Act of 1789, and the Invention of the Federal Courts," 1989 *Duke Law Journal* 1421, at 1430–1455.

the treaty rights of commercial creditors, it left untouched the large amount of real property confiscated, or otherwise forfeited, under wartime state legislation directed against those Americans who remained loyal to the Crown of Great Britain.

Those issues came before the Supreme Court in *Fairfax v. Hunter* and *Martin v. Hunter's Lessee,* matters well known to the Chief Justice. Prior to his appointment to the bench, Chief Justice Marshall, as a member of a family syndicate, had arranged to purchase from the Fairfax heirs that portion of the Fairfax tract that was considered "manor lands." These areas had been set aside by Lord Fairfax as his personal land and were therefore distinguishable from the ungranted proprietary lands, designated the "waste lands." A complicated series of cases probed the legality of the Fairfax title and the consequence of Virginia state legislation that purported to escheat the realty to the Commonwealth based upon the ancient rule that the real property of an alien enemy could not be inherited. As a financially interested party and as a principal attorney for the Marshall family syndicate, John Marshall knew the details of these transactions better than most members of the Court, but he disqualified himself from participation in the Court's decision in the matters.

Fairfax v. Hunter's Lessee raised the question whether Virginia's purported sequestration of the Fairfax estates in 1779 had been completed at that time or remained still to be accomplished in 1794 when the Jay treaty was negotiated.[12] Under the terms of the Jay Treaty, land titles of British subjects then valid might not be disturbed by state legislation or action. An 1810 case involving Maryland's wartime seizure of British-owned lands had held that the legislative confiscation was completed upon passage of the statute, thus barring any claims under the later Jay Treaty.[13] However, the Virginia statute provided that an inquest of office proceeding would be required to divest title from the British heirs and lodge it in the Commonwealth.[14] Delivering the Court's opinion, Judge Story held that because the final step in Virginia confiscation proceedings did not occur in regard to the Fairfax lands, the heir who took them by descent was protected by the terms of the 1794 treaty. This vindication of the Fairfax title was ignored by the Virginia Court of Appeals on remand, leading to Story's later opinion for the Court in *Martin's Lessee v. Hunter,*[15] strongly upholding the ap-

12. 7 Cranch 603–632 (1813), opinion by Judge Story.

13. *Smith v. Maryland,* 6 Cranch 286–307 (1810). Chief Justice Marshall did not sit in this case, presumably because of his financial interest in the Fairfax litigation soon to come before the Supreme Court.

14. The statutes involved are synopsized in *Fairfax v. Hunter,* 7 Cranch 603, at 609–610 (1813).

15. 1 Wheaton 304–382 (1816).

pellate authority of the Supreme Court in cases involving rights arising under treaties.

In a sequence of cases decided prior to the Fairfax appeals, the Court resolved questions concerning nationality and treason. Because of the peculiar circumstances of the American Revolution, there was a need to determine which residents of the revolting colonies were citizens of the new states and hence subject to punishment for treason in appropriate cases. The Court held that state law was controlling in regard to the time when an individual would have to choose between the independent state government and the Crown. Those who elected to retain their British status were subject to the forfeitures and other penalties imposed by the states upon enemy aliens.[16]

As *Ware v. Hylton* indicates, the peace treaty and the Jay treaty also dealt with the collection of prerevolutionary debts owed by Americans to British mercantile firms. Several states, the most prominent being Virginia, enacted short statutes of limitation and other procedural obstacles to the regular collection of these obligations. In addition, the submission of cases to local juries, composed in large measure of landowners also indebted to foreign creditors, made recovery highly unlikely. With the 1790 establishment of federal courts, large numbers of British debt cases were filed in the new tribunals. Richmond attorney John Marshall was among the most active defense counsel for Virginia debtors, and virtually every major political figure in the Commonwealth became his client.[17] Because of the future chief justice's engagement in public business from mid-1797 until he took his place on the Supreme Court bench, these professional linkages did not disqualify him from participating in Supreme Court cases presenting similar issues.

Three cases from the Virginia federal circuit and one from the circuit court for Georgia provide early affirmation of the *Ware v. Hylton* decision upholding the rights of British creditors. *Dunlop & Co. v. Ball* involved a presumption that a debt left unpaid for twenty years was presumed discharged.[18] For the Court, Marshall pointed out that the existence of war constituted a disability, during which the presumption would not apply. The Chief Justice, drawing upon Virginia decisions and presumably his

---

16. The cases are *M'Ilvaine v. Coxe's Lessee*, 2 Cranch 280 (1804), *M'Ilvaine v. Coxe's Lessee*, 4 Cranch 209 (1808), *Lambert's Lessee v. Paine*, 3 Cranch 97–136 (1806), and *Dawson's Lessee v. Godfrey*, 4 Cranch 321–324 (1808); for a more detailed discussion see Haskins and Johnson, *Foundations*, 496–511, 545–558; on citizenship by naturalization see James H. Kettner, *The Development of American Citizenship, 1608–1870* (Chapel Hill: University of North Carolina Press, 1978), particularly chapters 6 and 7.

17. *Marshall Papers*, vol. 5, 259–406.

18. 2 Cranch 180–185 (1804).

own knowledge, held that there was a general understanding among Virginians that until 1793 British debts could not be recovered. In two opinions issued concerning *Hopkirk v. Bell,* the Chief Justice dealt with possible exceptions to the presumption of payment rule. He held that the residence of an agent for collection in Virginia did not give rise to the payment presumption, nor might the expiration of time prior to the outbreak of the war be tacked to postwar delays in bringing action on the debt. Marshall remained adamant in the second appeal, holding that the presumption did not run, even when it was shown that a member of the British firm resided in Virginia for two years after the end of hostilities.[19]

The Georgia case, *Higginson v. Mein,* involved a debt secured by a real-property mortgage.[20] Pointing out that the debt was protected by the terms of the 1783 peace treaty, Marshall reasoned that the same rule should apply to the mortgage that served as security for the debt. Taken together, these cases broadened the opportunities for British creditors to litigate their claims in Virginia and throughout the United States. They reflect the Supreme Court's concern that the British treaties be given generous construction, thereby securing justice to creditors and increasing American prestige in international affairs. As we have seen, that concern and the decisions implementing it, stated most clearly *Martin v. Hunter's Lessee,* involved the Court in political difficulty with states anxious to defend their wartime policies and protect their citizens from foreign creditors and claimants.

Aside from commercial debts and property interests in realty, the Supreme Court was asked to rule on other prerevolutionary property arrangements, some of which could have been discredited by the termination of British sovereignty. These cases afforded the Court an opportunity to affirm the continuity of property rights despite the American Revolution. One situation involved church lands that were left undisturbed by postrevolutionary state legislation but that once had formed an essential part of the repudiated system of established religion. *Terrett v. Taylor* raised the question of the continuing validity of Virginia land grants made to Episcopal (that is, established) churches prior to the war. For the Court, Judge Story wrote that "the dissolution of the regal government no more destroyed the right to possess or enjoy this property than it did the right of any other corporation or individual to his or its own property." On the other hand, the change in government made it possible for the independent state of Virginia to repeal the exclusive establishment of the Episcopal Church and, with it, statutes imposing compulsory attendance at services and payment

---

19. 3 Cranch 454–458 (1806) and 4 Cranch 164–166 (1807).
20. 4 Cranch 415–420 (1808). The cases are discussed in more detail in Haskins and Johnson, *Foundations,* 545–551.

of taxes for support of the parish church.[21] A more complicated situation pertained to the Vermont case of *Town of Pawlett v. Clarke*. The original 1761 land grant from New Hampshire governor Benning Wentworth set aside one share of land for the use of a Church of England parish to be established in the town. However, no formally organized parish ever existed in Pawlett, and in 1805 the Vermont legislature enacted a statute granting such glebe lands to the respective towns. On behalf of a part-time Episcopalian clergyman retained by local church members to hold services in Pawlett, it was contended that the income from the glebe lands should be payable to him and the unincorporated society of Episcopalians in Pawlett. After a lengthy discussion of English ecclesiastical precedents (which provoked the ire of Judge Johnson), Story concluded that since an Episcopalian parish was never organized in Pawlett, the legal title under the colonial grant remained in abeyance and might legally be resumed by the Vermont legislature as successor in interest to the Crown. Had there been a church in existence in 1761, or had one come into existence at some time prior to 1805, the Crown or state could not resume title legally without the consent of the town and the incumbent minister, if there was any. Concurring in Story's opinion, Johnson commented acidly, "The difficulties in this case appear to me to arise from refining too much upon the legal principles relative to ecclesiastical property under the laws of England." He felt that until some party or group came into existence that was entitled to take the benefit of the grant, the state might revoke the purported grant at its pleasure.[22]

The continuity of private-property rights after the Revolution was affirmed subsequently by Judge Washington's opinion for the Court in *Society for the Propagation of the Gospel in Foreign Parts v. New Haven*. Based on a colonial land grant similar in many ways to that considered in *Town of Pawlett*, this case had an English charitable corporation as the grantee of a share in the town acreage. In 1794 the Vermont legislature granted the lands to the proprietors or trustees of towns in which the realty was situated. Relying upon *Terrett* and *Dartmouth College*, Judge Washington emphatically stated that rights arising from grants made by the Crown were binding upon successor state governments. He pointed out that a corporation, like an individual, was entitled to enjoy civil rights to property vested in its ownership. Those private rights were guaranteed by the 1783 and 1794 treaties, and they survived the War of 1812's disruption of amity between the United States and Britain: "Treaties stipulating for permanent rights, and general arrangements, and professing to aim at perpetuity, and

---

21. *Terrett v. Taylor*, 9 Cranch 43, 48–50, quotation at 50 (1814).
22. 9 Cranch 292–338, quotation at 337 (1815).

to deal with the case of war, as well as of peace, do not cease on the occurrence of war, but are, at most, only suspended while it lasts; and unless they are waived by the parties, or new and repugnant stipulations are made, they revive in their operation at the return of peace."[23] Once more the Supreme Court stressed the rule that private rights arising under treaty provisions were to be given every possible protection. It was only when property interests were demonstrably nonvested, and subject to the grantor's unilateral revocation, as in *Town of Pawlett,* that state action adverse to those rights would be tolerated. These cases laid the foundation for the Supreme Court's application of this principle to the *Dartmouth College* case in 1819.

ACQUISITION OF TERRITORY BY PURCHASE

Constitutional differences were not presented by the first territorial acquisition of the United States. This occurred in the 1783 peace treaty with Great Britain, which was negotiated under the authority of the Confederation Congress and ratified by that body. However, ratification of the Federal Constitution brought with it limitations on federal power that were based upon the enumeration of powers and supplementary activities supported by the necessary and proper clause. When President Thomas Jefferson confronted the constitutionality of the Louisiana Purchase, both he and his political opponents realized that territorial acquisition by treaty was outside the enumerated powers. Indeed, in a strict construction sense, such a use of diplomatic authority could scarcely be considered implied in the enumerated powers of waging war or conducting peaceful diplomacy. To their credit, the president and the Senate recognized a bargain when they saw it, and they elected to move forward with the acquisition even though its legality might be doubtful.

Territorial expansion through purchase was held constitutional in the landmark case *American and Ocean Insurance Company v. 356 Bales of Cotton (Canter, claimant),* decided in 1828. An admiralty decree for salvage entered by a Florida court established by Congress was questioned in the federal circuit court for South Carolina. Among the arguments against the Florida decree, the most significant was that federal courts erected under the provisions of Article III of the Constitution had admiralty jurisdiction exclusive of territorial courts, which were Article I courts. After a lengthy argument for the claimants, led by Daniel Webster, Chief Justice Marshall delivered the Supreme Court's opinion upholding the authority of Congress to erect

---

23. *Society for the Propagation of the Gospel in Foreign Parts v. New Haven,* 8 Wheaton 464, 481–483, 493, quotation at 494–495.

courts for the new territory. In deciding that issue, he felt impelled to consider the relationship of Florida to the United States and upheld acquisition by purchase in a short paragraph: "The Constitution confers absolutely on the government of the Union the powers of making war, and of making treaties; consequently that government possessed the power of acquiring territory, either by conquest or by treaty."[24] Appealing to international custom and usage, he observed that when a territory is taken in war, the conqueror's title is complete only when it is recognized by treaty. The ceded territory then becomes part of the conqueror's nation, subject to such terms and conditions as may be expressed in the treaty. On the other hand, such a transfer of nationality does not disturb the private relationships of the territorial inhabitants with each other, but their allegiance is transferred to the new sovereign power. Until the private law of the territory is altered by the new sovereign, it remains in full force.

How did the federal government acquire the power to govern a new territory? Either by the necessity of doing so, since the new land was not part of a state of the Union, or, as the decision decreed, "the right to govern may be the inevitable consequence of the right to acquire territory."[25] Whatever theoretical reasoning one adopted, the federal government's authority to act was unquestioned.

In enacting the 1823 law for the establishment of courts in Florida, Congress provided that in matters not touched upon by the statute, the laws of Florida (that is, the Spanish colonial laws) remained in full effect, and that would include the precession law of salvage. The congressional statute also empowered the superior court of the territory to exercise the jurisdiction conferred upon United States district courts operating as circuit courts in "all cases arising under the laws and Constitution of the United States." However, the admiralty power of federal courts, following the language of Article III, does not arise under the laws and Constitution. Quite the contrary, this ancient authority preceded both the Constitution and federal laws. It was within the competence of Congress to erect Florida courts of admiralty under the provisions of Article I, and in doing so they were not restricted by the judicial tenure requirements of Article III.[26] Thus the Florida salvage decree was valid.

Prior to the signing of the Florida cession treaty, substantial quantities of land were granted by the Spanish governor under questionable circumstances. As a consequence, only those grants made prior to January 24,

---

24. 1 Peters 510–546, quotation at 542 (1828); see also Ziegler, *International Law,* 50–54.
25. *Ibid., American and Ocean Insurance Company v. 356 Bales of Cotton (Canter, Claimant),* 1 Peters, 542–543.
26. *Ibid.,* 544, 546.

1818, were to be considered binding upon the United States; subsequent grants and those irregular in form were to be submitted to commissioners empowered to declare their validity. A military land grant to one Juan Percheman, issued in 1815 and surveyed shortly thereafter, was reviewed and rejected by the commissioners but ruled valid on appeal to the superior court for Eastern Florida, from which ruling the United States government appealed to the U.S. Supreme Court.[27]

Writing for the Court, Marshall held that while the two-thousand-acre grant to Percheman was not within the normal hundred-acre limit on gubernatorial land grants, it was specifically mentioned by Spanish royal dispatches as having been in excess of that amount. Thus the governor did not exceed his authority in making the grant, and similar larger grants had been approved by the commissioners. Perhaps with a view toward American hostility to and suspicion of Spanish land grants in Florida, the Chief Justice observed, "The modern usage of nations, which has become law, would be violated; that sense of justice and of right which is acknowledged and felt by the whole civilized world would be outraged, if private property should be generally confiscated, and private rights annulled." Argument of counsel indicated a variance between the Spanish and English texts of the 1819 cession treaty, the English version suggesting that Spanish grants "were to be ratified," while the Spanish text implied that they would "continue to be ratified." This variance, coupled with the demonstration that the Spanish term "concesiones de terrenos" was broader in scope than the English "grants," led Marshall to a more liberal approach to the defects in the Percheman claim than otherwise would have been the case. Both versions, he believed, should be construed in favor of the resident's rights where there were ambiguities in the meaning of the texts. Such a construction, he pointed out, also conformed to international custom.[28]

The accomplishments of the Marshall Court in the field of international law established a tradition of Supreme Court deference to the political branches of government in this field. That acquiescence in the decisions of the president and Congress was practiced even in *The Exchange v. M'Faddon* where private property rights were sacrificed to the higher cause of international peace and comity. In dealing with the 1783 peace treaty, the Court demonstrated its resolve to uphold treaty rights against state objection, and in *Fairfax v. Hunter* it resolved a threshold question of state law— whether an escheat proceeding was required—as essential to determining its federal-question jurisdiction of the matter. Thereafter such threshold

27. The diplomatic negotiations concerning Florida land grants, and the details of the appellee's case, are set forth in detail in Ziegler, *International Law*, 53–59, 71–79.
28. *Ibid.*, 68–70 (quotations), 86–87 (quotation), 96–98.

issues bearing upon matters of international law were considered to be within the Supreme Court's purview. Finally, in cases involving Revolutionary War property seizures and in regard to the Florida purchase, Marshall and his colleagues held fast to the view that a transfer of sovereignty does not divest private legal rights that arose prior to cession.

At the risk of worsening its relationship to the various states, the Marshall Court sought to apply traditional rules of international law to American activities. Recognizing that stability and integrity were essential to the place of the United States in the world of nations, Chief Justice Marshall and his colleagues made a significant contribution to international law and its effective domestic implementation within the Union.

PRIZE CASES AND THE LAW OF NATIONS

Undoubtedly one of the richest sources of international law developed during Marshall's chief justiceship was the body of Supreme Court decisions in prize cases. This form of litigation became obsolete some time between the Spanish-American War (1898) and American entry into the First World War (1917), a victim of modern methods of naval warfare designed to destroy and sink ships rather than capture them and divert their cargoes. However, it was an important adjunct of warfare in Marshall's day, and it retains interest for modern lawyers because of the large number of international law principles based upon prize cases.[29]

The capture of merchant ships and their cargoes was a form of economic warfare practiced by belligerents against each other. Commercial vessels belonging to a citizen of an enemy power were subject to capture, as were cargoes owned by enemy citizens carried by those vessels. Neutral vessels might also be captured if they violated some rule of international law, such as attempting to break a warring nation's blockade of its enemy's ports. Goods of enemy citizens carried in neutral vessels were, under certain conditions, also eligible for capture.

Captured ships and cargoes would be taken before an admiralty court of the captor's nation, or a similar court of a friendly power, which heard proofs concerning the captured ship and in appropriate cases might order the ship, the cargo, or both delivered to the captor. If the ship's documents and the testimony of the parties indicated that the capture was wrong as a matter of law, the vessel or cargo would be returned to the owner who

---

29. Holt identifies the prize court origins of federal court jurisdiction in " 'To Establish Justice,' " 1427–1430. The definitive treatment of prize courts before the Federal Constitution is Henry J. Bourguignon, *The First Federal Court: The Federal Appellate Prize Court of the American Revolution, 1775–1787* (Philadelphia: American Philosophical Society, 1977).

appeared as claimant in the prize court. A prize court decree decided the issues between the parties and was entitled to comity in the courts of all other nations, including the enemy power.

Warships engaged in taking prizes from the enemy fell into two categories. One group consisted of government-owned naval vessels whose officers and crews shared a portion of the value of the captured property, depending upon the difficulty of the capture as determined by the prize court. The more numerous second group was composed of privateer vessels, sailing under letters of marque and reprisal issued by the appropriate national authority. These letters of marque authorized the capture of enemy ships and cargoes. For privateers, the existence of a valid letter of marque was the principal factor distinguishing their activities from piracy on the high seas. Because of the substantial profits that awaited successful privateering ventures, a declaration of war carried with it a lucrative business opportunity for ship owners, maritime officers, and sailors. Absent the supervisory and adjudicative functions of the prize courts, the capture and condemnation of commercial vessels would very likely have destroyed wartime oceanic trade altogether.

Prize cases involved complicated questions of nationality and domicile. They required attention to the relative rights of belligerent and neutral vessels and the owners of those ships and cargoes. Because many legal issues turned upon the intention of one or more of the parties, assignment of burdens of proof was frequently critical to the outcome of a case. National policy and the possibility of retributive behavior by foreign states also played a role. All of these considerations combined to make prize cases a fertile source of precedents in international law. They also raised for Marshall's Court some vital constitutional issues concerning the relationship of judicial activity to the diplomatic, naval, and military policies of the executive and legislative branches of government.

When the United States declared war upon Great Britain on June 18, 1812, the Marshall Court had already become quite adept in deciding illegal trade cases. Initially these cases arose as prosecutions under the provisions of the Non-Intercourse Acts of 1799 and 1800, which prohibited American merchants from trading with the French Republic or its New World colonies. Although naval hostilities between the United States and France (1798–1800) did not rise to the level of a declared war, privateer and naval action resulted in the litigation of many captures, forfeitures, or prize claims in the federal district and circuit courts.[30] This Quasi-War with France ended with the Ellsworth Commission's negotiation of a consular convention with France on September 30, 1800. While this ended the pe-

---

30. The statutes and cases are discussed in Haskins and Johnson, *Foundations*, 408–415.

riod of nonintercourse, the convention merely shifted diplomatic attention to the strained relations with Great Britain. The differences at first involved the rights of neutral merchant vessels but subsequently included British impressment of American seamen for service in the Royal Navy. Public pressure developed in favor of renewed economic sanctions through trade restrictions against both Britain and France, who continued locked in the maritime struggle accompanying the Napoleonic Wars.

By the end of 1807 the Jefferson administration obtained congressional authorization to prohibit all transoceanic trade by American vessels. This embargo, an effort at economic coercion of the belligerents, involved the federal government in a massive enforcement activity, conducted for the most part through state officials. Over the course of the next year the scheme was supplemented by legislation designed to tighten controls over shipping from and to United States ports. Two modes of enforcement were employed: actions at common law upon penal bonds conditioned upon breach of the embargo and libels in admiralty for condemnation of ships and cargoes involved in embargo violations. A total of eleven embargo cases reached the Supreme Court from 1810 to 1815, and countless others were tried on circuit by the Supreme Court justices, among them the *Gilchrist* and *Williams* cases discussed in chapter four.[31]

In *The Venus* the Supreme Court was asked to decide whether an American merchant residing in London was exempt from condemnation of his property as being of British character. The majority held that all property situated in an enemy's territory was considered hostile unless the owner was in the course of removing to the United States at the time the capture was made. An unambiguous indication of an intent to remove was required, and the evidence probative of intent had to predate the time of seizure. Chief Justice Marshall dissented from this evidentiary standard, insisting that subsequent testimony might be admissible to prove a previous intention. He felt that American citizens residing in a hostile state should be presumed to have an intention to return home unless the contrary was shown. Marshall's differences with his colleagues in this regard reflected a sharp polarization in the Court over the applicability of British admiralty precedents in American prize law. In his view, British authorities should be examined carefully in terms of their policy ramifications before they were accepted by American courts. Sir William Scott, a prominent and much-

---

31. The legislation and cases are discussed at Haskins and Johnson, *Foundations,* 415–432. On March 1, 1809, the embargo acts were supplemented by the enactment of the Nonintercourse Act directed at trade with and imports from Britain and France. All of these regulations remained in effect until the American declaration of war on Great Britain. *Ibid.,* 432–437.

cited British admiralty judge, had "a mind that leans strongly in favor of the captors," according to Marshall.[32]

Marshall's desire to protect neutral property rights, based in part upon American accession to the Armed Neutrality in 1780, accounted for serious disagreement within the Supreme Court concerning what factors made ships or goods hostile in character. The disparity in judicial opinion was perhaps most obvious in the reversal of a New York federal circuit court decision in *The Nereide*.[33] In that case a merchant, Manuel Pinto of Buenos Aires, chartered a ship in London for the shipment of goods to Buenos Aires and a return voyage to London with a cargo from Buenos Aires. On the outward voyage, the *Nereide*, although armed with ten guns, was captured by an American privateer and brought into New York for adjudication. The federal circuit court condemned Pinto's property because of the British character of the vessel.

Examining the papers and testimony in the court below, Marshall pointed out that the mere fact that neutral goods were carried in an enemy ship did not, in American prize law, subject them to confiscation: "The character of the property . . . depends in no degree upon the character of the vehicle in which it is found." While the express provisions of the 1795 treaty between the United States and Spain did not address this aspect of the armed neutrality, the thrust of that doctrine was to enlarge the sphere of neutral commerce. Finally Marshall found no evidence that Pinto was responsible either for the arming of the *Nereide* or for her behavior in resisting capture, since the charter party reflected that Pinto controlled only the cargo.[34]

Judge Story agreed with Marshall that the general rule of international law protected neutral goods carried in hostile vessels, but he joined issue with the Chief Justice concerning the quality of Pinto's acts, asserting that they were unneutral. According to the charter party, Pinto agreed that the carrying vessel could sail in a British convoy. Sailing in a belligerent convoy was a hostile act, and if a vessel could not do so without risking condemnation, neither should cargo be permitted to take the enemy's protection. Furthermore, shipping cargo on an armed belligerent vessel was a hostile act that would subject the cargo to capture and condemnation.[35] In sharp

---

32. 8 Cranch 253–317, quotation at 299 (1814); see Ziegler, *International Law*, 170–180. The Court opinion was delivered by Justice Washington; Justice Story ostensibly did not participate but, in a short note, supported the majority position; Justice Livingston joined the Chief Justice in dissent, and Justice Johnson declined to give an opinion.

33. 9 Cranch 388–453 (1815).

34. *Ibid.*, 419–425, quotation at 419; see Ziegler, *International Law*, 248–257, on *The Nereide* as one of Marshall's ablest decisions; *ibid.*, 254.

35. *The Nereide*, 9 Cranch 445–449.

contrast to Story, Judge Johnson wrote an opinion concurring with Marshall but asserting an even broader conceptual basis for the protection of neutral rights.[36]

The unpopularity of the War of 1812, which many New Englanders considered to be "Mr. Madison's War," manifested itself in a variety of subterfuges to cover the conduct of illegal trade. It was not uncommon for American vessels, commanded and manned by American crews, to sail under the protection of British passports, which were guarantees of protection from capture or condemnation by Britain or her allies. Did the acceptance of such protection subject the vessel and cargo to condemnation in American prize courts? In *The Julia* Judge Story affirmed his decision in the Massachusetts circuit court, giving as the Court's opinion his circuit court opinion.[37] That opinion at the outset asserted Story's basic premise—that in war any dealings between the subjects of belligerents is illegal unless sanctioned by governmental authority and every aid that would make the enemy's war effort easier is strictly prohibited. Story posed and answered negatively the rhetorical question "Can an American citizen be permitted in this manner to carve out for himself a neutrality on the ocean, when his country is at war?"[38]

While Marshall's preference to defend neutral rights marks his contributions to the prize jurisprudence of the Court and stands in sharp contrast to Judge Story's views, this disagreement was based upon more than adverse intellectual positions. Undoubtedly the experiences of the two on circuit made a profound impact upon their reaction both to illegal trade and to seizure of enemy property. The second war with Britain was most unpopular in New England, as was the embargo that preceded it. This discontent led ultimately to a secession movement that culminated in the 1814 Hartford Convention. While New England's rejection of the Union was short-lived, because of the end of the war, popular opinion ran strongly against the Jeffersonian administration's trade policy and wartime activities. By way of contrast, the Jeffersonian majority in the South vigorously supported an aggressive national policy toward Britain. The net result was that Judge Story, presiding over the circuit courts in the New England states, found far more violations of the embargo and more instances of illegal trade than occurred in Marshall's circuit, Virginia and North Carolina. Story's experiences on circuit, which included personal hostility and

---

36. *Ibid.*, 433–436.
37. 8 Cranch 189–203 (1814).
38. 8 Cranch 181–203, quotation at 197 (1814). In a companion case, *The Aurora*, 8 Cranch 203–221 (1814), Judge Livingston upheld Story's opinion in the Rhode Island circuit court condemning an American vessel and cargo sailing under the protection of a British passport.

public animosity, persuaded him that only vigorous prosecution of the prize law and criminal statutes of the United States would halt behavior he considered treasonable. His insistence upon upholding captors' rights mirrored his better-known effort to establish a federal common law of crime.[39]

South American rebellions against the Spanish Empire, reflecting both the ill-fated participation of Spain in the Napoleonic Wars and the rise of indigenous national movements, generated a new crop of prize cases in the Supreme Court. In *United States v. Palmer* Chief Justice Marshall delivered the Court's opinion, which deferred to the decision of Congress concerning the international status of these rebellious states. According to Marshall, "If the government remains neutral, and recognizes the existence of a civil war, its courts cannot consider as criminal those acts of hostility which war authorizes."[40] On the other hand, the courts of the United States, as a neutral power, were not available to the belligerents as prize tribunals, but vessels brought before them would be restored to the captor without any exercise of jurisdiction.[41] Subsequently the Supreme Court held that since the United States was neutral in the struggles between Spain and her former colonies, the courts might not try marine torts or other claims asserted by one belligerent against another unless there was a clear showing that a breach of American neutrality had occurred. In such a case, the United States would act to redress its own wrong and not adopt a judicial position in favor of one combatant or the other.[42] When neither of two rival Haitian factions had been recognized as a belligerent, the federal statute prohibiting Americans from fitting out a vessel for assistance to a foreign prince or state was held not applicable.[43]

The Latin American national rebellions having exposed a serious deficiency in United States criminal law that precluded prosecution of foreign citizens or subjects for piracy on the high seas, Congress enacted a comprehensive statute defining and providing penalties for individuals acting as privateers under commissions not recognized by the United States.[44] How-

---

39. R. Kent Newmyer, *Supreme Court Justice Joseph Story: Statesman of the Old Republic* (Chapel Hill: University of North Carolina Press, 1985), 100–106.

40. 3 Wheaton 610–641, quotation at 634–635 (1818); see Ziegler, *International Law*, 37–40, on this decision as one of Marshall's most unpopular. *Ibid.*, 281–284.

41. *The Divina Pastora*, 4 Wheaton 52–63 (1819).

42. *La Amistad de Rues*, 5 Wheaton 385–393 (1820), opinion by Judge Story.

43. *Gelston v. Hoyt*, 3 Wheaton 246–336, at 328–329, opinion by Judge Story.

44. An Act to protect the commerce of the United States, and punish the crime of piracy, March 3, 1819, 3 Stat. 510–514 (1819), defining piracy to include acts so defined by the law of nations, was necessitated by the application of *United States v. Hudson and Goodwin*, 7 Cranch 32–34 (1812), to the maritime tort of recapture of a prize in *United States v. Coolidge*, 1 Wheaton 415–416 (1816). Since piracy prosecutions of non-American individu-

ever, the passage of this statute did not resolve all of the issues raised by the disorder in Latin America and the widespread issuance of letters of marque by would-be governments. American warships cruising to apprehend pirates and slave traders were mistaken for piratical armed cruisers and fired upon by armed merchantmen. The Supreme Court, in *The Marianna Flora,* was careful to explain that while warships might properly challenge other vessels on the high seas, the ships so approached had the right to take precautions for their own safety.[45] At the same time, American warships were protected from payment of damages if, in the presence of reasonable cause, they captured a vessel suspected of piratical activities.[46]

SLAVERY AND THE SLAVE TRADE

The maintenance of slavery as an American domestic institution received some sanction in the colonial-era English decision *Somerset v. Stewart* to the extent that the English courts recognized a system of chattel slavery within the American colonies that was unknown to English law.[47] However, in his opinion, Lord Mansfield insisted that slavery was such an odious institution that it could exist only by positive law. The absence of such a law in England compelled the court to release James Somerset from bondage. Of course, in the colonies that would become the United States, such positive laws did exist, and slavery continued despite the Declaration of Independence's ringing affirmation of the equality of all men.

Recourse to slavery as a labor system and the complementary adaptation of positive law to provide legal if not moral justification became increasingly regional during Marshall's chief justiceship. In the two decades immediately following the Treaty of Paris (1783), slavery was in decline, and the legal climate favored limiting or even abolishing the institution. The courts of Massachusetts declared that the state constitutional provision asserting

---

als and ships had relied upon a federal common law, the enactment of a statute specifically adopting the law of nations definition of piracy was needed. See the discussion at Dwight F. Henderson, *Congress, Courts, and Criminals: The Development of Federal Criminal Law, 1801–1829* (Westport: Greenwood Press, 1985), 127–154, and an exhaustive study in G. Edward White, *The Marshall Court and Cultural Change, 1815–35,* vols. 3 and 4, *History of the Supreme Court of the United States,* 10 vols. to date (New York: Macmillan Publishing Company, 1988), 870–879.

45. *The Marianna Flora,* 11 Wheaton 1–58, especially 42–43 (1826), held that a merchant ship did not act piratically if it fired in what it believed to be self-defense against a pirate.

46. *The Palmyra,* 12 Wheaton 1–18 (1827).

47. Loffts' Reports 1–18, 98 English Reports 499–510 (K.B., 1772); see also William M. Wiecek, *The Sources of Antislavery Constitutionalism in America, 1760–1848* (Ithaca: Cornell University Press, 1977), 20–39.

the equality of all men resulted in the abolition of slavery.[48] Other jurisdictions considered, and some adopted, schemes of gradual emancipation such as the one included in the 1821 New York Constitution. However, the discovery of rich cotton lands in Alabama and Mississippi, the evolution of sugar cane agriculture in Louisiana, and the development of a cotton gin in 1793 combined to make slavery once again economically viable in the South. This regional polarization into free and slave labor systems grew in significance between 1801 and 1835. While the Marshall Court did not have to face major questions concerning domestic slavery, it dealt with the peculiar institution, both within the Union and as an issue in international law, on several occasions.

When adopted, the Federal Constitution included a provision permitting Congress to abolish the slave trade after 1807. So incensed had Americans become at this barbarous commerce that after 1794, federal statutes regulated the conduct of the trade with the United States.[49] When abolition came in 1807, it was followed shortly by nationalist rebellions in Latin America that made enforcement of the prohibition difficult.

In *La Josefa Segunda* a Spanish slave trader was captured by a privateer commissioned by the rebelling government of Venezuela. Her prize master claimed that she was seeking food supplies when she was hovering off New Orleans and captured by United States customs officers. Judge Livingston affirmed the decree of the United States district court for Louisiana, condemning the ship for violating the slave trade prohibition. He observed that *Josefa Segunda*'s route following the Venezuelan capture was highly suspicious, that no log books existed to document her movements or necessities, and that a substantial profit could be made if the slaves on board were sold in New Orleans. He concluded,

If, on testimony so vague, so contradictory, and affording so little satisfaction, this court should award restitution, all the acts of Congress which have been passed to prohibit the importation of slaves into the United States may as well be expunged from the statute book; and this inhuman traffic . . . might, under the most frivolous pretexts, be carried on, not only with impunity, but with a profit which would keep in constant excitement the cupidity of those who think it no crime to engage in this unrighteous commerce. In the execution of these laws, no vigilance can be excessive.[50]

---

48. John D. Cushing, "The Cushing Court and the Abolition of Slavery in Massachusetts," 5 *American Journal of Legal History* 118 (1961).

49. Henderson, *Congress, Courts and Criminals*, 161–199.

50. 5 Wheaton 338–359, quotation at 356–357 (1820).

Until the Venezuelan cruiser had been denied ownership by a prize court or the *Josefa Segunda* was recaptured, the United States as a neutral nation was entitled to treat the captors as the owners of the ship and cargo and subject them to forfeiture. Subsequently the Supreme Court upheld the forfeiture of two ships under construction at Charleston, South Carolina, because their equipment indicated an intent to engage in the slave trade.[51] So intent was the Court upon suppressing the slave trade that it denied the wage claims of an American sailor who knowingly shipped on a forfeited slave ship, noting that "if one seaman may be engaged, why may not a crew? the offense is the same in essence, though not in magnitude. The general policy of the law is, to discountenance every contribution, even of the minutest kind, to this traffic in our ports."[52]

The first opportunity to deal at length with slave trade violations arose in *The Antelope*,[53] in which the situation was not at much variance with the facts in the *Josefa Segunda*. An American vessel from Baltimore was outfitted as a privateer and hoisted a South American flag once she was at sea. Having captured slaves from Spanish and Portuguese vessels off the coast of Africa, the privateer was wrecked, and armaments, slaves, and the American crew and captain were transferred to a captured ship, *The Antelope*. Caught hovering off Savannah Harbor, *The Antelope* was brought in for condemnation by a U.S. revenue cutter. The consuls of the two Iberian nations claimed the slaves as property of their subjects. As a prelude to his opinion for the Court, Chief Justice Marshall noted that it was essential that justices follow the mandates of law rather than succumb to feelings that otherwise might seduce them from their duty. He rejected the arguments advanced by counsel that the trade was contrary to the law of nations. Citing an English admiralty opinion by Sir William Scott, he pointed out that only positive national law could make it a crime, and even with such a national law, the offense was punishable only if the vessel involved belonged to the nation that passed the law and the condemnation was in that nation's courts. In no way could involvement in the slave trade be considered piracy.[54]

A difference of opinion concerning the slave trade existed between the federal circuits, and Marshall proceeded to resolve the issue now that it had come before the Supreme Court. Clearly it was against the law of nature, but it had long been recognized by the law of nations. Marshall said, "Whatever might be the answer of a moralist to this question, a jurist must

51. *The Emily and the Caroline*, 9 Wheaton 381–390 (1824).
52. *The St. Jago de Cuba*, 9 Wheaton 409–420, at 415 (1824), opinion by Judge Johnson.
53. *The Antelope*, 10 Wheaton 66–133 (1825).
54. *Ibid.*, 114–115, 118–119; for a good analysis of Marshall's opinion on this point see Ziegler, *International Law*, 301–311.

search for its legal solution in those principles of action which are sanctioned by the usages, the national acts, and the general assent of that portion of the world of which he considers himself a part." Long usage in Europe and America sanctioned the legality of slavery. Thus the slave trade was neither contrary to the law of nations nor piracy. A vessel engaging in this trade might not be stopped and searched on the high seas in time of peace; if an American cruiser seized a slave-trading vessel in those circumstances, the property had to be restored to the owners. The consequence was that the Spanish owners were given back the slaves they claimed, but those slaves for whom no Portuguese owners appeared were ordered surrendered to the United States to be disposed of according to law. After considerable delay, the 120 Africans determined to be "American" for lack of a Portuguese claimant were transported to Liberia, the settlement established by the American Colonization Society.[55]

Federal statutes prohibiting the slave trade were thus limited in their operation to situations that involved American vessels brought for adjudication in United States admiralty courts. Enforcement of the prohibition was inhibited by the Court's ruling that vessels might not be stopped on the high seas in peacetime and searched for evidence of participation in the slave trade. Furthermore, the illegality of the trade rested not upon broad principles of the law of nations but rather upon the precise verbiage of the statutes and the narrow jurisdiction of federal courts in enforcing those provisions. As Professor White argues, the Court's decision in *The Antelope* insulated the slavery and slave trade issue from natural-law considerations that it was willing to apply in regard to contract clause cases.[56] However, it is unlikely that they saw the inconsistency, and if they did, implausible that they viewed it as a preference for the rights of properties of white males.

The status quo preferences of the Court in regard to slavery can also be seen in *Mima Queen v. Hepburn,* a case appealed from the District of Columbia courts dealing with a petition for freedom. Unfortunately, the petitioning slave had only hearsay evidence concerning her ancestry, and Marshall, writing for the Court majority, saw no reason to except freedom petitions from the hearsay rule. Normally complaisant, Judge Duvall took strong exception to this decision, pointing out that it had long been the principle in Maryland that hearsay evidence rules should be relaxed in petitions for freedom. Since the county of Washington, where the case arose, was originally part of Maryland and drew its common-law foundations from that state, his comments were entitled to much greater weight than accorded

---

55. *The Antelope,* 121 (quotation), 122–123, 131–133; White, *Marshall Court,* 700–701.
56. White, *Marshall Court,* 701–703.

to them by his colleagues on the bench. Apparently he alone stood upon the ground that "it will be universally admitted that the right to freedom is more important than the right to property."

The opinion in *Mima Queen* suggests that, at least in 1813, the Court majority took a conservative approach to the question of slavery. That is, they declined to presume that a slave petitioning for freedom was free of bondage in the absence of clear proof concerning emancipation or status. To this extent it must be conceded that the property rights of the master were preferred to the liberty claim of the slave. Cranch's report indicates that all justices except Judge Todd were present on the delivery date and that the *Mima Queen* opinion was delivered on February 13. The manuscript minutes do not reflect the opinion's delivery date, but when the case was argued on February 5, 1813, the Chief Justice, along with Judges Washington, Livingston, Duvall, and Story were on the bench.[57] Presumably only those who heard argument participated in the decision. Three—Marshall, Washington, and Duvall—were slave owners, and Story was a confirmed opponent of slavery. Judge Washington was an officer of the American Colonization Society and continued so until his death, when he was succeeded by Marshall. Yet only Duvall, a Maryland planter with a sizeable plantation and a large slave work force, spoke out to ease the impact of the hearsay rule in freedom proceedings. While in private practice, Chief Justice Marshall had tried several cases involving slaves' claims for freedom based upon their alleged Indian ancestry.[58] As a consequence, he was well acquainted with Virginia precedents and procedure in the matter and had struggled with the difficulties of gaining evidence.

The focus of Marshall's opinion for the Court was upon the risks inherent in making a new exception to the hearsay rule. Pointing out that there were traditional exceptions to the rule, he continued: "The rule . . . which the court shall establish in this cause will not, in its application, be confined to cases of this particular description, but will be extended to others where rights may depend on facts which happened many years past. . . . If the circumstances that the eye witnesses of any fact be dead could justify the introduction of testimony to establish that fact from hearsay, no man could feel safe in any property, a claim to which might be supported by proofs so easily obtained."[59] If we accept, as we must, the then current view that

---

57. Minutes of the Supreme Court of the United States, Roll 1, Microcopy No. M215, National Archives, Washington, D.C.

58. See arguments in *Hannah v. Davis* (1787) and case papers in *Pleasants v. Pleasants* (1798), reprinted in *Marshall Papers,* vol. 1, 218–221, and vol. 5, 541–549, particularly 546, n. 3. *Hannah v. Davis* is an unreported decision; *Pleasants v. Pleasants* is reported at 2 Call 319 (1800).

59. 7 Cranch 290, at 295, 296.

slaves were the property of their owners, there remain two basic questions concerning the Court's position in *Mima Queen*. The first involved the impact of natural law presumptions concerning Africans purportedly existing under a regime of slavery. In *Somersett* English courts clearly took the position that slavery was contrary to natural law and thus could exist only upon proof of a positive law creating the master-slave relationship. American jurists, on the other hand, took the position that slavery existed by positive law, either statute or judicial decision; the very existence of that positive law provided a presumption of legitimacy in natural law. In other words, the local positive law was adopted as the framework upon which to erect a special territorially restricted natural law. The next step was to create within the Union a tacit agreement that each state and territory was entitled to adopt its own rules concerning the existence of slavery.

To the extent that the first question was answered by transforming positive law into a localized natural law, the second question was resolved. This involved the burden of proof and where it should be imposed. Was the master required to prove title to a slave, or was the slave expected to produce direct evidence of a right to freedom? If hearsay evidence drew into question the validity of a master's ownership, was a burden to be imposed upon him to negate that evidence? For the majority of the Supreme Court, the burden of proof rested squarely upon the petitioning slave, imposing an extremely demanding research task upon petitioners who lacked genealogical and historical research skills as well as the ability to read and write. Judge Duvall was quite correct that the issue was between property and freedom, given that choice, the justices chose the first

An interesting case concerning a common carrier's liability in tort presented the Court with an opportunity to revisit the question of property rights in slaves. In *Boyce v. Anderson* (1829) a group of slaves was left stranded after the steamboat carrying them caught fire and exploded on the Mississippi River. Subsequently the slaves were picked up from the shoreline by a tender of the steamboat *Washington*. In the course of coming alongside the steamboat, the yawl capsized and the slaves drowned. The circuit court refused to impose common carrier liability for loss of goods upon the *Washington*'s owners. On appeal, Chief Justice Marshall, for the Court, held that since slaves were not inanimate objects, tort rules governing a common carrier's liability for cargo did not apply. He observed that "a slave has volition, and has feelings which cannot be entirely disregarded. These properties cannot be overlooked in conveying him from place to place. He cannot be stowed away as a common package. Not only does humanity forbid this proceeding, but it might endanger his life or health." Since no contract for safe carriage had been made with the *Washington*'s owners, they were liable only if their agents or crew were found guilty of gross negligence. On the other hand, the steamboat owners' liability would arise upon proof of ordinary negligence if an agreement for carriage had been concluded.[60]

THE CHEROKEE CASES AND INTERNATIONAL LAW

Localization of natural-law concepts also occurred in regard to Indian rights under federal treaties, raised in the 1831–32 Supreme Court cases dealing with the portion of the Cherokee Nation located in territory claimed by the state of Georgia. In *Cherokee Nation v. Georgia* the tribe filed a bill in equity asking for an injunction against the state of Georgia, invoking the original jurisdiction of the Supreme Court to stop the state from imposing its laws upon the tribe.[61] Chief Justice Marshall, on behalf of the Court, denied the request, asserting that the Cherokee Nation was neither a foreign sovereign state nor a state of the Union. It was instead a dependent domestic nation that could not invoke the original jurisdiction of the Supreme Court. The matter came on for argument on March 12 and March 14, 1831. On those days the Chief Justice and Judges Johnson, Story, Thompson, McLean, and Baldwin were present. The Court's decision was announced on the last day of the term, March 18, at which time Judges Thompson and Story were no longer present.[62] Since Thompson's dissent is printed with the opinion of the Court,[63] he must have filed it earlier. Apparently the matter was not considered to be of such constitutional importance that the so-called four-judge rule was applied in this case. Only two associate justices concurred in Marshall's opinion for the Court.[64]

The Cherokee case was relatively simple in its factual background. Prior to the arrival of white settlers, the tribe had enjoyed full right of occupancy to its lands. Royal grants conferred upon European settlers only the right to purchase land from the tribe, which otherwise did not relinquish its sovereignty. In accordance with a series of treaties negotiated with royal governors, the Confederation Congress, and the Congress under the Federal Constitution, the sovereignty of the tribe was recognized. In 1802 an agreement between the federal government and Georgia transferred to the United States the lands previously included within the colonial chartered boundaries, and the United States agreed to extinguish peacefully all Cherokee titles to their land. That not having been done, in 1830 the state of

60. *Boyce v. Anderson*, 2 Peters 150, at 151–152, 154–156. The quotation is at *ibid.*, 154–155.
61. 5 Peters 1–80 (1831).
62. Minutes of the Supreme Court of the United States, Roll 1, Microcopy No. M215, National Archives, Washington, D.C.
63. 5 Peters 1, 50–80.
64. See the discussion of the four-judge rule at 105.

Georgia provided by a series of statutes for the transportation of the tribe to lands west of the Mississippi and for the imposition of Georgia law upon all Indians and lands within the state. Among other things, Georgia authorities had arrested a Cherokee named Corn Tassel within the tribe's territory and convicted him of a capital offense. In defiance of a writ of error directed to the Georgia courts by the U.S. Supreme Court, Georgia officials immediately executed the man.[65]

With an allusion to the Court's sympathies with the Cherokee tribe's predicament not unlike the regret he expressed in *Mima Queen*, Marshall outlined the circumstances surrounding the case: "A people once numerous, powerful and truly independent, found by our ancestors in the quiet and uncontrolled possession of an ample domain, gradually sinking beneath our superior policy, our arts and our arms, have yielded their lands by successive treaties, each of which contains a solemn guarantee of the residue, until they retain no more of their formerly extensive territory than is deemed necessary to their comfortable subsistence. To preserve this remnant the present application is made."[66] But was the bill within the Supreme Court's original jurisdiction? Referring to Article III of the Federal Constitution, Marshall conceded that the Cherokee were a state in the sense that both royal and federal governments had negotiated treaties with them. The question was whether they were a foreign state.[67] In this connection the relationship between the Cherokee and the United States was peculiar. Although within the territory of the United States and under its protection, they were seen to "occupy a territory to which we assert a title independent of their will" and thus to be "in pupilage" to the United States and to be a "domestic dependent nation."[68] When the Constitution was drafted, the framers did not intend to include Indians within the groups that might bring action in the Supreme Court against states of the Union. The separate mention of Indians in the commerce clause gave additional proof of the framers' intention that they were not to be considered foreign nations. Chief Justice Marshall concluded that the use of an injunction to restrain the Georgia legislature "savors too much of the exercise of political power" and insisted that the Supreme Court was not the proper tribunal to right whatever wrongs the Cherokee had suffered.[69]

Both Judge Johnson and Judge Baldwin, who concurred with the Chief

---

65. *Cherokee Nation v. Georgia*, 5 Peters 1, 1–15.

66. *Ibid.*, 15.

67. Counsel for the Cherokee had not attempted to argue that the tribe was a state of the Union, probably because there was no formal admission into the Union by a vote of Congress.

68. *Ibid.*, 17.

69. *Ibid.*, 18–19 (quotations), 20.

Justice, wrote opinions in support of their votes. Johnson's analysis seems to have been derived in large measure from the 1823 Court opinion in *Johnson and Graham's Lessee v. M'Intosh,* which held that American Indians had a right of occupancy in lands that would not defeat a grant issued in the name of the Crown or by a state or the United States.[70] Sovereignty in North America depended upon European claims of discovery. Chief Justice Marshall commented,

> We will not enter into the controversy, whether agriculturalists, merchants, and manufacturers, have a right, on abstract principles, to expel hunters from the territory they possess, or to contract their limits. Conquest gives a title which the courts of the conqueror cannot deny, whatever the private and speculative opinions of individuals may be, respecting the original justice of the claim. . . .
>
> The tribes of Indians inhabiting this country were fierce savages. . . . To leave them in possession of their country was to leave the country a wilderness; to govern them as a distinct people was impossible, because they were as brave and as high spirited as they were fierce, and were ready to repel by arms every attempt on their independence.[71]

Judge Johnson adopted these characterizations set forth in *Johnson and Graham's Lessee v. M'Intosh*[72] and then asked the rhetorical question "Must every petty kraal of Indians, designating themselves a tribe or nation, and having a few hundred acres of land to hunt on exclusively, be recognized as a State?"[73]

The third member of the Court majority, Judge Henry Baldwin, held to the view that the plain meaning of the Federal Constitution, coupled with the historical circumstances concerning Indian tribes, dictated that they not be considered foreign states. The political branches of the United States government treated them as dependent states or groups that did not exercise sovereignty but only rights of occupancy, and he would not go beyond the limits of judicial authority to examine those determinations.[74]

---

70. 8 Wheaton 543–605 (1823).

71. Quotations at 8 Wheaton 588, 590; for an analysis of Marshall's view of Indian title see Ziegler, *International Law,* 31–32, 47–50. Philip P. Frickey suggests that the *Johnson* case involved two white purchasers of titles long out of Indian ownership, and thus Marshall may have concluded the Europeans desiring to trace title should do so through a Crown grant. On the other hand, *Worcester v. Georgia,* 6 Peters 515 (1832), involved an issue of *current* title. "Marshalling Past and Present: Colonialism, Constitutionalism, and Interpretations in Federal Indian Law," 107 *Harvard Law Review* 381, at 389–390 (1993).

72. Most particularly at 5 Peters 1, 22–24.

73. *Ibid.,* 25.

74. *Ibid.,* 40–42, 50.

At the beginning of Baldwin's opinion there is some gratuitous praise for the "high authority" of Marshall's decision and the Chief Justice's "strong . . . moral influence." On the other hand, he noted that "the judge who stands alone [Thompson, apparently neglecting Story's concurrence] in decided dissent . . . must sink under the continued and unequal struggle unless he can fix himself by a firm hold on the Constitution and laws of the country. He must be presumed to be in the wrong until he proves himself to be in the right."[75] Apparently the Supreme Court in conference had engaged in some lengthy debate about the plain meaning of the constitutional provisions, and Thompson, with some support from Judge Story, had looked beyond the text and to the law of nations for his analysis.

As Marshall subsequently wrote to reporter Richard Peters, his opinion for the majority did not go beyond those narrow limits necessary to decide the case. In Marshall's view, Thompson's dissent went at large into the subject and ably represented the "other side."[76] Indeed, the painstaking nature of the dissenting opinion suggests that he expended considerable effort in its writing and perhaps received substantial help from his colleague in dissent, the scholarly Judge Story.

Testing the situation of the Cherokee against the definition of nationality expounded by Vattel, Thompson concluded that they were a sovereign state according to the law of nations. As he read Marshall's opinion, the determinative question was whether they were a sovereign nation under the Federal Constitution. Recognition of a foreign state was a function of the political branches of government; such a determination governed the Supreme Court's classification of the group as a sovereign foreign power. A long history of treaty negotiations between the United States and the Cherokee Nation provided ample evidence that the Indians had always been treated as a sovereign nation. The Treaty of Hopewell (1785) specifically provided that the tribe would extradite fugitive criminals upon the demand of Georgia authorities—"an explicit admission that the Cherokee territory is not within the jurisdiction of any State." The very idea that treaties were made with the Cherokee negated the conclusion that they were ever considered citizens or legal residents of a state.[77]

---

75. *Ibid.*, 32.
76. Marshall to Richard Peters, May 19, 1831, Peters Papers, Historical Society of Pennsylvania, Philadelphia.
77. 5 Peters 1, at 52, 53, 58–62, quotation at 62. The comment concerning citizenship is at 66. Judge Thompson was paraphrasing, or perhaps inaccurately quoting, the materials which appear in the Preliminaries, and in Book I, chapter 1, of Vattel's treatise, first published in 1758. See Emerich de Vattel, *The Law of Nations, or the Principles of the Law of Nature,* new edition, Joseph Chitty, editor (Philadelphia: T. & J. W. Johnosn, 1879), 1., lv., 1–2.

The commerce clause provision dealing with Indian tribes did not, by its separate mention of that group, exclude the possibility that the Cherokee were a foreign sovereign power. Since the major Indian groups were divided into bands or tribes, the separate mention of Indian tribes may well have been to permit regulation of trade with one tribe of the nation and not another group within the same nation. The provision would have been flawed if the term "Indian tribes" had been omitted. Historically the provisions of the Articles of Confederation reinforced the view that separate mention of Indians was simply to insure that trade with the various nations, tribes, and bands could be regulated as if it were foreign trade. Certainly no ad hoc conclusion concerning the status of the Cherokee could be drawn from the Federal Constitution's commerce clause.[78]

Citing Chancellor James Kent's opinion in *Jackson v. Goodell*[79] Thompson repeated the New York jurist's comments concerning the Oneida tribe, then almost indistinguishable from other New York residents. Despite the Oneida tribe's having placed itself and its lands under New York protection, the Oneida still retained their sovereignty. Reiterating the point he made earlier in his dissent, Thompson noted from Kent's opinion that a weak state allied with a more powerful nation might well lose most of its independence, but in law it still remained sovereign.[80]

Judge Thompson concluded that the case clearly involved rights claimed under a treaty of the United States, and thus fell within the category of a federal question case involving a state. Furthermore the resolution of the case would not involve the Court in the exercise of political power. Thus the issues raised were justiciable and the Court should consider the case upon the merits. Georgia's repressive legislation directly threatened and annihilated the Cherokee Nation's rights, and a writ of injunction was an appropriate remedy to uphold the treaty terms and guarantees made by the United States government.[81]

Professor Newmyer suggests in his biography of Judge Story that the Thompson dissent may have been a subtle invitation to the tribe, suggesting that a newly developed case might meet with better results. Story's notes on argument indicate that he supported the views Thompson expressed in the dissent, but in other situations Marshall shared Story and Thompson's concern for the Indians and their rights. It was at the Chief Justice's urging that the Thompson opinion was submitted for publication,

---

78. *Ibid.*, 63–66.

79. 20 Johnson's Reports 693–733 (New York Court of Impeachment and Errors, 1823); opinion begins at 703.

80. 5 Peters 1, at 66–68; compare Kent's opinion, 20 Johnson's Reports 693, at 711–712.

81. 5 Peters 1, 75–80.

and in the majority opinion, Marshall had suggested that without the jurisdictional bar to decision, the Indians might expect justice in another case. Newmyer observes, "What appeared to be a retreat under fire was in fact a call to the colors."[82]

In *Cherokee Nation v. Georgia* the majority relied upon jurisdictional concerns to sidestep a decision on the merits concerning the Indian tribe's rights under its treaties with the United States. The 3 to 2 decision avoided conflict with the political branches of government and the potential embarrassment of having the Court's decree ignored as its earlier writ of error had been. However, the Cherokee issue was not to be so easily dismissed, and *Worcester v. Georgia,* an appellate case brought before the Supreme Court by writ of error to the Georgia Superior Court, came on for argument in the 1832 term—an answer to the "call to the colors."

Samuel A. Worcester, Elizur Butler, and five other Methodist Church missionaries resided in Cherokee territory under a license from the federal government but without the gubernatorial license required by an 1830 Georgia statute. In September 1831 they were indicted by a Georgia state grand jury, and upon conviction were sentenced to four years at hard labor in the state penitentiary. Although the Superior Court for Gwinnett County, Georgia, returned a certified record to the U. S. Supreme Court, and the defendants duly served their notice of appeal upon the state's governor and attorney general, Georgia did not appear in the U. S. Supreme Court to answer the writ of error or to plead its case. Under the rule in *Cohens v. Virginia* a criminal case might be appealed from the highest state court having jurisdiction when a federal question was involved. Thus the jurisdictional weakness in *Cherokee* was not available for the resolution of *Worcester v. Georgia,* and the Court was compelled to consider the merits of the case.[83]

Delivering the Court's opinion, Chief Justice Marshall provided a strong endorsement for the tribal independence of the Cherokee. Royal charters may have given title to British subjects, as against claimants under other sovereigns, but they were "blank paper so far as the rights of the natives were concerned." While the Cherokee accepted United States protection in the Treaty of Hopewell, Marshall wrote, "protection does not imply the destruction of the protected." Citing Vattel and following Judge Thompson's lead in *Cherokee Nation,* the Chief Justice pointed out that a weak state may take the protection of a stronger without surrendering its independence or self-government.[84] Had Georgia's acts been merely extraterrito-

---

82. Newmyer, *Story,* 213–214.

83. Marshall's extensive discussion of jurisdiction appears in 6 Peters 515, at 536–541.

84. Quotations at *ibid.,* 546–552; see also 561 for the Vattel reference, which is paraphrased from Vattel, *Law of Nations,* new edition, Chitty, editor, 2.

rial, the U.S. Supreme Court might have lacked jurisdiction to reverse the case, but in this instance the state legislation was repugnant to the Constitution, the statutes, and the treaties of the United States.[85]

Judge John McLean's concurring opinion was even more forceful than Marshall's. In effect, McLean based his opinion upon a defense of the Supreme Court's jurisdiction under Section 25 of the Judiciary Act of 1789, which authorized federal-question cases appeals from the adverse decision of the highest state court exercising jurisdiction. Referring to the 1802 federal statute regulating trade with Indian tribes as well as the many British and federal treaties negotiated with the Cherokee, he observed, "It is vain and worse than vain, that the national Legislature enact laws, if those laws are to remain upon the statute books as monuments to the imbecility of the national power. It is in vain that the executive is called to superintend the execution of the laws, if he have no power to aid in their enforcement." It was a matter of federal supremacy, pure and simple: "By the treaties and laws of the United States, rights are guaranteed to the Cherokee, both as respects their territory and internal polity. By the laws of Georgia those rights are abolished; . . . which shall stand, the laws of the United States or the laws of Georgia?"[86]

The appeal to federal supremacy may well have been reflective of McLean's presidential ambitions, but it also preceded an even more forceful statement of federal supremacy later in the same year by President Jackson. Faced with South Carolina's nullification of the controversial tariff of 1832, the president was embarrassed by the possibility that *Worcester* might be the subject of a mandate from the Supreme Court that he enforce its order to the Georgia authorities. Georgia continued to defy the Supreme Court's mandate, but a direct clash between President Jackson and Georgia over this matter might exasperate growing tension with South Carolina over the 1832 tariff. Eventually a compromise, whereby Worcester and his colleagues were pardoned, was arranged in time for Jackson to move against South Carolina's nullifiers and request the passage of the Force Bill to supplement his ability to deal decisively with that state. The temporary coalescence of executive and judicial interests earned the full Supreme Court a dinner at the White House, and Judge Story was privileged to share a private conversation with Old Hickory over a glass of wine.[87]

In the Cherokee cases, as in the cases dealing with slavery and the slave trade, the Supreme Court tended to restrict natural-law arguments. When slavery issues were considered, the justices looked to positive law for guid-

---

85. *Ibid.*, 6 Peters 514, at 561.
86. Quotations at *ibid.*, 570, 578–579.
87. White, *Marshall Court*, 737–739.

ance—either to state law as to slave status or to national law to determine the legitimacy of the slave trade. Ultimately the rights of the Cherokee, to the extent that they were upheld at all, were left to stand upon the positive-law theory of federal supremacy. Professor White considers this to have been the beginning of the Supreme Court's abandonment of natural law as an independent source of rights. Yet Marshall himself, as we have seen in *Odgen v. Saunders,* was still tied to natural-law principles even in the face of a Court majority against him. For him, and perhaps for his colleagues as well, the law of nature, like the law of nations, was restricted in its application to "civilized" nations of Western Europe. In commercial matters within settled states, it could be invoked to protect private consensual agreements from state interference. However, in dealing with the freedom interests of purported slaves and the independence of Indian tribes, it was subordinated to positive law.

CONCLUSION

The international-law litigation before the U.S. Supreme Court under John Marshall demonstrates that while American national attention may have shifted to the settlement of the West, diplomatic relations and issues of international law continued unabated from 1801 to 1835. As the United States grew in national stature and economic power, the Court was expected to uphold American views concerning neutral rights on the high seas. It did so, at the same time recognizing the primary roles of Congress and the president in establishing wartime prize policy and rules for the recognition of new national states. Facing issues of slavery and Indian rights, they moved away from a pure natural-law position and sought the certainty inherent in international treaties and national constitutional principles. A new sense of pragmatism began to emerge in this area of the Court's work that would develop much more rapidly after Chief Justice Marshall's death.

IX

THE END OF AN ERA

As John Marshall's career as chief justice began to draw to a close, the Court's decisions, and the Court itself, began to change in a number of ways. We have noted the inroads of concurrency doctrine into contract clause jurisprudence. A similar trend in the enunciation of the federal commerce power manifested itself in the growing number of state police power challenges to congressional authority over interstate and foreign commerce. These developments did not reach maturity in Marshall's time, but they mark a transition toward the Taney Court's development of dual sovereignty.

Changes in the Court's view of the contract clause illustrate both concurrency and the way natural-law thinking separated the Chief Justice from his colleagues. In his *Ogden v. Saunders* dissent, Marshall's view of the contractual relationship became quite clear. Contract was founded upon the voluntary agreement of two or more parties; as such it had a natural-law basis and operated much as the social and political compact formed societies and the state. Thus there was no need for municipal law to authorize contracting activity, and both natural law and constitutional theory combined to negate legislative efforts to regulate contractual relationships. A growing number of Marshall's colleagues saw contract creation being based upon municipal law. Positive law was needed to permit individuals to contract, and their agreements were limited by the municipal law of the time and place of contracting.

After 1827 Marshall's declining influence became pronounced not only because of these philosophical differences but also because of age differentials and diverging political beliefs. Circumstances had much to do with the Chief Justice's increased isolation from his associate justices. Judge Bushrod Washington, the only justice remaining on the Court who had been there when Marshall was appointed, died in 1829. Washington's death deprived the Chief Justice of strong and affectionate support both on and off the bench. Yet even Washington refused to support Marshall's natural-law basis for contract and refused to join in the *Ogden* dissent.

Death caused rapid turnover in the Court's membership during the 1820s. Brockholst Livingston died in 1823, Thomas Todd in 1826, and Robert Trimble in 1828. As new justices joined the Court, they found that Marshall's health frequently resulted in absences. After 1831 he labored under the twin afflictions of poor health and grief over his wife's death in December 1831.

Despite these changed circumstances, the Chief Justice won the unanimous concurrence of his colleagues in his 1833 *Barron v. Baltimore* opinion, which held that the Fifth Amendment operated as a limitation upon the federal government but did not restrict the activities of state authorities.[1] The case involved city redirection of streams that deposited silt in Barron's wharf, which was thus rendered useless for landing cargo ships. Although this was arguably necessary to accommodate urban needs, it destroyed virtually all of the wharf's economic value. A trial court jury awarded damages to Barron, but the Maryland Court of Appeals reversed its judgment, and the owner's last hope for compensation was the Supreme Court of the United States. He alleged that the Fifth Amendment of the Federal Constitution required compensation for private property taken for public use.

Marshall rejected the invitation to apply the Fifth Amendment's protection against state action. He pointed out that historically the Bill of Rights amendments found their origin in the ratifying conventions. It was there that opponents of the Constitution made clear the need for formal restrictions upon the federal government, but it was also true that they were not concerned about the abuse of state powers that were at least theoretically controlled by state constitutional provisions. This original intention was supported by a textual analysis of the original constitution. Great care was taken to delineate those prohibitions that applied to the state governments and those that limited the federal government. Marshall reasoned that had the framers of the Bill of Rights wished to make its provisions applicable to the states, they would have made express provision within the text of the document or its amendments. Short in compass and crisp in its textual analysis, *Barron* remained the definitive answer to this question until after the ratification of the Fourteenth Amendment in 1868.

The Chief Justice was also able to persuade the majority of the Court to vote with him in the two Cherokee cases, *Cherokee Nation v. Georgia* and *Worcester v. Georgia*.[2] Both involved the status of the Cherokee tribe, then located in the mountainous areas of Georgia, North Carolina, and Tennessee. *Cherokee* was an original jurisdiction case, brought upon the assumption that the tribe was a foreign nation suing a state of the federal Union. Mar-

1. 7 Peters 243–251 (1833).
2. 5 Peters 1–80 (1831) and 6 Peters 515–598 (1832).

shall's opinion for the Court revolved around the question of jurisdiction, ultimately deciding that the Cherokee were a "domestic dependent nation," and since they were not a sovereign foreign nation, they lacked standing to bring an original jurisdiction case.[3] However, Judge Smith Thompson dissented, pointing out that the Cherokee had always exercised control over their lands, and by virtue of an 1802 congressional statute, the tribe governed that territory to the exclusion of all other sovereigns.[4] Second, it was apparent that no loss of productivity would occur if the Cherokee were suffered to remain in Georgia. Indeed, it was their prosperity, in farming and in mining, that attracted the cupidity of their Georgia neighbors.

The *Cherokee* opinions provide insight into the Supreme Court during Marshall's declining years. Smith Thompson carried Joseph Story with him in silent dissent, opposing Marshall's effort to sidestep a politically dangerous decision. Judge Johnson sided with Marshall and wrote a lengthy opinion against accepting jurisdiction of the case. Such a realignment suggests that sympathy with the plight of the Cherokee played a significant part in the decision and that other justices, such as Judge Johnson, may have approached the case with some deep-seated biases.[5] In a letter written to Joseph Story in 1828, the Chief Justice expressed strong compassion for the plight of Native Americans: "Every oppression now exercised on a helpless people depending upon our magnanimity and justice for the preservation of their existence, impresses a deep stain on the American character. I often think with indignation on our disreputable conduct (as I think it) in the affairs of the Creeks in Georgia, and I look with some alarm on the course now pursuing in the North west."[6] Although the Chief Justice's compassion and sense of injustice are manifest in this observation, it is also readily apparent that the situation he describes is not that of one sovereign nation dealing with another. Quite the contrary, the Indian tribes are viewed as defenseless and passive recipients of unmerited harsh treatment by the state governments. However, these considerations were put to one side in the *Cherokee Nation* decision. President Jackson's refusal to interpose federal authority between the tribe and the state of Georgia provided a clear signal to Marshall that a decision upon the merits might well be avoided for as long as possible.

---

3. 5 Peters 1, quotation at 15.
4. *Ibid.*, 53–56.
5. Professor White's discussion of the two Cherokee cases provides a careful analysis of the cultural attitudes of the justices, which may seem overly harsh but draws credibility from their private correspondence and inferences in the opinions. G. Edward White, *The Marshall Court and Cultural Change, 1815–35*, vols. 3 and 4, *History of the Supreme Court of the United States*, 10 vols. to date (New York: Macmillan Publishing Company, 1988), 703–740.
6. Marshall to Story, October 29, 1828, Story Papers, Massachusetts Historical Society.

The Cherokee problem was not destined to disappear with a simple dismissal on jurisdictional grounds. The next Court term set the justices on a collision course with President Andrew Jackson's firm resolve to remove the tribe from Georgia. *Worcester v. Georgia* (1832) involved a non-Indian Methodist missionary imprisoned by Georgia officials for having entered Indian territory without state permission.[7] Convicted under two Georgia statutes passed in 1829 and 1830, Worcester was condemned to four years at hard labor in the penitentiary. The statutes required that all whites residing on Cherokee lands take an oath of allegiance to Georgia; they also provided that Georgia law would supersede that of the Cherokee Nation and that no further authority could be exercised by the Cherokee tribe over its territory. Since Samuel Worcester was a citizen of Vermont sent to preach to the Cherokee by the Methodist Church's American Board of Commissioners for Foreign Missions, he could claim that rights conferred by federal statutes were violated by the Georgia conviction.[8] Worcester's plight permitted the Supreme Court to consider the Cherokee tribe's status on a federal-question appeal even though, the year before, the question of separate nation status had prevented the Court from taking original jurisdiction.

For the Court, Chief Justice Marshall wrote that although the monarchs of Europe claimed a right of discovery, those rights were applicable only to other European powers and did not change the relationship of the native peoples to their land. Neither did the Crown claim any right to interfere with the internal affairs of the Indian tribes. Indeed, an effort was made to join the native peoples to the Crown by means of alliances, thereby gaining freedom from the threat of attack and assurance against their confederation with rival European powers. This situation continued throughout the period of the Revolution and was also true under the Articles of Confederation.[9]

In addition, the Constitution provided that the United States should regulate commerce with the Indian tribes, and in 1819 Congress enacted a statutory scheme for civilizing the tribes. The Georgia statutes were in direct conflict with the peaceable relations subsisting between the United States and the Cherokee. They violated Congress's control over commerce with the tribe, and they violated territorial guarantees made by the federal government. Consequently they were repugnant to the Constitution and void. Worcester had been convicted under an unconstitutional statute, and his conviction was reversed.[10]

7. 6 Peters 515.

8. For the details and the text of the statutes involved see 6 Peters 515, at 521–531.

9. *Ibid.*, 559.

10. *Ibid.*, 556–563.

Judge John McLean, a Jackson appointee, concurred with the Chief Justice but wrote a separate opinion that hesitated to attribute national independence to the Cherokee. He was willing to concede that the tribe held a right of occupancy and that some limited sovereignty characterized its status: "The law of nature, which is paramount to all other laws, gives the right to every nation to the enjoyment of a reasonable extent of country, so as to derive the means of subsistence from the soil. . . . At no time has the sovereignty of the country been recognized as existing in the Indians, but they have been always admitted to possess many of the attributes of sovereignty."[11] On the other hand, the residence of tribal units within the limits of a state had not until recently been considered incompatible with state sovereignty. In McLean's view, this situation was merely temporary, for ultimately the Indian tribes would either exchange their territory on equitable principles or consent to become amalgamated into their surrounding political communities. Meanwhile, it was held, the Federal Constitution, laws, and treaties "throw a shield over the Cherokee Indians. They guarantee to them their rights of occupancy, of self-government, and the full enjoyment of those blessings which might be attained in their humble condition."[12] The Georgia statutes being repugnant to the Constitution, and the federal laws and treaties applicable to the Cherokee, were unconstitutional and void. McLean's fellow Jacksonian Henry Baldwin remained unconvinced and filed a single paragraph in dissent, relying upon his *Cherokee* dissent, which denied any separate state status to the Indian tribe.

The litigation over Cherokee sovereignty was to end not with a sharp clash between the Supreme Court and President Jackson but rather, as noted previously, in national distraction over the growing nullification controversy.[13] The State of Georgia refused to recognize the Supreme Court's mandate reversing Worcester's conviction. After a short time Worcester sought and obtained a pardon from Georgia's governor. He acted upon the advice of his Methodist Church superiors, who responded to a plea that any further judicial challenge might trigger a confrontation between Georgia and the federal government. That in turn could thrust Georgia into alliance with South Carolina's states' rights nullification position and possibly destroy the Union.[14]

---

11. *Ibid.*, 579–580.

12. *Ibid.*, 591–595, quotation at 595.

13. See the discussion of the Cherokee cases at chapter 2, 81–84.

14. William G. McLoughlin, *Cherokee Renascence in the New Republic* (Princeton: Princeton University Press, 1986), 445–446; the political complexities of the release of Worcester are considered at length in Edwin A. Miles, "After John Marshall's Decision: Worcester v. Georgia and the Nullification Crisis," 39 *Journal of Southern History* 519–544 (1973).

The Cherokee issue was forgotten in an effort to preserve a Union already being racked by sectionalism. This spirit was responsible for a rapprochement between Marshall's Court and President Jackson. When the 1833 Court term began, the justices were invited to the White House dinner at which Old Hickory graciously arranged to have a private drink with Judge Story, whom he had once characterized as "the most dangerous man in America." South Carolina's threat of nullification and the resultant danger to the Union temporarily unified Story and his colleagues with the president who would succeed in dispossessing the Cherokee and sending them on the Trail of Tears.[15]

As Chief Justice Marshall's life drew to a close, it was this growing sectional challenge that dominated American life and depressed his spirits. Senator Beveridge notes in his biography of the Chief Justice that Marshall found himself allied with James Madison in the fear that states' rights and sectionalism would destroy the Union they had constructed with such effort and care. To Joseph Story he wrote, in September 1832, "I yield slowly and reluctantly to the conviction that our constitution cannot last. . . . The union has been prolonged thus far by miracles, I fear they cannot continue."[16]

Despite these gloomy predictions concerning the future of the nation, Chief Justice Marshall might well have looked back over his thirty-five years in the Supreme Court's leadership. He had taken a Court badly shaken by the swift enactment of the Eleventh Amendment and so firmly established its jurisdiction that it not only advanced federal supremacy but did so in a way that insured the future constitutional structure of the United States. By contemporary standards, not one of his opinions appears to be flawless, but it is important to recall that prior to his chief justiceship there were relatively few judicial opinions available in print. All but a few issues of federal constitutional law were then untouched by the Supreme Court. Similarly, the impact of international law upon a republican state lacked clarification, and issues of private law essential to the prosperity of the United States were only beginning to present themselves.

Not only did Marshall establish the Court's practice of issuing majority opinions, but his mode of analyzing constitutional issues provided American federal law with a precise vocabulary and a clear view of what the issues would be in defining the nature of the Union. Aware of his own adage that it was a Constitution that he was defining, the Chief Justice took care to draw the skeletal form of federal governmental structure and to delineate

---

15. White, *Marshall Court*, 737–739.

16. Alfred J. Beveridge, *The Life of John Marshall*, 4 vols. (New York: Houghton Mifflin Company, 1916–19), vol. 4, 555–560, quotation at 559.

the division between federal and state power. Yet it was also characteristic of his thought that he pragmatically left room for future interpretation and construction of his own decisions and modification of their interpretations of the Federal Constitution. To this day, discourse about constitutional law must begin with Marshall's basic principles.

Within the Supreme Court's procedures and practice, Chief Justice Marshall consistently worked to enhance the highest court's prestige and power. This can be seen by the important role that jurisdictional issues play in the evolution of American constitutional law. In Marshall's day this may well have been an intentional exertion of the Court's power not only to decide the issues in cases but also to resolve fine points of Court authority. Finally, there is no doubt that Marshall left his impress upon the office of chief justice. We tend to measure the work of his successors by the standards he set. Do subsequent chief justices effectively manage the Court's business so that dissent is minimized and the Court may speak with a unified voice? Do they succeed in maintaining the Court's position as a co-equal branch of the federal government, whatever political considerations may lead them toward compromise on issues of justiciability? Do they symbolically represent for the American people, and the legal profession, the ideal of a rule of law that rises above the willfulness of men?

A catalog of Marshall's achievements can go on endlessly, but it is readily apparent that his intellectual leadership of the Court, and his managerial and personal skills, made the Court of 1835 vastly different from the Court he had joined in 1801. No one achievement predominates. Many of the Chief Justice's leading decisions have been modified with the passage of a century and a half. Some of the Court's practices and procedures have also been altered since his death. Undoubtedly the stature of the Court has fluctuated, as has the leadership of its chief justices. However, the clear impress of Marshall's mind and the influence of his heart remain as treasured professional legacies of a life well spent in the service of a beloved country.

In Marshall's case, and perhaps in the case of all those who lead, it is the heart rather than the mind which is critical to success. Ancient civilizations, particularly Biblical Israel, considered the blood and the circulatory system to be the repository of a human being's spirit. Indeed, the heart, rather than the brain, was considered by many primitive peoples to contain not only an individual's emotions but also the person's intellectual and judgmental functions. Those ancient, and now largely rejected philosophical concepts, provide a better understanding of Marshall's heart, and thus his impact upon the U. S. Supreme Court and American law. Lawyers and judges are social and political pathologists; it is hard to remain an idealist about human nature while serving as a member of the legal profession. Yet

Marshall, although acutely aware of the shortcomings that he and others shared, never lost his enthusiasm for life nor his interest, respect, and deep concern for people. This emerges, as through a glass darkly, when one reads his letters, his opinions, and the many anecdotes told about him. It was what made a highly competent lawyer into a great chief justice.

APPENDIX A

Points of Law Decided in the United States Supreme Court
and the United States Circuit Courts, 1801–1835

Abbreviations

ADML	Admirality
APPP	Appeals and Error
BORG	Business Organizations
CIVI	Civil Procedure
CLAW	Constitutional Law
CNTR	Contracts
COMM	Commercial Law
COUR	Courts
CRIM	Criminal Law
EQ	Equity
FLAW	Family Law
GVTO	Government Officers
ILAW	International Law
LABR	Labor Law
PPRO	Personal Property
REAL	Real Property
SILA	Security Instruments
STAT	Status of Persons
TAXL	Taxation
TCC	Transportation and Common Carriers
TRTT	Torts

DISTRICT OF COLUMBIA *
1801 - 1835

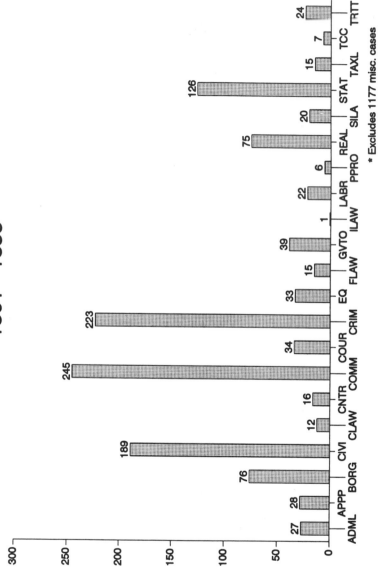

* Excludes 1177 misc. cases

CONNECTICUT *
1807 - 1835

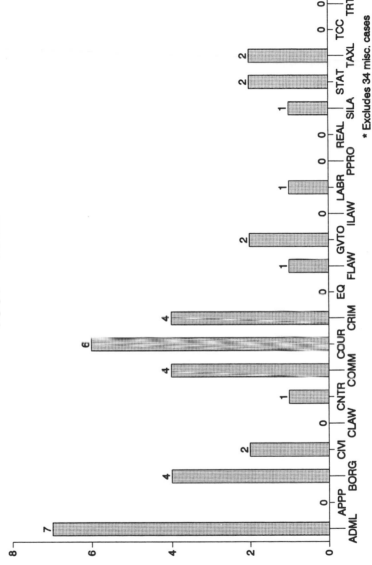

* Excludes 34 misc. cases

ADML 7
APPP 0
BORG 4
CIVI 2
CLAW 0
CNTR 1
COMM 4
COUR 6
CRIM 4
EQ 0
FLAW 1
GVTO 2
ILAW 0
LABR 1
PPRO 0
REAL 0
SILA 1
STAT 2
TAXL 2
TCC 0
TRTT 0

MAINE*
1812 - 1835

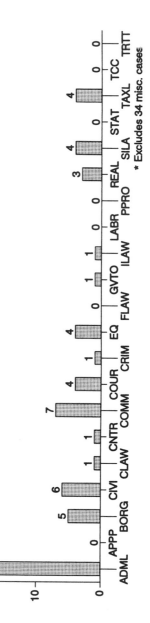

* Excludes 34 misc. cases

MASSACHUSETTS*
1801 - 1835

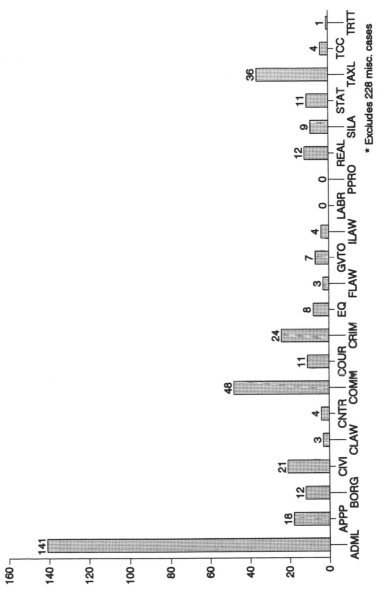

* Excludes 228 misc. cases

NEW JERSEY *
1803 - 1831

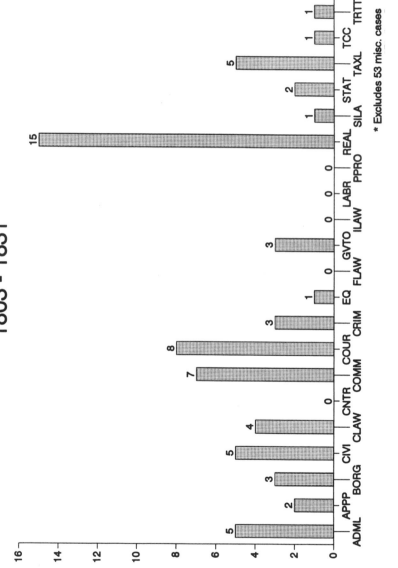

* Excludes 53 misc. cases

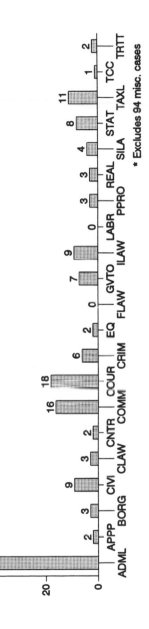

NEW YORK *
1802 - 1835

* Excludes 94 misc. cases

OHIO *
1822 - 1835

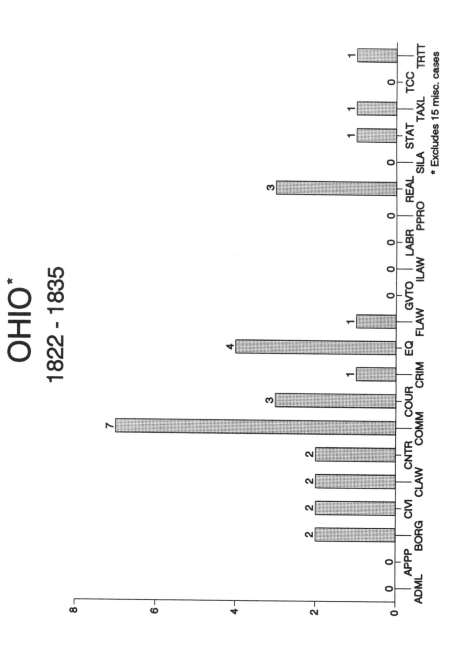

* Excludes 15 misc. cases

PENNSYLVANIA*
1801 - 1835

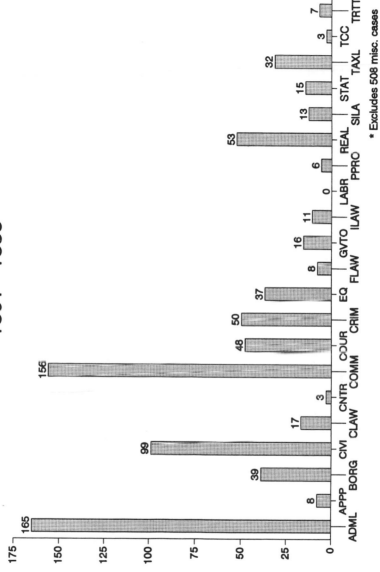

* Excludes 508 misc. cases

RHODE ISLAND*
1812 - 1835

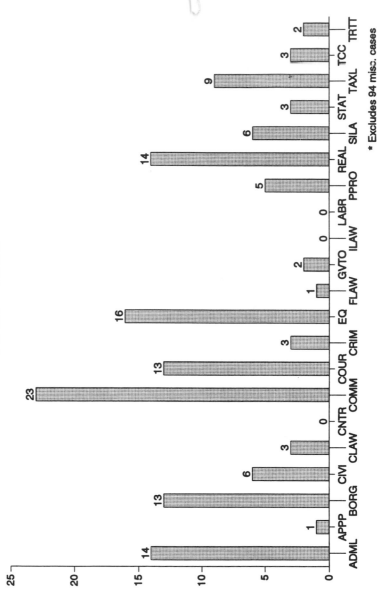

* Excludes 94 misc. cases

SOUTH CAROLINA*

1801 - 1831

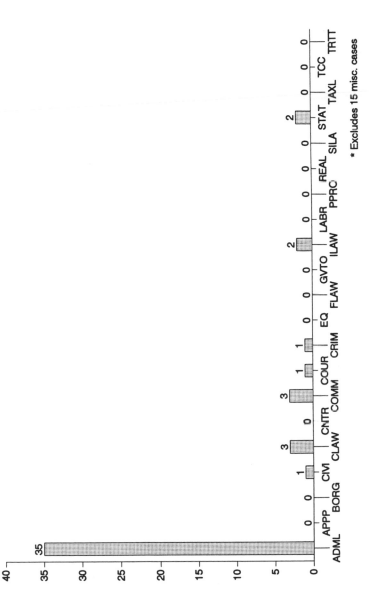

* Excludes 15 misc. cases

TENNESSEE*
1808 - 1834

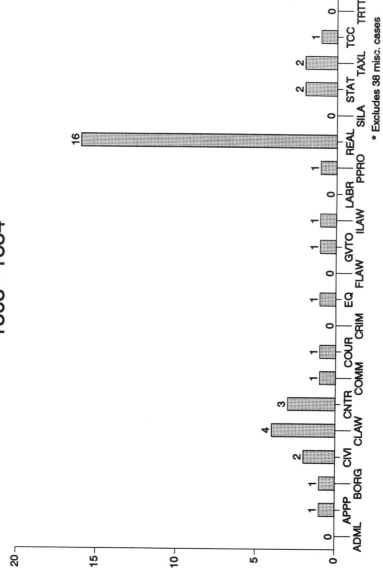

* Excludes 38 misc. cases

VIRGINIA *
1802 - 1833

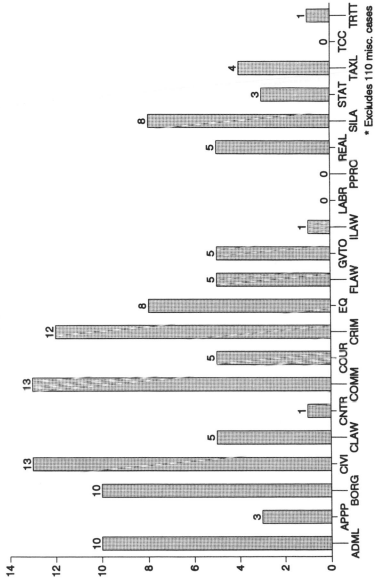

* Excludes 110 misc. cases

APPENDIX B

Points of Law Decided by Supreme Court Justices in the
United States Circuit Courts, 1801–1835

Since Marshall Court justices performed judicial duties in the circuit courts as well as in the Supreme Court, it is helpful to compare the subject matter of litigation that confronted them at both levels of their jurisdiction. The following graphs compare the legal precedents enunciated in selected United States Circuit Courts with those set forth in the Supreme Court of the United States. Because the focal point of the inquiry is the work of each Marshall Court justice, only those for which a full spectrum of data is available from both the Supreme Court and the circuit court have been included in this appendix.

Readers are cautioned against treating these graphs as statistical comparisons. First and foremost, the reporting of cases in the circuit courts was quite uneven and depended upon the interests and diligence of the unofficial reporter who undertook that responsibility. Second, although the Supreme Court justice presiding in a circuit court usually wrote the opinions, that duty was upon occasion delegated to the district judge sitting on the court with him. Third, only a selection of case categories is provided, and graphs depict only those justices whose opinions are reported in both a circuit court and the Supreme Court. Fourth, data are displayed on different scales since the volume of cases and digest citations varies greatly from court to court and from justice to justice.

When circuit court reports are available for a Marshall Court justice, the West digest topics associated with each case have been identified and grouped into general categories listed on the vertical axis of the circuit court graph. The aggregate number of digest citations drawn from that circuit court, and attributable to the Supreme Court justice, is indicated on the horizontal axis. Thus for each justice considered, the graph provides an pictorial representation of the legal issues decided in that circuit court. However, caution must be observed in making comparisons either between the various justices, or between the circuit courts over which they presided, particularly in regard to the actual number of cases involved.

The presentations of Supreme Court subject matter on the right hand pages were constructed in the same manner. The variations in the number of citations on the horizontal axis represent the amount of case law attributable to each justice. Again the actual number of citations, as well as the total number of cases decided, varies greatly among justices. Some case assignment patterns may be identified, suggesting that a justice's expertise in some categories may have resulted in the assignment. On the other hand, delivery and authorship of a Court opinion, is also dictated by a justice's vote on the case, and we must also conclude that the initiative and energy of certain justices also contributed to their overall contribution to the Court's precedents.

Observation of the graphs for each justice, illustrated on facing pages, will suggest that a Marshall Court justice's work on circuit varied from what engaged his attention while in Washington. Commercial law was very significant, both in the circuit courts and in the Supreme Court, pointing to the important role the justices played in "fleshing out" the private law implications of the commerce clause. The New York and Massachusetts circuits provided a large number of admiralty cases for trial by Justices Story, Livingston, and Thompson, and they were also a substantial part of Supreme Court opinions delivered by those justices. However, for other justices there is little correlation between the circuit court precedents, and those which they authored in the Supreme Court.

These graphs suggest that circuit duties presented a great variety of legal issues for decision by Supreme Court justices. For those who did not write a large number of Court opinions, their circuit court opinions represent their most significant judicial work. We can only speculate whether this broad and varied experience on the circuits may have been tapped by their fellow justices who are more highly regarded by history because they authored Supreme Court opinions. However, it is abundantly clear that riding the circuit was a challenging and demanding duty for Marshall Court justices.

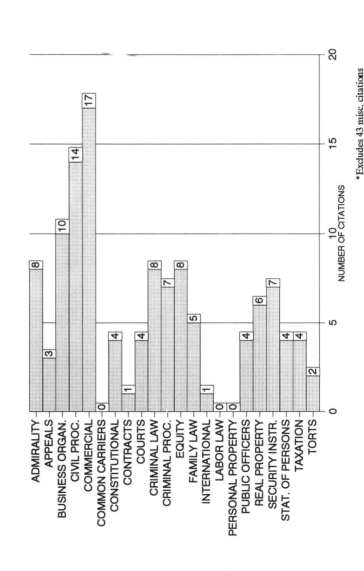

MARSHALL
CIRCUIT COURT (1802-1833) *

NUMBER OF CITATIONS

ADMIRALITY — 8
APPEALS — 3
BUSINESS ORGAN. — 10
CIVIL PROC. — 14
COMMERCIAL — 17
COMMON CARRIERS — 0
CONSTITUTIONAL — 4
CONTRACTS — 1
COURTS — 4
CRIMINAL LAW — 8
CRIMINAL PROC. — 7
EQUITY — 8
FAMILY LAW — 5
INTERNATIONAL — 1
LABOR LAW — 0
PERSONAL PROPERTY — 0
PUBLIC OFFICERS — 4
REAL PROPERTY — 6
SECURITY INSTR. — 7
STAT. OF PERSONS — 4
TAXATION — 4
TORTS — 2

*Excludes 43 misc. citations

MARSHALL
SUPREME COURT (1801-1835) *

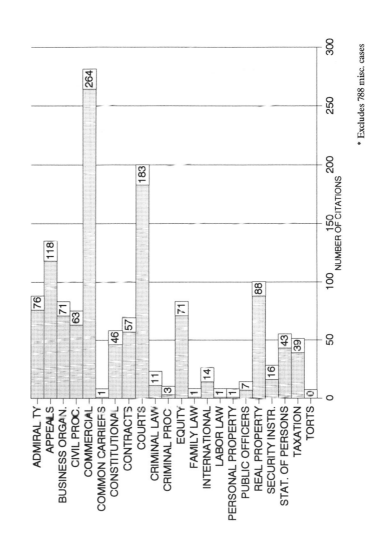

Category	Value
ADMIRALTY	76
APPEALS	118
BUSINESS ORGAN.	71
CIVIL PROC.	63
COMMERCIAL	264
COMMON CARRIERS	1
CONSTITUTIONAL	46
CONTRACTS	57
COURTS	183
CRIMINAL LAW	11
CRIMINAL PROC.	3
EQUITY	71
FAMILY LAW	1
INTERNATIONAL	14
LABOR LAW	1
PERSONAL PROPERTY	1
PUBLIC OFFICERS	7
REAL PROPERTY	88
SECURITY INSTR.	16
STAT. OF PERSONS	43
TAXATION	39
TORTS	0

NUMBER OF CITATIONS

* Excludes 788 misc. cases

BALDWIN
CIRCUIT COURT (1830-1835) *

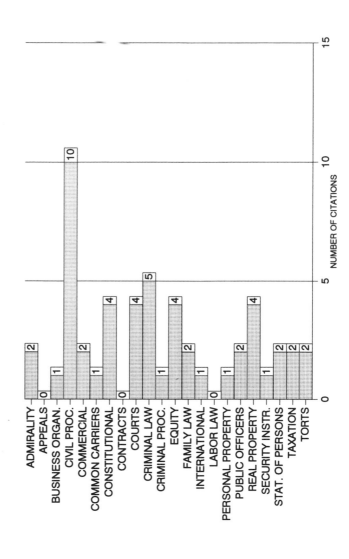

NUMBER OF CITATIONS

* Excludes 43 misc. cases

BALDWIN
SUPREME COURT (1830-1835) *

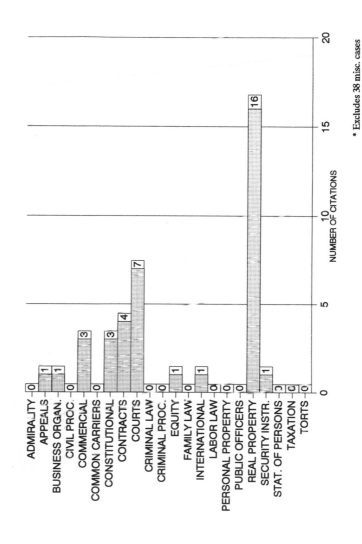

NUMBER OF CITATIONS

* Excludes 38 misc. cases

LIVINGSTON
CIRCUIT COURT (1808-1822) *

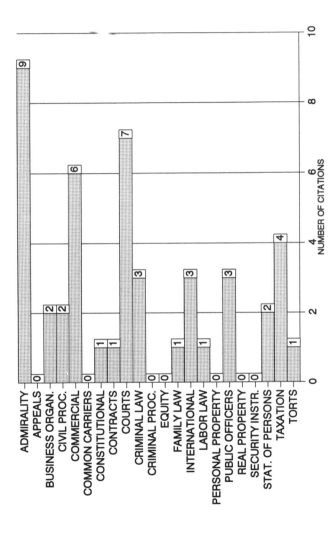

* Excludes 43 misc. cases

LIVINGSTON
SUPREME COURT (1809-1823) *

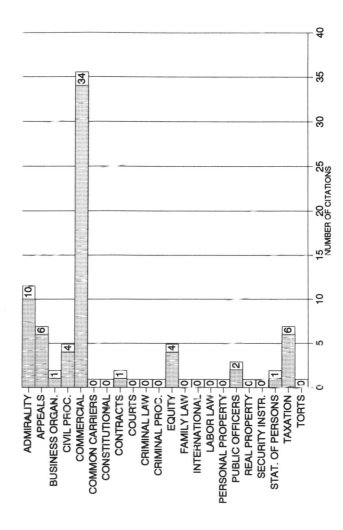

NUMBER OF CITATIONS

* Excludes 64 misc. cases

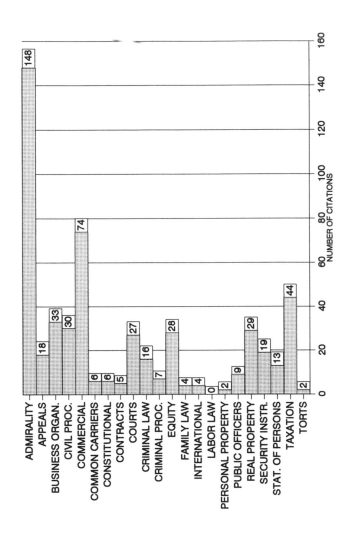

STORY
CIRCUIT COURT (1811-1835) *

Category	Value
ADMIRALITY	148
APPEALS	18
BUSINESS ORGAN.	33
CIVIL PROC.	30
COMMERCIAL	74
COMMON CARRIERS	6
CONSTITUTIONAL	6
CONTRACTS	5
COURTS	27
CRIMINAL LAW	16
CRIMINAL PROC.	7
EQUITY	28
FAMILY LAW	4
INTERNATIONAL	4
LABOR LAW	0
PERSONAL PROPERTY	2
PUBLIC OFFICERS	9
REAL PROPERTY	29
SECURITY INSTR.	19
STAT. OF PERSONS	13
TAXATION	44
TORTS	2

NUMBER OF CITATIONS

* Excludes 341 misc. cases

STORY
SUPREME COURT (1812-1835) *

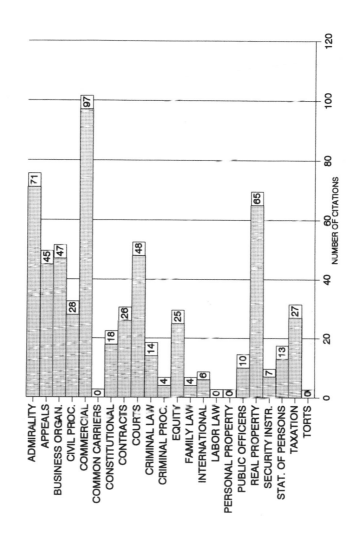

NUMBER OF CITATIONS

* Excludes 421 misc. cases

THOMPSON
CIRCUIT COURT (1823-1835) *

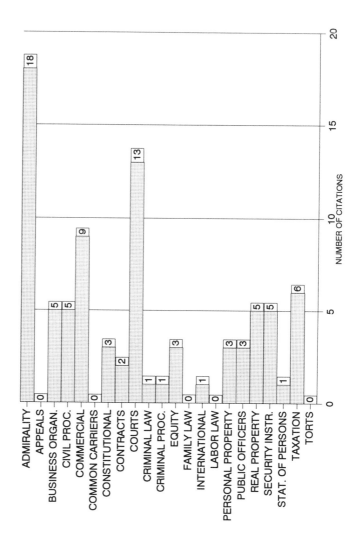

NUMBER OF CITATIONS

* Excludes 52 mis∴ cases

THOMPSON
SUPREME COURT (1824-1835) *

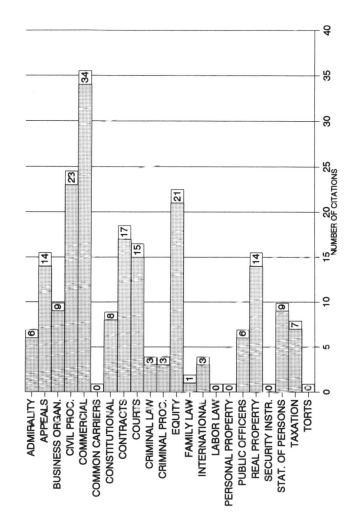

NUMBER OF CITATIONS

ADMIRALITY 6
APPEALS 14
BUSINESS ORGAN. 9
CIVIL PROC. 23
COMMERCIAL 34
COMMON CARRIERS 0
CONSTITUTIONAL 8
CONTRACTS 17
COURTS 15
CRIMINAL LAW 3
CRIMINAL PROC. 3
EQUITY 21
FAMILY LAW 1
INTERNATIONAL 3
LABOR LAW 0
PERSONAL PROPERTY 0
PUBLIC OFFICERS 6
REAL PROPERTY 14
SECURITY INSTR. 0
STAT. OF PERSONS 9
TAXATION 7
TORTS 0

* Excludes 100 misc. cases

WASHINGTON
CIRCUIT COURT (1803-1829) *

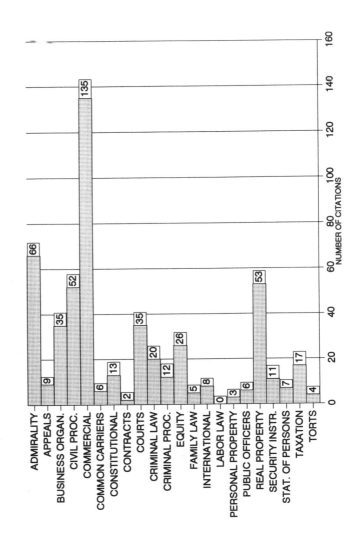

* Excludes 384 misc. cases

WASHINGTON
SUPREME COURT (1806-1829) *

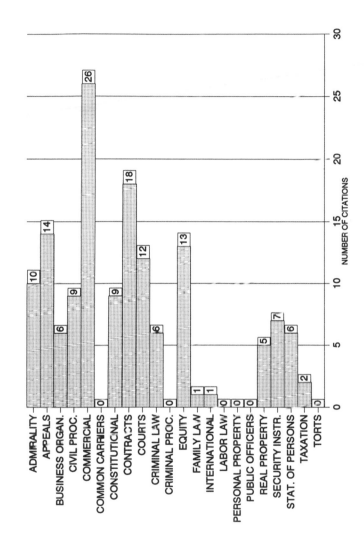

NUMBER OF CITATIONS

* Excludes 100 misc. cases

BIBLIOGRAPHY

BOOKS

Abernethy, Thomas P. *The Burr Conspiracy.* New York: Oxford University Press, 1954.

Baker, Leonard. *John Marshall: A Life in Law.* New York: Macmillan, 1974.

Baxter, Maurice G. *Daniel Webster and the Supreme Court.* Amherst: University of Massachusetts Press, 1966.

―――. *The Steamboat Monopoly: Gibbons v. Ogden, 1824.* New York: Alfred A. Knopf, 1972.

Beveridge, Albert J. *The Life of John Marshall.* 4 vols., Boston: Houghton Mifflin Company, 1916–1919.

Bickel, Alexander M. *The Least Dangerous Branch: The Supreme Court at the Bar of Politics.* Indianapolis: Bobbs-Merrill, 1962.

Bourguignon, Henry J. *The First Federal Court: The Federal Appellate Prize Court of the American Revolution, 1775–1787.* Philadelphia: American Philosophical Society, 1977.

Burr, Aaron. *Political Correspondence and Public Papers of Aaron Burr.* Mary-Jo Kline and Joanne Woods Ryan, editors, 2 vols., Princeton: Princeton University Press, 1983.

Casto, William R. *The Supreme Court in the Early Republic: The Chief Justiceships of John Jay and Oliver Ellsworth.* Columbia: University of South Carolina Press, 1995.

Chapin, Bradley. *The American Law of Treason: Revolutionary War and Early National Origins.* Seattle: University of Washington Press, 1964.

Choper, Jesse H. *Judicial Review and the National Political Process: A Functional Reconsideration of the Role of the Supreme Court.* Chicago: University of Chicago Press, 1980.

Clinton, Robert L. *Marbury v. Madison and Judicial Review.* Lawrence: University Press of Kansas, 1989.

Coleman, Peter J. *Debtors and Creditors in America: Insolvency, Imprisonment for Debt, and Bankruptcy, 1607–1900.* Madison: State Historical Society of Wisconsin, 1974.

Correspondence of the American Revolution . . . . Jared Sparks, editor, 4 vols., Boston: Little, Brown, 1853.

Corwin, Edward S. *Court Over Constitution.* Princeton: Princeton University Press, 1938.

————. *The Doctrine of Judicial Review and Other Essays*. Princeton: Princeton University Press, 1914.

————. *John Marshall and the Constitution: A Chronicle of the Supreme Court*. New Haven: Yale University Press, 1919.

————. *The Twilight of the Supreme Court*. New Haven: Yale University Press, 1934.

Courts and Law in Early New York: Selected Essays. Leo Hershkowitz and Milton M. Klein, editors, Port Washington: Kennikat Press, 1978.

Crosskey, William W. *Politics and the Constitution in the History of the United States*. 2 vols., Chicago: University of Chicago Press, 1953.

Currie, David P. *The Constitution in the Supreme Court: The First Hundred Years, 1789–1888*. Chicago: University of Chicago Press, 1985.

Dargo, George. *Jefferson's Louisiana: Politics and the Clash of Legal Traditions*. Cambridge: Harvard University Press, 1975.

Dumbauld, Edward. *Thomas Jefferson and the Law*. Norman: University of Oklahoma Press, 1978.

Dunne, Gerald T. *Justice Joseph Story and the Rise of the Supreme Court*. New York: Simon and Schuster, 1970.

Elsmere, Jane Schaffer. *Justice Samuel Chase*. Muncie: Janevar Publishing Company, 1980.

Ely, James W., Jr. *The Chief Justiceship of Melville W. Fuller, 1888–1910*. Columbia: University of South Carolina Press, 1995.

————. *The Guardian of Every Other Right: A Constitutional History of Property Rights*. New York: Oxford University Press, 1992.

Faulkner, Robert K. *The Jurisprudence of John Marshall*. Princeton: Princeton University Press, 1970.

Frankfurter, Felix. *The Commerce Clause under Marshall, Taney and Waite*. Chapel Hill: University of North Carolina Press, 1937; reprinted, Chicago: Quadrangle Books, Inc., 1964.

Frankfurter, Felix, and James M. Landis. *The Business of the Supreme Court: A Study in the Federal Judicial System*. New York: Macmillan, 1928.

Freehling, William W. *Prelude to Civil War: The Nullification Controversy in South Carolina, 1816–1836*. New York: Harper & Row, 1966.

Gilmore, Grant, and Charles L. Black, Jr. *The Law of Admiralty*. 2nd edition, Mineola, New York: Foundation Press, 1975.

Goebel, Julius, Jr. *Antecedents and Beginnings to 1801*, vol. 1, *History of the Supreme Court of the United States*. New York: Macmillan, 1971.

Gunther, Gerald, editor. *John Marshall's Defense of McCulloch v. Maryland*. Gerald Gunther, editor, Stanford: Stanford University Press, 1969.

Haskins, George L., and Herbert A. Johnson. *Foundations of Power, 1801–15: Volume 2, History of the Supreme Court of the United States*. New York: Macmillan, 1981.

Henderson, Dwight F. *Congress, Courts, and Criminals: The Development of Federal Criminal Law, 1801–1829*. Westport: Greenwood Press, 1985.

Hoffer, Peter C., and N[atalie] E.H. Hull. *Impeachment in America, 1635–1805*. New Haven: Yale University Press, 1984.

Hough, Charles. *Reports of Cases in the Vice Admiralty of the Province of New York and in* the Court of Admiralty of the State of New York, 1715–1788. New Haven: Yale University Press, 1925.

Jackson, Percival. *Dissent in the Supreme Court: A Chronology*. Norman: University of Oklahoma Press, 1969.

Jacobs, Clyde E. *The Eleventh Amendment and Sovereign Immunity*. Westport: Greenwood Press, 1972.

Jay, John. *John Jay, the Winning of the Peace: Unpublished Papers, 1780–1784*. Richard B. Morris, editor, New York: Harper & Row, 1980.

Jennings, Walter W. *The American Embargo, 1807–1809*. Iowa City: University of Iowa, 1931.

Jones, W. Melville. *Chief Justice John Marshall: A Reappraisal*. W. Meville Jones, editor, Ithaca: Cornell University Press, 1956; reprinted, New York: Da Capo Press, 1970.

Justices of the United States Supreme Court, 1789–1969: Their Lives and Major Opinions. Leon Friedman and Fred L. Israel, editors, 4 vols., New York: Chelsea House, 1969.

Kettner, James H. *The Development of American Citizenship, 1608–1870*. Chapel Hill: University of North Carolina Press, 1978.

Lawrence, Alexander A. *James Moore Wayne, Southern Unionist*.Chapel Hill: University of North Carolina Press, 1943.

Levy, Leonard W. *Jefferson and Civil Liberties: The Darker Side*. Cambridge: Harvard University Press, 1963.

Luce, W. Ray. *Cohens v. Virginia (1821): The Supreme Court and States Rights: A Reevaluation of Influence and Impacts*. New York: Garland Publishing, 1990.

Marshall, John. *A History of the Colonies Planted by the English on the Continent of North America . . . .* Philadelphia: A. Small, 1824.

———. *An Autobiographical Sketch by John Marshall*. John Stokes Adams, editor, Ann Arbor: University ofMichigan Press, 1937.

———. *The Life of George Washington . . .* . 1st edition, 5 vols., Philadelphia: C. P. Wayne, 1804–07.

———. *The Life of George Washington . . .* . 2nd edition, 2 vols., Philadelphia: J. Crissy, 1836–39.

———*The Papers of John Marshall*. Herbert A. Johnson, Charles T. Cullen, William C. Stinchcombe, Charles F. Hobson, et al., editors. 8 vols. to date, Chapel Hill: University of North Carolina Press, 1974–date.

Mason, Frances Norton. *My Dearest Polly: Letters of Chief Justice John Marshall to his Wife . . .* . Richmond: Garrett & Massie, 1961.

McClellan, James P. *Joseph Story and the American Constitution: A Study in Political and Legal Thought with Selected Writings*. Norman: University of Oklahoma Press, 1971.

McGrath, C. Peter. *Yazoo: Law and Politics in the Early Republic: The Case of Fletcher v. Peck*. New York: Norton, 1967.

McLoughlin, William G. *Cherokee Renascence in the New Republic*. Princeton: Princeton University Press, 1986.

Miller, F. Thorton. *Juries and Judges versus the Law: Virginia's Provincial Legal Perspective, 1783–1828*. Charlottesville: University Press of Virginia, 1994.

Morgan, Donald G. *Justice William Johnson, the First Dissenter: the Career and Constitutional Philosophy of a Jeffersonian Judge.* Columbia: University of South Carolina Press, 1954.

Nedelsky, Jennifer. *Private Property and the Limits of American Constitutionalism: The Madisonian Framework and Its Legacy.* Chicago: University of Chicago Press, 1990.

Newmyer, R Kent. *Supreme Court Justice Joseph Story: Statesman of the Old Republic.* Chapel Hill: University of North Carolina Press, 1985.

New York, Reports of Cases in the Vice Admiralty of the Province of New York and in the Court of Admiralty of the State of New York, 1715–1788. Charles M. Hough, editor, New Haven: Yale University Press, 1925.

North, Douglas C. *The Economic Growth of the United States, 1790–1860.* New York: Norton, 1966.

O'Connor, John E. *William Paterson: Lawyer and Statesman, 1745–1806.* New Brunswick: Rutgers University Press, 1979.

Origins of the Federal Judiciary: Essays on the Judiciary Act of 1789. Maeva Marcus, editor, New York: Oxford University Press, 1992.

Orth, John V. *The Judicial Power of the United States: The Eleventh Amendment in American History.* New York: Oxford University Press, 1987.

Presser, Stephen B. *The Original Misunderstanding: The English, the Americans and the Dialectic of Federalist Jurisprudence.* Durham: Carolina Academic Press, 1991.

Roper, Donald M. *Mr. Justice Thompson and the Constitution.* New York: Garland Publishing, Inc., 1987.

Rudko, Frances H. *John Marshall and International Law: Statesman and Chief Justice.* Westport: Greenwood Press, 1991.

Scott, William B. *In Pursuit of Happiness: American Conceptions of Property from the Seventeenth to the Twentieth Century.* Bloomington: Indiana University Press, 1977.

Sears, Louis M. *Jefferson and the Embargo.* Durham: Duke University Press, 1927.

Shevory, Thomas C., editor *John Marshall's Achievement: Law, Politics, and Constitutional Interpretation.* Westport: Greenwood Press, 1989.

———. *John Marshall's Law: Interpretation, Ideology and Interest.* Westport: Greenwood Press, 1994.

Snowiss, Sylvia. *Judicial Review and the Law of the Constitution.* New Haven: Yale University Press, 1990.

Steamer, Robert J. *Chief Justice: Leadership and the Supreme Court.* Columbia: University of South Carolina Press, 1986.

Story, Joseph. *The Miscellaneous Letters of Joseph Story.* William W. Story, editor, Boston: Charles C. Little and James Brown, 1852.

———. *Commentaries on the Law of Bills of Exchange, Foreign and Inland . . . .* Boston: Charles C. Little and James Brown, 1843.

Warren, Charles. *The Story-Marshall Correspondence (1819–1831),* Series 1, No. 7, *Anglo American Legal History Series.* New York: New York University School of Law, 1942.

———. *The Supreme Court in United States History,* revised edition, 2 vols., Boston: Little, Brown & Company, 1922–26.

Weisenberger, Francis P. *The Life of John McLean: A Politician on the United States Supreme Court.* Columbus: Ohio State University Press, 1937.

Wheaton, Henry. *A Digest of the Law of Marine Captures and Prizes.* New York: R. M'Dermut & D. D. Arden, 1815.

White, G. Edward. *The Marshall Court and Cultural Change, 1815–35,* vols. 3 & 4, *History of the Supreme Court of the United States.* New York: Macmillan, 1988.

White, Leonard D. *The Jeffersonians: A Study in Administrative History.* New York: Free Press, 1951.

Wiecek, William M. *The Sources of Antislavery Constitutionalism in America, 1760–1848.* Ithaca: Cornell University Press, 1977.

Wirt, William. *The Letters of a British Spy.* 9th edition, Baltimore: F. Lucas, 1831.

Witt, Elder, editor. *The Supreme Court at Work.* Washington: Congressional Quarterly, 1990.

The Writings of George Washington . . . . Jared Sparks, editor, 12 vols., Boston: American Stationers, 1834–37.

Wolfe, Christoper. *The Rise of Modern Judicial Review: From Constitutional Interpretation to Judge-Made Law.* New York: Basic Books, 1986; 2d edition, New York: Rowan and Littlefield, 1994.

Ziegler, Benjamin. *The International Law of John Marshall: A Study in First Principles.* Chapel Hill: University of North Carolina Press, 1939.

ARTICLES AND ESSAYS

Abel, Albert S. "Commerce Regulation before Gibbons v. Ogden: Interstate Transportation Enterprise," 18 *Mississippi Law Journal* 335–380 (1947).

Akmar, Akhil R. "Jurisdiction Stripping and the Judiciary Act of 1789," in *Origins of the Federal Judiciary: Essays on the Judiciary Act of 1789.* Maeva Marcus, editor, New York: Oxford University Press, 1992.

———. "Marbury, Section 13, and the Original Jurisdiction of the Supreme Court," 56 *University of Chicago Law Review* 443–499 (1989).

———. "The Two-Tiered Structure of the Judiciary Act of 1789," 138 *University of Pennsylvania Law Review* 1499–1566 (1990).

Alfange, Dean, Jr. "Marbury v. Madison and Original Understandings of Judicial Review: In Defense of Traditional Wisdom," 1993 *Supreme Court Review,* 329–446.

Baker, Stewart A. "Federalism and the Eleventh Amendment," 48 *University of Colorado Law Review* 139–188 (1977).

Bartosic, Florian. "With John Marshall from William and Mary to Dartmouth College, 7 *William and Mary Law Review* 259–266 (1966).

Blaustein, Albert P., and Roy M. Mersky. "Bushrod Washington," in *Justices of the United States Supreme Court, 1789–1969.* Leon Friedman and Fred L. Israel, editors, 4 vols., New York: Chelsea House, 1969.

Bloch, Susan Low, and Maeva Marcus. "John Marshall's Selective Use of History in Marbury v. Madison," 1986 *Wisconsin Law Review* 301–337.

Boyd, Stephen R. "The Contract Clause and the Evolution of American Federalism, 1789–1815," 44 *William and Mary Quarterly,* 3d Series, 529–548 (1987).

Brisbin, Richard A., Jr. "John Marshall on History, Virtue, and Legality," in *John Marshall's Achievement: Law, Politics, and Constitutional Interpretation,* Thomas C. Shevory, editor, Westport: Greenwood Press, 1989.

Broderick, Albert. "From Constitutional Politics to Constitutional Law: The Supreme Court's First Fifty Years," 65 *North Carolina Law Review* 945–956 (1987).

Bruchey, Stuart. "The Impact of Concern for the Security of Property Rights in the Legal System of the Early American Republic," 1980 *Wisconsin Law Review* 1135–1158.

Campbell, Bruce A. "John Marshall, the Virginia Political Economy, and the Dartmouth College Decision," 19 *American Journal of Legal History* 40–65 (1975).

Campbell, Thomas P. "Chancellor Kent, Chief Justice Marshall and the Steamboat Cases," 25 *Syracuse Law Review* 497–534 (1974).

Conant, Michael. "The Commerce Clause, the Supremacy Clause and the Law Merchant: Swift v. Tyson and the Unity of Commercial Law," 14 *Journal of Maritime and Commercial Law,* 153–178 (1984).

Corwin, Edward S. "Marbury v. Madison and the Doctrine of Judicial Review," 12 *Michigan Law Review* 538–572 (1914).

Cozine, R. Kirkland. "The Emergence of Written Appellate Briefs in the Nineteenth-Century United States," 38 *American Journal of Legal History* 482–530 (1994).

Currie, David P. "The Most Insignificant Justice: A Preliminary Inquiry," 50 *University of Chicago Law Review,* 466–480 (1983).

Cushing, John D. "The Cushing Court and the Abolition of Slavery in Massachusetts, 5 *American Journal of Legal History* 118–144 (1961).

Custer, Lawrence B. "Bushrod Washington and John Marshall: A Preliminary Inquiry," 4 *American Journal of Legal History* 34–48 (1960).

Dilliard, Irving. "Gabriel Duvall," in *Justices of the United States Supreme Court, 1789–1969.* Leon Friedman and Fred L. Israel, editors, 4 vols., New York: Chelsea House, 1969.

Dumbauld, Edward. "John Marshall and the Law of Nations," 104 *University of Pennsylvania Law Review* 38–56 (1955).

Dunne, Gerald T. "Brockholst Livingston," in *Justices of the United States Supreme Court, 1789–1969.* 4 vols., Leon Friedman and Fred L. Israel, editors, New York: Chelsea House, 1969.

———. "Smith Thompson," in *Justices of the United States Supreme Court, 1789–1969.* Leon Friedman and Fred L. Israel, editors, 4 vols., New York: Chelsea House, 1969.

———. "The Story-Livingston Correspondence (1812–1822)," 10 *American Journal of Legal History* 226–236 (1966).

Easterbrook, Frank. "The Most Insignificant Justice: Further Evidence," 50 *University of Chicago Law Review* 481–503 (1983).

Engdahl, David E. "John Marshall's 'Jeffersonian' Concept of Judicial Review," 42 *Duke Law Journal* 279–339 (1993).

Field, Martha A. "The Eleventh Amendment and Other Sovereign Immunity Doctrines," 126 *University of Pennsylvania Law Review* 515–549 (1977).

Fisher, William W., III. "Ideology, Religion, and the Protection of Private Property," 39 *Emory Law Journal* 65–134 (1990).

Fletcher, William A. "A Historical Interpretation of the Eleventh Amendment: A

Narrow Construction of an Affirmative Grant of Jurisdiction Rather than a Prohibition against Jurisdiction," 35 *Stanford Law Review* 1033–1131 (1983).

Freund, Paul A. "Appointment of Justices: Some Historical Perspectives," 101 *Harvard Law Review* 1146–1163 (1988).

Frickey, Philip P. "Marshalling Past and Present: Colonialism, Constitutionalism, and Interpretations in Federal Indian Law," 107 *Harvard Law Review* 381–440 (1993).

Friedman, Barry. "A Different Dialogue: The Supreme Court, Congress and Federal Jurisdiction," 85 *Northwestern University Law Review* 1–61 (1990).

Friedman, Leon. "Alfred Moore," in *Justices of the United States Supreme Court, 1789–1969*. 4 vols., Leon Friedman and Fred L. Israel, editors, New York: Chelsea House, 1969.

Gatell, Frank Otto. "Henry Baldwin," in *Justices of the United States Supreme Court, 1789–1969*. Leon Friedman and Fred L. Israel, editors, 4 vols., New York: Chelsea House, 1969.

———. "James Moore Wayne," in *Justices of the United States Supreme Court, 1789–1969*. Leon Friedman and Fred L. Israel, editors, 4 vols., New York: Chelsea House, 1969.

———. "John McLean," in *Justices of the United States Supreme Court, 1789–1969*. Leon Friedman and Fred L. Israel, editors, 4 vols., New York: Chelsea House, 1969.

Gibbons, John J. "The Eleventh Amendment and State Sovereign Immunity: A Reinterpretation," 83 *Columbia Law Review* 1889–2005 (1983).

Hale, Robert L. "The Supreme Court and the Contract Clause," 57 *Harvard Law Review* 512–557 (1944)

Hartnett, Edward. "A New Trick from an Old and Abused Dog: Section 1441 (c) Lives and Now Permits the Remand of Federal Question Cases," 63 *Fordham Law Review* 1099–1182 (1995).

Haskins, George L. "John Marshall and the Commerce Clause of the Constitution," 104 *University of Pennsylvania Law Review* 23–27 (1955).

Holt, Wythe W. " 'To Establish Justice': Politics, the Judiciary Act of 1789, and the Invention of the Federal Courts," 1989 *Duke Law Journal* 1421–1531.

Hovenkamp, Herbert. "Technology, Politics, and Regulated Monopoly: An American Historical Perspective," 62 *Texas Law Review* 1263–1312 (1984).

Hurst, James Willard. "English Sources of the American Law of Treason," 1945 *Wisconsin Law Review* 315–356.

———. "The Historic Background of the Treason Clause of the United States Constitution," 6 *Federal Bar Journal* 305–313 (1945).

———. "Treason in the United States," 58 *Harvard Law Review* 226–272, 395–444, 806–857 (1944–45).

Isaacs, Nathan. "John Marshall on Contracts, A Study in Early American Juristic Theory," 7 *Virginia Law Review* 413–428 (1921).

Israel, Fred L. "Thomas Todd," in *Justices of the United States Supreme Court, 1789–1969*. Leon Friedman and Fred L. Israel, editors, 4 vols., New York: Chelsea House, 1969.

Jackson, Vicki C. "The Supreme Court, the Eleventh Amendment, and State Sovereign Immunity," 98 *Yale Law Journal* 1–126 (1988).

Johnson, Herbert A. "Albert J. Beveridge," *Dictionary of Literary Biography: Twentieth Century American Historians,* Clyde V. Wilson, editor, vol. 17, 116–127. Detroit: Gale Research Company, 1983.

———. "The Constitutional Thought of William Johnson," 89 *South Carolina Historical Magazine* 132–145 (1988).

———. "Federal Union, Property, and the Contract Clause," in *John Marshall's Achievement: Law, Politics, and Constitutional Interpretation,* Westport: Greenwood Press, 1989.

———. "Gibbons v. Ogden before Marshall," in *Courts and Law in Early New York: Selected Essays.* Leo Hershkowitz and Milton M. Klein, editors, Port Washington: Kennikat Press, 1978.

———. "Impeachment and Politics," 63 *South Atlantic Quarterly* 552–563 (1964).

———. "Toward a Reappraisal of the 'Federal' Government, 1783–1789," 8 *American Journal of Legal History* 314–325 (1964).

———. "William Cushing," in *Justices of the United States Supreme Court, 1789–1969.* Leon Friedman and Fred L. Israel, editors, 4 vols., New York: Chelsea House, 1969.

Kainen, James. "Nineteenth Century Interpretations of the Federal Contract Clause: The Transformation from Vested to Substantive Rights against the State," 31 *Buffalo Law Review* 381–480 (1982).

Kraus, Michael. "William Patterson," in *Justices of the United States Supreme Court, 1789–1969.* Leon Friedman and Fred L. Israel, editors, 4 vols., New York: Chelsea House, 1969.

Mann, W. Howard. "The Marshall Court: Nationalization of Private Rights and Personal Liberty from the Authority of the Commerce Clause, 38 *Indiana Law Journal* 117–238 (1963).

Massey, Calvin R. "State Sovereignty and the Tenth and Eleventh Amendments," 56 *University of Chicago Law Review* 61–151 (1987).

Mendelson, Wallace. "New Light on Fletcher v. Peck and Gibbons v. Ogden," 58 *Yale Law Journal* 567–573 (1949).

Miles, Edwin A. "After John Marshall's Decision: Worcester v. Georgia and the Nullification Crisis," 39 *Journal of Southern History* 519–544 (1973).

Morgan, Donald G. "Marshall, the Marshall Court, and the Constitution," in *Chief Justice John Marshall: A Reappraisal.* W. Melville Jones, editor, Ithaca: Cornell University Press, 1956; reprint, New York: Da Capo, 1970.

———. "William Johnson," in *Justices of the United States Supreme Court, 1789–1969.* Leon Friedman and Fred L. Israel, editors, 4 vols., New York: Chelsea House, 1969.

Nadelman, Kurt H. "On the Origin of the Bankruptcy Clause," 1 *American Journal of Legal History* 215–228 (1957).

Nelson, William E. "Changing Concepts of Judicial Review: The Evolution of Constitutional Theory in the States, 1790–1860," 120 *University of Pennsylvania Law Review* 1166–1185 (1972).

O'Fallon, James. "Marbury," 44 *Stanford Law Review* 219–260 (1992).

Palmer, Robert C. "The Federal Common Law of Crime," 4 *Law and History Review,* 267–323 (1986).

Powell, H. Jefferson. "The Oldest Question of Constitutional Law," 79 *Virginia Law Review* 633–689 (1993)

———. "The Political Grammar of Early Constitutional Law," 71 *North Carolina Law Review* 949–1009 (1993).

Presser, Stephen B. "The Supra-Constitution, the Courts and the Federal Common Law of Crimes: Some Comments on Palmer and Preyer," 4 *Law and History Review* 325–335 (1986).

Preyer, Kathryn [Turner]. "The Appointment of Chief Justice Marshall," 17 *William and Mary Quarterly,* 3rd Series, 143–163 (1961).

———. "Federal Policy and the Judiciary Act of 1802," 22 *William and Mary Quarterly,* 3rd Series, 3–32 (1965).

———. "Jurisdiction to Punish: Federal Authority, Federalism and the Common Law of Crimes in the Early Republic," 4 *Law and History Review* 223–265 (1986).

———. "The Midnight Judges . . .," 109 *University of Pennsylvania Law Review* 494–523 (1961).

Pushaw, Robert J., Jr. "Article III's Case/Controversy Distinction and the Dual Functions of Federal Courts," 69 *Notre Dame Law Review* 447–532 (1994).

Redish, Martin H. "Text, Structure and Common Sense in the Interpretation of Article III," 138 *University of Pennsylvania Law Review* 1633–1649 (1990).

Reynolds, William L. III. "Luther Martin, Maryland and the Constitution," 47 *Maryland Law Review* 291–321 (1987).

Roper, Donald M. "Judicial Unanimity and the Marshall Court—A Road to Reappraisal," 9 *American Journal of Legal History* 118–134 (1964).

Rossum, Ralph A. "Congress, the Constitution, and Appellate Jurisdiction of the Supreme Court: The Letter and Spirit of the Exceptions Clause," 24 *William and Mary Law Review* 385–428 (1983).

Rowe, Gary D. "The Sound of Silence: United States v. Hudson & Goodwin, the Jeffersonian Ascendancy and the Abolition of the Federal Common Law of Crimes," 101 *Yale Law Journal* 919–948 (1992).

Schroeder, Oliver, Jr. "The Life and Judicial Work of William Johnson, Jr., 95 *University of Pennsylvania Law Review* 344–386 (1946–47).

Seddig, Robert G. "John Marshall and the Origins of Supreme Court Leadership," 36 *University of Pittsburgh Law Review* 785–833 (1975).

Shaiman, S. Lawrence. "The History of Imprisonment for Debt and Insolvency Laws in Pennsylvania as they Evolved from the Common Law," 5 *American Journal of Legal History* 205–225 (1960).

Shevory, Thomas C. "John Marshall as a Republican: Order and Conflict in American Political History," in *John Marshall's Achievement: Law, Politics, and Constitutional Interpretation.* Thomas C. Shevory, editor, Westport: Greenwood Press, 1989.

Tabb, Charles Jordan. "The Historical Evolution of the Bankruptcy Discharge," 65 *American Bankruptcy Law Journal* 325–371 (1991).

Thompson, Barton H., Jr. "The History of the Judicial Impairment 'Doctrine' and its Lessons for the Contract Clause," 44 *Stanford Law Review* 1373–1466 (1992).

Warren, Charles. "Legislative and Judicial Attacks on the Supreme Court of the United States—A History of the Twenty-fifth Section of the Judiciary Act," 47 *American Law Review* 1–34 and 161–189 (1913).

Wechsler, Herbert. "The Appellate Jurisdiction of the Supreme Court: Reflections on the Law and the Logistics of Direct Review," 34 *Washington and Lee Law Review* 1043–1064 (1977).

White, G. Edward. "The Working Life of the Marshall Court, 1815–1835," 70 *Virginia Law Review* 1–52 (1984).

MANUSCRIPT COLLECTIONS AND MISCELLANEOUS SOURCES

Cardwell, Margaret. Collection. Cambridge, Mass.

Ess, Henry N. III. Collection. New York, N.Y.

Historical Society of Pennsylvania, Philadelphia, Pa.
    Cadwalader Collection
    Richard Peters Papers

Johnson, Herbert A. "A Statistical Analysis of Marshall Court Opinions," a paper delivered at the 25th annual meeting of the Southern Historical Association, Washington, D.C., on October 30, 1969.

Library of Congress, Washington, D.C.
    John Marshall Papers

Maryland Historical Society, Baltimore, Md.
    Samuel Chase Papers.

Massachusetts Historical Society, Boston, Mass.
    Joseph Story Papers.

Morristown National Historical Park Library, Morristown, N.J.
    Miscellaneous Manuscripts.

The National Archives, Washington, D.C.
    RG 46
    RG 59, Records of the Department of State
    RG 128, John Marshall Papers
    RG 267

New York Public Library, New York, N.Y.
    Berg Collection

The Pierpont Morgan Library, New York, N.Y.
    Henry Wheaton Papers

Rutgers University Libraries, New Brunswick, N.J.
    Special Collections

Southern Historical Collection, University of North Carolina, Chapel Hill, N.C.
    William Gaston Papers

Supreme Court of the United States, Minutes of the, Roll 1, Microcopy No. M215, National Archives, Washington, D.C..

United States Supreme Court Library, Washington, D.C.

University of Virginia, Alderman Library, Charlottesville, Va.
   McGregor Collection
Wickham, Littleton Tazewell. Collection. Richmond, Virginia.
College of William and Mary, Swem Library
   John Marshall Papers
   Tucker-Coleman Papers

TABLE OF CASES

The Active v. United States, 7 Cranch 100 (1812), 193n. 5

The Adeline and Cargo, 9 Cranch 244 (1815), 203n. 36

Alexander v. Baltimore Marine Insurance Company, 4 Cranch 370 (1808), 204n. 40

American and Ocean Insurance Company v. 356 Bales of Cotton (Canter, claimant), 1 Peters 511 (1828), 203n. 39, 234n. 25

The Amiable Isabella, 6 Wheaton 1 (1821), 34

La Amistad de Rues, 5 Wheaton 385 (1820), 241n. 42

The Antelope, 10 Wheaton 66 (1825), 46, 47, 95n. 22, 195, 244–245

The Aurora, 8 Cranch 203 (1814), 240n. 38

Bank of Columbia v. Lawrence, 1 Peters 578 (1828), 207–208n. 52

Bank of Columbia v. Patterson's Administrator, 7 Cranch 299 (1813), 216–217n. 88

Bank of Kentucky v. Wister, 2 Peters 318 (1829), 215n. 79

Bank of the Metropolis v. Jones, 8 Peters 12 (1834), 217n. 89

Bank of the United States v. Carneal, 2 Peters 543 (1829), 208n. 54

Bank of the United States v. Corcoran, 2 Peters 121 (1829), 208n. 54

Bank of the United States v. Deveaux, 5 Cranch 61 (1809), 122n. 13

Bank of the United States v. Dunn, 6 Peters 51 (1832), 217n. 89

Bank of the United States v. Donnally, 8 Peters 361 (1834), 209n. 61

Bank of the United States v. Planter's Bank of Georgia, 9 Wheaton 904 (1824), 157–158, 214–215

Bank of the United States v. Smith, 11 Wheaton 171 (1826), 207–208nn. 52, 53

Bank of the United States v. Tyler, 4 Peters 366 (1830), 207n. 51

Bank of the United States v. Weisiger, 2 Peters 331 (1829), 207n. 51

Barclay v. Howell's Lessee, 6 Peters 498 (1832), 123

Barron v. Baltimore, 7 Peters 243 (1833), 93, 94, 257

Bas v. Tingy, 4 Dallas 37 (1800), 184n. 62

Blaine v. The Charles Carter, 4 Cranch 332 (1808), 199nn. 27, 28

Bollman, Ex Parte, 4 Cranch 75 (1807), 124–125

Boyce v. Anderson, 2 Peters 150 (1829), 247–248

Boyce & Henry v. Edwards, 4 Peters 111 (1830), 209n. 59

Boyle v. Zachary & Turner, 6 Peters 635 (1832), 212 n. 69

Bracken v. College of William and Mary, 3 Call 573 (1790), 176–177, 179

Briscoe v. Commonwealth's Bank of Kentucky, 9 Peters 85 (1835), 106 n. 50

Brown v. Maryland, 12 Wheaton 419 (1827), 45, 93, 169–171, 187

Brown v. United States, 8 Cranch 110 (1814), 227 n. 7

Calder v. Bull, 3 Dallas 386 (1796), 173

Cassell v. Carroll, 11 Wheaton 134 (1826), 219–220

Charles River Bridge v. Warren Bridge, 11 Peters 420 (1837), 84, 180

Chisholm v. Georgia, 2 Dallas 419 (1793), 139, 184 n. 62

Cherokee Nation v. Georgia, 5 Peters 1 (1831), 42, 81–84, 94

Chesapeake and Ohio Canal Company v. Knapp, 9 Peters 541 (1835), 216–217 n. 88

Church v. Hubbart, 2 Cranch 187 (1804), 205 n. 42

Clark v. Young, 1 Cranch 181 (1803), 207 n. 51

Clark's Executor v. Van Riemsdyck, 9 Cranch 153 (1815), 212 n. 70

Cohens v. Virginia, 6 Wheaton 264 (1821), 75–77, 78, 80, 92–93, 147, 152–154, 157, 253

Commonwealth v. Morrison, 9 Kentucky (2 Marshall) 75 (1819), 147 n. 30

Conard v. Atlantic Insurance Company of New York, 1 Peters 386 (1828), 201

Coolidge v. Payson, 2 Wheaton 66 (1817), 209 n. 59

Cooper v. Aaron, 358 U.S. 1 (1958), 58 n. 11

Craig v. Missouri, 4 Peters 410 (1830), 48, 154–157, 215 n. 79

Croudson v. Leonard, 4 Cranch 434 (1808), 205 n. 43

Dartmouth College v. Woodward, 4 Wheaton 518 (1819), 33, 43, 60, 73, 74, 92, 93, 104, 175 n. 34, 176–181, 187, 232–233

Dawson's Lessee v. Godfrey, 4 Cranch 321 (1808), 230 n. 16

The Divina Pastora, 4 Wheaton 52 (1819), 241 n. 41

Doddridge v. Thompson, 9 Wheaton 469 (1824), 222

Dred Scott v. Sandford, 19 Howard 393 (1857), 95 n. 23

Dugan v. United States, 3 Wheaton 172 (1818), 158 n. 66

Dunlop & Company v. Ball, 2 Cranch 180 (1804), 230

Durousseau v. United States, 6 Cranch 307 (1810), 154 n. 53

Duvall v. Craig, 2 Wheaton 45 (1817), 40 n. 93

Elkison v. Deliesseline, 8 Federal Cases (No. 4,366) 493 (S.C. Cir. Ct., 1823), 33, 131– 133, 137, 168 n. 12

The Emily and the Caroline, 9 Wheaton 381 (1824), 195–196, 244 n. 51

The Exchange v. M'Faddon, 7 Cranch 116 (1812), 142, 226–227, 235

Fairfax's Devisee v. Hunter's Lessee, 7 Cranch 603 (1813), 69, 71, 72, 105, 149–151, 217–218, 229–230, 235

Fleckner v. Bank of the United States, 8 Wheaton 338 (1823), 216–217 n. 88

Fletcher v. Peck, 6 Cranch 87 (1810), 33, 60, 92, 93, 174, 175–176, 178 n. 45, 179, 187

French's Executor v. Bank of Columbia, 4 Cranch 141 (1807), 208

Gelston v. Hoyt, 3 Wheaton 246 (1818), 241 n. 43

The General Smith, 4 Wheaton 438 (1819), 198, 199 n. 25

Gibbons v. Ogden, 9 Wheaton 1 (1824), 60, 78 n. 71, 80, 87, 92–93, 133, 162–169, 170, 175 n. 34

Gilchrist v. Collector of Charleston, 10 Federal Cases (No. 5,420) 200 (S.C. Cir. Ct., 1808), 193, 238

Golden v. Prince, 10 Federal Cases (No. 5,509) 542 (Pa. Cir. Ct.,1814), 136

Gordon v. Caldcleugh, 3 Cranch 268 (1806), 141 n. 12

Gracie v. Marine Insurance Company of Baltimore, 8 Cranch 75 (1814), 204 n. 40

Green v. Biddle, 8 Wheaton 1 (1823), 7, 78–81, 105, 109, 187–189

Green v. Neal, 6 Peters 291 (1832), 217 n. 92

Hannah v. Davis (1787) unreported, 246 n. 58

Harris v. Johnston, 3 Cranch 31 (1806), 207 n. 51

Harrison v. Nixon, 9 Peters (34 US) 483, 123

Harrison v. Sterry, 5 Cranch 289 (1809), 211

Head & Amory v. Providence Insurance Company, 7 Cranch 331 (1812), 204 n. 40

Henderson v. Griffin, 5 Peters 151 (1831), 217 n. 91

Higginson v. Mein, 4 Cranch 415 (1808), 231

Hite v. Fairfax, 4 Call 42 (Va. Ct. App., 1786), 12

Hopkirk v. Bell, 4 Cranch 164 (1807), 231

Houston v. Moore, 5 Wheaton 1 (1820), 102, 102 n. 38, 160–161, 164

Hunt v. Wickliffe, 2 Peters 201 (1829), 222

Hunter v. United States, 5 Peters 173 (1831), 212 n. 70

Jackson v. Goodell, 20 Johnson 693 (N.Y. Ct. Impeachments and Errors, 1823), 252

The James Wells v. United States, 7 Cranch 22 (1812), 193 n. 6

Johnson and Graham's Lessee v. McIntosh, 8 Wheaton 543 (1823), 250–251

Kirk v. Smith ex dem Penn, 9 Wheaton 241 (1824), 218–219

La Josefa Segunda, 5 Wheaton 338 (1820), 195, 243–244

The Julia, 8 Cranch 181 (1814), 123 nn. 16, 17, 240

King v. Delaware Insurance Company, 6 Cranch 71 (1810), 204 n. 40

King v. Riddle, 7 Cranch 168 (1812), 212 n. 72

Kirkman v. Hamilton, 6 Peters 20 (1832), 209 n. 60

Lambert's Lessee v. Paine, 3 Cranch 97 (1806), 230 n. 16

Lanusse v. Barker, 3 Wheaton 102 (1818), 40 n. 93

Lawrason v. Mason, 3 Cranch 492 (1806), 206 n. 47

Lindsey v. Miller's Lessee, 6 Peters 666 (1832), 223

Liter v. Green, 2 Wheaton 306 (1817), 40 n. 93

Little v. Barreme, 7 Cranch 577 (1813), 192

Livingston v. Dorgenois, 7 Cranch 57 (1813), 77

Madrazzo, Ex Parte, 7 Peters 627 (1833), 148

Magruder v. Union Bank of Georgetown, 3 Peters 87 (1830), 207–208 n. 52

Mandeville v. Union Bank of Georgetown, 9 Cranch 9 (1815), 206n. 48

Mandeville & Jameson v. Riddle & Company, 1 Cranch 290 (1803), 206n. 46

Manro v. Almeidu, 10 Wheaton 473 (1823), 199n. 25

Marbury v. Madison, 1 Cranch 137 (1803), 3, 4, 5, 7, 57–63, 68, 76, 141, 152, 153, 159, 183n 59

The Marianna Flora, 11 Wheaton 1 (1826), 242

Martin v. Hunter's Lessee, 1 Wheaton 304 (1816), 7, 69–72, 76–78, 91–92, 105, 141, 149–152, 157, 229–230, 231, 235

Maryland Insurance Company v. LeRoy, 7 Cranch 26 (1812), 204n. 41

Maryland Insurance Company v. Woods, 6 Cranch 45 (1810), 204n. 40

Mason v. The Blaireau, 2 Cranch 264 (1804), 202n. 34

Mason v. Haile, 12 Wheaton 370 (1827), 212n. 69

Mayor of London v. Wood, 12 Modern (Exchequer 1702), 215n. 81

M'Culloch v. Maryland, 4 Wheaton 316 (1819), 7, 60, 73–76, 92, 140–147, 158, 161, 164, 169, 171, 179, 181, 210

McDonald v. Magruder, 3 Peters 470 (1830), 207–208n. 52

M'Gruder v. Bank of Washington, 9 Wheaton 598 (1824), 207–208n. 52

M'Ilvaine v. Coxe's Lessee, 4 Cranch 209 (1808), 100n. 35

M'Millan v. M'Neill, 4 Wheaton 209 (1819), 183, 184

Mechanic's Bank of Alexandria v. Seton, 1 Peters 299 (1828), 216

Mechanic's Bank of Alexandria v. Bank of Columbia, 5 Wheaton 326 (1820), 216n. 88

The Merino, The Constitution, The Louisa, 9 Wheaton 391 (1824), 196

Mills v. Bank of the United States, 11 Wheaton 431 (1826), 208n. 56

Mima Queen v. Hepburn, 7 Cranch 290 (1813), 43, 245–247

Minor v. Mechanic's Bank of Alexandria, 1 Peters 46 (1828), 216n. 85

Murray v. The Charming Betsey, 2 Cranch 64 (1804), 202n. 35

The Nereide, 9 Cranch 388 (1815), 239–240

New Jersey v. Wilson, 7 Cranch 164 (1812), 174n. 30

New York v. Miln, 11 Peters 102 (1837), 84

Nicholls v. Webb, 8 Wheaton 325 (1823), 208n. 57

The Octavia, 1 Wheaton 20 (1816), 123n. 16

Ogden v. Saunders, 12 Wheaton 213 (1827), 24, 45, 46, 47, 50, 62, 81, 93, 94, 106, 171, 179–180, 182, 184–186, 211–212, 213n. 74, 255, 256

Olivera v. Union Insurance Company, 3 Wheaton 183 (1818), 24

Osborn v. Bank of the United States, 9 Wheaton 738 (1824), 78n. 71, 157–159, 161

The Palmyra, 12 Wheaton 1 (1827), 20n. 35, 242n. 46

Parsons v. Armor, 3 Peters 413 (1830), 209n. 58

The Paulina's Cargo, 7 Cranch 52 (1812), 193n. 5

Peisch v. Ware, 4 Cranch 347 (1808), 197, 225 n. 2

Penhallow v. Doane's Administrator, 3 Dallas 54 (1795), 148

Peyroux v. Howard, 7 Peters 324 (1833), 198 n. 24, 201 n. 32

Pleasants V. Pleasants, 2 Call 319 (1800), 246 n. 58

Providence Bank v. Billings, 4 Peters 514 (1830), 81, 93, 180 n. 52

Ramsay v. Allegre, 12 Wheaton 611 (1827), 198–199

Reily v. Lamar, Beall and Smith, 2 Cranch 344 (1804), 212

Respublica v. De Longchamps, 138 n. 2

Reynolds v. McArthur, 2 Peters 417 (1829), 222–223

Richards v. Maryland Insurance Company, 8 Cranch 84 (1814), 211 n. 66

Riddle & Company v. Mandeville & Jameson, 5 Cranch 322 (1809), 206 nn. 46, 47

Robinson v. Campbell, 3 Wheaton 208 (1818), 40 n. 93

The St. Jago de Cuba, 9 Wheaton 409 (1824), 195 n. 13, 196, 200, 244 n. 52

The Santissima Trinidad and the St. Ander, 7 Wheaton 283 (1822), 227–228

Satterlee v. Matthewson, 2 Peters 380 (1829), 173 n. 28

Schimmelpennich v. Bayard, 1 Peters 264 (1828), 209 n. 59

Sheppard v. Taylor, 5 Peters 675 (1831), 194–195

The Short Staple v. United States, 9 Cranch 55 (1815), 193 n. 6

Slacum v. Pomeroy, 6 Cranch 221 (1810), 206

Smith v. Maryland, 6 Cranch 286 (1810), 151, 229 n. 13

Society for the Propagation of the Gospel in Foreign Parts v. New Haven, 8 Wheaton 464 (1823), 214 n. 77, 232–233

Society for the Propagation of the Gospel in Foreign Parts v. Town of Pawlet, 4 Peters 480 (1830), 214 n. 77

Somersett v. Stewart, Lofft's Reports 1–18, 98 English Reports (Full Reprint) 499 (K.B., 1772), 242, 247

Stevens v. The Sandwich, 23 Federal Cases (No. 13,409) 29 (Md. D.Ct., 1801), 198–199

Stratton v. Jarvis & Brown, 8 Peters 4 (1828), 203 n. 38

Strawbridge v. Curtiss, 3 Cranch 267 (1806), 122 n. 13, 159 n. 70, 215 n. 80

Stuart v. Laird, 1 Cranch 299 (1803), 55–57, 100, 112–114

Sturges v. Crowninshield, 4 Wheaton 122 (1819), 73–74, 78 n. 71, 92 n. 11, 103, 136, 181–187, 211 n. 73

Swartwout, Ex Parte, 4 Cranch 75 (1807), 127, 129, 130

The Sybil, 4 Wheaton 98 (1819), 203 n. 38

Talbot v. Seeman, 1 Cranch 1 (1801), 201–202

Terrett v. Taylor, 9 Cranch 43 (1815), 174 nn. 31, 32, 231–233

The Thomas Jefferson, 10 Wheaton 428 (1825), 198 n. 23

Thornton v. Wynn, 12 Wheaton 183 (1827), 208 n. 59

Town of Pawlet v. Clark, 9 Cranch 292 (1815), 174n. 31, 232–233

Townsley v. Sumrall, 2 Peters 170 (1829), 209n. 59

Union Bank v. Hyde, 6 Wheaton 572 (1821), 208n. 58

Union Bank of Georgetown v. Laird, 2 Wheaton 390 (1817), 216n. 84

Union Bank of Georgetown v. Magruder, 7 Peters 287 (1833), 208n. 55

United States v. Amedy, 11 Wheaton 392 (1826), 214n. 76

United States v. Arredondo, 6 Peters 691 (1832), 46, 220–221

United States v. Bevans, 3 Wheaton 336 (1818), 198

United States v. Burr, 4 Cranch 469–506 (1807), 124–131, 137

United States v. Coolidge, 1 Wheaton 415 (1816), 41, 142, 241n. 44

United States v. The Brig Eliza, 7 Cranch 113 (1812), 193n. 6

United States v. Fisher, 2 Cranch 358 (1804), 145n. 24, 181n. 54, 210–211

United States v. Hall & Worth, 6 Cranch 171 (1810), 193n. 6

United States v. Hudson & Goodwin, 7 Cranch 32 (1812), 130n. 40

United States v. Le Jeune Eugenie, 26 Federal Cases (No. 15,551) 832 (Mass. Cir. Ct., 1818), 42

United States v. More, 3 Cranch 159 (1805), 154n. 53

United States v. Palmer, 3 Wheaton 610 (1818), 241

United States v. Peters, 5 Cranch 115 (1809), 138n. 2, 147–148

United States v. The William, 28 Federal Cases (No. 16,700) 614 (Mass. Cir. Ct., 1808), 67–68, 193n. 8

The Venus, 8 Cranch 253 (1814), 238–239

Violett v. Patton, 5 Cranch 142 (1809), 206n. 46

The Virgin v. Vyfhuis, 8 Peters 538 (1834), 200

Ware v. Hylton, 3 Dallas 199 (1796), 11, 69, 138, 230

Wheaton v. Peters, 8 Peters 591 (1834), 45, 108–111

Wheaton v. Peters, 29 Federal Cases (No. 17,486) 862 (Pa. Cir. Ct., 1832), 110n. 66

Williams v. Armroyd, 7 Cranch 423 (1813), 227

Williams v. Bank of the United States, 2 Peters 96 (1829), 208n. 54

Willson v. Black Bird Creek Marsh Company, 2 Peters 245 (1829), 81, 93, 167n. 9, 171, 187

Wilson v. Mason, 1 Cranch 45 (1801), 221

Wood v. Owings and Smith, 2 Cranch 239 (1804), 210n. 64

Worcester v. Georgia, 6 Peters 515 (1832), 42n. 104, 48, 82–84, 94n. 19, 154, 248–255, 257–261

Yeaton v. Bank of Alexandria, 5 Cranch 49 (1809), 206n. 47

Young v. Bryan, 6 Wheaton 146 (1821), 209

Youngstown Sheet & Tube Company v. Sawyer, 343 U.S. 579 (1952), 192

Index

Adams, John, 9, 10, 11, 12, 22, 23, 26, 30, 54, 55, 57, 112, 225

Adams, John Quincy, 32, 33, 38, 47, 48, 131

Adams-Onis Treaty (1819), 46

Admiralty, 136–136, 138, 201–203, 225, 233, 244; jurisdiction of, 34, 99, 190–199, 203; maritime liens, 136, 198–201; Story-Johnson disagreement, 99, 197–199

Alexandria Gazette, 74, 75

Aliens, 12, 54

American Board of Foreign Missions, 83

American Colonization Society, 245, 246

American Revolution, 27, 28, 35, 41, 43, 60, 69, 138, 140, 197, 214, 218, 221, 230, 231, 232, 259

"Amphictyon" Letters, 74–75

Appeals, 122–123

Armed Neutrality (1780), 239

Articles of Confederation, 26, 138, 147, 178–179, 252, 259

Associate justices, 6–7, 22–50; relationships to Marshall, 36, 37, 38, 49, 135–136, 256–258, 260

Baldwin, Henry, 47, 49, 83, 89, 98–99, 110, 111, 117, 119, 120, 123, 156, 220, 223, 248, 249, 250–251, 260

Bank of the United States, 49, 78, 84, 92, 140, 142–146, 159–160, 164; federal court jurisdiction, 122, 157–161, 215–217

Bankruptcy, 181–185, 210–213; insolvency and, 93, 181–187, 210 n.63

Bankruptcy Act (1800), 210–213

Batture Controversy (1813), 77

Beveridge, Albert J., 3, 70, 71, 176, 261

Bill of Rights, 257

Bills of credit, 154–157, 214–215

Blackstone, Sir William, 14

Blair, John, 25, 26

Blennerhassett's Island, 126–128, 131

Boardinghouse, Justices', 2, 97–99, 103, 111

Bollman, Erick, 124–125

Bottomry bond, 199–201

British debts, 11, 230–231

British Parliament, 178–179, 225

Brockenbrough, William, 75

Burr, Aaron, 7, 65–66, 68, 71, 113, 124–131

Butler, Elizur, 82–84, 253

Bynkershoek, Cornelius van, 41, 50

Callender, James T., 30, 63

Campbell, Mary Johnson, 49–50

Charleston, S.C., 32, 33

Chase, Samuel, 22, 26, 27, 28–32, 38, 43, 56, 57, 63–65, 88, 100, 113, 117, 120, 124, 199–200

Cherokee cases, 81–84, 94–95, 109, 248–255, 257–261

Choice of law, 209–219

Circuit Courts, United States, 31, 55–57, 107, 113–120, 133–134; appeals from, 113–114, 121, 123–124;

Circuit Courts, U.S. (*continued*)
  certified questions from, 116–117,
  120; organization of, 113, 120–121,
  135; riding circuit, physical demands,
  25, 26, 112–113, 134–135; Supreme
  Court justices in, 6, 55–57, 113–114,
  120–121
Clark, Tom, 192
Clay, Henry, 79, 105, 188, 218–219
Coke, Sir Edward, 14, 96–97
Colleges, 176–177
Commerce, 163, 165–166
Commerce clause, 33, 80, 167, 169–171,
  256; exclusive federal power, 132,
  133, 167; limitation of, 80–81, 93,
  166–167
Commercial law, 205–213
Common carrier, 248
Common law, federal, 34, 99, 130–131,
  142; crime in, 41, 81, 141-142; Story,
  Joseph, and, 81, 99, 241
Common market, 162
Compact theory of Union, 144–145,
  165–166
Concurrent power, 164, 166
Confiscation of land, 150
Conflicts of law, 206
Construction, 180
Contract clause, 24, 33, 60, 79, 136,
  173–175, 177–178, 180, 182-183, 187–
  189, 256; corporations and, 81, 93,
  176–181; natural law and, 50–51, 174,
  256
Contracts, 93, 180–181, 185–187
Cooper, Thomas, 30, 33
Copyright, 110–111
Corn Tassel, 82, 249
Corporations, 176–181, 213–214, 216–
  217, 232–233; complete diversity rule,
  121–122, 159–160, 215–216
Corwin, Edward S., 4
Council of Revision, 45
Courts, Federal, 54–55
Craig, Hiram, 154–157
Cranch, William, 100, 108–111, 246

Criminal procedure (federal), 126–127,
  131
Cushing, William, 22, 25, 26, 30, 38, 88,
  100, 113, 117, 120, 129

Dallas, Alexander J., 49
Dartmouth College, 176–181
Davis, John, 67, 193
Declaration of Independence, 242
De homine replegiando, 132
Denmark Vesey slave uprising, 131
Dissent, 68–69, 99
District of Columbia, 205–210, 245–246
Diversity cases, 121, 159, 191
Divorce, 180
Dormancy, 167, 171, 181
Double jeopardy, 129
Duvall, Gabriel, 37, 38, 43–44, 84, 88,
  89, 90, 92, 105, 117, 120, 156, 177,
  182, 185–187, 245, 246, 247

Eleventh Amendment, 82, 92, 139, 147–
  149, 152, 214, 216, 261; party of rec-
  ord rule, 148, 158 n. 67, 214
Elkison, Henry, 131–134
Ellsworth, Oliver, 29–30, 65, 100, 108,
  112, 139, 225, 228, 237
Embargo, 33, 38, 66–68, 191, 193, 238
Eminent domain, 173
Emmett, Thomas Addis, 105, 165
English Promissory Note Act (1704),
  206
Episcopal Church, 231–232
Evarts Act of 1891, 113
Everett, Edward, 38
Evidence, 246–247
Exclusive powers, 45, 164–165, 182
Executive privilege, 126
Expositive interpretation, 61

Fairfax proprietary lands, 11, 12, 69–72,
  73, 91, 105, 139, 148–151, 221,
  229–230
Federal Coastal Licensing Act (1793),
  167

Federal Constitution, 4, 155–156; construction of, 145–146, 166, 167
Federalism, 53–54, 139, 140–142, 152–154, 164, 161
Federalist Party, 10, 55, 58, 63, 67, 71, 112, 141
Federalist Papers, 154
Federal questions, 76, 149–152, 217–218
Fifth Amendment, 93–94, 173, 257
Florida land grants, 220–221, 234–235
Four Judge Rule, 105–106
Fourteenth Amendment, 257
French Directory, 224
French Republic, 192
French Revolution, 14
"Friend of the Constitution" Essays, 75
Fries Rebellion, 30, 63

Ghent, Treaty of (1815), 71
Gibbons, Thomas, 163, 167
Great Compromise, 26
Griffin, Cyrus, 125
Grotius, Hugo, 50

Habeas corpus, 132
Haitian Rebellion, 202
Hamilton, Alexander, 10, 65, 143
"Hampden" Letters, 75
Hartford Convention (1814), 71, 240
Harvard, 39, 40, 42
Higher law. See Natural law
Hobbes, Thomas, 14
Hopewell, Treaty of (1785), 251, 253
Hopkinson, Joseph, 110, 111, 143–144, 164, 176
Hughes, Charles Evans, 85

Illegal trade, 191–195, 240–241
Impeachment, 32, 57, 63–65, 129
Indian tribes, 46, 48, 59, 81–84, 94, 172, 174, 248, 250, 252, 253, 257–260; status of, 48, 81–84, 249, 251, 257–259
Insolvency laws, state, 5, 46, 181–187, 210 n. 64, 210–213

International law, 50, 130, 131, 135, 138, 142, 220, 235, 239
Interpretivism, 4, 61
Interstate compacts, 78
Interstate conflict, 163
Iredell, James, 25, 26

Jackson, Andrew, 14, 47, 48, 49, 50, 84, 94, 95, 124, 254, 258–261
Jay, John, 9, 25, 26, 34, 35, 53, 112, 139
Jay Treaty of 1794, 11, 69, 71, 205, 229, 230, 232
Jefferson, Thomas, 17, 18, 25, 27, 30, 31–33, 34, 35, 36, 38, 40, 43, 44, 55, 57, 59, 62, 63, 65, 67, 68, 69, 76–77, 80, 83, 98, 99, 100, 125, 126, 129, 144, 168, 184, 191, 192, 193, 233, 238
Jeffersonian Republican, 10, 38, 54, 57, 58–59, 64–66, 68, 113, 129, 130, 141, 168, 240
Johnson, Richard M., 80
Johnson, William, 5, 31–34, 35, 38, 39, 44, 46, 48, 49, 50, 67, 81, 84, 88, 89, 92, 97, 98, 99, 103–104, 105, 113, 117, 118, 120, 122–123, 124, 132–135, 156–159, 160, 167–168, 175–176, 177, 182, 184, 185, 188–189, 190, 193, 196, 197–199, 204, 215–216, 232, 240, 248, 249–250, 258
Judges and justices, 57, 64, 97; disqualification, 56–57, 149, 229, 230
Judicial decision-making, 46, 53, 97–99
Judicial independence, 58, 68, 97
Judicial power, 53, 159, 235–236
Judicial review, 58 n. 11, 59–62, 69, 71–72, 254; historiography, 3–4, 59–61
Judiciary Act (1789), 56, 59, 60, 72, 77, 106, 113, 132, 138, 149, 152–154, 155–157, 217, 225, 254
Judiciary Act (1793), 106
Judiciary Act (1801), 9, 55–57, 63, 100, 112
Judiciary Act (1802), 55–57, 58, 63, 106, 112, 120

Jurisdiction, 147–148, 153–154, 159, 190, 203, 262; federal courts, 59, 76, 122, 157–158, 160–161, 190; federal question, 149, 157–158, 235, 253, 259; U. S. Supreme Court, 77, 82, 125, 150–151, 153, 159, 189, 249, 257–258

Kent, James, 45, 252
Kentucky land grants, 221–222

Latrobe, Benjamin H., 108
Legislative power (state), 175–176
Livingston, Edward, 77
Livingston, Henry Brockholst, 31, 34–35, 44, 67–68, 79, 88, 89, 92, 103, 105, 116, 117, 118, 120, 122, 124, 177, 182, 191, 243, 246, 257
Locke, John, 13, 14
Lottery, 152–154
Louisiana Purchase (1803), 190, 233

Macon, Nathaniel, 44
Madison, Dolly, 98
Madison, James, 38, 44, 57, 152, 261
Mandamus, 58, 59, 148
Mansfield, Lord, 242
Manuscript opinions, 2
Marbury, William, 57–62
Marine insurance, 191, 203–205
Marshall, John: anonymous essays, 74–75, 147; behavior, 16–21, 65-66; biographies of, 5; *Bracken v. College of William and Mary*, 176–177, Burr trial, 65–66, 128–129; conflict avoidance, 58; constitutional thought, 5, 13–15; dissenting opinions, 93–94; economic thought, 14–15, 162; Fairfax proprietary grants, 11–12, 69–72, 73, 91, 105, 139, 148–151, 221, 229–230; health, 257; historiography concerning, 1–6, 60–62; House of Representatives, 10; Jefferson, Thomas, and, 17, 77; jurisprudential differences from associates, 90, 256–257; Kentucky land grants, 78, 221–222; lawyer, 11, 23, 69, 228, 230, 246; leadership, 12, 54, 85, 256, 262–263;

majority opinions, 60, 87–94, 261–262; marriage, 18; *Martin v. Hunter's Lessee*, 70–71. 91–92; military service, 19–20, 37; natural law, 50–51, 81; nomination as chief justice, 9; papers of, 2; personal appearance, 16–17, 85; Richmond Hustings Court, 11 n. 5; secretary of state, 9–11, 30; style of opinions, 91–92; textual exposition, 60; Virginia House of Delegates, 23; Virginia ratifying convention, 23; William and Mary, College of, 23; XYZ Mission (1797–1798), 10, 11, 124
Marshall, John, The Papers of , 2, 5
Marshall, Mary Willis (wife of John Marshall), 16, 18, 20, 41, 98, 257
Martin, Luther, 144 n. 19
McLean, John, 47–49, 83, 89, 97, 98, 99, 110–111, 117, 119, 121, 122–123, 156–157, 223, 248, 254, 260
Methodist Church, 83–84, 253, 259–260
Milan Decree, 227
Militia, 160
Missouri Compromise, 46
Monroe, James, 19, 44, 45, 46, 48, 108
Moore, Alfred, 23, 25, 31, 35, 120
"Mr. Madison's War" (War of 1812), 3, 71, 99, 123, 134, 141, 142, 145, 202, 203, 225, 232, 240

Napoleonic War, 66, 191, 192, 224, 238, 241
Nash, Thomas (a.k.a. Jonathan Robbins), 10
National Archives, 2–3
Nationalism, 93, 251
Natural law, 61–62, 81, 94, 178–179, 187, 254–256; slavery and, 95, 244, 245, 256
Necessary and proper clause, 145–146
Negotiable instruments, 190, 207–208, 209
Negro Seamen's Act, 113, 131–134, 168
Neutrality, 191, 224–225; South American revolutions, 225, 227–228, 241–242

New York Constitution, 45, 243
Non-Importation Act (1806), 191, 192
Non-Intercourse Acts (1799 and 1800), 237
Nullification controversy (1831–33), 50, 84, 261

Occupying claimant laws (Kentucky), 78–81, 187–189
Ogden, Aaron, 163, 165, 167
Ohio military reserve, 222–223
"Old Hickory" (Andrew Jackson), 84, 254, 261
Opinions, 2–4, 44, 99, 100–105, 108–111, 184–185, 261; seriatim, 99, 184–185
Original intention, 4, 61, 130

Patents, 167
Paterson, William, 26–27, 56–57, 100, 120
Patronage, 55
Peace Treaty of 1783, 11, 71, 224, 228–229, 231–233, 235
Per curiam opinions, 100
Peters, Richard, Jr., 109–111, 251
Peters, Richard, Sr., 30, 128, 148
Philadelphia Aurora, 30
Philadelphia Convention (1787), 4, 13, 26, 27, 151, 162, 174–175, 186, 205
Philadelphia Union, 74
Pickering, John, 63, 106
Pinkney, William, 34, 143, 145, 177, 198
Piracy, 193, 244
Political questions, 46, 61, 227, 241
Precedent, 151–152
Princeton, 44, 49
Privy Council (British), 60, 140
Prize cases, 135, 147, 191, 205, 236–237
Process Act (1789), 106
Property rights, 58, 229–233
Proprietary colonies, 218–220
Provincial Congresses, 26, 28
Public officers, 193, 220

Quasi-War with France (1798–1800), 139, 192, 202, 225, 237–238

Quit rents, 219–220

Randolph, John, 64, 125
Real property, 187, 217–223
Rehnquist, William, 85
Religious establishment, 232–232
Remedies, 188
Repeal Act (1802), 56
Richmond Enquirer, 66, 72, 74
Richmond junto, 77
Ritchie, Thomas, 72
Rittenhouse, David, 147–148
Roane, Spencer, 69, 72, 75, 76–77
Roosevelt, Franklin D., 3
Rutledge, John, 26

Salvage cases, 201–203
Scott, Sir William, 238–239, 244
Secession, 71
Sedition Act (1798), 10, 27–28, 30–31, 54, 63, 100, 141
Separation of powers, 140
Shay's Rebellion (1786), 25
"Sidney, Algernon" (Spencer Roane), 76–77
"Silver Heels" (John Marshall), 19
Slavery, 25, 43–44, 46, 75 n. 60, 131, 133, 196, 242–243, 245–248
Slave trade, 42, 95, 195–197, 243–245
Smith, Jeremiah, 63
Social compact, 256
Somerset, James, 242
South Carolina's Negro Seaman's Act, 33, 113, 131–134, 168
Sovereignty, 139–140, 165, 178–179, 189, 214–215, 260
Spanish-American War (1898), 236
Spanish Crown, 124
State power, 45, 178
States, 187–189
State's rights, 71, 80, 170–171
Statutory construction, 62
Stony Point, 20, 37
Story, Joseph, 5, 20, 21, 23, 24, 34, 35–44, 48, 69, 70, 71, 72, 74, 78, 79, 81, 84, 88, 89, 90–92, 97, 98, 99, 102–103,

Story, Joseph (*continued*)
    104, 105, 110, 111, 113, 116, 117, 119,
    120, 122–124, 133, 134, 135, 136, 141,
    142, 149, 150, 151, 156, 157, 160–161,
    174, 177, 179–180, 182, 185–187, 188,
    190, 194, 197–199, 200, 201, 202–203,
    209, 214, 218, 228, 229, 231–232,
    239–240, 246, 248, 251, 252, 254, 258,
    261
Story, Sarah Waldo Wetmore, 40–41,
    98, 99
Supremacy, 59, 73, 74, 76, 83, 132, 140–
    141, 152, 154, 254, 259-260
Supreme Court, United States, 2–3,
    6–7, 21–22, 31–32, 51–54, 61–62, 68,
    72–74, 77–78, 79–81, 93, 96–98, 101–
    102, 105–106, 107, 108, 124–125,
    225–226; appellate jurisdiction of, 54,
    71–72, 77–78; argument before, 104,
    107, 142–143; conferences of, 19, 85,
    98, 102–104; justices, relationships
    between, 86, 97–98, 256–260; original
    jurisdiction, 82, 94; procedural rules,
    106–108
Swarthout, Samuel, 124–125

Taney, Roger B., 43, 46, 49, 180, 256
Taxation, 143–144, 146
Tazewell, Littleton Waller, 20, 42, 106
Territories (U.S.), 203, 233–234
Textual interpretation, 4, 60–61, 257
Thompson, Smith, 35, 40, 42, 44–47,
    48, 50, 84, 89, 90, 92, 93, 97, 98, 99,
    109, 110, 111, 116, 117, 119, 122, 156,
    170–171, 184, 185, 191, 195, 216,
    220–221, 248, 251, 252, 253, 258
Todd, Thomas, 31, 36, 37, 47, 79, 88, 89,
    98, 105, 117, 121, 135, 177, 246, 257
Tracy, Uriah, 29, 64
Trail of Tears, 94, 261
Treason, 124–131; defined, 124–125,
    127–128, 130, 230,
Treaties, 82–83, 132–133, 150, 220–221,
    224–225, 229, 231, 235, 237, 239;
    Peace Treaty of 1783, 138–139, 149,
150, 217–220, 228–229; Treaty of
    Hopewell (1785), 251, 253; Treaty of
    Paris (1783), 242; Treaty of Washing-
    ton (1819), 194
Trimble, Robert, 44, 46–47, 89, 117,
    119, 121, 184, 185, 257
Tucker, St. George, 106, 134
Tyler, John, 106, 407

U.S.-British Commercial Convention
    (1815), 132
U.S.-French Treaty (1778), 224–225
U.S. House of Representatives, 43, 47,
    49, 50, 63, 64, 106–107
U.S. Senate, 63–66

Van Buren, Martin, 45, 79
Vested property rights, 173–174, 232
Virginia Continental Line, 19–20
Virginia Court of Appeals, 69–70, 75,
    91, 150, 179, 218, 229
Virginia House of Delegates, 19, 23
Virginia-Kentucky Compact (1789), 79,
    187–189

War of 1812, 71, 99, 123, 134, 141, 142,
    145, 202, 203, 225, 232, 240
Warren, Earl, 4, 61, 85
Warren Court, 61
Washington, Bushrod, 21–25, 30, 31, 34,
    36, 37–38, 39, 49, 70, 74, 78, 79, 88,
    89, 92, 103, 105, 110, 111, 116, 117,
    118, 120, 121, 122, 124, 135, 136, 160,
    164, 173, 177, 179–180, 182, 184, 185,
    187, 188–189, 190, 196, 211, 212, 232,
    246, 256
Washington, George, 10, 14, 15, 16, 25,
    26, 28–29, 37, 225
Washington, The Life of George, 14, 15–16
Wayne, James Moore, 47, 49, 89, 117,
    120
Webster, Daniel, 44, 142, 144–145, 164,
    167, 176–177, 218–219, 233,
Wheaton, Henry, 34, 75, 77, 108–111; as
    reporter, 39–40, 108–111
Whig Party, 48, 50

Wickham, John, 66, 129
Wilkinson, James, 124–126
William and Mary, College of, 23, 176
Wilson, James, 72, 23, 25, 26, 121
Wine, 19
Wirt, William, 16, 17, 145, 164, 165, 167, 176
Wolcott, Alexander, 38
Wolfe, Christopher, 61

Worcester, Samuel, 82–84, 94, 253, 259
World War I, 236
Wythe, George, 23

XYZ Mission (1797–1798), 10, 11, 124

Yale College, 49
Yazoo Lands, 81–84